Diehl

Insider- und Börsenrecht

German Insider and Stock Exchange Law

Insider- und Börsenrecht

Eine Einführung in das deutsche Recht
mit deutsch-englischer Textausgabe
des Wertpapierhandelsgesetzes, des Börsengesetzes,
der Börsenzulassungs-Verordnung
und des Wertpapier-Verkaufsprospektgesetzes

von
Dr. Konrad Mohr

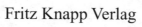

Fritz Knapp Verlag   Frankfurt am Main

German Insider and Stock Exchange Law

An introduction to the German Law
with German text and synoptic English translation
of the Securities Trading Act, the Stock Exchange Act,
the Stock Exchange Admissions Regulation
and the Securities Sales Prospectus Act

by
Dr. Konrad Mohr

Fritz Knapp Verlag Frankfurt am Main

ISBN 3-7819-2842-X

© 1994 by Verlag Fritz Knapp GmbH, Frankfurt am Main

Technische Gesamtherstellung:
Hassmüller KG Graphische Betriebe, Frankfurt am Main

Printed in Germany

Inhalt

	Seite
Vorwort	6
Table of Contents	8
Introduction	13
Gesetz über den Wertpapierhandel	58
Börsengesetz	122
Börsenzulassungs-Verordnung	218
Wertpapier-Verkaufsprospektgesetz	314

Contents

	Page
Foreword	7
Table of Contents	8
Introduction	13
Securities Trading Act	59
Stock Exchange Act	123
Stock Exchange Admissions Regulation	219
Securities Sales Prospectus Act	315

Vorwort

In weiten Kreisen wurde es als Mangel empfunden, daß es in der Bundesrepublik Deutschland keine gesetzlichen Vorschriften gegen Insiderhandel gibt. Auch die Ausgestaltung der Aufsicht über die Börsen wurde als nicht mehr zeitgerecht und nicht den erforderlichen internationalen Standards entsprechend empfunden. Das Zweite Finanzmarktförderungsgesetz vom 26. Juli 1994 hat insbesondere in diesen beiden Bereichen Abhilfe geschaffen. Verbesserung des Anlegerschutzes und Stärkung der internationalen Wettbewerbsfähigkeit des Finanzplatzes Deutschland durch vertrauensbildende Maßnahmen waren oberste Richtschnur des Gesetzgebers.

Das Zweite Finanzmarktförderungsgesetz enthält in seinem ersten Teil, dem Wertpapierhandelsgesetz, die neue gesetzliche Regelung gegen Insiderhandel, die Neufassung der bisher im Börsengesetz geregelten Pflichten über die Ad-hoc-Publizität, die Umsetzung der Transparenzrichtlinie zur Durchsichtigmachung der Eigentümerstruktur einer Gesellschaft sowie – nach anfänglichem Zögern des Gesetzgebers – die Rules of Conduct für Wertpapier-Dienstleistungsunternehmen, mit denen die Vorrangigkeit des Anlegerinteresses mit grundsätzlichen und detaillierten Verhaltenspflichten festgeschrieben ist. Der Anlegerschutzgedanke wird wieder aufgenommen in den umfangreichen Neuregelungen des Börsengesetzes, enthalten in einem weiteren Teil des Zweiten Finanzmarktförderungsgesetzes, z. B. über die Festlegung der Pflichten der Banken bei Ausführung von Kundenorders sowie die einzuhaltenden Regeln bei der Kursermittlung. Weitere Änderungen des Börsengesetzes betreffen die Anpassung an veränderte organisatorische Verhältnisse, insbesondere das Vordringen elektronischer Handelssysteme sowie insbesondere die Neugestaltung der Aufsicht über die Börse mit einer Erweiterung der Rechtsaufsicht zur Marktaufsicht und der Installierung einer unabhängigen Handelsüberwachungsstelle.

Die Zusammenschau der Regelungen des neuen Wertpapierhandelsgesetzes und der Regelungen des Börsengesetzes mit seinen umfangreichen Neuerungen läßt das Ausmaß der durchgesetzten Verbesserungen des Anlegerschutzes erkennen. Die Neustrukturierung der Aufsicht erfordert die Darbietung und Erläuterung dieser beiden für den gesamten Wertpapierbereich künftig grundlegenden Gesetze. Da die Fragen der Zulassung von Wertpapieren zum Börsenhandel im Börsengesetz nur mit einigen grundlegenden Vorschriften beschrieben sind, die Einzelheiten sich aber aus der Börsenzulassungsverordnung ergeben, wird diese ebenfalls mitbehandelt und wegen des engen Sachzusammenhanges das Wertpapier-Verkaufsprospektgesetz.

Foreword

The lack of legal prohibitions against insider trading in Germany was seen as a serious defect in many banking circles. Oversight was considered neither adequate to the needs of the times nor to international standards. The Second Financial Market Advancement Law of 26 July 1994 was drafted expressly to correct these areas. Investor protection and strengthening the international competitiveness of "Financial Center Germany" through confidence building measures led lawmakers' priorities.

The Second Financial Market Advancement Law contains in Part One, with the Securities Trading Act, the new legal regulations against insider trading, the new version of duties about ad hoc publicity (earlier covered in the Stock Exchange Law), articulation of the new transparency guidelines to clarify company ownership structures and finally – after some parliamentary hesitations – for companies providing services related to securities, Rules of Conduct imposing detailed and thorough obligations. Investor protection is taken up again in the wide-reaching new regulations of the Stock Exchange Act, in the second part of the Second Financial Market Advancement Law covering, for example, duties imposed on banks when executing client's orders, as well as rules for ascertaining prices. Further changes of the Stock Exchange Act include adaptations to changed circumstances, primarily the emergence of electronic trading systems, and new stock exchange oversight in the direction of market oversight, from earlier self-regulation, and the installation of an independent trading monitoring office.

This synopsis of new rulings in the new Securities Trading Act, and changes in the regulations of the Stock Exchange Act, makes clear the extent of improvement in investor protection. The restructuring of oversight responsibilities through the newly created Federal Securities Trading Authority on the one hand, as well as the changes in stock exchange oversight on the other, require examination because they are key to future German securities law.

The admission of securities to trading is dealt with in only a few basic provisions in the Stock Exchange Act, leaving the details to be filled in by the Stock Exchange Admissions Regulations, so these will also be examined, as well as the Securities Sales Prospectus Act, owing to the overlapping obligations attaching to it.

Table of Contents

Introduction

A) Preliminary Remarks   Page

    I. Insider Law 13

    II. Stock Exchange Law 15
        1) The Stock ExchangeAct 15
        2) The Stock Exchange Admissions Regulation/
            The Securities Sales Prospectus Act 16

B) Securities Trading Act

    I. Insider Law 17
        1) Insider 18
            a) Primary Insider, b) Secondary Insider
        2) Insider Information (Insider Facts) 20
        3) Substantial Influence on Prices 22
        4) Insider Securities 23
        5) Prohibitions 24
        6) Penalties 27

    II. Ad hoc Publicity 28
        1) Facts to be Publicised 28
        2) Procedure 30

    III. Changes in Voting Rights 32
        1) Basic Rules 32
        2) Shares to be Attributed or not Taken into Account 33
        3) Procedure 34

    IV. Rules of Conduct 35
        1) General and Specific Rules 35
        2) Organizational Obligations 36

C) Stock Exchange Law

    I. Trading 37
        1) General Remarks 37
        2) Bank and Customer Orders 38
        3) Brokers and Prices 39
        4) Electronic Trading 41

II. Admission of Securities 42
  1) Official Market 43
    a) General Prerequisites, Procedure, b) Prospectus,
    c) Consequences of Admission, d) Prospectus Liability
  2) Regulated Market 46
  3) Free Market 47
III. Futures Trading 47
  1) Disallowed Business 47
  2) Allowed, Official Business 47
  3) Allowed, Unofficial Business 48

D) Securities Sales Prospectus Act

  I. Basic Rules 49
  II. Exceptions 50
  III. The Prospectus 50
  IV. Liability, Fines 51
  V. International Cooperation 52

E) Supervision

  I. Federal Supervisory Authority for Securities Trading 52
  II. Stock Exchange Supervisory Agency 55
  III. Trading Monitoring Office 56
  IV. Federal Banking Supervisory Authority 56

Securities Trading Act

	Table of Contents	59
Chapter One	Scope of Application, Definitions (§§ 1–2)	63
Chapter Two	Federal Supervisory Authority for Securities Trading (§§ 3–11)	65
Chapter Three	Insider Monitoring (§§ 12–20)	79
Chapter Four	Information and Publicity Requirements relating to Variations in Voting Rights in Listed Companies (§§ 21–30)	93
Chapter Five	Rules of Conduct for Enterprises Providing Services relating to Securities (§§ 31–37)	107

| Chapter Six | Rules relating to Criminal Provisions and Fines (§§ 38–40) | 115 |
| Chapter Seven | Transitional Provisions (§ 41) | 119 |

Stock Exchange Act

Table of Contents 123
I. General Provisions for Stock Exchanges
   and their Organs (§§ 1–28) 129
II. Brokers and Fixing of Prices (§§ 29–35) 163
III. Admission of Securities to Official Listing
   on Stock Exchanges (§§ 36–49) 175
IV. Futures Trading (§§ 50–70) 195
V. The Admission of Securities to Stock Exchange Trading
   with Unofficial Listing (§§ 71–97) 207

Stock Exchange Admissions Regulation

Table of Contents 219

Chapter One Admission of Securities to Official Listing

Part One
Conditions for Admission (§§ 1–12) 227

Part Two
Prospectus

Sub-Part One
Contents of the Prospectus (§§ 13–32) 237

Sub-Part Two
Contents of Prospectus in Special Cases
(§§ 33–42) 269

Sub-Part Three
Publication of the Prospectus (§§ 43–44) 283

Sub-Part Four
Exemption from the Obligation to Publish
a Prospectus (§§ 45–47) 285

	Part Three
	Admissions Procedure (§§ 48–52) 291
Chapter Two	Obligations of an Issuer of Admitted Securities
	Part One
	Interim Report
	Sub-Part One
	Contents of the Interim Report (§§ 53–56) 297
	Sub-Part Two
	Contents of the Interim Report in Special Cases
	(§§ 57–60) 301
	Sub-Part Three
	Publication of the Interim Report (§§ 61–62) 303
	Part Two
	Miscellaneous Obligations (§§ 63–70) 305
Chapter Three	Breach of Regulations and Fining Provisions (§ 71) .. 313

Securities Sales Prospectus Act

	Table of Contents 315
Chapter One	Area of Application (§§ 1–4) 319
Chapter Two	Offer for Sale of Securities for which Application is made for an Official Listing (§§ 5–6) 325
Chapter Three	Offer for Sale of Securities for which no Application is made for an Official Listing (§§ 7–8) 327
Chapter Four	Publication of the Sales Prospectus (§§ 9–12) 329
Chapter Five	Infringement of the Obligation concerning Prospectuses (§ 13) 333
Chapter Six	Procedures in the European Economic Community; Charges; Fining Provisions (§§ 14–17) 333

Introduction

A. PRELIMINARY REMARKS

New aspects and decisive new data for "Financial Center Germany" have been supplied by the Second Financial Market Advancement Law (*Zweites Finanzmarktförderungsgesetz*) of 26 July 1994.

I. Insider Law

The first part of the Second Financial Market Advancement Law contains the Securities Trading Act articulating for the first time German law prohibiting insider trading.

Until the appearance of this law, only some aspects of the problem were covered by legal regulation. The members of the board of a stock corporation, for example, are to conduct their business orderly and conscientiously, and are particulary to observe secrecy on confidential data, company secrets, and trade and business secrets which become known to them through their tasks on the board, according to § 93 subparagraph 1 AktG (Stock Corporation Act). The same applies to members of the supervisory board (§ 116 AktG).

Claims for damages can be made against the members of the board or the members of the supervisory board, as well as criminal prosecution, should they fail to comply (§ 404 AktG).

There is a special further regulation for auditors. In accordance with § 323 HGB (Commercial Code), auditors are required to observe secrecy and are prohibited from unauthorisedly exploiting company and trade secrets which they have obtained in the course of the execution of their appointed activities. Failure to comply can result in claims for damages or criminal proceedings against them.

Aside from such specific regulations, there were no German laws governing the complexities of insider trading like those instituted long ago in the US or more recently in other European countries. Instead,

Introduction

voluntary self-regulation was tried in an attempt to control the problem.

The earlier insider guidelines and rules for traders and consultants were based on the recommendations of a commission of stock market experts and representatives from central offices within the German economy. A working group from the German Stock Exchanges developed procedural rules; inspection commissions were set up at all the exchanges. Since decisions of the institutions mentioned do not have the force of law, regulations governing insider trading and other regulations could only be applied when those concerned voluntarily agreed to submit to them under private law. These guidelines were acknowledged by the majority of the stock corporations whose shares are traded on the stock exchanges as well as practically the entire banking industry and a few investment consultants. Corporations not acknowledging the regulations were identified in the stock exchange quotation sheets.

According to these voluntary guidelines certain persons defined as insiders committed themselves not to exploit insider information to their own or a third party's advantage in transactions concerning "insider securities". Credit institutions and investment consultants committed themselves to recommend securities only in the interest of the customer and not to reduce or increase their own portfolio or to otherwise recommend or deal them to improve their own situation. Laid down in the insider guidelines were sanctions which directed insiders to pass their profits on to the corporation concerned. In the case of consultants, the only possible sanction was the removal of their names from the lists held by the stock exchanges.

There reigned mixed judgement as to the efficiency of these guidelines from the start. The procedural guidelines were seen as ineffectual. Over the years only a few procedures were instituted and most ended in nothing.

Despite this, many active in the economy long insisted on continuing the voluntary restrictions and the superfluity of legal regulations. Opinion changed only with the realization that if insider trading was not controlled "Financial Center Germany" would remain competitively disadvantaged. Spurred on by the European Insider Guide-

Introduction

lines of 1989, Germany has finally introduced statutory regulations covering insider trading. The results of these efforts is the Second Financial Market Advancement Law. All future cases will be dealt with under the new law which supersedes the former guidelines.

The new rules in the Second Financial Market Advancement Law require special interpretation; falling back on the interpretation of the older regulations would be misleading. The European Insider Guidelines, however, may become of importance, and also how other European countries have variously interpreted them.

II. Stock Exchange Law

1) The Stock Exchange Act

The Stock Exchange Act of 1896, revised several times, has been overhauled to a large extent by the Second Financial Market Advancement Law, not only in details, but also in basics. This was done to improve "Financial Center Germany's" international image and competitive position.

Under the new law, the regulated supervision of the stock exchanges is substantially strengthened. An office monitoring trading on the stock exchanges, including electronic trading systems, has been introduced.

Laws governing brokers' activities have been reformulated, especially concerning official brokers' own account business.

The Stock Exchange's overall organisation has been restructured, creating a new Stock Exchange Board of Governors responsible for management, with the Stock Exchange Council now mainly responsible for the supervision of the Board of Governors.

The admissions procedures for traders on the Stock Exchange were also revised and adjusted.

Many of the new regulations cover de facto changes in Stock Exchange trading over the past several years, for example the introduction of electronic trading systems (especially IBIS), the creation of

Introduction

the DTB (Deutsche Terminbörse – German Options and Financial Futures Exchange), as well as the introduction of an order routing system for floor trading. These developments are hardly over. Over the next few years further legal and regulatory changes can be anticipated.

2) The Stock Exchange Admissions Regulation/ The Securities Sales Prospectus Act

The Stock Exchange Admissions Regulations of 1987 replaced older, less comprehensive regulations. The Securities Sales Prospectus Act was introduced in 1990.

The Stock Exchange Admissions Regulation governs the admission of securities to official listing on the stock exchange. The basic rules are laid down in §§ 36 ff. of the Stock Exchange Act. The Stock Exchange Admissions Regulations regulates details including the contents of the prospectus, the issuer's individual requirements, and the securities which are to be admitted.

The Securities Sales Prospectus Act supplements the Stock Exchange Admissions Regulation and not only concerns the admission of securities to listing on the stock exchange but also the sale of securities not admitted to official listing and the requirements of a valid sales prospectus.

The reporting requirements contained in the new Securities Trading Act, many of the requirements in the Admission Regulations and the Securities Sales Prospectus Act stem from EC Directives. They aim to facilitate the free movement of capital within the European Community and thereby help to create a more uniform and transparent EC-capital market.

Introduction

B. SECURITIES TRADING ACT

I. Insider Law

§ 14 of the Securities Trading Act covers the prohibitions for both "primary" and "secondary" insiders. The law does not use the expressions primary and secondary insider, but they have become common usage.

A primary insider (§ 14 sub-paragraph one of the Securities Trading Act) is prohibited from:
- exploiting his knowledge of insider facts (*Tatsachen*) to acquire or dispose of insider securities for his own or another account or for another person,
- communicating or giving access to insider facts to another party without authorisation,
- recommending that someone acquire or dispose of insider securities based on his knowledge of insider facts.

A secondary insider (§ 14 subparagraph two of the Securities Trading Act) is prohibited from:
- exploiting his knowledge of these facts to acquire or dispose of insider securities for his own or another account or for another person.

The following require further explanation:
1. Who is an insider? Who is a primary insider and who is a secondary insider?
2. Which facts are, according to the new law, insider facts?
3. When does such information substantially affect the price?
4. Which securities are insider securities?
5. What actions are prohibited and what are the fines and penalties?

Introduction

1) Insider

a) **Primary insiders** are members of the business management or supervisory bodies of the issuers. In the case of a stock corporation, these are the management board and the supervisory board. For a limited liability company these are the managing directors and if a supervisory board exists, the members of the supervisory board – whether the supervisory board was formed voluntarily or in compliance with legal requirements. In the case of a partnership limited by shares, those partners personally liable, as well as the members of the supervisory board, are primary insiders. For partnerships, the personally liable partners are primary insiders.

The persons mentioned are primary insiders as well if they exercise that position for an enterprise connected with the issuer. The expression "connected enterprise" has not been further explained. However it may be assumed that § 15 AktG applies.

According to § 15 AktG, a business is connected not only when the company is a majority owned enterprise of another company, but also without it being a majority owned enterprise if the relationship of a dependent and controlling company exists; if, within the eyes of the law, it is a company of the same concern or group; or if the companies are a contractual part of a special contract between business enterprises.

Anyone, as well, with knowledge of insider facts because of his share of the capital of the issuer or one of the companies connected with the issuer, is a primary insider, irrespective of how large the share is. A small shareholder can be a primary insider if he has insider knowledge "based on his shares". Although German stock corporation law is designed so that individual shareholders normally cannot receive any special information or "facts", in the case of the insider law, it is irrelevant whether these rules of stock corporation law are followed. Important is only whether the fact was given owing to the possession of an interest, or shares, in the company.

A third group of primary insiders are persons receiving insider information or facts in the execution of their appointed activities (*bestimmungsgemäß*). This will no doubt raise of demarcation ques-

Introduction

tions. Obviously, certain persons always mentioned in this context – lawyers, notaries, auditors, accountants, and business consultants working for the issuing company – belong to this group. The members of an advisory board of a company belong to this group as well, as the advisory board is not a body in the sense of a supervisory board.

More difficult is the case of the employees employed by the issuing company. Only those employees receiving insider knowledge "in the execution of their appointed activities" are to be classed as primary insiders. This is not only the secretary to the board of directors, but all employees involved in working on the process in question, i.e. typically employees in staff divisions or, if for example new research developments are involved, employees of the Research and Development departments. The messenger delivering messages from one board director's office to another, however, also finds himself in this group if he has to deliver an oral message; if documents are sealed, and the messenger then acquires knowledge without authorization, he has then arrived at this knowledge not "in the execution of his appointed activities".

Employees of third parties or companies can also be primary insiders – not only the employees of the lawyers, auditors, etc., but also the employees of the company's bank or, in the case of important delivery or purchase contracts, the employees of the contractual partner concerned. Furthermore, the employees of stock exchanges or supervisory authorities can be primary insiders.

Other primary insiders outside the company would be for example printers involved in the printing of documents or prospectuses or the like (see for example the Chiarella case in the US courts) because here the person concerned gains knowledge of the facts "in the execution of his appointed activities". But a psychiatrist treating someone with insider knowledge who gains insider facts by asking his patient clever questions is not a primary insider.

The question whether business journalists and financial analysts could be primary insiders has created special interest. This question must be raised especially when information is offered in "background conversations" or the like. Leaving aside the question of authorized disclosure, it is assumed that these persons are primary insiders since

Introduction

they do not receive this information accidentally, rather in their capacity as journalists or analysts, so that this information or fact is meant for these persons only in their appropriate capacity.

b) **Secondary insiders** are persons who are not primary insiders and who have knowledge of insider information. It is irrelevant how one has come by the information – from a primary insider or otherwise.

Therefore, not only the psychiatrist who asks clever questions, but also the nosy cleaner who rummages in the board director's wastepaper basket in search of information and the secretary who listens in on a confidential conversation are secondary insiders. Those persons who gain knowledge of an insider fact by pure coincidence are secondary insiders in the same way as those who gain that knowledge through industrial espionage or theft.

The minimum requirement is always that the person concerned has knowledge of insider information or facts. If someone receives an investment tip without the person giving the tip revealing the insider information which prompted the recommendation, then this person is not a secondary insider.

As only those persons who have exploited insider information can be punished as secondary insiders, the person must be aware that the facts concerned are insider facts.

2) Insider Information (Insider Facts)

Information can only be an insider fact if it is not public knowledge. A fact is publicly known if an undefined number of people can gain knowledge of this fact. Leaving aside the question of the obligations to publish new facts under § 15 of the Act (ad-hoc publicity), this is so if the information has been made public in accordance with stock exchange rules or if it has been publicised in the economic press or other public media. According to legislative intent, it is sufficient if so-called sector publicity has been established. This is so when the market participants have gained knowledge of the facts. This is why distribution via information services such as dpa, Reuters or similar is sufficient.

Introduction

Insider information must relate to insider securities or to one or more issuers of insider securities. It is not clear whether this means that general market data is to be classed as insider information if they do not relate to a single issuer but are significant to all issuers. Information for instance, about a basic change in the tax rules for motor vehicles would directly affect the auto and the oil industries, as well as associated sectors, and therefore certain individual issuers. Information about the Bundesbank discount rate affects the entire economy and relates therefore not only to individual issuers, but to all issuing companies. This question arises especially for general commercial conditions or a political event (recall the case when Rothschild, knowing the outcome of the Battle of Waterloo before the market, made arrangements on the stock exchange). The majority would assume that such general circumstances could also be insider facts.

The statute does not use the word insider information, it uses the word insider fact (*Tatsache*). This is meant to emphasise that opinions and evaluations do not constitute insider information. The statute states in § 13 sub-paragraph 2 that evaluations made based on facts publicly known are not insider facts. This refers to analyses such as those produced by business journalists, financial analysts, analysis departments of banks or insurance companies, or consultants. These analyses are usually based only on publicly known facts – sector publicity. However, if information from background conversations is included in these evaluations, then the evaluation may possibly be classified as insider information. No doubt this will lead to some rethinking and adjustment, especially for financial analysts.

It is important not to overlook the distinction that an evaluation which is based on publicly known facts does not constitute insider information, is different from the question whether the fact that an evaluation has taken place at all constitutes insider information. The fact that, for instance, a rating agency has changed a company's rating may well be considered insider information before that information or fact has been made public.

Introduction

3) Substantial Influence on Prices

Furthermore, information can only be regarded as being insider information if it is sufficiently important and is therefore suited to affect the price of an insider security. Typical examples would be news of a capital reduction, the conclusion of a control agreement, or a profit transfer agreement; especially significant innovations; the conclusion of a contract; changes in the rate of dividends; the intended purchase of a large amount of shares or their sale on the stock exchange; a suspension of the quotation or the cancellation of a debenture issue.

Given that insider facts are not only those created within the company itself, insider facts are also facts which arise e.g. from the trade in securities. For instance, if a bank trader sees that large purchase orders have come in and he therefore recognises that the price will increase, he will then be guilty of insider dealing if he quickly buys some shares for himself. As you see, front-running has been prohibited in the new law (for front running see also p. 35).

Finally, to define the term insider information or insider fact, it is a prerequisite that the price of insider securities not just be affected, but substantially affected. This will probably present the most difficulties when applying the law. The reasoning for the draft of the law does not give any help in interpreting it. Partly, it is thought to use the stock exchange regulation via plus- or minus-announcements (for shares, a change of more than 5% of the market value, and for fixed interest securities 1.5% of the nominal value) or even double minus or double plus announcements (for shares, a change of more than 10% of the market value, and for fixed interest securities more than 3% of the nominal value). However, it is probable that such ceilings will be only one factor among others in determining the meaning of substantial influence on the price.

Each case will be unique, since the price trend for a specific security depends on many circumstances, including the volatility of the security, the depth of the market (liquidity) for it, market circumstances, for example whether the market is unsettled or quiet and many others. As long as the courts or authorities do not specify the rules in

Introduction

more detail, it will be reasonable to be reserved, rather than test the limits of the rules.

4) Insider Securities

The prohibition of insider dealing only refers to the acquisition and disposition of insider securities. Insider securities are securities as defined in § 2 of the Securities Trading Act. In principle, all types of shares or certificates representing shares, bonds, profit participation certificates, warrants, and other securities comparable to shares and bonds could be included. It is not necessary that documents have been issued.

Securities are insider securities not only if they have been admitted to the domestic stock exchange for official trading or are traded on the regulated market, but also when they have been included in the free market (for explanations see pp 42 ff.). However, it suffices if the securities have been appropriately admitted to trading in another member state of the European Community or in another contracting state of the European Economic Area Treaty.

Since often trading "before introduction" is pertinent, the term insider securities has been widened to include those for which the application for admission or inclusion have been made or publicly announced.

If further conditions are met, the following are also to be regarded as insider securities:

– rights to subscription, acquisition or disposition of securities,
– rights to payment of a margin which is measured in a change of the value of the securities
– futures contracts on a shares or bonds index or interest futures contracts (financial futures contracts) as well as the subscription, acquisition, or disposal of financial futures contracts, if the financial futures contracts deal with securities or if they refer to an index in which securities are included,
– other futures contracts obliging the holder to acquire or dispose of securities.

Introduction

5) Prohibitions

The prohibitions of § 14 of the Securities Trading Act distinguish, as mentioned above on p 17, between the actions of a primary and a secondary insider.

a) The primary insider is prohibited from the acquisition or disposition of insider securities, the passing on of information about them, and the making of recommendations concerning them.

– The prohibition from acquisition or disposal applies whether one is trading for one's own account, for the account of others, or on behalf of another. The board director or employee of a company who does not acquire or dispose of the securities himself but has the company do it will be regarded as trading for another party in the same way as someone who usually trades for someone else. Trading "for the account of others" is trading as a commission agent according to §§ 383 ff. of the Commercial Code, especially for banks when carrying out customer orders.

The knowledge of insider facts must be exploited in order to be a crime. This means that one knows that one is dealing with insider information. However, if someone "closes his eyes" to the knowledge that it is an insider fact, then, for practical matters a judge may very well assume actual knowledge.

There is no instance of exploiting insider information if both immediate partners to the contract have knowledge of the insider facts. (The prohibition standard does not make it a necessary condition that the business is conducted at the stock exchange or by a professional trader so as to include direct deals).

There has been no exploitation in the sense of the prohibition standards if one is simply acting on one's own decision, i.e. if the insider fact has been produced by oneself. This means that, for example, the fact that someone is buying a block of shares may often be an insider fact if that person's knowledge is exploited by a third party – the third party might then be guilty of violating the prohibition standards. However, the person initially deciding to buy the block of shares and who executes this decision is of course innocent of violating the prohibitions.

Introduction

Carrying out price support operations insider is based on a business decision and would normally not be covered under the prohibition standards.

The same applies to a person who, owing to the peculiarities of his profession, (i.e. official or independent brokers, or market makers), comes into the possession of insider facts, but uses these in accordance with his professional duties without gaining any special advantage.

If the trader of a credit institution has knowledge of insider facts, then he is not normally guilty of violating the prohibition standards in principle when he merely carries out a customer order. However, if it is a discretionary *(interessewahrende)* customer order, then in general he will be hindered from carrying out this order if he has knowledge of insider facts. Conflicts for a bank dealer can arise when the dealer recognises, due to insider knowledge, that a customer's order is going to be disadvantageous to the customer and, according to the contractual relationship with the customer, he has to recommend that the customer not go ahead with it.

Only acquisition or disposition of securities is prohibited here, but not abstaining from an acquisition or disposition in order to make a profit or avoid a loss.

– Another action which a primary insider is prohibited is telling or making accessible insider facts to another without authorisation.

If a board member tells an auditor or consultant information so that they can execute their appointed activities, this is authorised passing on of insider information. In general, the question must be asked whether the flow of information corresponds internally and externally with what is legally intended or is in compliance with general business procedures. Passing on information to journalists or analysts while showing them around the plant or in background conversation will therefore be very narrowly defined. In principle, this will only be possible in that rules regarding the obligation to inform and publicise have been complied with in accordance with § 15 of the Securities Trading Act beforehand (compare pp. 31 ff. below).

Not only is unauthorised informing prohibited, so is "making facts available" without authorization. This means that cases where information is not passed on directly are also covered, whether somebody

Introduction

has "just by chance" left sensitive information out in the open to allow a third party to gain this knowledge. Also to be mentioned is the case of revealing a secret password to enable a person to gain access to electronically stored information.

– A primary insider is prohibited as well from recommending the acquisition or disposal of insider securities based on knowledge of insider facts.

This covers instances where, for example, an investment consultant makes a recommendation to his customer without telling him the insider facts triggering this recommendation. If a customer trusts his investment consultant because of years of good experience, then it is often unnecessary for the investment consultant to reveal the insider facts upon which he is basing his recommendations. The customer needs only the recommendation. However, an investment consultant acting in this manner is guilty of violating the prohibition.

b) The prohibition only affects the secondary insider if he exploits his knowledge of insider facts to acquire or dispose of insider securities for his own account or the account of another or on behalf of others. This means that the prohibition against informing or giving a recommendation to another does not apply to him.

This gives rise to the following situations:
– If primary insider P informs a third party of an insider fact, then the third party becomes secondary insider S. It is irrelevant if S receives the information directly from P or if it is made accessible to him indirectly. In any case, P is guilty of violating the prohibition against informing outside third parties. S is now a secondary insider and therefore cannot acquire or dispose of insider securities without violating the prohibition. S, being only a secondary insider, can pass that information on to another third party or make a recommendation without principally violating the prohibitions.
– When a primary insider does not reveal the insider fact but merely recommends a third party to acquire or dispose of insider securities, the primary insider is still guilty of violating the prohibition. The third party, however, with no knowledge of the insider fact, does not thereby become a secondary insider. He can acquire or dispose of insider securities without violating the prohibitions.

Introduction

- If S is a secondary insider based on his knowledge of an insider fact (S1) and he passes this fact on to a third person, this third person becomes in turn a secondary insider, owing to his knowledge of the insider fact (S2). If S2 acquires or disposes of the insider security, he violates the prohibitions, S1, who merely passed on the information, does not violate the prohibitions because in contrast to primary insiders, secondary insiders are not prohibited from passing on information. But S1 risks charges of aiding or abetting S2 to commit a criminal offence.

- If someone is a secondary insider (S1) owing to his knowledge of insider information and does not pass on the insider fact to a third party, but merely makes a recommendation, then the third party does not become a secondary insider because he lacks knowledge of the insider fact. If, based on the recommendation, he decides to acquire or dispose of shares, he does not violate any prohibitions. S1 does not violate the prohibitions because he has only made a recommendation. He cannot be prosecuted for aiding or abetting either, because the violation never took place.

We will have to wait and see how often we come across in practice the line of defence outlined in the last example. There are, to be sure, already proposals to change this point of the law.

6) *Penalties*

The law provides for a prison sentence of up to 5 years or a fine if a person is found guilty of violating the prohibitions of § 14 of the Securities Trading Act. This framework of penalties is quite harsh in comparison with other regulations governing penalties in German criminal law. These penalties apply as well to violations of the corresponding foreign prohibitions.

It is not necessary for the insider to have made a profit for him to be punished. But if he has made a profit, according the the Penal Code, he can be made to forfeit it.

To what extent an insider would be exposed to civil damage claims remains to be clarified.

Introduction

II. Ad hoc Publicity

The quicker the information affecting prices is publicised, the less chance there is of insider information being exploited. § 15 of the Securities Trading Act dictates certain legal obligations to publicise for issuers of securities admitted to trading on a domestic stock exchange.

This affects only securities admitted to official trading or on the regulated market, i.e. not securities only included in the free market.

Issuers of securities admitted to official trading or to regulated market must publish not publicly known new facts occurring in their area of activity immediately if these facts, because of their effect on the net worth, financial position or the general course of business of the issuer, can substantially affect the stock exchange price of the listed securities.

1) Facts to be Publicised

The first condition is that it is a fact which is not publicly known. "Sector publicity" is sufficient to define whether it is publicly known or not – i.e., it must be possible for market participants to take note of the fact. The possibility to take note of the fact is given when the fact has been made public using a generally accessible information system (e.g. dpa, Reuters etc.). The odd business may be tempted to "accidentally" let a fact become public to avoid the complicated procedures involved in the legal obligation to publicise and their duty to inform. One may assume that the Federal Supervisory Authority will instigate an investigation when they suspect "accidental" violations of the legal obligations to inform and publicise and possibly violations of the insider prohibitions as well.

Insider facts, in the sense of prohibited insider dealings, are not necessarily at the same time facts which have to be made public in accordance with § 15 of the Securities Trading Act. Often procedures develop in stages. Only after reaching a certain stage does the legal obligation to publicise apply, in accordance with §15 of the Securities Trading Act, whereas beforehand the same circumstances already consti-

Introduction

tute an insider fact in the sense of prohibited insider trading. For instance, if a company is planning to take over another company, then, according to § 15 of the Securities Trading Act, the company is obliged to publicise the fact only after the board has reached a decision regarding the takeover, but possibly only when the supervisory board has given its agreement. But if the assistant who prepared the board's decision informs a third party of this planned takeover, then he, as a primary insider, is guilty of violating the insider prohibitions, since news of a takeover clearly constitutes an insider fact.

Only facts in the area of activity of the issuer need to be publicised, whereas with insider facts it is only necessary that they refer to one or more issuers of insider securities or to insider securities. This means that according to § 15 of the Securities Trading Act, information referring only to securities is not covered by the legal obligation to publicise or by the duty to inform (e.g. if large purchase or sales orders are present, or if comments have been made by financial analysts, or if purchasing or sales recommendations have been made by a consultant). General market-related information or other general information is also not covered.

New facts which might substantially affect the price must be made publicly known. That which was discussed above on page 22 regarding insider facts applies. However, there is a limitation in that § 15 of the Securities Trading Act specifies that the substantial influence on the price must be based on the effect on the net worth and financial situation or on the general course of business.

The expressions net worth, financial situation and general course of business come from accounting law and commercial law principles which apply to the management report. It depends on whether the event or events in question would trigger a duty to inform in the management report. The criteria are that the management report has to inform about the situation of the company in such a way that a true and fair view of the situation of the business is established.

Therefore, facts which have to be made public can, for example, be in the area of change in the net worth situation, acquisition or disposal of considerable blocks of shares; control or profit transfer agreements; merger agreements; company lease or company surrender agreements;

Introduction

integrations; spin offs; conversions; divisions; offers of takeover or appraisal transactions.

Facts which may change the financial situation and which therefore have to be made public could be, for example, an increase or decrease in capital; other capital adjustments; the issue of non-voting preference shares; the issue of participation certificates; notices of loss in accordance with § 92 AktG; imminent cessations of payment due to indebtedness; creditors' meetings because of liquidity problems; or the calling in of substantial loans.

The following are facts which may affect results and which therefore have to be made public: considerable extraordinary profits or expenses due to special circumstances; a change in the income prospects due to changes in the specialised area of the business which are not generally known; problems with the financial standing of important customers; dissolution of considerable hidden reserves.

Facts which may signal changes in general business procedure and which have to be made public are, for example, large contracts and changes in significant supply and purchase contracts, personnel redundancies or short-time work; the granting of important patents; the introduction of law suits or government administrative procedures with possible high risks; basic changes in production methods or sales policies.

To establish whether or not the price could be substantially influenced, the reasoning of the draft law refers to the duty of the issuer to obtain the professional advice of a credit institution which accompanies the issue or professional advice and expertise from a person acquainted with the situation of the capital markets.

2) Procedure

Before the issuer publicises facts which will affect the price, he must inform the board of directors of the stock exchange where the securities are traded (and if the securities are the basis of derivatives also the board of directors of the stock exchange where such deriv-

Introduction

atives are traded), and the Federal Supervisory Authority. This is to enable the stock exchange to suspend the quotation if necessary.

The issuer must inform the stock exchange and the Federal Supervisory Authority of such circumstances immediately. The issuer should examine the duty to inform and legal obligation to disclose results carefully. If necessary, he is to ask for expert advice. Experience shows that sensitive information often cannot be kept confidential over a longer period, obligating the issuer to inform those concerned at short notice.

After the stock exchange and the Federal Supervisory Authority have been informed, the information has to be made public. It is sufficient to comply with sector publicity using commonly available information systems. If the fact to be made public can be described in just a few words, then using such information systems will usually be sufficient. It is more difficult when the contents are more complex since, generally speaking, information systems transmit only short messages over the screen. If assurance cannot be obtained that the information system will pass on the text without editorial changes, the facts will have to be published in the authorised journals for the publication of mandatory stock exchange announcements. Earlier publication by press release or other means is prohibited.

For detailed information, the Federal Supervisory Authority may permit the issuer to publish a summary, if the detailed information is available at the issuer's payment agents free of charge, and the issuer has referred to this fact in the summary.

Once the information has been made public, the issuer must immediately take steps to insert a note in the Federal Gazette. Finally, the issuer must immediately send the publication to the Federal Supervisory Authority and the stock exchange where the issue is traded.

The issuer can apply to the Federal Supervisory Authority to be released from the obligation to make a fact public which has the (insider relevant) potential to affect the price if the ad hoc publicity would damage the legitimate interests of the issuer. It is not sufficient if the publicity might only possibly interfere with the interests of the issuer. It must be the case that the issuer's legitimate interests would be damaged by immediately making the information public.

Introduction

Obviously, the question as to whether the interests of the public are damaged or not is not decisive here, but rather whether the interests of the issuer will be damaged.

A typical case where it may be possible to obtain a release from the legal obligation to disclose a company's results might be when attempting to establish a financial rescue plan. Making information public prematurely could destroy rescue possibilities.

Violations of the duty to inform and the legal obligation to publish in accordance with § 15 of the Securities Trading Act will be prosecuted as an administrative offence and heavy fines of up to 500,000 German marks are possible.

III. Changes in Voting Rights

1) Basic Rules

The Securities Trading Act introduces a further reporting obligation relating to changes in voting rights in companies quoted on the Stock Exchange (§ 21 Securities Trading Act).

When a shareholder reaches, exceeds, or falls below the threshold values of 5%, 10%, 25%, 50% or 60% this must be officially registered. The legal procedure by which these thresholds are reached is irrelevant. The affected shareholder must promptly notify the company and the Federal Supervisory Authority however, within seven calendar days at the latest if he has attained, exceeded, or fallen below the specified threshold values. In addition, he must report the exact percentage of voting rights. Finally, he must give his address.

This affects only shareholdings in domestic companies which are admitted for official trading on a stock exchange in a member state of the European Community or a contracting state of the European Economic Area Treaty. Thus, companies only admitted for regulated trading or only included in free market trading are unaffected.

Introduction

2) Shares Attributed or not Taken into Account

As there could be a tendency, in building up or reducing a block of shares, to circumvent the reporting obligations by purchases (sales) via third parties, a comprehensive regulation concerning the attribution of voting rights (§ 22 Securities Trading Act) has been created. There may also be cases where it may also be improper for the purposes of this Act to take into account certain voting rights; therefore, the instances when voting rights are not to be taken into account have been specified in a further provision (§ 23 Securities Trading Act).

Attributions are made specifically in the following cases:

– when the shares belong to a company controlled by the person whose duty it is to report (registrant),

– when a third party acquires the shares for the account of the registrant or for a company which is controlled by the registrant,

– when the registrant has a right of purchase or where a beneficiary right is created for the registrant, or when the papers have been transferred as security and the exercise of voting rights remains with the registrant,

– when voting right pool agreements have been made,

– of particular importance is when securities entrusted for safekeeping are assigned, when the keeper can exercise the voting rights of the shares at his discretion in the absence of specific instructions from the shareholder.

The Securities Trading Act allows for instances where voting rights are not to be taken into account. However such cases can only be asserted after the Federal Supervisory Authority, following the appropriate application, so decides.

It is particularly important to mention that shares which are held in a trading portfolio do not need to be included on application. Distinguishing characteristics, such as those developed for bank accounting purposes, may be applied here. In practice, some trading portfolios can reach significant percentage levels.

A further prerequisite is that the applicant is a company which provides services related to securities. Finally, there is the requirement

Introduction

that shares are acquired without any intention of exerting influence on the management of the company.

For other companies not fulfilling the above requirement, it is under certain circumstances possible to apply for exemption of certain voting rights if there is no intention of exerting influence on the management of the company.

When voting rights may not be taken into consideration, they may also not be exercised, at least not when exercising them would trigger a reporting requirement according to § 21 of the Securities Trading Act.

3) Procedure

If the company has received the necessary notification from the registrant, it must publish this notification promptly in a national authorized journal, however within nine calendar days at the latest. If the shares are also admitted to official trading on a stock exchange of another member state of the European Community or in another contracting state of the European Economic Area Treaty, corresponding notification must also be given in a stock exchange authorized journal in the relevant state.

In the case of a company with its principal place of business abroad but whose shares are admitted to official trading on a domestic stock exchange, the requirement to publish is the same as for domestic issuers.

To avoid misleading publications, the person making the notification (registrant) must, at the request of the Federal Supervisory Authority or the company quoted on the stock exchange, provide proof of the existence of the reported shareholding (§ 27 Securities Trading Act).

While the reporting requirements remain unfulfilled, the voting rights from the shares cannot be exercised.

The Federal Supervisory Authority has extensive powers to review and determine whether reporting and publication requirements have been met. Cooperation with the responsible authorities of the other

Introduction

states of the European Communities and other contracting states of the European Economic Area Treaty, and other states where applicable, is prescribed in the Act.

IV. Rules of Conduct

For some time it was uncertain whether general rules of conduct for companies providing services related to securities should also be incorporated into the Securities Trading Act, or whether this should be left to the anticipated Third Financial Market Advancement Act. The rules of conduct were finally drawn up on the insistence of the Bundesbank in particular.

1) General and Specific Rules

The emphasis is, first of all, on the general and self-evident obligation of companies providing services related to securities to work with the necessary expertise, care and conscientiousness in the interests of clients. Avoiding conflicts of interest is crucial. If conflicts of interest cannot be avoided, the client's brief must be carried out with all due consideration of the client's interests.

The further obligations are also subject to the principle that everything must be done for and in the interests of the client. To help prevent exploiting a client's inexperience or unfamiliarity with securities transactions, firms are required to ascertain the experience and knowledge of the client in the field of securities.

In particular, emphasis is placed on instances when the client's interests could be jeopardized by the recommendation of the purchase or sale of certain securities or their derivatives. It is precisely those cases involving conflicts of interests with the independent transactions of the company providing services related to securities and those of the customer which are of special significance.

Front running is also covered (see § 32 sub-paragraph 1 No. 3). As mentioned earlier (see p. 22) front running is principally an offense against the insider rules. However, it may be that the insider effect is

Introduction

not sufficient to influence the market price to the required substantial extent and therefore does not qualify as a violation of the prohibitions. In any case, front running is always a violation of the rules of conduct.

2) Organizational Obligations

Of special practical significance are the organizational obligations required of companies providing services related to securities to help insure that a transaction which is not in the client's interest and which, in particular, could lead to conflicts of interest, is ruled out from the outset. Each company providing services related to securities must be organized in such a way that when carrying out its business, conflicts of interest between the company and the client, and between different clients, are reduced to an absolute minimum. The companies must have appropriate internal control procedures to eliminate as far as possible contraventions of the requirements of the Securities Trading Act.

The entire body of compliance rules have now been addressed. It is especially important, particularly with the German universal banking system, that "Chinese walls" are erected between the various bank departments to prevent the uncontrolled spread of information. Most of the larger banks have already implemented the necessary procedures. From now on, such measures are a legal requirement.

Companies providing services relating to securities must comply with certain obligations to keep books and records for a specified period to make the monitoring effective. The order and associated instructions from the client, the execution thereof, the name of the employee taking the order, and the date and time for each procedure must all be duly recorded.

The monitoring of these rules of conduct is again the responsibility of the Federal Supervisory Authority, which has extensive inspection and monitoring rights.

Introduction

C. STOCK EXCHANGE LAW

I. Trading

1) General Remarks

In the Federal Republic of Germany, floor trading is conducted at eight exchanges. Besides Frankfurt am Main, these include the stock exchanges in Düsseldorf, Munich, Stuttgart, Berlin, Hamburg, Hannover and Bremen. Frankfurt is of especial importance, given that about 75% of securities trading turnover is conducted there.

A distinction is to be made between traditional floor trading, now, like elsewhere around the world, with computer support, which runs like an auction, and computerized trading such as on IBIS (Integrated Stock Exchange Information System) or on the DTB (*Deutsche Terminbörse*) for dealings in futures and options.

Stock exchanges require an allowance from the responsible Stock Exchange Supervisory Agency to operate. This Supervisory Agency is a State Agency of the respective *Länder* (for example Hesse or Bavaria) where the stock exchange is located. The fact that stock exchange supervision is a prerogative of the *Länder* and not the Federal Government, explains many legalities and characteristics of the German stock market. This also goes to explain why there is no central oversight for the securities trade in the form of a single agency like the SEC but instead a splintering into various oversight agencies.

The traders on the floor represent mostly banks, and there are also official brokers (*Kursmakler*), and independent brokers (*Freimakler*). Official brokers and independent brokers may only trade with banks or with each other and are for this reason not to be confused with brokers active in the financial industry in the US, for example.

§7 of the Stock Exchange Act lists the rules for admission to the stock exchange, some of which have been tightened under the new law.

Introduction

2) Bank and Customer Orders

It is characteristic of the German universal banking system that trade in securities is done through banks. That is the reason that in § 1 of the Banking Act, the acquistition and disposal of securities for others is singled out as a legal peculiarity of banking activity. Banks take their customer's orders, carry them out on the stock exchange or elsewhere, and handle the custody and administration of securities for the accounts of their customers as well, another legal peculiarity of German banks.

According to § 10 of the redrafted Stock Exchange Act, banks as a general rule have to carry out orders for the buying and selling of securities which are admitted to trading on a domestic stock exchange or on the free market through trading on the stock exchange. The customer is to determine where the transaction is to take place, and whether the trade is to be done on the floor or electronically. If the customer does not give specific instructions, the order or trade is as a general rule to be carried out on the floor unless the best interest of the customer calls for a different execution. The same is true for where the trade is to be carried out.

If the customer gives specific instructions in individual cases or for a certain number of trades not to carry out the order on the stock exchange, then the bank is to follow these instructions.

For fixed interest bonds which are the subject of an issue the total nominal value of which is less than two billion German Marks the previous provisions for execution do not apply.

Trade in fixed income securities takes place mostly over the telephone outside the exchange, especially for institutional investors.

Banks execute customer orders in the legal form of a commission agency according to § 383 seq. of the Commercial Code. Transfer of ownership is effected according to the model system of the German Safe Custody Act and the efficient handling through the German Securities Settlements Organization.

Introduction

3) Brokers and Prices

As outlined, customer orders are, when in doubt, to be directed to the floor traders. In this traditional floor trading the official brokers play a special role. They exercise a public office and are appointed by the stock exchange supervisory agencies, and stand under special oversight. Apart from the exercise of these official duties, they are independent professionals.

The official brokers determine the official price for the paper which is admitted to official trading. The official price in Germany has a special meaning. In many individual regulations of the civil law and commercial law special reference is given to the official stock exchange price. The official price is to be ascertained so that it reflects the actual trading conditions on the exchange (§ 29 sub-paragraph 3 Stock Exchange Act). Claim to consideration in the fixing of the official price is only possible when the trade is carried out through an official broker (§ 31 Stock Exchange Act). This results in de facto constraints to conduct business through the official broker.

Each official broker is assigned a specific segment of securities. During trading hours he is to trade only in these papers and is obligated to make an effort to carry out each order. If an order exists on the other side, he is obliged to carry it out. So long as an order on the other side does not exist, he is not required to carry out a trade at his own risk.

Vice versa, the question arises to what extent the official broker may conduct his own trades when he decides to do so. The revisions of the Stock Exchange Act of 1994 clarified the situation. For calculated prices, the official broker may only take over a contingent remaining amount while in other variable trading he is not subject to such a restriction.

Variable trading is carried out for securities with large turnover. At the start of floor trading, an opening price, according to the system of calculated prices, is ascertained. After that the price will develop according to the trading situation and is fixed in variable trading until noon. At noon, the spot price is ascertained again according to the system of calculated prices, and after that, variable trading takes place

Introduction

until the close of trading. Here once again, the last price is fixed according to the system of calculated prices.

The system of calculated prices is based on the concept that prices are to be ascertained so as to guarantee the highest possible turnover. There are a large number of buy and sell orders, partly limited, partly not, facing each other, so to speak. The calculation of the greatest possible turnover and with that the possible price is prepared these days by computers. If residual amounts appear, then the official broker can step in for his own account. For other variable trades, a price is ascertained according to when a particular deal offers itself or becomes possible.

The revision of the Stock Exchange Act is especially stringent in regard to the formation of the orderly fixing of stock exchange prices. It requires especially that the offers be made accessible to the participants and that they be in a position to accept them. Before the determination of a stock exchange price, the trading participants are to be made aware of the spread between offer and bid prices (different, naturally, for calculated prices). The stock exchange prices and the basis turnover must be made known to the trading participants at once. It is further regulated that in a Stock Exchange Order, before the fixing of a stock exchange price, the trading participants are to be made aware of the price of the highest limited buying order and of the lowest limited selling order.

If there are strong variations in the price development, the trading participants are to be made aware of this in advance according to certain rules. Notification is to be made by a plus announcement when a stock price rises more than 5 percent, in the case of fixed interest securities, 1.5 percent of the nominal worth. If a stock price rises more than 10 percent or 3 percent for a fixed interest security, then a double plus announcement is to be made. A triple plus announcement is to be made in cases when a share price rises more than 20 percent. Correspondingly, minus announcements are to be made when prices fall. After the respective announcement has been made, the official broker is to call for a representative of the Board of Governors before determining the new price.

Addenda to fixed prices are also to indicate certain circumstances to the trading participants such as whether offers or bids could not be bal-

Introduction

anced or even had to be rationed, or if a price was fixed but no trades executed.

Details are to be found in the "Conditions for Trading on German Stock Exchanges", as well as other rules for the carrying on of business, and in the respective Stock Exchange Orders of the respective floor exchanges.

Independent brokers exercise similar functions as the official brokers when they ascertain prices for securities which are only included on the free market or admitted on the regulated market. Similar rules apply to price fixing as for the official brokers. Aside from this, independent brokers are in every respect independent traders attempting to draw orders from the banks, trading with each other and with the official brokers.

Brokers are not representatives of the respective parties. Instead, they exercise an intermediary function.

Automatic clearing between the participants takes place over an automated stock exchange settlement system.

In practice, the opportunity for "open transaction for undisclosed parties" (*Aufgabegeschäft*) plays a large role for the brokers. If a broker has an order outstanding, but no corresponding order on the other side to match it, he can still fill the order subject to the proviso that the party on the other side will be named later. Open transaction can only be carried through up to a ceiling depending on the deposit left on account at the stock exchange.

The automatic routing system BOSS allows the banks to communicate their trades to the official brokers or independent brokers directly. If the affected independent broker does not carry out the trade himself, he hands it on to the official broker. The official broker's order book fills with orders in this way.

4) Electronic Trading

Floor trading, now with computer support, corresponds to the traditional picture of stock exchange trading, common at least since its

Introduction

introduction in the Stock Exchange Law of 1896. In recent years developments in the direction of computer trading systems have changed the landscape. It cannot be easily predicted to what extent the traditional floor trading scheme will be pushed into the background by the increased use of computer trading systems. But for some time activity has been in this direction.

For example, IBIS (Integriertes Börsen- und Informations-System) has been operating since 1991. Transactions are carried out through the automated matching of buy and sell orders, without the mediation of brokers. IBIS runs both simultaneously with floor trading and before and after normal trading times. A very high percentage of trading in securities with high volume is now conducted over IBIS. From the administrative point of view, IBIS is not a separate stock exchange, but rather a supplement to floor trading.

The DTB (*Deutsche Terminbörse*) is, on the other hand, a separate stock exchange. It works according to the marketmaker system. Brokers as such are not active in the system. Trades are transacted within the clearing system and between the clearing banks and the customers.

The margin which the clearinghouse demands of the clearing banks, and the clearing banks of its customers, is calculated by permanent calculation of positions so that risks are hedged.

II. Admission of Securities

Requirements for the admission of securities for trading on the stock exchange differ depending on the market segment, that is, whether the security is to be

- admitted to official trading
- admitted to the regulated market
- included in the free market

The consequences of admission differ too, depending on the market segment.

Introduction

1. *Official Market*

The regulations are to be found in §§ 36–49 of the Stock Exchange Act and in the Stock Exchange Admissions Regulation.

a) General Prerequisites, Procedure

General prerequisites for the admission to official trading are that the prospective value of the shares to be admitted be at least 2.5 million German Marks. For other securities the nominal value must be at least 0.5 million German Marks (§ 2 Stock Exchange Admissions Regulation). Additionally, the issuer must have existed as an enterprise for at least three years and to have made available its annual reports for the three years preceding the application (§ 3 Stock Exchange Admissions Regulation). A sufficient distribution of the shares is also a prerequisite, this is satisfied if at least 25 percent of the total nominal value of the securities to be admitted is acquired by the public or if, because of the great number of shares and their wide distribution, regular stock exchange trade is assured even with a lower percentage (§ 9 Stock Exchange Admissions Regulation).

Application for admission must be made by the issuer and a credit institution which is admitted to trading on a domestic exchange. The admission is to include a copy of the stock exchange admission prospectus. The specific documents required follow § 48 of the Stock Exchange Admissions Regulation.

The admissions application goes from the Listing Board to publication in an authorized journal as well as announcement on the stock exchange. The Listing Board then decides on the admissions application. Admission of the issue may not follow sooner than three work days following the publication of the admission application.

If the application is approved, then the prospectus is to be published either in an authorized journal or is to be made available at the offices of the paying agent. So the admission is to be published, as well as the prospectus (§ 51 Stock Exchange Admissions Regulation).

Only after these preliminaries can the security be introduced. This normally takes place – at the earliest – on the third work day after the

Introduction

first publication of the prospectus. The introduction itself must also be accompanied by a credit institution admitted to trading on a domestic stock market.

b) Prospectus

The contents of the stock exchange prospectus are laid down in detail in §§ 13 ff. of the Stock Exchange Admissions Regulation.

The prospectus is to include information about the security, especially the specific conditions of issuance, all technicalities and information about the expected net proceeds of the issue, the stock exchanges where application was or will be made, and the payment and deposit offices.

The prospectus is also to contain information about the issuer itself, to include the legal form of the company and the objects of the business.

Exact information is to be given about the capital of the issuer (§ 19 Stock Exchange Admissions Regulation).

Information about the Board of Directors, Supervisory Board, and certified public accountants is to be included.

The most critical and important points are the information about the business activity of the issuer (§ 20 Stock Exchange Admissions Regulation) and information about the net worth, financial situation, and results of the issuer (§ 21 Stock Exchange Admissions Regulation). Questions about legal or arbitration proceedings, important patents, and figures on the most important investments including future investments which are already agreed upon belong here. Developments in current business activity, business prospects as well as a detailed presentation of the previous year's annual accounts are to be offered.

c) Consequences of Admission

One consequence of admission is the ad hoc publicity requirement, earlier covered in the Stock Exchange Act, now newly formulated in

Introduction

§ 15 of the Securities Trading Act (see p. 28 ff.). Another consequence of admission is the necessity to publish at least one interim report per year (§ 44 b Stock Exchange Act and §§ 53 ff. Stock Exchange Admissions Regulation). The interim report has to allow assessment of the business development of the issuer for the first six months of the business year and present turnover, classified by field of activity, and results before or after taxes.

There exists the further general obligation to treat all shareholders of admitted securities equally under like circumstances and the general obligation to inform the public and the Listing Board about the issuer and the admitted securities.

d) Prospectus Liability

The prospectus is to be examined by the Listing Board. The importance of the prospectus lies however in the liability which intervenes if the information in the prospectus is inaccurate.

The law distinguishes between the incorrectness of a prospectus and the incompleteness of a prospectus:

In the case of the incorrectness of a prospectus, those responsible for the prospectus are liable, if they knew of the incorrectness or without gross negligence should have known. For an incomplete prospectus, liability incurs only if this is due to fraudulent concealment or fraudulent omission of a sufficient audit on the part of those responsible for the prospectus.

Those liable to recourse are all those who authorized the prospectus and those from whom the prospectus emanates. The prospectus is authorized by those taking responsibility for it. This includes the credit institution that, with the issuer, made the application for admission and those persons who, following § 14 of the Stock Exchange Admission Regulation, made the declaration that to their knowledge the information was correct and no essential conditions were left out. Not only are those who authorized the prospectus liable, but also the actual originators of the prospectus – who may have used those apparently responsible as a pretext for their own purposes.

Introduction

Those entitled to damages are only those who came into possession of the securities, through domestic purchase, and which were admitted on the basis of the disputed prospectus. If the sale of the securities goes ahead after the publication of the prospectus, a causal connection between its contents and the acquisition of the securities is to be supposed. It can also be the case that the securities were placed before the prospectus was published, for example if subscription rights were taken up based on the Stock Corporation Act. Then the required causality is lacking.

If there is contributory negligence on the part of the damaged party, all claims to liability do not apply. It is not the case, as otherwise common in civil law, where a damages division would follow.

In principle, the party liable to pay damages is liable for all damages. The Stock Exchange Act gives, however, a compensation authorization which allows the party liable for damages to accept the return of the securities against payment of the certified buying price or the price of the securities upon admission.

Damage claims resulting from liability of a prospectus become barred by the statute of limitations after five years of the admission of the security.

2) Regulated Market

The prerequisites of admission to the regulated market are given in §§ 71-77 of the Stock Exchange Act, as well as in the respective Stock Exchange Orders of the individual exchanges.

In the regulated market, admission is made easier. For this reason, many prerequisites for the admission to official trading are refrained from. It is, for example, not necessary that a company already exist for three years. The volume of the nominal value of the securities to be placed need not exceed 0.5 million German Marks. A prospectus is not necessary, instead, a company report is sufficient. An interim report is also unnecessary. The provisions pertaining to ad hoc publicity remain, however, applicable.

Introduction

Other rules are to a great extent similar to those applicable to official trading.

3) Free Market

The rules differ according to the specific exchange and their committees of independent brokers.

No prospectus is necessary (however, the rules of the Securities Sales Prospectus Act must be followed). No company report is necessary and there is no necessity to publish interim reports. One reason is that the consent of the issuer is not required for inclusion in the free market.

III. Futures Trading

The legal framework for futures trading in Germany has a colorful past and many peculiarities. The intricacies of the legalities (which would fill a well stocked law library) are not to be handled in detail, rather some basics.

1) Disallowed Business

The question whether a futures transactions is prohibited or allowed can be decided by Regulation by the Federal Ministry of Finance. Business transacted nevertheless is null and void.

Previous prohibitions against the trade in grain futures were finally annulled by the Second Financial Market Advancement Law. The establishment of commodities futures exchanges is now possible and is encouraged by other new provisions in the Stock Exchange Act.

2) Allowed, Official Business

If a transaction is allowed, the next distinction is between official and unofficial business. Official business is a transaction admitted by the stock exchange to stock exchange futures trading. This is effective,

Introduction

if on both sides there is the capacity to conclude futures deals or if the transaction has been settled.

There is the capacity to conclude futures trades when on both sides persons officially registered in the trade register, or stock exchange professionals, conduct the trade. In cases when only one side is a person officially registered in the trade register, the required capacity to conclude futures trades can be supplied by information. The contents of the required information is supplied in § 53 sub-paragraph 2 of the Stock Exchange Act.

Such transactions are held to be valid.

3) Allowed, Unofficial Business

These are transactions outside a domestic stock exchange or on a foreign stock exchange. Similar rules apply as in cases of allowed, official business. However § 61 Stock Exchange Act stipulates that for foreign transactions, no further claims may be raised as would be possible under German Law, with the proviso that the required capacity to conclude futures deals is lacking, that furthermore the ordinary residence of the persons concerned is in Germany, and that the person has rendered the declaration of intent in Germany.

D. SECURITIES SALES PROSPECTUS ACT

With the passing of the Securities Sales Prospectus Act, which entered into force on 1 Jan. 1991 (and the accompanying Sales Prospectus Regulation – not reprinted here), the German legislature translated an E.C. directive into national law. Alongside the goal of institutional protection of the capital market, the intention is to guarantee individual protection for investors. The rules are designed to contribute to the creation of an effective Europe-wide capital market law.

In part, these rules supplement prospectus law as defined by the Stock Exchange Act and the Stock Exchange Admissions Regulations, in part they break new ground.

Introduction

I. Basic Rules

The basic regulation states that for securities publicly offered for sale for the first time on the domestic market and not admitted to trading on a domestic stock exchange, the issuer is to publish a prospectus. Subsequently, the Act distinguishes between whether an application is made for admission to official listing on a domestic stock exchange or not.

The question as to which securities the Act covers is not completely clear. "Securities" is not explained in detail. It will hardly be possible to fall back on the definition from the Securities Trading Act, first passed in 1994.

A public offer for sale occurs when the offer is targeted at an unspecified group of people. An offer for sale to a group of people which is merely restricted exists particularly in cases of "private placement". If, after the completion of the private placement, securities are then sold by individual "intermediate buyers" to multiple end purchasers, this also constitutes a public offer for sale. Incidentally, it is immaterial in what form the offer for sale is directed at the unspecified group of people, e.g. by direct mail, or through advertisements in the media. Furthermore, it is irrelevant whether a sales offer already exists according to civil law, or merely a request to submit offers for sale via potential investors.

The obligation to publish the sales prospectus applies to the person making the offer. This may be the issuer, but need not be; it can also be a third party, particularly the issuing banks. The Act does not impose any requirement to hand over the prospectus. Rather, the only requirements are those relating to publication, deposition and making the prospectus available. The decision as to whether to make use of the information offered in the sales prospectus is left to the investor.

Any publication referring to or giving information about the sales offer of the securities must refer to the prospectus and its publication. Should any changes occur in the intervening period between publication and sale, there is a legal requirement to update the prospectus.

Introduction

II. Exceptions

§§ 2-4 of the Act contain specific exceptions from the requirement to publish a sales prospectus. There are exceptions in relation to certain types of sales offers, e.g. if securities are offered for sale to a group of people who, by virtue of access to other information sources, are sufficiently informed and therefore not in need of protection; or if employers make sales offers to their employees.

There are further exceptions regarding specific issuers. In particular, there is a wide-ranging exemption from the requirement to publish a sales prospectus when bonds are offered for sale via credit institutions. As credit institutions are subject to regular supervision by the Federal Banking Supervisory Authority, the lack of a sales prospectus would appear harmless, for reasons associated with the protection of investors.

Finally, there are exceptions regarding specific securities, Eurosecurities in particular, provided these are not offered for sale in a general advertising campaign, or door-to-door.

III. The Prospectus

The requirements regarding the contents of the sales prospectus vary according to whether or not an application has been made for official listing on a domestic stock exchange.

If so, the sales prospectus must conform to stock exchange admissions prospectus requirements. In practice, this means that only one prospectus is drawn up. If, however, the securities are first offered for sale and only afterwards an application is made for admission to official listing, then the prospectus must initially comply only with the requirements of the Securities Sales Prospectus Act. Should it not fulfill the conditions laid down by the Stock Exchange Admissions Regulations when a subsequent application is made for admission to official listing, a second prospectus must be drawn up which does.

Introduction

If no application has been made for admission to official listing on a domestic stock exchange, the general rule applying is that the sales prospectus must contain such particulars as are necessary to enable the public to make an accurate assessment of the issuer and the securities (§ 7, sub-paragraph 1 of the Act). The detailed requirements are listed in the Sales Prospectus Regulations. According to these, the contents of the prospectus are adapted to the rules applicable to the company report as required in the admissions procedure to the regulated market.

In the case of securities for which an application has been made for official listing, before publication, the sales prospectus must be approved by the Listing Board of the stock exchange. For securities for which no application has been made for admission to official listing, there is no requirement for an approval of the sales prospectus. The sales prospectus merely has to be deposited before publication with the Federal Supervisory Authority for Securities Trading.

IV. Liability, Fines

The relevant provisions of §§ 45-48 of the Stock Exchange Act (see p. 12 ff.) apply in respect to liability for infringement of the requirement to publish a prospectus. Accordingly, any entitlement to compensation lapses in five years following the date of publication.

Specific violations of the requirement to publish a prospectus can be punished by fines as breach of regulation, i.e. if the prospectus is not published or not published at the correct time; if it is published before approval by the Listing Board (in the case of an application for official listing); if it is not deposited or not deposited at the correct time with the Depositing Office (Federal Supervisory Authority) and if publication is not carried out or not carried out in the prescribed form.

Introduction

V. International Cooperation

The Act contains extensive rules in respect to cooperation within the European Economic Community and the states of the European Economic Area Treaty. The responsible authorities cooperate within the framework of their responsibilities and powers and can share requisite information.

In some cases, the domestic Listing Board may be required to obtain a statement from the responsible authority of another state.

If sales offers are made in several member states of the European Economic Community or in other contracting states of The European Economic Area Treaty, the domestic Listing Board must under certain conditions approve the sales prospectus already approved by the responsible authority of the other state without further review (§ 15 of the Act). If exemptions have been granted by the responsible authority of the other state or if divergences have been authorized, further exceptions come into effect.

E. SUPERVISION

As mentioned previously, according to the Securities Trading Act a Federal Supervisory Authority was newly created to supervise trading in securities. This Authority will also include a separate securities council. The Stock Exchange Act has been reformulated to supervise the stock exchanges in the different *Länder*. Trading monitoring offices will be established at the stock exchanges. The tasks of these institutions will now be described in more detail.

I. Federal Supervisory Authority for Securities Trading

The Federal Supervisory Authority for Securities Trading will receive the information from the issuers regarding price influencing facts in accordance with § 15 of the Securities Trading Act (compare

Introduction

page 30 ff. above). Once the issuer has made the information public, in accordance with the new regulations, he will furnish the Federal Supervisory Authority with evidence of this publication. The Federal Supervisory Authority will monitor compliance with § 15 of the Securities Trading Act. It can request information and have documents presented. The staff of the Federal Supervisory Authority can have access to the offices of the issuer during normal working hours in order to pursue their monitoring duties.

Furthermore, the Federal Supervisory Authority monitors the trading of insider securities on and off the stock exchange in order to prevent prohibited insider dealings from taking place. All credit institutions and other business admitted to trading on the stock exchange are obliged to inform the Federal Supervisory Authorities of all transactions in securities or derivatives the day after the transaction took place at the latest, and it is irrelevant whether they concluded the transaction in connection with a service relating to securities or as an own account deal (compare § 9 of the Securities Trading Act). Own account deals must be specially indicated.

With this information, the Federal Supervisory Authority is in a position to follow the market and to determine when violations of insider laws might have taken place. The relevant computerised monitoring system is in the process of being set up and appropriate software is being developed.

Once the Federal Supervisory Authority suspects that a violation of the insider laws might have occurred, it can request information from credit institutions or other businesses. It can demand the identity of the person who gave the order and the persons entitled or obliged, and changes in the portfolio of the insider securities. It can also demand the presentation of documents. Again, the staff of the Federal Supervisory Authority is authorised to enter offices during normal working hours.

In addition, the Federal Supervisory Authority can demand information about insider facts and persons having knowledge of these facts from the issuer. These persons, as well as those who gave the orders for these deals, are obliged to furnish any information requested of them.

Introduction

If the Federal Supervisory Authority has substantiated suspicions that a criminal offence has occurred, it then passes this information along to the Public Prosecutor. The Federal Supervisory Authority does not conduct prosecutions, rather the Public Prosecutor, with the support of the police.

The clear intention of the law is for the Federal Supervisory Authority to cooperate intensively with the supervising authorities of other countries (§ 19 Securities Trading Act).

The Federal Supervisory Authority will also receive information about substantial changes in participations in corporations whose shares are quoted on the stock exchange (§ 21 Securities Trading Act). When the listed corporation has published the necessary information, the Federal Supervisory Authority is to receive a notification to the effect that the information has been made public.

The Federal Supervisory Authority will release the listed corporation from having to make information public if it makes an application to that effect in writing and if, once the Authority has considered the circumstances, it is of the opinion that publication would not be in the interest of the public or would cause the corporation substantial damage.

The Federal Supervisory Authority has appropriate authorisation to cooperate with the responsible authorities in foreign countries (§ 30 Securities Trading Act), similar to the authorisation for insider monitoring.

Furthermore, the Federal Supervisory Authority monitors adherence to the rules of conduct laid down in §§ 31 ff. of the Securities Trading Act. To do this, annual checks are made. In the case of credit institutions, this check is carried out with the securities deposit audit.

Finally, the Federal Supervisory Authority is the depositing office for prospectuses, to be deposited according to the Securities Sales Prospectus Act.

The Securities Council within the Federal Supervisory Authority is made up of members from each Land. The securities council is also involved in the monitoring. It advises the Federal Supervisory Authority when the Authority enacts regulations and guidelines as well as

Introduction

with other measures of the Federal Supervisory Authority (§ 5 Securities Trading Act).

II. Stock Exchange Supervisory Agency

The Stock Exchange Supervisory Agency is, in accordance with the Stock Exchange Act, an authority of the *Länder* Government. The Supervisory Agency monitors the stock exchange in accordance with the Stock Exchange Act. Their supervision monitors adherence to the stock exchange rules and regulations and ensures that trading on the stock exchange and settlements are executed correctly.

Until now, the supervision of the Stock Exchange Supervisory Agency was limited to questions of legality, but its jursidiction has been significantly increased to include the supervision of stock exchange trading and settlements. The state commission which was part of the stock exchange is now included in the Supervisory Agency of the *Land*.

Until now, it was possible to delegate the direct supervision of the stock exchange to self administrating bodies, and this was widely done. The supervision of the stock exchange was essentially self administered. This power to delegate supervision is now hardly present.

The Stock Exchange Supervisory Agencies in the *Länder* will continue to supervise the official brokers and independent brokers.

The stock exchange supervisory authorities have extensive information and monitoring rights and can demand information be presented to facilitate all of their tasks.

Introduction

III. Trading Monitoring Offices

The new version of the Stock Exchange Act sets up new institutions in the shape of trading monitoring offices. These will be independent organs of the stock exchange. They have been removed from the usual organisational structure and hierarchies of the stock exchange. The trading monitoring offices main tasks will be to systematically and completely record and evaluate data regarding stock exchange transactions and business settlements on the stock exchange as well as to carry out any necessary investigations. Initially, the trade monitoring office's primary task will be to develop an automatic monitoring system. Electronic checking programs are being developed.

The Stock Exchange Supervisory Agency of the *Länder* Governments can instruct the trading monitoring offices. The directors of the monitoring offices can only be appointed with the agreement of the Stock Exchange Supervisory Agency of the individual *Land*; those persons carrying out the monitoring tasks in the trade monitoring offices can only be removed from office against their wishes in agreement with the Stock Exchange Supervisory Agency of the individual *Land*. Furthermore, the trading monitoring office must report to the Stock Exchange Supervisory Agency of the individual *Land* at regular intervals.

IV. Federal Banking Supervisory Authority

The Federal Banking Supervisory Authority continues to supervise credit institutions as in the past. This means that in future credit institutions will be monitored by the Federal Banking Supervisory Authority where credits or other banking business, including securities business are concerned and, which is new, by the Federal Supervisory Authority for Securities Trading for services relating to securities and trading as stipulated in the Securities Trading Act.

The structure of the supervision can, in parts, only be explained by the federal system of the Federal Republic of Germany. Combining the supervisory offices into one authority would have either affected the

Introduction

rights of the Federal Government or the rights of the individual *Länder*.

However, apart from that, it still remains to be seen how the different supervisory offices will work together, especially whether the necessary supervision can become effective – how overlaps can be avoided on the one hand, and how the necessary cooperation can be achieved on the other.

Those involved assume that by implementing this supervisory system, the requisite international standards will be achieved.

Gesetz über den Wertpapierhandel
(Wertpapierhandelsgesetz – WpHG)*
vom 26. Juli 1994 (BGBl. I, S. 1749)

Inhaltsübersicht

§

Erster Abschnitt	**Anwendungsbereich, Begriffsbestimmungen**	
	Anwendungsbereich	1
	Begriffsbestimmungen	2
Zweiter Abschnitt	**Bundesaufsichtsamt für den Wertpapierhandel**	
	Organisation	3
	Aufgaben	4
	Wertpapierrat	5
	Zusammenarbeit mit Aufsichtsbehörden im Inland	6
	Zusammenarbeit mit zuständigen Stellen im Ausland	7
	Verschwiegenheitspflicht	8
	Meldepflichten	9
	Zwangsmittel	10
	Kosten	11
Dritter Abschnitt	**Insiderüberwachung**	
	Insiderpapiere	12
	Insider	13
	Verbot von Insidergeschäften	14
	Veröffentlichung und Mitteilung kursbeeinflussender Tatsachen	15
	Laufende Überwachung	16
	Verarbeitung und Nutzung personenbezogener Daten	17
	Strafverfahren bei Insidervergehen	18
	Internationale Zusammenarbeit	19
	Ausnahmen	20

---

* Artikel 1 des Gesetzes über den Wertpapierhandel und zur Änderung börsenrechtlicher und wertpapierrechtlicher Vorschriften (Zweites Finanzmarktförderungsgesetz)

Securities Trading Act
of July 26, 1994 (Federal Gazette I 1749)

Table of Contents

		§
Chapter One	**Scope of Application, Definitions**	
	Scope of Application	1
	Definitions	2
Chapter Two	**Federal Supervisory Authority for Securities Trading**	
	Organisation	3
	Duties	4
	Securities Council	5
	Cooperation with Other Domestic Agencies	6
	Cooperation with Responsible Foreign Authorities	7
	Duty of Confidentiality	8
	Reporting Obligations	9
	Enforcement	10
	Costs	11
Chapter Three	**Insider Monitoring**	
	Insider Securities	12
	Insider	13
	Prohibition of Insider Dealings	14
	Publication and Communication of Facts Influencing Market Prices	15
	Continous Monitoring	16
	Processing and Use of Personal Data	17
	Criminal Proceedings for Insider Offences	18
	International Cooperation	19
	Exceptions	20

Wertpapierhandelsgesetz

	§
Vierter Abschnitt	**Mitteilungs- und Veröffentlichungspflichten bei Veränderungen des Stimmrechtsanteils an börsennotierten Gesellschaften**

    Mitteilungspflichten des Meldepflichtigen 21
    Zurechnung von Stimmrechten 22
    Nichtberücksichtigung von Stimmrechten 23
    Mitteilung durch Konzernunternehmen 24
    Veröffentlichungspflichten der börsennotierten Gesellschaft 25
    Veröffentlichungspflichten von Gesellschaften mit Sitz im Ausland 26
    Nachweis mitgeteilter Beteiligungen 27
    Ruhen des Stimmrechts 28
    Befugnisse des Bundesaufsichtsamtes 29
    Zusammenarbeit mit zuständigen Stellen im Ausland 30

Fünfter Abschnitt **Verhaltensregeln für Wertpapierdienstleistungen**

    Allgemeine Verhaltensregeln 31
    Besondere Verhaltensregeln 32
    Organisationspflichten 33
    Aufzeichnungs- und Aufbewahrungspflichten 34
    Überwachung der Verhaltensregeln 35
    Prüfung der Meldepflichten und Verhaltensregeln 36
    Ausnahmen 37

Sechster Abschnitt **Straf- und Bußgeldvorschriften**

    Strafvorschriften 38
    Bußgeldvorschriften 39
    Zuständige Verwaltungsbehörde 40

Siebter Abschnitt **Übergangsbestimmungen**

    Erstmalige Mitteilungs- und Veröffentlichungspflicht 41

Securities Trading Act

		§
Chapter Four	**Information and Publicity Requirements relating to Variations in Voting Rights in Listed Companies**	
	Reporting Requirements	21
	Attribution of Voting Rights	22
	Voting Rights not Taken into Account	23
	Information provided by a Group of Enterprises . . .	24
	Obligation of Listed Companies to Publish Information	25
	Publication Obligations of Foreign Companies	26
	Evidence of Notified Shareholdings	27
	Suspension of Voting Rights	28
	Powers of the Federal Supervisory Authority	29
	Cooperation with Responsible Authorities Abroad	30
Chapter Five	**Rules of Conduct for Enterprises Providing Services Relating to Securities**	
	General Rules of Conduct	31
	Special Rules of Conduct	32
	Organizational Obligations	33
	Duties to Maintain and Retain Records	34
	Monitoring of Rules of Conduct	35
	Auditing Compliance with Reporting Requirements and Rules of Conduct	36
	Exceptions	37
Chapter Six	**Rules Relating to Criminal Provisions and Fines**	
	Criminal Provisions	38
	Fines Provisions	39
	Relevant Administrative Authority	40
		§
Chapter Seven	**Transitional Provisions**	
	Providing Information and Publication of Information for the First Time	41

Wertpapierhandelsgesetz

Erster Abschnitt
Anwendungsbereich, Begriffsbestimmungen

§ 1
Anwendungsbereich

Dieses Gesetz ist anzuwenden auf den börslichen und außerbörslichen Handel mit Wertpapieren und Derivaten sowie auf Veränderungen der Stimmrechtsanteile von Aktionären an börsennotierten Gesellschaften.

§ 2
Begriffsbestimmungen

(1) Wertpapiere im Sinne dieses Gesetzes sind, auch wenn für sie keine Urkunden ausgestellt sind,

1. Aktien, Zertifikate, die Aktien vertreten, Schuldverschreibungen, Genußscheine, Optionsscheine,

2. andere Wertpapiere, die mit Aktien oder Schuldverschreibungen vergleichbar sind,

wenn sie auf einem Markt gehandelt werden können, der von staatlich anerkannten Stellen geregelt und überwacht wird, regelmäßig stattfindet und für das Publikum unmittelbar oder mittelbar zugänglich ist.

(2) Derivate im Sinne dieses Gesetzes sind an einem inländischen oder ausländischen Markt im Sinne des Absatzes 1 gehandelte Rechte, deren Börsen- oder Marktpreis unmittelbar oder mittelbar von der Entwicklung des Börsen- oder Marktpreises von Wertpapieren oder ausländischen Zahlungsmitteln oder der Veränderung von Zinssätzen abhängt.

(3) Wertpapierdienstleistungen im Sinne dieses Gesetzes sind

1. die Anschaffung und die Veräußerung von Wertpapieren oder Derivaten für andere,

2. die Anschaffung und die Veräußerung von Wertpapieren oder Derivaten im Wege des Eigenhandels für andere,

3. die Vermittlung von Geschäften über die Anschaffung und die Veräußerung von Wertpapieren oder Derivaten,

wenn der Umfang der Dienstleistungen einen in kaufmännischer Weise eingerichteten Geschäftsbetrieb erfordert.

– Securities Trading Act

Chapter One

Scope of Application, Definitions

§ 1
Scope of Application

This Act shall apply to trading in securities and derivatives, both on and off the stock exchange, and to variations in the voting rights of shareholders in companies quoted on the stock exchange.

§ 2
Definitions

(1) Securities within the meaning of this Act, even if no authorised documentation has been issued, are:

1. shares, certificates representing shares, bonds, participating certificates, options certificates,

2. other securities equivalent to shares or bonds

which are capable of being traded on a regular basis on a market that is regulated and supervised by state recognised authorities and to which the public has direct or indirect access.

(2) Derivatives within the meaning of this Act are legal rights which are traded on a domestic or foreign market, as defined in sub-paragraph 1, the stock exchange or market price of which depends directly or indirectly on the development of the stock exchange or market price of securities or foreign currencies or on a variation of interest rates.

(3) Services relating to securities within the meaning of this Act are:

1. the acquisition and disposal of securities or derivatives for others,

2. the acquisition and disposal of securities or derivatives as own account business for others,

3. acting as intermediary for transactions involving the acquisiton and disposal of securities and derivatives

where the scope and volume of the services provided require a commercially organised business operation.

Wertpapierhandelsgesetz

(4) Wertpapierdienstleistungsunternehmen sind

1. Kreditinstitute mit Sitz im Inland sowie Zweigstellen von Unternehmen im Sinne des § 53 Abs. 1 Satz 1 und des § 53b Abs. 1 Satz 1 des Gesetzes über das Kreditwesen oder von Unternehmen, die aufgrund einer Rechtsverordnung gemäß § 53c des Gesetzes über das Kreditwesen gleichgestellt oder freigestellt sind,

2. andere Unternehmen mit Sitz im Inland, die an einer inländischen Börse zur Teilnahme am Handel zugelassen sind,

die Wertpapierdienstleistungen erbringen.

Zweiter Abschnitt
Bundesaufsichtsamt für den Wertpapierhandel

§ 3
Organisation

(1) Das Bundesaufsichtsamt für den Wertpapierhandel (Bundesaufsichtsamt) wird als eine selbständige Bundesoberbehörde im Geschäftsbereich des Bundesministeriums der Finanzen errichtet.

(2) Der Präsident des Bundesaufsichtsamtes wird auf Vorschlag der Bundesregierung durch den Bundespräsidenten ernannt. Die Bundesregierung hat bei ihrem Vorschlag die für das Börsenwesen zuständigen Fachministerien der Länder anzuhören.

§ 4
Aufgaben

(1) Das Bundesaufsichtsamt übt die Aufsicht nach den Vorschriften dieses Gesetzes aus. Es hat im Rahmen der ihm zugewiesenen Aufgaben Mißständen entgegenzuwirken, welche die ordnungsmäßige Durchführung des Wertpapierhandels beeinträchtigen oder erhebliche Nachteile für den Wertpapiermarkt bewirken können. Das Bundesaufsichtsamt kann Anordnungen treffen, die geeignet sind, diese Mißstände zu beseitigen oder zu verhindern.

(4) Enterprises providing services relating to securities are:
1. domestic credit institutions and branches of enterprises within the meaning of § 53 sub-paragraph 1 sentence 1 and of § 53b sub-paragraph 1 sentence 1 of the Banking Act or of enterprises that are the equivalent thereof or are exempted under a Regulation made in accordance with § 53c of the Banking Act,
2. other domestic enterprises which are admitted to trading on a domestic stock exchange

which provide services relating to securities.

Chapter Two

Federal Supervisory Authority for Securities Trading

§ 3

Organisation

(1) A Federal Supervisory Authority for Securities Trading ("Federal Supervisory Authority") shall be established as an independent senior federal authority under the aegis of the Federal Ministry of Finance.

(2) The president of the Federal Supervisory Authority shall, following nomination by the Federal Government, be appointed by the president of the Federal Republic of Germany. In nominating a candidate, the federal government is to give hearing to the ministries of the *Länder* responsible for stock exchange matters.

§ 4

Duties

(1) The Federal Supervisory Authority shall exercise supervision in accordance with the provisions of this Act. It shall, within the framework of the duties assigned to it, take steps to counteract any irregularities which could adversely affect the proper conduct of securities trading or substantially harm the securities market. The Federal Supervisory Authority may make Orders for the purpose of eliminating or preventing such irregularities.

Wertpapierhandelsgesetz

(2) Das Bundesaufsichtsamt nimmt die ihm nach diesem Gesetz zugewiesenen Aufgaben und Befugnisse nur im öffentlichen Interesse wahr.

§ 5
Wertpapierrat

(1) Beim Bundesaufsichtsamt wird ein Wertpapierrat gebildet. Er besteht aus Vertretern der Länder. Die Mitgliedschaft ist nicht personengebunden. Jedes Land entsendet einen Vertreter. An den Sitzungen können Vertreter der Bundesministerien der Finanzen, der Justiz und für Wirtschaft, der Deutschen Bundesbank und des Bundesaufsichtsamtes für das Kreditwesen teilnehmen. Der Wertpapierrat kann Sachverständige insbesondere aus dem Bereich der Börsen, der Marktteilnehmer, der Wirtschaft und der Wissenschaft anhören. Der Wertpapierrat gibt sich eine Geschäftsordnung.

(2) Der Wertpapierrat wirkt bei der Aufsicht mit. Er berät das Bundesaufsichtsamt, insbesondere

1. bei dem Erlaß von Rechtsverordnungen und der Aufstellung von Richtlinien für die Aufsichtstätigkeit des Bundesaufsichtsamtes,

2. hinsichtlich der Auswirkungen von Aufsichtsfragen auf die Börsen- und Marktstrukturen sowie den Wettbewerb im Wertpapierhandel,

3. bei der Abgrenzung von Zuständigkeiten zwischen dem Bundesaufsichtsamt und den Börsenaufsichtsbehörden sowie bei Fragen der Zusammenarbeit.

Der Wertpapierrat kann beim Bundesaufsichtsamt Vorschläge zur allgemeinen Weiterentwicklung der Aufsichtspraxis einbringen. Das Bundesaufsichtsamt berichtet dem Wertpapierrat mindestens einmal jährlich über die Aufsichtstätigkeit, die Weiterentwicklung der Aufsichtspraxis sowie über die internationale Zusammenarbeit.

(3) Der Wertpapierrat wird mindestens einmal jährlich vom Präsidenten des Bundesaufsichtsamtes einberufen. Er ist ferner auf Verlangen von einem Drittel seiner Mitglieder einzuberufen. Jedes Mitglied hat das Recht, Beratungsvorschläge einzubringen.

(2) The Federal Supervisory Authority shall perform the duties imposed on it and exercise the authority given it by this Act solely in the public interest.

§ 5
Securities Council

(1) The Federal Supervisory Authority is to form a Securities Council. It is to be made up of representatives of the Länder. Membership shall not be personal membership. Each Land is to send a representative. The Federal Ministries of Finance, Justice, Economy, the German Federal Bank and the Federal Banking Supervisory Authority shall be entitled to attend meetings of the Securities Council. The Securities Council may give hearing to experts on stock exchange matters, persons concerned in the market, the economy and academics. The Securities Council shall formulate its own standing orders.

(2) The Securities Council shall assist in the exercise of supervision. It shall advise the Federal Supervisory Authority, in particular on the following matters:

1. the making of Regulations and the formulation of guidelines applicable to the supervisory work of the Federal Supervisory Authority,
2. the effects of matters arising out of supervision on stock exchange and market structures as well as competition in securities trading,
3. the demarcation of responsibilities between the Federal Supervisory Authority and the Stock Exchange Supervisory Agencies, and questions of cooperation between them.

The Securities Council shall be entitled to make proposals to the Federal Supervisory Authority on the general development of supervisory practice. The Federal Supervisory Authority shall report to the Securities Council at least once a year on its supervisory activities, the development of supervisory practice, and international cooperation.

(3) A meeting of the Securities Council shall be convened at least once a year by the president of the Federal Supervisory Authority. In addition, meetings may be convened by one third of the members. Each member shall have the right to put forward suggestions for discussion.

Wertpapierhandelsgesetz

§ 6
Zusammenarbeit mit Aufsichtsbehörden im Inland

(1) Das Bundesaufsichtsamt kann sich bei der Durchführung seiner Aufgaben anderer Personen und Einrichtungen bedienen.

(2) Die Börsenaufsichtsbehörden werden im Wege der Organleihe für das Bundesaufsichtsamt bei der Durchführung von eilbedürftigen Maßnahmen für die Überwachung der Verbote von Insidergeschäften nach § 14 an den ihrer Aufsicht unterliegenden Börsen tätig. Das Nähere regelt ein Verwaltungsabkommen zwischen dem Bund und den börsenaufsichtsführenden Ländern.

(3) Das Bundesaufsichtsamt für das Kreditwesen, das Bundesaufsichtsamt für das Versicherungswesen, die Deutsche Bundesbank, soweit sie die Beobachtungen und Feststellungen im Rahmen ihrer Tätigkeit nach Maßgabe des Gesetzes über das Kreditwesen macht, die Börsenaufsichtsbehörden sowie das Bundesaufsichtsamt haben einander Beobachtungen und Feststellungen mitzuteilen, die für die Erfüllung ihrer Aufgaben erforderlich sind.

§ 7
Zusammenarbeit mit zuständigen Stellen im Ausland

(1) Dem Bundesaufsichtsamt obliegt die Zusammenarbeit mit den für die Überwachung von Börsen oder anderen Wertpapiermärkten und den Wertpapierhandel zuständigen Stellen anderer Staaten. Die Vorschriften des Börsengesetzes und des Verkaufsprospektgesetzes über die Zusammenarbeit der Zulassungsstelle der Börse mit entsprechenden Stellen anderer Staaten bleiben hiervon unberührt.

(2) Das Bundesaufsichtsamt darf im Rahmen der Zusammenarbeit mit den in Absatz 1 Satz 1 genannten Stellen Tatsachen übermitteln, die für die Überwachung von Börsen oder anderen Wertpapiermärkten, des Wertpapierhandels, von Kreditinstituten, Finanzinstituten oder Versicherungsunternehmen oder damit zusammenhängender Verwaltungs- oder Gerichtsverfahren erforderlich sind. Bei der Übermittlung von Tatsachen hat das Bundesaufsichtsamt den Zweck zu bestimmen, für den diese Tatsachen verwendet werden dürfen. Der Empfänger ist darauf hinzuweisen, daß die übermittelten Tatsachen einschließlich personenbezogener Daten nur zu dem Zweck verarbeitet oder benutzt werden dürfen, zu dessen Erfüllung sie übermittelt wurden.

§ 6
Cooperation with Other Domestic Agencies

(1) The Federal Supervisory Authority may retain other persons and institutions for the purpose of carrying out its duties.

(2) The Stock Exchange Supervisory Agencies shall act by way of delegation on behalf of the Federal Supervisory Authority where urgent steps need to be taken to monitor prohibitions against insider dealings within the meaning of § 14 on stock exchanges for the supervision of which they are responsible. Detailed provisions shall be regulated by an inter-agency agreement between the Federal Government and the Federal States responsible for stock exchange supervision.

(3) The Federal Banking Supervisory Authority, the Federal Insurance Supervisory Authority, the German Federal Bank, to the extent that it makes observations and findings within the scope of its duties under the Banking Act, the Stock Exchange Supervisory Agencies and the Federal Supervisory Authority shall inform one another of any observations or findings which are necessary for the performance of their duties.

§ 7
Cooperation with Responsible Foreign Authorities

(1) The Federal Supervisory Authority shall have the duty to ensure cooperation with the relevant authorities of other states responsible for the supervision of stock exchanges or other securities markets and securities trading. The provisions of the Stock Exchange Act and the Securities Sales Prospectus Act on cooperation between the Listing Board of the stock exchange and the corresponding authorities of other states shall not be affected thereby.

(2) The Federal Supervisory Authority may, in the context of cooperation with the authorities referred to in sub-paragraph 1 sentence 1 provide information necessary for the purpose of supervising stock exchanges or other securities markets, securities trading, credit institutions, financial institutions or insurance enterprises or any court or administrative proceedings connected therewith. In doing so it shall stipulate the purpose of which such information may be used. It shall notify the recipient that any information provided, including personal data, may only be used or processed for the purpose of which it has been provided. Personal data shall not be transmitted

Wertpapierhandelsgesetz

Eine Übermittlung personenbezogener Daten unterbleibt, soweit Grund zu der Annahme besteht, daß durch sie gegen den Zweck eines deutschen Gesetzes verstoßen wird. Die Übermittlung unterbleibt außerdem, wenn durch sie schutzwürdige Interessen des Betroffenen beeinträchtigt würden, insbesondere wenn im Empfängerland ein angemessener Datenschutzstandard nicht gewährleistet wäre.

(3) Werden dem Bundesaufsichtsamt von einer Stelle eines anderen Staates Tatsachen mitgeteilt, so dürfen diese nur unter Beachtung der Zweckbestimmung durch diese Stelle offenbart oder verwertet werden.

(4) Die Regelungen über die internationale Rechtshilfe in Strafsachen bleiben unberührt.

§ 8
Verschwiegenheitspflicht

(1) Die beim Bundesaufsichtsamt Beschäftigten und die nach § 6 Abs. 1 beauftragten Personen dürfen die ihnen bei ihrer Tätigkeit bekanntgewordenen Tatsachen, deren Geheimhaltung im Interesse eines nach diesem Gesetz Verpflichteten oder eines Dritten liegt, insbesondere Geschäfts- und Betriebsgeheimnisse sowie personenbezogene Daten, nicht unbefugt offenbaren oder verwerten, auch wenn sie nicht mehr im Dienst sind oder ihre Tätigkeit beendet ist. Dies gilt auch für andere Personen, die durch dienstliche Berichterstattung Kenntnis von den in Satz 1 bezeichneten Tatsachen erhalten. Ein unbefugtes Offenbaren oder Verwerten im Sinne des Satzes 1 liegt insbesondere nicht vor, wenn Tatsachen weitergegeben werden an

1. Strafverfolgungsbehörden oder für Straf- und Bußgeldsachen zuständige Gerichte,

2. kraft Gesetzes oder im öffentlichen Auftrag mit der Überwachung von Börsen oder anderen Wertpapiermärkten, des Wertpapierhandels, von Kreditinstituten, Finanzinstituten oder Versicherungsunternehmen betraute Stellen sowie von diesen beauftragte Personen,

soweit diese Stellen die Informationen zur Erfüllung ihrer Aufgaben benötigen. Für die bei diesen Stellen beschäftigten Personen gilt die Verschwiegenheitspflicht nach Satz 1 entsprechend. An eine Stelle eines anderen Staates dürfen die Tatsachen nur weitergegeben werden, wenn diese Stelle und die von ihr beauftragten Personen einer dem Satz 1 entsprechenden Verschwiegenheitspflicht unterliegen.

where there are grounds to suppose that such transmission would violate the intent of any German law. Furthermore, information shall not be provided if the legitimate interests of any person concerned could thereby be hurt, in particular where the recipient country does not guarantee an adequate standard of data protection.

(3) When the Federal Supervisory Authority is provided with information by the authorities of another state, such information shall only be used or made known for the purposes of which it has been provided.

(4) The provisions relating to international mutual judicial assistance in criminal cases shall not be affected thereby.

§ 8

Duty of Confidentiality

(1) Persons employed by the Federal Supervisory Authority and any persons retained by them in accordance with § 6 sub-paragraph 1 may not, even after termination of their employment or retirement, make unauthorised disclosure of or make use of any information which has come to their knowledge in the course of their employment and which ought to be kept confidential in the interests of any person upon whom obligations are imposed by this Act or of any third party, in particular trade and business secrets and personal data. The same shall also apply to other persons who acquire information by reason of receiving reports of matters of the kind referred to in sentence 1. There is no instance of unauthorised use or disclosure of the kind referred to in sentence 1 when information is passed on to

1. any prosecuting authority or any court which has the power to impose criminal penalties or fines,
2. authorities or persons retained by any authority, responsible under the law or on behalf of the government, for the supervision of stock exchanges, other securities markets or securities trading, credit institutions, financial institutions or insurance enterprises

where such authorities need the information to perform their duties. The duty of confidentiality referred to in sentence 1 shall correspondingly apply to any persons engaged by such authorities. Where such authorities are located in another state, information shall only be passed on to them if they, together with any persons retained by them, are subject to a duty of confidentiality in accordance with sentence 1.

Wertpapierhandelsgesetz

(2) Die Vorschriften der §§ 93, 97, 105 Abs. 1, § 111 Abs. 5 in Verbindung mit § 105 Abs. 1 sowie § 116 Abs. 1 der Abgabenordnung gelten nicht für die in Absatz 1 Satz 1 oder 2 bezeichneten Personen, soweit sie zur Durchführung dieses Gesetzes tätig werden. Sie finden Anwendung, soweit die Finanzbehörden die Kenntnisse für die Durchführung eines Verfahrens wegen einer Steuerstraftat sowie eines damit zusammenhängenden Besteuerungsverfahrens benötigen, an deren Verfolgung ein zwingendes öffentliches Interesse besteht, und nicht Tatsachen betroffen sind, die den in Absatz 1 Satz 1 oder 2 bezeichneten Personen durch eine Stelle eines anderen Staates im Sinne von Absatz 1 Satz 3 Nr. 2 oder durch von dieser Stelle beauftragte Personen mitgeteilt worden sind.

§ 9

Meldepflichten

(1) Kreditinstitute mit Sitz im Inland, Zweigstellen von Unternehmen im Sinne des § 53 Abs. 1 Satz 1 und des § 53b Abs. 1 Satz 1 des Gesetzes über das Kreditwesen oder von aufgrund einer Rechtsverordnung gemäß § 53c des Gesetzes über das Kreditwesen gleichgestellten oder freigestellten Unternehmen sowie andere Unternehmen, die ihren Sitz im Inland haben und an einer inländischen Börse zur Teilnahme am Handel zugelassen sind, sind verpflichtet, dem Bundesaufsichtsamt jedes Geschäft in Wertpapieren oder Derivaten, die zum Handel an einem Markt im Sinne des § 2 Abs. 1 in einem Mitgliedstaat der Europäischen Gemeinschaften oder in einem anderen Vertragsstaat des Abkommens über den Europäischen Wirtschaftsraum zugelassen oder in den Freiverkehr einer inländischen Börse einbezogen sind, spätestens an dem auf den Tag des Geschäftsabschlusses folgenden Werktag, der kein Samstag ist, mitzuteilen, wenn sie das Geschäft im Zusammenhang mit einer Wertpapierdienstleistung oder als Eigengeschäft abschließen. Die Verpflichtung nach Satz 1 gilt auch für Geschäfte in Aktien und Optionsscheinen, bei denen ein Antrag auf Zulassung zum Handel an einem Markt im Sinne des § 2 Abs. 1 oder auf Einbeziehung in den Freiverkehr gestellt oder öffentlich angekündigt ist. Die Verpflichtung nach den Sätzen 1 und 2 gilt auch für Unternehmen, die ihren Sitz im Ausland haben und an einer inländischen Börse zur Teilnahme am Handel zugelassen sind, hinsichtlich der von ihnen an einer inländischen Börse oder im Freiverkehr im Zusammenhang mit einer Wertpapierdienstleistung oder als Eigengeschäft geschlossenen Geschäfte.

Securities Trading Act

(2) The provisions of §§ 93, 97, 105 sub-paragraph 1, §111 sub-paragraph 5 in conjunction with § 105 sub-paragraph 1 and § 116 sub-paragraph 1 of the Taxes Order shall not apply to the persons referred to in sub-paragraph 1 sentences 1 or 2 if such persons are acting to enforce the terms of this Act. They shall, however, apply when the tax authorities require the information for the purpose of bringing proceedings relating to a tax offence under the criminal law or for tax proceedings connected therewith, the prosecution of which is a matter of overriding public interest, and where information is not involved which has been passed on to the persons referred to in sub-paragraph 1 sentences 1 or 2 by an authority of another state within the meaning of sub-paragraph 1 sentence 3 No. 2 or by any persons retained by such an authority.

§ 9
Reporting Obligations

(1) Domestic credit institutions, branches of enterprises within the meaning of § 53 sub-paragraph 1 sentence 1 and § 53b sub-paragraph 1 sentence 1 of the Banking Act or of enterprises that are the equivalent thereof or are exempted in accordance with Regulations under § 53c of the Banking Act and other domestic enterprises which are admitted to trading on a domestic stock exchange, shall be obliged to inform the Federal Supervisory Authority of every transaction in securities or derivatives which are admitted for trading on a market within the meaning of § 2 sub-paragraph 1 in any member state of the European Community or in any other contracting state of the European Economic Area Treaty, or are included for trading on the free market of a domestic stock exchange by no later than the working day, not being a Saturday, following the day on which the transaction was completed, if the transaction was connected with a service relating to securities or was an own account transaction. This obligation shall also apply to transactions in shares and options in relation to which an application for admission to a market within the meaning of § 2 sub-paragraph 1 or for inclusion on the free market has been made or publicly announced. The obligations set out in sentences 1 and 2 shall also apply to foreign enterprises which are admitted to trading on a domestic stock exchange where such enterprises undertake transactions on a domestic stock exchange or on the free market in conjunction with the provision of services relating to securities or transact own account business.

Wertpapierhandelsgesetz

(2) Die Mitteilung hat auf Datenträgern oder im Wege der elektronischen Datenfernübertragung zu erfolgen. Sie muß für jedes Geschäft die folgenden Angaben enthalten:

1. Bezeichnung des Wertpapiers oder Derivats und Wertpapierkennummer,

2. Datum und Uhrzeit des Abschlusses oder der maßgeblichen Kursfeststellung,

3. Kurs, Stückzahl, Nennbetrag der Wertpapiere oder Derivate,

4. die an dem Geschäft beteiligten Kreditinstitute, Zweigstellen und Unternehmen im Sinne des Absatzes 1,

5. die Börse oder das elektronische Handelssystem der Börse, sofern es sich um ein Börsengeschäft handelt,

6. Kennzeichen zur Identifikation des Geschäftes.

Geschäfte für eigene Rechnung sind gesondert zu kennzeichnen.

(3) Das Bundesministerium der Finanzen kann durch Rechtsverordnung, die nicht der Zustimmung des Bundesrates bedarf,

1. nähere Bestimmungen über Inhalt, Art, Umfang und Form der Mitteilung und über die zulässigen Datenträger und Übertragungswege erlassen,

2. zusätzliche Angaben vorschreiben, soweit diese zur Erfüllung der Aufsichtsaufgaben des Bundesaufsichtsamtes erforderlich sind,

3. zulassen, daß die Mitteilungen der Verpflichteten auf deren Kosten durch die Börse oder einen geeigneten Dritten erfolgen, und die Einzelheiten hierzu festlegen,

4. für Geschäfte, die Schuldverschreibungen oder bestimmte Arten von Derivaten zum Gegenstand haben, zulassen, daß Angaben nach Absatz 2 nicht oder in einer zusammengefaßten Form mitgeteilt werden,

5. die in Absatz 1 genannten Kreditinstitute, Zweigstellen und Unternehmen von der Mitteilungspflicht nach Absatz 1 für Geschäfte befreien, die an einem Markt im Sinne des § 2 Abs. 1 in einem anderen Mitgliedstaat der Europäischen Gemeinschaften oder in einem anderen Vertragsstaat des Abkommens über den Europäischen Wirtschaftsraum abgeschlossen werden, wenn in diesem Staat eine Mitteilungspflicht mit gleichwertigen Anforderungen besteht,

(2) The information shall be made available on computer disc or by electronic data transmission. It shall include, for each transaction, the following information:

1. the designation of the security or derivative and identification number of the security,
2. the date and time of the transaction or fixing of the relevant price,
3. the price, number, and face value of the securities or derivatives,
4. the credit institutions, branches and enterprises, within the meaning of sub-paragraph 1, participating in the transaction,
5. the stock exchange or the stock exchange electronic dealing system, if the transaction is a stock exchange transaction,
6. a transaction number for the purpose of identifying the transaction.

Transactions carried out on an own account basis shall be identified separately.

(3) The Federal Ministry of Finance may pass Regulations which shall not require the consent of the Bundesrat

1. making detailed provisions about the content, manner, extent and form of notification and permissible computer disc formats and data transmission of the information;
2. prescribing additional information to be provided to the extent necessary for the performance of the supervisory duties of the Federal Supervisory Authority;
3. providing that the persons obliged to provide the information do so, via the stock exchange or a suitable third party, at their own expense, and make detailed provisions to that effect;
4. allowing the information referred to in sub-paragraph 2 to be provided in summary form or not at all in the case of transactions relating to bonds or certain kinds of derivatives;
5. exempting credit institutions, branches and enterprises of the kind referred to in sub-paragraph 1 from the obligation to provide information in accordance with sub-paragraph 1 if the transaction concerned is concluded on a market within the meaning of § 2 sub-paragraph 1 in another member state of the European Community or of another contracting state of the European Economic Area Treaty where there is a duty to provide information with similar requirements;

Wertpapierhandelsgesetz

6. bei Sparkassen und Kreditgenossenschaften, die sich zur Ausführung des Geschäfts einer Girozentrale oder einer genossenschaftlichen Zentralbank oder des Zentralkreditinstituts bedienen, zulassen, daß die in Absatz 1 vorgeschriebenen Mitteilungen durch die Girozentrale oder die genossenschaftliche Zentralbank oder das Zentralkreditinstitut erfolgen, wenn und soweit der mit den Mitteilungspflichten verfolgte Zweck dadurch nicht beeinträchtigt wird.

(4) Das Bundesministerium der Finanzen kann die Ermächtigung nach Absatz 3 durch Rechtsverordnung auf das Bundesaufsichtsamt übertragen.

§ 10
Zwangsmittel

Das Bundesaufsichtsamt kann seine Verfügungen, die es innerhalb seiner gesetzlichen Befugnisse trifft, mit Zwangsmitteln nach den Bestimmungen des Verwaltungs-Vollstreckungsgesetzes durchsetzen. Es kann auch Zwangsmittel gegen juristische Personen des öffentlichen Rechts anwenden. Die Höhe des Zwangsgeldes beträgt abweichend von § 11 des Verwaltungs-Vollstreckungsgesetzes bis zu 50 000 Deutsche Mark.

§ 11
Kosten

(1) Die Kosten des Bundesaufsichtsamtes sind dem Bund zu erstatten

1. zu 75 Prozent durch Kreditinstitute mit Sitz im Inland und Zweigstellen von Unternehmen im Sinne des § 53 Abs. 1 Satz 1 und des § 53b Abs. 1 Satz 1 des Gesetzes über das Kreditwesen oder von Unternehmen, die aufgrund einer Rechtsverordnung gemäß § 53c des Gesetzes über das Kreditwesen gleichgestellt oder freigestellt sind, sofern diese Kreditinstitute oder Zweigstellen das Effektengeschäft im Inland betreiben dürfen,

2. zu 5 Prozent durch die Kursmakler, Freimakler und andere zur Teilnahme am Börsenhandel zugelassene Unternehmen, die nicht unter Nummer 1 fallen,

3. zu 10 Prozent durch Emittenten mit Sitz im Inland, deren Wertpapiere an einer inländischen Börse zum Handel zugelassen oder mit ihrer Zustimmung in den Freiverkehr einbezogen sind.

6. in the case of savings banks or mutual societies which use a giro bank, a mutual central bank or central credit institution to carry out the transaction, permitting registration as prescribed in sub-paragraph 1, to be effected by the giro bank, mutual central bank or central credit institution, provided that the purpose for which the information is required is not thereby adversely affected.

(4) The Federal Ministry of Finance may, by Regulation, delegate the exercise of its powers under sub-paragraph 3 to the Federal Supervisory Authority.

§ 10

Enforcement

The Federal Supervisory Authority may enforce compliance with any directions it has given within the scope of its statutory authority in accordance with the provisions of the Administrative Enforcement Act. It may also take enforcement steps against legal entities under public law. Notwithstanding § 11 of the Administrative Enforcement Act, the amount of any fine may be up to 50,000 German Marks.

§ 11

Costs

(1) The running costs of the Federal Supervisory Authority shall be reimbursed to the Federal Government as follows:

1. 75% by domestic credit institutions and branches of enterprises within the meaning of § 53 sub-paragraph 1 sentence 1 and § 53b sub-paragraph 1 sentence 1 of the Banking Act or by enterprises which are the equivalent thereof or are exempted in accordance with a regulation under § 53c of the Banking Act to the extent that such credit institutions or branches are permitted to carry out securities business in Germany,

2. 5% by official brokers, independent brokers and other enterprises admitted to trade on the stock exchange not falling within the definition under No.1 above,

3. 10% by domestic issuers whose securities are admitted to trading on a domestic stock exchange or are included with their consent on the free market.

Wertpapierhandelsgesetz

In den Fällen der Nummern 1 und 2 werden die Kosten nach Maßgabe des Umfangs der Geschäfte in Wertpapieren und Derivaten anteilig umgelegt. Im Fall der Nummer 3 werden die Kosten auf die Emittenten nach Maßgabe der Börsenumsätze ihrer zum Handel zugelassenen oder in den Freiverkehr einbezogenen Wertpapiere anteilig umgelegt.

(2) Die nach Absatz 1 Satz 2 Verpflichteten und die inländischen Börsen haben dem Bundesaufsichtsamt auf Verlangen Auskünfte über den Geschäftsumfang und die Börsenumsätze zu erteilen. Die Kostenforderungen werden vom Bundesaufsichtsamt nach den Vorschriften des Verwaltungs-Vollstreckungsgesetzes durchgesetzt.

(3) Das Nähere über die Erhebung der Umlage nach Absatz 1 und über die Beitreibung bestimmt das Bundesministerium der Finanzen durch Rechtsverordnung, die nicht der Zustimmung des Bundesrates bedarf; es kann in der Rechtsverordnung Mindestbeträge festsetzen. Das Bundesministerium der Finanzen kann die Ermächtigung durch Rechtsverordnung auf das Bundesaufsichtsamt übertragen.

(4) Die Kosten, die dem Bund durch die Prüfung nach § 36 Abs. 1 entstehen, sind von den betroffenen Unternehmen gesondert zu erstatten und auf Verlangen des Bundesaufsichtsamtes vorzuschießen.

Dritter Abschnitt

Insiderüberwachung

§ 12

Insiderpapiere

(1) Insiderpapiere sind Wertpapiere, die

1. an einer inländischen Börse zum Handel zugelassen oder in den Freiverkehr einbezogen sind, oder

2. in einem anderen Mitgliedstaat der Europäischen Gemeinschaften oder einem anderen Vertragsstaat des Abkommens über den Europäischen Wirtschaftsraum zum Handel an einem Markt im Sinne des § 2 Abs. 1 zugelassen sind.

Der Zulassung zum Handel an einem Markt im Sinne von § 2 Abs. 1 oder der Einbeziehung in den Freiverkehr steht gleich, wenn der Antrag

In cases 1 and 2, the costs shall be assessed by reference to volume of business in securities and derivatives. In case 3, the costs attributable to issuers shall be assessed by reference to turnover on the stock exchange of securities or derivatives admitted to trading on the stock exchange or included on the free market.

(2) Those obliged to reimburse under the terms of sub-paragraph 1 sentence 1, and domestic stock exchanges shall, on request, provide the Federal Supervisory Authority with information about the business volume and stock exchange turnover. The reimbursement of costs may be enforced by the Federal Supervisory Authority, in accordance with the terms of the Administrative Enforcement Act.

(3) Detailed provisions as to the manner of assessing and recovering of costs in accordance with sub-paragraph 1 shall be formulated by the Federal Ministry of Finance by means of Regulations which do not require the consent of the Bundesrat; such Regulations may provide for minimum contribution levels. The Federal Ministry of Finance may, by Regulation, delegate its powers to the Federal Supervisory Authority.

(4) Monitoring costs due the Federal Government under § 36 sub-paragraph 1 shall be separately reimbursed by the enterprises concerned and, if required by the Federal Supervisory Authority, paid in advance.

Chapter Three

Insider Monitoring

§ 12

Insider Securities

(1) Insider securities are securities which
1. are admitted for trading to a domestic stock exchange or are included on the free market,
2. are admitted in another member state of the European Community or another contracting state of the European Economic Area Treaty to trading on a market within the meaning of § 2 sub-paragraph 1.

Where an application for admission for trading or inclusion on the free market has been made or announced publicly, this shall be the equivalent of

Wertpapierhandelsgesetz

auf Zulassung oder Einbeziehung gestellt oder öffentlich angekündigt ist.

(2) Als Insiderpapiere gelten auch

1. Rechte auf Zeichnung, Erwerb oder Veräußerung von Wertpapieren,
2. Rechte auf Zahlung eines Differenzbetrages, der sich an der Wertentwicklung von Wertpapieren bemißt,
3. Terminkontrakte auf einen Aktien- oder Rentenindex oder Zinsterminkontrakte (Finanzterminkontrakte) sowie Rechte auf Zeichnung, Erwerb oder Veräußerung von Finanzterminkontrakten, sofern die Finanzterminkontrake Wertpapiere zum Gegenstand haben oder sich auf einen Index beziehen, in den Wertpapiere einbezogen sind,
4. sonstige Terminkontrakte, die zum Erwerb oder zur Veräußerung von Wertpapieren verpflichten,

wenn die Rechte oder Terminkontrakte in einem Mitgliedstaat der Europäischen Gemeinschaften oder einem anderen Vertragsstaat des Abkommens über den Europäischen Wirtschaftsraum zum Handel an einem Markt im Sinne des § 2 Abs. 1 zugelassen oder in den Freiverkehr einbezogen sind und die in den Nummern 1 bis 4 genannten Wertpapiere in einem Mitgliedstaat des Abkommens über den Europäischen Wirtschaftsraum zum Handel an einem Markt im Sinne des § 2 Abs. 1 zugelassen oder in den Freiverkehr einbezogen sind. Der Zulassung der Rechte oder Terminkontrakte zum Handel an einem Markt im Sinne des § 2 Abs. 1 oder ihrer Einbeziehung in den Freiverkehr steht gleich, wenn der Antrag auf Zulassung oder Einbeziehung gestellt oder öffentlich angekündigt ist.

§ 13
Insider

(1) Insider ist, wer

1. als Mitglied des Geschäftsführungs- oder Aufsichtsorgans oder als persönlich haftender Gesellschafter des Emittenten oder eines mit dem Emittenten verbundenen Unternehmens,
2. aufgrund seiner Beteiligung am Kapital des Emittenten oder eines mit dem Emittenten verbundenen Unternehmens oder
3. aufgrund seines Berufs oder seiner Tätigkeit oder seiner Aufgabe bestimmungsgemäß

admission to a market within the meaning of § 2 sub-paragraph 1 or inclusion on the free market.

(2) The following are also deemed to be insider securities:
1. rights to subscribe to, acquire or dispose of securities,
2. rights to payment of a margin arrived at by reference to a change in the price of securities,
3. futures contracts relating to a shares or bonds index or interest futures contracts ("financial futures contracts") as well as rights to subscribe to, acquire or dispose of financial futures contracts to the extent that the subject matter of such financial futures contracts is securities or relates to an index in which securities are included,
4. other futures contracts which give rise to an obligation to acquire or dispose of securities,

if such rights or futures contracts are admitted to trading in a member state of the European Community or another contracting state of the European Economic Area Treaty on a market within the meaning of § 2 sub-paragraph 1, or are included on a free market and the securities referred to in Nos. 1 to 4 above are admitted to trading in a member state of the European Economic Area Treaty to a market within the meaning of § 2 sub-paragraph 1 or are included on a free market. The admission of rights or futures to trading on a market within the meaning of § 2 sub-paragraph 1 or the inclusion on a free market shall be deemed to apply if an application for admission or inclusion has been made or announced publicly.

§ 13

Insider

(1) An insider is any person who
1. as a member of any managing or supervisory organ or as a personally liable partner of an issuer or of an enterprise connected with an issuer,
2. by reason of his participation in the capital of the issuer or of an enterprise connected with the issuer or
3. by reason of his profession, business or function and when executing his appointed activities

Wertpapierhandelsgesetz

Kenntnis von einer nicht öffentlich bekannten Tatsache hat, die sich auf einen oder mehrere Emittenten von Insiderpapieren oder auf Insiderpapiere bezieht und die geeignet ist, im Falle ihres öffentlichen Bekanntwerdens den Kurs der Insiderpapiere erheblich zu beeinflussen (Insidertatsache).

(2) Eine Bewertung, die ausschließlich aufgrund öffentlich bekannter Tatsachen erstellt wird, ist keine Insidertatsache, selbst wenn sie den Kurs von Insiderpapieren erheblich beeinflussen kann.

§ 14
Verbot von Insidergeschäften

(1) Einem Insider ist es verboten,

1. unter Ausnutzung seiner Kenntnis von einer Insidertatsache Insiderpapiere für eigene oder fremde Rechnung oder für einen anderen zu erwerben oder zu veräußern,

2. einem anderen eine Insidertatsache unbefugt mitzuteilen oder zugänglich zu machen,

3. einem anderen auf der Grundlage seiner Kenntnis von einer Insidertatsache den Erwerb oder die Veräußerung von Insiderpapieren zu empfehlen.

(2) Einem Dritten, der Kenntnis von einer Insidertatsache hat, ist es verboten, unter Ausnutzung dieser Kenntnis Insiderpapiere für eigene oder fremde Rechnung oder für einen anderen zu erwerben oder zu veräußern.

§ 15
Veröffentlichung und Mitteilung kursbeeinflussender Tatsachen

(1) Der Emittent von Wertpapieren, die zum Handel an einer inländischen Börse zugelassen sind, muß unverzüglich eine neue Tatsache veröffentlichen, die in seinem Tätigkeitsbereich eingetreten und nicht öffentlich bekannt ist, wenn sie wegen der Auswirkungen auf die Vermögens- und Finanzlage oder auf den allgemeinen Geschäftsverlauf des Emittenten geeignet ist, den Börsenpreis der zugelassenen Wertpapiere erheblich zu beeinflussen, oder im Fall zugelassener Schuldverschreibungen die Fähigkeit des Emittenten, seinen Verpflichtungen nachzukommen, beeinträchtigen kann. Das Bundesaufsichtsamt kann den Emittenten auf Antrag von der Veröffentlichungspflicht befreien, wenn die Veröffentlichung der Tatsache geeignet ist, den berechtigten Interessen des Emittenten zu schaden.

has knowledge of a fact which is not publicly available, relating to one or more issuers of insider securities or to insider securities, and which is prone, if it were to become publicly available, to substantially influence the market price of an insider security ("insider fact").

(2) An evaluation which is made exclusively on the basis of publicly available facts is not an insider fact even if it is likely to substantially influence the market price of insider securities.

§ 14
Prohibition of Insider Dealings

(1) An insider is forbidden

1. to acquire or dispose of insider securities for his own account or the account of others or on behalf of another by exploiting his knowledge of an insider fact,
2. to communicate or give access to an insider fact without authorization to another person,
3. to recommend the acquiring or disposing of insider securities to another person on the basis of his knowledge of an insider fact.

(2) It is forbidden for a third party who has knowledge of an insider fact to acquire or dispose of insider securities for his own account or on account of another or on behalf of another by exploiting such knowledge.

§ 15
Publication and Communication of Facts Influencing Market Prices

(1) An issuer of securities admitted to trading on a domestic stock exchange must publish forthwith any new facts which become available within its sphere of activity and which are not publicly available if by reason of its likely effect on the net worth and financial position or on the general course of business of the issuer, were it made known, could substantially influence the stock exchange price of admitted securities or, in the case of admitted bonds, could adversely affect the ability of the issuer to comply with its obligations. The Federal Supervisory Authority may, on application, exempt the issuer from its obligation, if making the facts public could damage the legitimate interests of the issuer.

Wertpapierhandelsgesetz

(2) Der Emittent hat die nach Absatz 1 zu veröffentlichende Tatsache vor der Veröffentlichung

1. der Geschäftsführung der Börsen, an denen die Wertpapiere zum Handel zugelassen sind,

2. der Geschäftsführung der Börsen, an denen ausschließlich Derivate im Sinne des § 2 Abs. 2 gehandelt werden, sofern die Wertpapiere Gegenstand der Derivate sind, und

3. dem Bundesaufsichtsamt

mitzuteilen. Die Geschäftsführung darf die ihr nach Satz 1 mitgeteilte Tatsache vor der Veröffentlichung nur zum Zwecke der Entscheidung verwenden, ob die Feststellung des Börsenpreises auszusetzen oder einzustellen ist.

(3) Die Veröffentlichung nach Absatz 1 Satz 1 ist

1. in mindestens einem überregionalen Börsenpflichtblatt oder

2. über ein elektronisch betriebenes Informationsverbreitungssystem, das bei Kreditinstituten, Zweigstellen von Unternehmen im Sinne des § 53 Abs. 1 Satz 1 und des § 53b Abs. 1 Satz 1 des Gesetzes über das Kreditwesen, anderen Unternehmen, die ihren Sitz im Inland haben und an einer inländischen Börse zur Teilnahme am Handel zugelassen sind, und Versicherungsunternehmen weit verbreitet ist,

in deutscher Sprache vorzunehmen. Eine Veröffentlichung in anderer Weise darf nicht vor der Veröffentlichung nach Satz 1 erfolgen. Im Bundesanzeiger ist unverzüglich ein Hinweis auf die Veröffentlichung nach Satz 1 bekanntzumachen. Das Bundesaufsichtsamt kann bei umfangreichen Angaben gestatten, daß eine Zusammenfassung gemäß Satz 1 veröffentlicht wird, wenn die vollständigen Angaben bei den Zahlstellen des Emittenten kostenfrei erhältlich sind und in der Veröffentlichung hierauf hingewiesen wird; Satz 3 gilt hierfür entsprechend.

(4) Der Emittent hat die Veröffentlichung nach Absatz 3 Satz 1 unverzüglich der Geschäftsführung der in Absatz 2 Satz 1 Nr. 1 und 2 erfaßten Börsen und dem Bundesaufsichtsamt zu übersenden.

(5) Das Bundesaufsichtsamt kann von dem Emittenten Auskünfte und die Vorlage von Unterlagen verlangen, soweit dies zur Überwachung der Einhaltung der in den Absätzen 1 bis 4 geregelten Pflichten erforderlich ist. Während der üblichen Arbeitszeit ist seinen Bediensteten und den von ihm beauftragten Personen, soweit dies zur Wahrnehmung seiner Aufgaben erfor-

Securities Trading Act

(2) The issuer shall, before publication, notify

1. the Board of Governors of the stock exchange to which the securities have been admitted,
2. the Board of Governors of any stock exchanges on which exclusively derivatives within the meaning of §2 sub-paragraph 2 are traded if the securities are the object of those derivatives, and
3. the Federal Supervisory Authority

of any fact to be published according to sub-paragraph 1. The Board of Governors may use such a fact before publication only for the purpose of deciding whether to suspend or discontinue the fixing of a stock exchange price.

(3) Publication under sub-paragraph 1 sentence 1 shall be effected

1. in at least one national authorised stock exchange journal or
2. by means of an electronic data distribution system of a type widely used by credit institutions, branches and enterprises within the meaning of § 53 sub-paragraph 1 sentence 1 and § 53b sub-paragraph 1 sentence 1 of the Banking Law, and which can be widely distributed to other domestic enterprises which are admitted to trading on a domestic stock exchange, and to insurance enterprises

and shall be in the German language. Publication in any other manner shall not be effected before publication in accordance with sentence 1. An announcement shall be placed forthwith in the Federal Gazette for the publication in accordance with sentence 1. The Federal Supervisory Authority may, in the case of lengthy information, permit publication in summary form, provided that full information is available free of charge at the paying offices of the issuer and such availability is referred to in the notice; sentence 3 applies.

(4) The issuer shall forthwith send details of publication under sub-paragraph 3 sentence 1 to the Board of Governors of the stock exchanges referred to in sub-paragraph 2 sentence 1 Nos. 1 and 2 and to the Federal Supervisory Authority.

(5) The Federal Supervisory Authority may require the issuer to provide information or documents for the purpose of checking compliance with the obligations laid down in sub-paragraphs 1 to 4. The issuer shall permit the former's officers or persons retained by it to enter its property or business

Wertpapierhandelsgesetz

derlich ist, das Betreten der Grundstücke und Geschäftsräume des Emittenten zu gestatten. § 16 Abs. 6 und 7 gilt entsprechend.

(6) Verstößt der Emittent gegen die Verpflichtung nach Absatz 1, 2 oder 3, so ist er einem anderen nicht zum Ersatz des daraus entstehenden Schadens verpflichtet. Schadensersatzansprüche, die auf anderen Rechtsgrundlagen beruhen, bleiben unberührt.

§ 16
Laufende Überwachung

(1) Das Bundesaufsichtsamt überwacht das börsliche und außerbörsliche Geschäft in Insiderpapieren, um Verstößen gegen die Verbote nach § 14 entgegenzuwirken.

(2) Hat das Bundesaufsichtsamt Anhaltspunkte für einen Verstoß gegen ein Verbot nach § 14, so kann es von den in § 9 Abs. 1 Satz 1 genannten Kreditinstituten, Zweigstellen und Unternehmen Auskünfte über Geschäfte in Insiderpapieren verlangen, die sie für eigene oder fremde Rechnung abgeschlossen oder vermittelt haben. Das Bundesaufsichtsamt kann vom Auskunftspflichtigen die Angabe der Identität der Auftraggeber, der berechtigten oder verpflichteten Personen sowie der Bestandsveränderungen in Insiderpapieren verlangen, soweit es sich um Insiderpapiere handelt, für welche die Anhaltspunkte für einen Verstoß vorliegen oder deren Kursentwicklung von solchen Insiderpapieren abhängt.

(3) Im Rahmen der Auskunftspflicht nach Absatz 2 kann das Bundesaufsichtsamt vom Auskunftspflichtigen die Vorlage von Unterlagen verlangen. Während der üblichen Arbeitszeit ist seinen Bediensteten und den von ihm beauftragten Personen, soweit dies zur Wahrnehmung seiner Aufgaben erforderlich ist, das Betreten der Grundstücke und Geschäftsräume der in Absatz 2 Satz 1 genannten Kreditinstitute, Zweigstellen und Unternehmen zu gestatten. Das Betreten außerhalb dieser Zeit, oder wenn die Geschäftsräume sich in einer Wohnung befinden, ist ohne Einverständnis nur zur Verhütung von dringenden Gefahren für die öffentliche Sicherheit und Ordnung zulässig und insoweit zu dulden. Das Grundrecht der Unverletzlichkeit der Wohnung (Artikel 13 des Grundgesetzes) wird insoweit eingeschränkt.

(4) Hat das Bundesaufsichtsamt Anhaltspunkte für einen Verstoß gegen ein Verbot nach § 14, so kann es von den Emittenten von Insiderpapieren und den mit ihnen verbundenen Unternehmen, die ihren Sitz im Inland haben

Securities Trading Act

premises during normal business hours if necessary to carry out its duties. § 16 sub-paragraphs 6 and 7 apply.

(6) If an issuer acts in breach of its obligations under sub-paragraphs 1, 2 and 3 it shall not be liable for damages to any third party who suffers damage arising therefrom. Other claims to damages arising out of any different legal basis shall not be affected thereby.

§ 16
Continuous Monitoring

(1) The Federal Supervisory Authority shall supervise dealings in insider securities, both on and off the stock exchange, so as to counteract breaches of § 14.

(2) If the Federal Supervisory Authority has grounds to suspect a breach of § 14, it may require the credit institutions, branches and enterprises referred to in § 9 sub-paragraph 1 sentence 1 to provide information on dealings in insider securities, whether effected on their own account or on account of others or as intermediaries. The Federal Supervisory Authority may require persons obliged to furnish information to identify the person instructing them, the persons acquiring rights or obligations, and any changes in holdings of insider securities if insider securities are involved when there are indications that breaches have occurred or if its price development depends on such insider securities.

(3) In connection with the obligation to provide information in accordance with sub-paragraph 2, the Federal Supervisory Authority may require persons obliged to furnish information to produce documents. Further, its officers and any other persons retained by it may enter the property or business premises of any credit institutions, branches and enterprises referred to in sub-paragraph 2 sentence 1 during normal business hours as long as this is necessary to carry out their duties. Premises may be entered without consent outside regular business hours, or where the premises are in a dwelling, only in circumstances where there is an immediate threat to public safety and order and therefore to be tolerated. The constitutional right of the inviolability of a person's dwelling (Article 13 of the Basic Law) is thereby restricted.

(4) If the Federal Supervisory Authority has grounds to suspect a breach of the prohibitions of § 14, it may require the issuers of insider securities and

Wertpapierhandelsgesetz

oder deren Wertpapiere an einer inländischen Börse zum Handel zugelassen sind, sowie den Personen, die Kenntnis von einer Insidertatsache haben, Auskünfte über Insidertatsachen und über andere Personen verlangen, die von solchen Tatsachen Kenntnis haben.

(5) Das Bundesaufsichtsamt kann von Personen, deren Identität nach Absatz 2 Satz 2 mitgeteilt worden ist, Auskünfte über diese Geschäfte verlangen.

(6) Der zur Erteilung einer Auskunft Verpflichtete kann die Auskunft auf solche Fragen verweigern, deren Beantwortung ihn selbst oder einen der in § 383 Abs. 1 Nr. 1 bis 3 der Zivilprozeßordnung bezeichneten Angehörigen der Gefahr strafgerichtlicher Verfolgung oder eines Verfahrens nach dem Gesetz über Ordnungswidrigkeiten aussetzen würde. Der Verpflichtete ist über sein Recht zur Verweigerung der Auskunft zu belehren.

(7) Widerspruch und Anfechtungsklage gegen Maßnahmen nach den Absätzen 2 bis 5 haben keine aufschiebende Wirkung.

§ 17
Verarbeitung und Nutzung personenbezogener Daten

(1) Das Bundesaufsichtsamt darf ihm nach § 16 Abs. 2 Satz 2 mitgeteilte personenbezogene Daten nur für Zwecke der Prüfung, ob ein Verstoß gegen ein Verbot nach § 14 vorliegt, und der internationalen Zusammenarbeit nach Maßgabe des § 19 speichern, verändern und nutzen.

(2) Personenbezogene Daten, die für Prüfungen oder zur Erfüllung eines Auskunftsersuchens einer zuständigen Stelle eines anderen Staates nach Absatz 1 nicht mehr erforderlich sind, sind unverzüglich zu löschen.

§ 18
Strafverfahren bei Insidervergehen

(1) Das Bundesaufsichtsamt hat Tatsachen, die den Verdacht einer Straftat nach § 38 begründen, der zuständigen Staatsanwaltschaft anzuzeigen. Es kann die personenbezogenen Daten der Betroffenen, gegen die sich der Verdacht richtet oder die als Zeugen in Betracht kommen, der Staatsanwaltschaft übermitteln.

(2) Dem Bundesaufsichtsamt sind die Anklageschrift, der Antrag auf Erlaß eines Strafbefehls und der Ausgang des Verfahrens mitzuteilen, soweit

enterprises connected with them and which have their principal place of business in Germany, or whose securities are admitted to trading on a domestic stock exchange, as well as any persons having knowledge of insider facts, to provide details of such insider facts and of other persons having knowledge thereof.

(5) The Federal Supervisory Authority may demand information pertaining to such dealings from any persons who have been identified pursuant to sub-paragraph 2 sentence 1.

(6) A person obliged to provide information may refuse to give information in reply to questions where, if answered, such questions could make him or a relative as defined in § 383 sub-paragraph 1, No. 1-3 of the Civil Procedure Code, liable to prosecution or legal proceedings for breach of regulation. A person who would normally be obliged to give information shall be informed of his right to remain silent.

(7) Any objection or appeal against the measures referred to in sub-paragraphs 2 to 5 shall not delay enforcement.

§ 17
Processing and Use of Personal Data

(1) The Federal Supervisory Authority may store, alter or use personal data supplied to it under § 16 sub-paragraph 2 sentence 2 only for the purpose of investigating whether there has been a breach of § 14 or for the purpose of international cooperation under § 19.

(2) Personal data compiled for an investigation or in compliance with a request for information from a relevant authority of another state under sub-paragraph 1 which is no longer required, shall be deleted forthwith.

§ 18
Criminal Proceedings for Insider Offences

(1) The Federal Supervisory Authority is to notify any facts substantiating the suspicion that a criminal offence may have been committed under § 38 to the relevant public prosecutor. It may pass personal data regarding any potential suspect or witness to the public prosecutor.

(2) Any indictment, applications for the issuance of an order for summary punishment, and the outcome of any criminal proceedings shall be brought

Wertpapierhandelsgesetz

dies für die Wahrnehmung seiner Aufgaben nach diesem Abschnitt erforderlich ist.

§ 19
Internationale Zusammenarbeit

(1) Das Bundesaufsichtsamt übermittelt den zuständigen Stellen anderer Mitgliedstaaten der Europäischen Gemeinschaften oder anderer Vertragsstaaten des Abkommens über den Europäischen Wirtschaftsraum die für die Überwachung der Verbote von Insidergeschäften erforderlichen Informationen. Es macht von seinen Befugnissen nach § 16 Abs. 2 bis 5 Gebrauch, soweit dies zur Erfüllung des Auskunftsersuchens der in Satz 1 genannten zuständigen Stellen erforderlich ist.

(2) Bei der Übermittlung von Informationen sind die zuständigen Stellen im Sinne des Absatzes 1 Satz 1 darauf hinzuweisen, daß sie unbeschadet ihrer Verpflichtungen in strafrechtlichen Angelegenheiten, die Verstöße gegen Verbote von Insidergeschäften zum Gegenstand haben, die ihnen übermittelten Informationen ausschließlich zur Überwachung des Verbotes von Insidergeschäften oder im Rahmen damit zusammenhängender Verwaltungs- oder Gerichtsverfahren verwenden dürfen.

(3) Das Bundesaufsichtsamt kann die Übermittlung von Informationen verweigern, wenn

1. die Weitergabe der Informationen die Souveränität, die Sicherheit oder die öffentliche Ordnung der Bundesrepublik Deutschland beeinträchtigen könnte oder

2. aufgrund desselben Sachverhalts gegen die betreffenden Personen bereits ein gerichtliches Verfahren eingeleitet worden ist oder eine unanfechtbare Entscheidung ergangen ist.

(4) Das Bundesaufsichtsamt darf die ihm von den zuständigen Stellen im Sinne des Absatzes 1 Satz 1 übermittelten Informationen, unbeschadet seiner Verpflichtungen in strafrechtlichen Angelegenheiten, die Verstöße gegen Verbote von Insidergeschäften zum Gegenstand haben, ausschließlich für die Überwachung der Verbote von Insidergeschäften oder im Rahmen damit zusammenhängender Verwaltungs- oder Gerichtsverfahren verwenden. Eine Verwendung dieser Informationen für andere Zwecke der Überwachung nach § 7 Abs. 2 Satz 1 oder in strafrechtlichen Angelegenheiten in diesen Bereichen oder ihre Weitergabe an zuständige Stellen anderer Staaten für Zwecke nach Satz 1 bedarf der Zustimmung der übermittelnden Stellen.

to the attention of the Federal Supervisory Authority if necessary to enable it to carry out its obligations under this chapter.

§ 19
International Cooperation

(1) The Federal Supervisory Authority shall provide any information necessary for the purpose of monitoring prohibitions against insider dealing to the relevant authority of other member states of the European Community or another contracting state of the European Economic Area Treaty. It shall make use of its powers under § 16 sub-paragraphs 2 to 5 as necessary to obtain information on behalf of the authorities referred to in sentence 1.

(2) In passing on information, it shall direct the authorities referred to in sub-paragraph 1 sentence 1 that without prejudice to their obligations in any criminal proceedings, they may make use of information sent to them only for the purpose of monitoring prohibitions against insider dealing, or in connection with administrative or legal proceedings connected therewith.

(3) The Federal Supervisory Authority may refuse to pass on information if

1. doing so could adversely affect the sovereignty, security or public order of the Federal Republic of Germany or

2. arising out of the same subject matter, legal proceedings have already been commenced against the persons concerned or an order has been made which is not susceptible of appeal.

(4) Without prejudice to its obligations in relation to criminal proceedings which have as their object breaches of prohibitions against insider dealing, the Federal Supervisory Authority may make use of information provided to it by the authorities referred to in sub-paragraph 1 sentence 1 exclusively for the purpose of monitoring prohibitions against insider dealing or in connection with administrative or legal proceedings connected therewith. Any use of such information for purposes other than monitoring in accordance with § 7 subparagraph 2 sentence 1 or for the purpose of criminal proceedings in this area or the passing of the information to the relevant authorities in other states for purposes other than in accordance with sentence 1 shall require the consent of the authority providing the information.

Wertpapierhandelsgesetz

(6) Das Bundesaufsichtsamt kann für die Überwachung der Verbote von Insidergeschäften im Sinne des § 14 und entsprechender ausländischer Verbote mit den zuständigen Stellen anderer als der in Absatz 1 Satz 1 genannten Staaten zusammenarbeiten und diesen Stellen Informationen nach Maßgabe des § 7 Abs. 2 übermitteln. Absatz 1 Satz 2 ist entsprechend anzuwenden.

§ 20

Ausnahmen

Die Vorschriften dieses Abschnitts sind nicht auf Geschäfte anzuwenden, die aus geld- oder währungspolitischen Gründen oder im Rahmen der öffentlichen Schuldenverwaltung vom Bund, einem seiner Sondervermögen, einem Land, der Deutschen Bundesbank, einem ausländischen Staat oder dessen Zentralbank oder einer anderen mit diesen Geschäften beauftragten Organisation oder mit für deren Rechnung handelnden Personen getätigt werden.

Vierter Abschnitt

Mitteilungs- und Veröffentlichungspflichten bei Veränderungen des Stimmrechtsanteils an börsennotierten Gesellschaften

§ 21

Mitteilungspflichten des Meldepflichtigen

(1) Wer durch Erwerb, Veräußerung oder auf sonstige Weise 5 Prozent, 10 Prozent, 25 Prozent, 50 Prozent oder 75 Prozent der Stimmrechte an einer börsennotierten Gesellschaft erreicht, überschreitet oder unterschreitet (Meldepflichtiger), hat der Gesellschaft sowie dem Bundesaufsichtsamt unverzüglich, spätestens innerhalb von sieben Kalendertagen, das Erreichen, Überschreiten oder Unterschreiten der genannten Schwellen sowie die Höhe seines Stimmrechtsanteils unter Angabe seiner Anschrift schriftlich mitzuteilen. Die Frist beginnt mit dem Zeitpunkt, zu dem der Meldepflichtige Kenntnis davon hat oder nach den Umständen haben mußte, daß sein Stimmrechtsanteil die genannten Schwellen erreicht, überschreitet oder unterschreitet.

(2) Börsennotierte Gesellschaften im Sinne dieses Abschnitts sind Gesellschaften mit Sitz im Inland, deren Aktien zum amtlichen Handel an einer

Securities Trading Act

(5) The Federal Supervisory Authority may cooperate with and pass on information in accordance with § 7 sub-paragraph 2 to the responsible authorities of states other than those referred to in sub-paragraph 1 sentence 1 for the purpose of monitoring prohibitions against insider dealing within the meaning of § 14. Sub-paragraph 1 sentence 2 are to apply correspondingly.

§ 20
Exceptions

The provisions of this chapter shall not apply to transactions effected by reason of monetary or currency policy or by reason of the administration of the public debt by the Federal Government, by one of its special funds, by a Land, by the German Federal Bank, by a foreign state or the central bank of a foreign state or any other organisation engaged in connection with such transactions, or any persons acting on their account.

Chapter Four

Information and Publicity Requirements relating to Variations in Voting Rights in Listed Companies

§ 21
Reporting Requirements

(1) Any person who reaches, exceeds or falls below 5%, 10%, 25%, 50% or 75% of the voting rights in a listed company, whether by acquiring or disposing of shares or otherwise (hereafter called "registrant"), shall forthwith, and at the latest within seven calendar days, inform the company and the Federal Supervisory Authority in writing that he has reached, exceeded or fallen below the aforesaid thresholds, the extent of his voting rights, and notify the Authority of his address. The time period begins from the point when the registrant became aware or should have become aware according to circumstances that his voting rights have reached, exceeded or fallen below the aforementioned thresholds.

(2) A listed company within the meaning of this chapter is a domestic company, the shares of which are admitted to official trading on a stock

Wertpapierhandelsgesetz

Börse in einem Mitgliedstaat der Europäischen Gemeinschaften oder in einem anderen Vertragsstaat des Abkommens über den Europäischen Wirtschaftsraum zugelassen sind.

§ 22

Zurechnung von Stimmrechten

(1) Für die Mitteilungspflichten nach § 21 Abs. 1 stehen den Stimmrechten des Meldepflichtigen Stimmrechte aus Aktien der börsennotierten Gesellschaft gleich,

1. die einem Dritten gehören und von diesem für Rechnung des Meldepflichtigen oder eines von dem meldepflichtigen kontrollierten Unternehmens gehalten werden,

2. die einem Unternehmen gehören, das der Meldepflichtige kontrolliert,

3. die einem Dritten gehören, mit dem der Meldepflichtige oder ein von ihm kontrolliertes Unternehmen eine Vereinbarung getroffen hat, die beide verpflichtet, langfristig gemeinschaftliche Ziele bezüglich der Geschäftsführung der börsennotierten Gesellschaft zu verfolgen, indem sie ihre Stimmrechte einvernehmlich ausüben,

4. die der Meldepflichtige einem Dritten als Sicherheit übertragen hat, es sei denn, der Dritte ist zur Ausübung der Stimmrechte aus diesen Aktien befugt und bekundet die Absicht, die Stimmrechte auszuüben,

5. an denen zugunsten des Meldepflichtigen ein Nießbrauch bestellt ist,

6. die der Meldepflichtige oder ein von ihm kontrolliertes Unternehmen durch einseitige Willenserklärung erwerben kann,

7. die dem Meldepflichtigen zur Verwahrung anvertraut sind, sofern er die Stimmrechte aus diesen Aktien nach eigenem Ermessen ausüben kann, wenn keine besonderen Weisungen des Aktionärs vorliegen.

(2) Die zuzurechnenden Stimmrechte sind in den Mitteilungen nach § 21 Abs. 1 für jede der Nummern in Absatz 1 getrennt anzugeben.

(3) Ein kontrolliertes Unternehmen ist ein Unternehmen, bei dem dem Meldepflichtigen unmittelbar oder mittelbar

1. die Mehrheit der Stimmrechte der Aktionäre oder Gesellschafter zusteht,

2. als Aktionär oder Gesellschafter das Recht zusteht, die Mehrheit der Mitglieder des Verwaltungs-, Leitungs- oder Aufsichtsorgans zu bestellen oder abzuberufen, oder

exchange in a member state of the European Community or in another contracting state of the European Economic Area Treaty.

§ 22
Attribution of Voting Rights

(1) Voting rights attaching to the shares of a stock exchange listed company
1. which belong to a third person and are held by him on account of a registrant or by an enterprise controlled by him,
2. which belong to an enterprise controlled by a registrant,
3. which belong to a third person with whom a registrant or an enterprise controlled by him has reached an agreement whereby both are obliged to pursue long-term common goals in respect to the management of the stock exchange listed company, such that they vote by mutual consent,
4. which a registrant has transferred to a third person as security unless the third person is entitled to exercise the voting rights attaching to the shares and asserts his intention to do so,
5. in relation to which a registrant enjoys a beneficial right,
6. the transfer of which a registrant or an enterprise controlled by him can require by unilateral declaration,
7. which are given in custody to a registrant where he can exercise at his discretion the voting rights attaching to the shares, unless specific directions are given by the shareholder

shall be treated for a registrant the same way as those referred to in § 21 sub-paragraph 1.

(2) Information as to voting rights which are to be attributed shall be notified in accordance with § 21 sub-paragraph 1 by reference to the separate categories set out in sub-paragraph 1 above.

(3) A directly or indirectly controlled enterprise is any enterprise in which a registrant
1. has the majority of shareholders' or members' voting rights,
2. whether as shareholder or associate has the right to appoint or dismiss the majority of members of the administrative, management or supervisory organs of the enterprise, or

Wertpapierhandelsgesetz

3. als Aktionär oder Gesellschafter aufgrund einer mit anderen Aktionären oder Gesellschaftern dieses Unternehmens getroffenen Vereinbarung die Mehrheit der Stimmrechte allein zusteht.

§ 23
Nichtberücksichtigung von Stimmrechten

(1) Das Bundesaufsichtsamt läßt auf schriftlichen Antrag zu, daß Stimmrechte aus Aktien der börsennotierten Gesellschaft bei der Berechnung des Stimmrechtsanteils unberücksichtigt bleiben, wenn der Antragsteller

1. ein zur Teilnahme am Handel an einer Börse in einem Mitgliedstaat der Europäischen Gemeinschaften oder in einem anderen Vertragsstaat des Abkommens über den Europäischen Wirtschaftsraum zugelassenes Unternehmen ist, das Wertpapierdienstleistungen erbringt,

2. die betreffenden Aktien im Handelsbestand hält oder zu halten beabsichtigt und

3. darlegt, daß mit dem Erwerb der Aktien nicht beabsichtigt ist, auf die Geschäftsführung der Gesellschaft Einfluß zu nehmen.

(2) Das Bundesaufsichtsamt läßt auf schriftlichen Antrag eines Unternehmens mit Sitz in einem Mitgliedstaat der Europäischen Gemeinschaften oder in einem anderen Vertragsstaat des Abkommens über den Europäischen Wirtschaftsraum, das nicht die Voraussetzungen des Absatzes 1 Nr. 1 erfüllt, zu, daß Stimmrechte aus Aktien der börsennotierten Gesellschaft für die Meldeschwelle von 5 Prozent unberücksichtigt bleiben, wenn der Antragsteller

1. die betreffenden Aktien hält oder zu halten beabsichtigt, um bestehende oder erwartete Unterschiede zwischen dem Erwerbspreis und dem Veräußerungspreis kurzfristig zu nutzen und

2. darlegt, daß mit dem Erwerb der Aktien nicht beabsichtigt ist, auf die Geschäftsführung der Gesellschaft Einfluß zu nehmen.

(3) Bei der Prüfung des Jahresabschlusses eines Unternehmens, dem gemäß Absatz 1 oder 2 eine Befreiung erteilt worden ist, hat der Abschlußprüfer in einem gesonderten Vermerk festzustellen, ob das Unternehmen die Vorschriften des Absatzes 1 Nr. 2 oder des Absatzes 2 Nr. 1 beachtet hat, und diesen Vermerk zusammen mit dem Prüfungsbericht den gesetzlichen Vertretern des Unternehmens vorzulegen. Das Unternehmen ist verpflichtet, den Vermerk des Abschlußprüfers unverzüglich dem Bundes-

3. whether as shareholder or associate, by reason of any agreement made with other shareholders or associates, enjoys the majority of voting rights.

§ 23
Voting Rights not Taken into Account

(1) The Federal Supervisory Authority shall, on written application, allow voting rights in shares in a stock exchange listed company to be left out of account in calculating voting rights if the applicant

1. is an enterprise providing services relating to securities admitted to trade on a stock exchange in a member state of the European Community or in another contracting state of the European Economic Area Treaty,
2. holds or intends to hold the shares concerned in a trading portfolio,
3. demonstrates that it does not intend, by the acquisition of the shares, to exercise influence over the management of the company.

(2) The Federal Supervisory Authority shall, on written application by an enterprise having its principal place of business in a member state of the European Community or in another contracting state of the European Economic Area Treaty which does not comply with the requirements of sub-paragraph 1 number 1, permit voting rights in shares in a listed company to be left out of account in calculating the 5% registration threshold if the applicant

1. holds or intends to hold the shares concerned in order to utilise existing or anticipated differences between the acquisition and disposal price on a short term basis and
2. demonstrates that it does not intend by the acquisition of the shares to exercise influence over the management of the company.

(3) When auditing the annual accounts of an enterprise which has been exempted under sub-paragraphs 1 or 2, the auditors shall note specifically whether the enterprise has complied with the provisions of sub-paragraph 1 number 2 or sub-paragraph 2 number 1 and present this note together with his report to the legal representatives of the enterprise. The enterprise shall be obliged to present the auditors' note forthwith to the Federal Supervisory Authority. The Federal Supervisory Authority may revoke an

Wertpapierhandelsgesetz

aufsichtsamt vorzulegen. Das Bundesaufsichtsamt kann die Befreiung nach Absatz 1 oder 2 außer nach den Vorschriften des Verwaltungsverfahrensgesetzes widerrufen, wenn die Verpflichtungen nach Satz 1 oder 2 nicht erfüllt worden sind. Wird die Befreiung zurückgenommen oder widerrufen, so kann das Unternehmen einen erneuten Antrag auf Befreiung frühestens drei Jahre nach dem Wirksamwerden der Rücknahme oder des Widerrufs stellen.

(4) Stimmrechte aus Aktien, die aufgrund einer Befreiung nach Absatz 1 oder 2 unberücksichtigt bleiben, können nicht ausgeübt werden, wenn im Falle ihrer Berücksichtigung eine Mitteilungspflicht nach § 21 Abs. 1 bestünde.

§ 24
Mitteilung durch Konzernunternehmen

Gehört der Meldepflichtige zu einem Konzern, für den nach den §§ 290, 340i des Handelsgesetzbuchs ein Konzernabschluß aufgestellt werden muß, so können die Mitteilungspflichten nach § 21 Abs. 1 durch das Mutterunternehmen oder, wenn das Mutterunternehmen selbst ein Tochterunternehmen ist, durch dessen Mutterunternehmen erfüllt werden.

§ 25
Veröffentlichungspflichten der börsennotierten Gesellschaft

(1) Die börsennotierte Gesellschaft hat Mitteilungen nach § 21 Abs. 1 unverzüglich, spätestens neun Kalendertage nach Zugang der Mitteilung, in deutscher Sprache in einem überregionalen Börsenpflichtblatt zu veröffentlichen. In der Veröffentlichung ist der Meldepflichtige mit Name oder Firma und Wohnort oder Sitz anzugeben. Die börsennotierte Gesellschaft hat im Bundesanzeiger unverzüglich bekanntzumachen, in welchem Börsenpflichtblatt die Mitteilung veröffentlicht worden ist.

(2) Sind die Aktien der börsennotierten Gesellschaft an einer Börse in einem anderen Mitgliedstaat der Europäischen Gemeinschaften oder in einem anderen Vertragsstaat des Abkommens über den Europäischen Wirtschaftsraum zum amtlichen Handel zugelassen, so hat die Gesellschaft die Veröffentlichung nach Absatz 1 Satz 1 und 2 unverzüglich, spätestens neun Kalendertage nach Zugang der Mitteilung, auch in einem Börsenpflichtblatt dieses Staates oder, sofern das Recht dieses Staates eine andere Form der Unterrichtung des Publikums vorschreibt, in dieser anderen Form vorzuneh-

Securities Trading Act

exemption granted under sub-paragraphs 1 or 2 other than in accordance with the provisions of the Administrative Proceedings Act if the requirements of sentences 1 or 2 have not been complied with. If exemption is withdrawn or revoked, the enterprise may make a fresh application for exemption no sooner than three years after the withdrawal or revocation took effect.

(4) Voting rights on shares exempted under sub-paragraphs 1 or 2 may not be exercised if in the event such shares were taken into account a reporting requirement would arise under § 21 sub-paragraph 1.

§ 24

Information provided by a Group of Enterprises

If the obligation to register rests with a group in respect to which consolidated accounts have to be prepared under §§ 290, 340i of the Commercial Code, the obligation to register under § 21 sub-paragraph 1 may be fulfilled by the parent company or, where the parent company is itself a subsidiary, by the latter's parent company.

§ 25

Obligation of Listed Companies to Publish Information

(1) Any company listed on the stock exchange must publish in the German language information of the kind referred to in § 21 sub-paragraph 1 forthwith and at the latest within nine calendar days after receipt thereof in at least one national authorised stock exchange journal. The notice published shall contain details of the name or firm and residential address or principal place of business of the person obliged to give information (registrant). The stock exchange listed company must forthwith publish a notice in the Federal Gazette giving details about the national authorised journal in which the announcement was published.

(2) If shares in a company listed on the stock exchange are admitted to official quotation on a stock exchange in another member state of the European Community or in another contracting state of the European Economic Area Treaty, the company shall publish a notice in accordance with sub-paragraph 1 sentences 1 and 2 forthwith and at the latest within nine calender days after receipt of the information, also in an authorised journal of such state or make the information known to the public in such other form as may

Wertpapierhandelsgesetz

men. Die Veröffentlichung muß in einer Sprache abgefaßt werden, die in diesem Staat für solche Veröffentlichungen zugelassen ist.

(3) Die börsennotierte Gesellschaft hat dem Bundesaufsichtsamt unverzüglich einen Beleg über die Veröffentlichung nach den Absätzen 1 und 2 zu übersenden. Das Bundesaufsichtsamt unterrichtet die in Absatz 2 genannten Börsen über die Veröffentlichung.

(4) Das Bundesaufsichtsamt befreit auf schriftlichen Antrag die börsennotierte Gesellschaft von den Veröffentlichungspflichten nach den Absätzen 1 und 2, wenn es nach Abwägung der Umstände der Auffassung ist, daß die Veröffentlichung dem öffentlichen Interesse zuwiderlaufen oder der Gesellschaft erheblichen Schaden zufügen würde, sofern im letzteren Fall die Nichtveröffentlichung nicht zu einem Irrtum des Publikums über die für die Beurteilung der betreffenden Wertpapiere wesentlichen Tatsachen und Umstände führen kann.

§ 26

Veröffentlichungspflichten von Gesellschaften mit Sitz im Ausland

(1) Erreicht, übersteigt oder unterschreitet der Stimmrechtsanteil des Aktionärs einer Gesellschaft mit Sitz im Ausland, deren Aktien zum amtlichen Handel an einer inländischen Börse zugelassen sind, die in § 21 Abs. 1 Satz 1 genannten Schwellen, so ist die Gesellschaft, sofern nicht die Voraussetzungen des Absatzes 3 vorliegen, verpflichtet, diese Tatsache sowie die Höhe des Stimmrechtsanteils des Aktionärs unverzüglich, spätestens innerhalb von neun Kalendertagen, in einem überregionalen Börsenpflichtblatt zu veröffentlichen. Die Frist beginnt mit dem Zeitpunkt, zu dem die Gesellschaft Kenntnis hat, daß der Stimmrechtsanteil des Aktionärs die in § 21 Abs. 1 Satz 1 genannen Schwellen erreicht, überschreitet oder unterschreitet.

(2) Auf die Veröffentlichungen nach Absatz 1 ist § 25 Abs. 1 Satz 2 und 3, Abs. 3 und 4 entsprechend anzuwenden.

(3) Gesellschaften mit Sitz in einem anderen Mitgliedstaat der Europäischen Gemeinschaften oder in einem anderen Vertragsstaat des Abkommens über den Europäischen Wirtschaftsraum, deren Aktien sowohl an einer Börse im Sitzstaat als auch an einer inländischen Börse zum amtlichen Handel zugelassen sind, müssen Veröffentlichungen, die das Recht des Sitzstaates aufgrund des Artikels 10 der Richtlinie 88/627/EWG des Rates vom 12. Dezember 1988 über die bei Erwerb und Veräußerung einer bedeutenden

be prescribed by the law of such state. Publication shall be in a language that is recognised for such publications by such state.

(3) A company listed on the stock exchange shall be obliged to send the Federal Supervisory Authority forthwith a printed copy of the notice published in accordance with sub-paragraphs 1 and 2 as evidence of publication. The Federal Supervisory Authority shall give notice of publication to the stock exchanges referred to in sub-paragraph 2.

(4) The Federal Supervisory Authority shall, on written application, exempt a company listed on the stock exchange from its obligation to publish in accordance with sub-paragraphs 1 and 2 if, after considering the circumstances, it is of the view that publication would be contrary to the public interest or would lead to substantial damage to the company, provided, in the latter case, non-publication will not mislead the public as to material facts and circumstances in the assessment of the securities affected.

§ 26

Publication Obligations of Foreign Companies

(1) If the voting share of a shareholder in a foreign company the shares of which are admitted to official quotation on a domestic stock exchange reaches, exceeds or falls below the thresholds referred to in § 21 sub-paragraph 1 sentence 1, the company shall, except in the circumstances set out in sub-paragraph 3, be obliged to publish this fact as well as the level of voting shares rights of the shareholder concerned forthwith and at the latest within nine calendar days in a national authorised stock exchange journal. The time period shall begin when the company has knowledge that the shareholder's voting rights have reached, exceeded or fallen below the thresholds referred to in § 21 sub-paragraph 1 sentence 1.

(2) § 25 sub-paragraph 1 sentences 2 and 3 and sub-paragraphs 3 and 4 apply to publications under sub-paragraph 1.

(3) Companies having their principal place of business in another member state of the European Community or in another contracting state of the European Economic Area Treaty, shares of which are admitted to official quotation, both on a stock exchange in the state of the principal place of business as well as on a domestic stock exchange, must publish notices in the Federal Republic in national authorised journals in German in the manner prescribed by the law of the principal place of business, by reason of article 10 of guide-

Wertpapierhandelsgesetz

Beteiligung an einer börsennotierten Gesellschaft zu veröffentlichenden Informationen (ABl. EG Nr. L 348 S. 62) vorschreibt, im Inland in einem überregionalen Börsenpflichtblatt in deutscher Sprache vornehmen. § 25 Abs. 1 Satz 3 gilt entsprechend.

§ 27
Nachweis mitgeteilter Beteiligungen

Wer eine Mitteilung nach § 21 Abs. 1 abgegeben hat, muß auf Verlangen des Bundesaufsichtsamtes oder der börsennotierten Gesellschaft das Bestehen der mitgeteilten Beteiligung nachweisen.

§ 28
Ruhen des Stimmrechts

Stimmrechte aus Aktien, die einem Meldepflichtigen oder einem von ihm unmittelbar oder mittelbar kontrollierten Unternehmen zustehen, dürfen für die Zeit, für welche die Mitteilungspflichten nach § 21 Abs. 1 nicht erfüllt werden, nicht ausgeübt werden.

§ 29
Befugnisse des Bundesaufsichtsamtes

(1) Das Bundesaufsichtsamt kann von der börsennotierten Gesellschaft und deren Aktionären Auskünfte und die Vorlage von Unterlagen verlangen, soweit dies zur Überwachung der Einhaltung der in diesem Abschnitt geregelten Pflichten erforderlich ist. Die Befugnisse nach Satz 1 bestehen auch gegenüber Personen und Unternehmen, deren Stimmrechte nach § 22 Abs. 1 zuzurechnen sind. § 16 Abs. 6 ist anzuwenden.

(2) Das Bundesaufsichtsamt kann Richtlinien aufstellen, nach denen es für den Regelfall beurteilt, ob die Voraussetzungen für einen mitteilungspflichtigen Vorgang oder eine Befreiung von den Mitteilungspflichten nach § 21 Abs. 1 gegeben sind. Die Richtlinien sind im Bundesanzeiger zu veröffentlichen.

(3) Das Bundesaufsichtsamt kann die Veröffentlichungen nach § 25 Abs. 1 und 2 auf Kosten der börsennotierten Gesellschaft vornehmen, wenn die Gesellschaft die Veröffentlichungspflicht nicht, nicht richtig, nicht vollständig oder nicht in der vorgeschriebenen Form erfüllt.

Securities Trading Act

line 88/627/EG (ABl, EG No. L 348 S. 62) of 12 December 1988 of the Council concerning information to be published in conjunction with the acquisition and disposal of a substantial holding in a stock exchange listed company. § 25 sub-paragraph 1 sentence 3 applies.

§ 27
Evidence of Notified Shareholdings

Any person who has provided information under § 21 sub-paragraph 1 must, at the request of the Federal Supervisory Authority or of the stock exchange listed company concerned, provide evidence of the shareholding which has been notified.

§ 28
Suspension of Voting Rights

Voting rights arising out of shares to which a registrant is entitled or an enterprise controlled directly or indirectly by such a registrant may not be exercised for the period during which the reporting requirements under § 21 sub-paragraph 1 have not been complied with.

§ 29
Powers of the Federal Supervisory Authority

(1) The Federal Supervisory Authority may require a stock exchange listed company and its shareholders to provide information or to produce documents as necessary, to monitor compliance with the obligations set out in this Chapter. These powers may also be exercised in respect to persons and enterprises whose voting rights are to be attributed under § 22 sub-paragraph 1. § 16 sub-paragraph 6 applies.

(2) The Federal Supervisory Authority may formulate guidelines as to the norms to be generally applied in establishing whether prerequisites for compliance with or exceptions from the reporting requirements under § 21 sub-paragraph 1 exist. Such guidelines shall be published in the Federal Gazette.

(3) The Federal Supervisory Authority may publish notices in accordance with § 25, sub-paragraphs 1 and 2 at the expense of a stock exchange listed company if the company itself fails to fulfil the publishing requirements or fails to do so correctly or fully or in the prescribed form.

Wertpapierhandelsgesetz

§ 30
Zusammenarbeit mit zuständigen Stellen im Ausland

(1) Das Bundesaufsichtsamt arbeitet mit den zuständigen Stellen der anderen Mitgliedstaaten der Europäischen Gemeinschaften, der anderen Vertragsstaaten des Abkommens über den Europäischen Wirtschaftsraum sowie in den Fällen der Nummern 1 und 4 auch mit den entsprechenden Stellen von Drittstaaten zusammen, um insbesondere darauf hinzuwirken, daß

1. Meldepflichtige mit Wohnsitz, Sitz oder gewöhnlichem Aufenthalt in einem dieser Staaten ihre Mitteilungspflichten ordnungsmäßig erfüllen,

2. börsennotierte Gesellschaften ihre Veröffentlichungspflicht nach § 25 Abs. 2 ordnungsmäßig erfüllen,

3. die nach den Vorschriften eines anderen Mitgliedstaates der Europäischen Gemeinschaften oder eines anderen Vertragsstaates des Abkommens über den Europäischen Wirtschaftsraum in diesem Staat Meldepflichtigen mit Wohnsitz, Sitz oder gewöhnlichem Aufenthalt im Inland ihre Mitteilungspflichten ordnungsmäßig erfüllen,

4. Gesellschaften mit Sitz im Ausland, deren Aktien an einer inländischen Börse zum amtlichen Handel zugelassen sind, ihre Veröffentlichungspflichten im Inland ordnungsmäßig erfüllen.

(2) Das Bundesaufsichtsamt darf den zuständigen Stellen der anderen Mitgliedstaaten oder Vertragsstaaten Tatsachen einschließlich personenbezogener Daten übermitteln, soweit dies zur Überwachung der Einhaltung der Mitteilungs- und Veröffentlichungspflichten erforderlich ist. Bei der Übermittlung ist darauf hinzuweisen, daß die zuständigen Stellen, unbeschadet ihrer Verpflichtungen in strafrechtlichen Angelegenheiten, die Verstöße gegen Mitteilungs- oder Veröffentlichungspflichten zum Gegenstand haben, die ihnen übermittelten Tatsachen einschließlich personenbezogener Daten ausschließlich zur Überwachung der Einhaltung dieser Pflichten oder im Rahmen damit zusammenhängender Verwaltungs- oder Gerichtsverfahren verwenden dürfen.

(3) Dem Bundesaufsichtsamt stehen im Fall des Absatzes 1 Nr. 3 die Befugnisse nach § 29 Abs. 1 zu.

§ 30
Cooperation with Responsible Authorities Abroad

(1) The Federal Supervisory Authority shall cooperate with the relevant authorities of other member states of the European Community and other contracting states of the European Economic Area Treaty, in relation to cases 1 to 4, as well as with the authorities of third party states in order to ensure, in particular

1. that registrants having their place of residence, principal place of business or habitual abode in such a state properly fulfil their obligations to register;
2. that stock exchange listed companies properly fulfil the publishing requirements in accordance with § 25 sub-paragraph 2,
3. that persons obliged to provide information under the law of another member state of the European Community or another contracting state the European Economic Area Treaty, having their place of residence, principal place of business or ordinary residence in the Federal Republic of Germany, comply with their obligations to provide information in such foreign states,
4. that companies having their principal place of business abroad, but the shares of which are officially quoted on a domestic stock exchange, comply properly with their obligations to notify domestically,

(2) The Federal Supervisory Authority may provide facts, including personal data, to the relevant authorities of other member states or contracting states if doing so is necessary for supervisory purposes and to comply with reporting and publishing requirements. When providing information attention is to be drawn to the fact that the relevant authorities, irrespective of their obligations in relation to any criminal matters arising out of breaches of obligations to inform and to publish, may only use the information provided, including personal data, for the purpose of monitoring compliance with those obligations or for administrative or court proceedings connected therewith.

(3) The Federal Supervisory Authority may use the powers provided under § 29 sub-paragraph 1 for any case under sub-paragraph 1 No. 3.

Wertpapierhandelsgesetz

Fünfter Abschnitt
Verhaltensregeln für Wertpapierdienstleistungsunternehmen

§ 31
Allgemeine Verhaltensregeln

(1) Ein Wertpapierdienstleistungsunternehmen ist verpflichtet,

1. Wertpapierdienstleistungen mit der erforderlichen Sachkenntnis, Sorgfalt und Gewissenhaftigkeit im Interesse seiner Kunden zu erbringen,
2. sich um die Vermeidung von Interessenkonflikten zu bemühen und dafür zu sorgen, daß bei unvermeidbaren Interessenkonflikten der Kundenauftrag unter der gebotenen Wahrung des Kundeninteresses ausgeführt wird.

(2) Es ist ferner verpflichtet,

1. von seinen Kunden Angaben über ihre Erfahrungen oder Kenntnisse in Geschäften, die Gegenstand von Wertpapierdienstleistungen sein sollen, über ihre mit den Geschäften verfolgten Ziele und über ihre finanziellen Verhältnisse zu verlangen,
2. seinen Kunden alle zweckdienlichen Informationen mitzuteilen,

soweit dies zur Wahrung der Interessen der Kunden und im Hinblick auf Art und Umfang der beabsichtigten Geschäfte erforderlich ist.

(3) Die Absätze 1 und 2 gelten auch für Unternehmen mit Sitz im Ausland, die Wertpapierdienstleistungen gegenüber Kunden erbringen, die ihren gewöhnlichen Aufenthalt oder ihre Geschäftsleitung im Inland haben, sofern nicht die Wertpapierdienstleistung einschließlich der damit im Zusammenhang stehenden Nebenleistungen ausschließlich im Ausland erbracht wird.

§ 32
Besondere Verhaltensregeln

(1) Einem Wertpapierdienstleistungsunternehmen oder einem mit ihm verbunden Unternehmen ist es verboten,

1. Kunden des Wertpapierdienstleistungsunternehmens den Ankauf oder Verkauf von Wertpapieren oder Derivaten zu empfehlen, wenn und soweit die Empfehlung nicht mit den Interessen der Kunden übereinstimmt;

Securities Trading Act

Chapter Five

Rules of Conduct for Enterprises Providing Services relating to Securities

§ 31

General Rules of Conduct

(1) An enterprise providing services relating to securities shall be obliged
1. to provide these services with the requisite knowledge, care and conscientiousness in the interests of its customers,
2. to take steps to avoid conflicts of interest or, where conflicts of interest cannot be avoided, to carry out its customer's instructions with due regard to the interests of such customer.

(2) It shall be obliged in addition
1. to require from its customers information regarding their knowledge or experience of business related to securities services, their goals in any transaction undertaken, and their financial circumstances,
2. to provide its customers with all pertinent information available

insofar as this is necessary to protect the interests of the customer, and in regard to the manner and extent of the intended transactions.

(3) Sub-paragraphs 1 and 2 also apply to enterprises having their principal place of business abroad which provide services relating to securities to customers but who have their ordinary residence or management in the Federal Republic of Germany except to the extent that such services, including any connected supplementary services, are exclusively provided abroad.

§ 32

Special Rules of Conduct

(1) An enterprise providing services relating to securities or an enterprise connected with such an enterprise is prohibited
1. from recommending its customers to acquire or dispose of securities or derivatives if such recommendation is not in the best interests of its customers;

Wertpapierhandelsgesetz

2. Kunden des Wertpapierdienstleistungsunternehmens den Ankauf oder Verkauf von Wertpapieren oder Derivaten zu dem Zweck zu empfehlen, für Eigengeschäfte des Wertpapierdienstleistungsunternehmens oder eines mit ihm verbundenen Unternehmens Preise in eine bestimmte Richtung zu lenken;

3. Eigengeschäfte aufgrund der Kenntnis von einem Auftrag eines Kunden des Wertpapierdienstleistungsunternehmens zum Ankauf oder Verkauf von Wertpapieren oder Derivaten abzuschließen, die Nachteile für den Auftraggeber zur Folge haben können.

(2) Den Geschäftsinhabern eines in der Rechtsform des Einzelkaufmanns betriebenen Wertpapierdienstleistungsunternehmens, bei anderen Wertpapierdienstleistungsunternehmen den Personen, die nach Gesetz oder Gesellschaftsvertrag mit der Führung der Geschäfte des Unternehmens betraut und zu seiner Vertretung ermächtigt sind, sowie den Angestellten eines Wertpapierdienstleistungsunternehmens, die mit der Durchführung von Geschäften in Wertpapieren oder Derivaten, der Wertpapieranalyse oder der Anlageberatung betraut sind, ist es verboten,

1. Kunden des Wertpapierdienstleistungsunternehmens den Ankauf oder Verkauf von Wertpapieren oder Derivaten unter den Voraussetzungen des Absatzes 1 Nr. 1 oder zu dem Zweck zu empfehlen, für den Abschluß von Geschäften für sich oder Dritte Preise von Wertpapieren oder Derivaten in eine bestimmte Richtung zu lenken;

2. aufgrund der Kenntnis von einem Auftrag eines Kunden des Wertpapierdienstleistungsunternehmens zum Ankauf oder Verkauf von Wertpapieren oder Derivaten Geschäfte für sich oder einen Dritten abzuschließen, die Nachteile für den Auftraggeber zur Folge haben können.

(3) Die Absätze 1 und 2 gelten unter den in § 31 Abs. 3 bestimmten Voraussetzungen auch für Unternehmen mit Sitz im Ausland.

§ 33

Organisationspflichten

Ein Wertpapierdienstleistungsunternehmen

1. ist verpflichtet, die für eine ordnungsmäßige Durchführung der Wertpapierdienstleistung notwendigen Mittel und Verfahren vorzuhalten und wirksam einzusetzen;

2. muß so organisiert sein, daß bei der Erbringung der Wertpapierdienstleistung Interessenkonflikte zwischen dem Wertpapierdienstleistungsunternehmen und seinen Kunden oder Interessenkonflikte zwischen verschie-

2. from recommending its customers to acquire or dispose of securities or derivatives for the purpose of influencing the price movements of own account transactions or of a connected enterprise;
3. from carrying on own account business based on knowledge derived from an instruction given by a customer to acquire or dispose of securities or derivatives which could adversely affect that customer.

(2) The owners of an enterprise providing services relating to securities which is carried on in the legal form of a sole trader or, in the case of other enterprises providing services relating to securities, the persons who under its memorandum and articles of association and under the law are entrusted with the management and representation of the enterprise, together with the employees of such an enterprise employed in carrying out transactions in securities or derivatives, securities analysis or investment advice, are prohibited

1. from recommending customers of the enterprise to acquire or dispose of securities or derivatives in the circumstances set out in sub-paragraph 1 No. 1, or for the purpose of concluding transactions for themselves or for third parties that will influence the price movements of securities or derivatives;
2. by reason of their knowledge of any instruction given by a customer of the enterprise to acquire or dispose of securities or derivatives from engaging in transactions for themselves or for third parties which could adversely affect that customer.

(3) The provisions of sub-paragraphs 1 and 2 also apply in the circumstances set out in § 31 sub-paragraph 3 to enterprises having their principal place of business abroad.

§ 33

Organizational Obligations

Any enterprise providing services relating to securities
1. shall be obliged to maintain and employ such facilities and procedures which are necessary to enable it properly to carry on the business of providing services relating to securities;
2. must be organised so as to minimise conflicts of interest between itself and its customers, or between its customers, in providing services relating to securities;

Wertpapierhandelsgesetz

denen Kunden des Wertpapierdienstleistungsunternehmens möglichst gering sind;

3. muß über angemessene interne Kontrollverfahren verfügen, die geeignet sind, Verstößen gegen Verpflichtungen nach diesem Gesetz entgegenzuwirken.

§ 34

Aufzeichnungs- und Aufbewahrungspflichten

(1) Ein Wertpapierdienstleistungsunternehmen ist verpflichtet,

1. bei der Erbringung von Wertpapierdienstleistungen den Auftrag und hierzu erteilte Anweisungen des Kunden sowie die Ausführung des Auftrags und

2. den Namen des Angestellten, der den Auftrag des Kunden angenommen hat, sowie die Uhrzeit der Erteilung und Ausführung des Auftrags

aufzuzeichnen.

(2) Das Bundesministerium der Finanzen kann nach Anhörung der Deutschen Bundesbank durch Rechtsverordnung, die nicht der Zustimmung des Bundesrates bedarf, die Wertpapierdienstleistungsunternehmen zu weiteren Aufzeichnungen verpflichten, soweit diese zur Überwachung der Verpflichtungen der Wertpapierdienstleistungsunternehmen durch das Bundesaufsichtsamt erforderlich sind. Das Bundesministerium der Finanzen kann die Ermächtigung durch Rechtsverordnung auf das Bundesaufsichtsamt übertragen.

(3) Die Aufzeichnungen nach den Absätzen 1 und 2 sind mindestens sechs Jahre aufzubewahren. Für die Aufbewahrung gilt § 257 Abs. 3 und 5 des Handelsgesetzbuchs entsprechend.

§ 35

Überwachung der Verhaltensregeln

(1) Das Bundesaufsichtsamt kann, soweit dies zur Überwachung der Einhaltung der in diesem Abschnitt geregelten Pflichten erforderlich ist, von den Wertpapierdienstleistungsunternehmen, den mit diesen verbundenen Unternehmen und den in § 32 Abs. 2 genannten Personen Auskünfte und die Vorlage von Unterlagen verlangen. § 16 Abs. 6 ist anzuwenden. Während der üblichen Arbeitszeit ist den Bediensteten des Bundesaufsichtsamtes, soweit dies zur Wahrnehmung seiner Aufgaben nach diesem Abschnitt erforderlich ist, das Betreten der Grundstücke und Geschäftsräume der Wertpapierdienstleistungsunternehmen und der mit diesen verbundenen Unternehmen zu gestatten.

Securities Trading Act

3. must maintain internal control procedures designed to counteract breaches of obligations under this Act.

§ 34

Duties to Maintain and Retain Records

(1) Any enterprise providing services relating to securities shall be obliged

1. when providing services relating to securities, to maintain a record of any instructions and directions given in connection therewith by its customers and of the execution of such instructions and
2. to maintain a record of the name of the employee who accepted the customer's instruction, and the time of the instruction and execution.

(2) The Federal Ministry of Finance may, after hearing the German Federal Bank, make orders which shall not require the consent of the Bundesrat, imposing additional recording requirements on enterprises providing services relating to securities if it is necessary to ensure proper monitoring of the obligations of the enterprises by the Federal Supervisory Authority. The Federal Ministry of Finance may delegate such authority to the Federal Supervisory Authority by way of Regulation.

(3) Records kept, pursuant to sub-paragraphs 1 and 2, shall be preserved for at least six years. § 257 sub-paragraphs 3 and 5 of the Commercial Code apply.

§ 35

Monitoring of Rules of Conduct

(1) The Federal Supervisory Authority may, to the extent that it is necessary for the purpose of monitoring compliance with the obligations provided for in this chapter, require enterprises providing services relating to securities, enterprises connected therewith and the persons referred to in § 32 sub-paragraph 2 to provide information and produce documents. § 16 sub-paragraph 6 applies. Employees of the Federal Supervisory Authority shall be entitled to enter the property and business premises of enterprises providing services relating to securities, or enterprises connected therewith during normal business hours for the purpose of monitoring compliance with its obligations under this chapter.

Wertpapierhandelsgesetz

(2) Das Bundesaufsichtsamt kann Richtlinien aufstellen, nach denen es für den Regelfall beurteilt, ob die Anforderungen nach den §§ 31 bis 33 erfüllt sind. Die Deutsche Bundesbank, das Bundesaufsichtsamt für das Kreditwesen sowie die Spitzenverbände der betroffenen Wirtschaftskreise sind vor dem Erlaß der Richtlinien anzuhören; Richtlinien zu § 33 sind im Einvernehmen mit dem Bundesaufsichtsamt für das Kreditwesen zu erlassen. Die Richtlinien sind im Bundesanzeiger zu veröffentlichen.

§ 36

Prüfung der Meldepflichten und Verhaltensregeln

(1) Das Bundesaufsichtsamt hat bei Wertpapierdienstleistungsunternehmen die Einhaltung der Meldepflichten nach § 9 und der in diesem Abschnitt geregelten Pflichten in der Regel einmal jährlich zu prüfen. Bei den in § 2 Abs. 4 Nr. 1 genannten Kreditinstituten und Zweigstellen soll die Prüfung in der Regel zusammen mit der Depotprüfung nach § 30 des Gesetzes über das Kreditwesen durch den Depotprüfer erfolgen. Dem Bundesaufsichtsamt für das Kreditwesen ist eine Ausfertigung des Prüfungsberichts zu übermitteln.

(2) Das Bundesministerium der Finanzen kann durch Rechtsverordnung, die nicht der Zustimmung des Bundesrates bedarf, nähere Bestimmungen über Art, Umfang und Zeitpunkt der Prüfung nach Absatz 1 erlassen, soweit dies zur Erfüllung der Aufgaben des Bundesaufsichtsamtes erforderlich ist, insbesondere um Mißständen im Handel mit Wertpapieren und Derivaten entgegenzuwirken, um auf die Einhaltung der Meldepflichten nach § 9 und der in diesem Abschnitt geregelten Pflichten hinzuwirken und um zu diesem Zweck einheitliche Unterlagen zu erhalten. Das Bundesministerium der Finanzen kann die Ermächtigung durch Rechtsverordnung auf das Bundesaufsichtsamt übertragen.

§ 37

Ausnahmen

(1) Die Verpflichtungen nach den §§ 31 bis 34 gelten nicht für

1. Unternehmen, die Wertpapierdienstleistungen ausschließlich für ihr Mutterunternehmen oder ihre Tochterunternehmen im Sinne des § 1 Abs. 6 und 7 des Gesetzes über das Kreditwesen oder andere Tochterunternehmen ihres Mutterunternehmens erbringen;

Securities Trading Act

(2) The Federal Supervisory Authority may lay down guidelines setting out norms to establish whether the requirements of §§ 31 to 33 have been complied with. The German Federal Bank, the Federal Banking Supervisory Authority and the central organisations in the economy concerned shall be consulted before such guidelines are laid down; guidelines relating to § 33 shall be laid down with the understanding of the Federal Banking Supervisory Authority. Guidelines shall be published in the Federal Gazette.

§ 36

Auditing Compliance with Reporting Requirements and Rules of Conduct

(1) The Federal Supervisory Authority shall monitor enterprises providing services relating to securities to ensure compliance with the registration obligations provided for by § 9 and this chapter once a year. In the case of credit institutions and branches of the kind referred to in § 2 sub-paragraph 4 No. 1, such monitoring shall be carried out, as a rule, by the securities deposit auditor at the same time as the securities deposit audit, made pursuant to § 30 of the Banking Act. A copy of the monitoring report shall be sent to the Federal Banking Supervisory Authority.

(2) The Federal Ministry of Finance may, without the consent of the Bundesrat, make Regulations providing in detail the manner, scope and timing of monitoring pursuant to sub-paragraph 1 to such extent as may be necessary to enable the Federal Supervisory Authority to comply with its obligations, in particular so as to counteract irregularities in the trading of securities or derivatives, to ensure compliance with registration obligations under § 9 and the obligations provided for in this chapter and to ensure uniformity of documentation to that end. The Federal Ministry of Finance may, by Regulation, delegate its powers to the Federal Supervisory Authority.

§ 37

Exceptions

(1) The obligations set out in §§31 to 34 shall not apply to

1. enterprises providing services relating to securities exclusively for their parent company or subsidiaries within the meaning of § 1 sub-paragraphs 6 and 7 of the Banking Act or other subsidiaries of their parent company;

Wertpapierhandelsgesetz

2. die öffentliche Schuldenverwaltung des Bundes, eines seiner Sondervermögen, eines Landes, eines anderen Mitgliedstaates der Europäischen Gemeinschaften oder eines anderen Vertragsstaates des Abkommens über den Europäischen Wirtschaftsraum, die Deutsche Bundesbank sowie die Zentralbanken der anderen Mitgliedstaaten oder Vertragsstaaten.

(2) Die §§ 31, 32 und 34 gelten nicht für Geschäfte, die an einer Börse zwischen zwei Wertpapierdienstleistungsunternehmen abgeschlossen werden. Wertpapierdienstleistungsunternehmen, die an einer Börse ein Geschäft als Kommissionär abschließen, unterliegen insoweit den Pflichten nach § 34. § 33 gilt nicht für ein Wertpapierdienstleistungsunternehmen, das ausschließlich Geschäfte betreibt, die in Satz 1 genannt sind.

Sechster Abschnitt
Straf- und Bußgeldvorschriften

§ 38
Strafvorschriften

(1) Mit einer Freiheitsstrafe bis zu fünf Jahren oder mit Geldstrafe wird bestraft, wer

1. entgegen einem Verbot nach § 14 Abs. 1 Nr. 1 oder Abs. 2 ein Insiderpapier erwirbt oder veräußert,
2. entgegen einem Verbot nach § 14 Abs. 1 Nr. 2 eine Insidertatsache mitteilt oder zugänglich macht oder
3. entgegen einem Verbot nach § 14 Abs. 1 Nr. 3 den Erwerb oder die Veräußerung eines Insiderpapiers empfiehlt.

(2) Einem Verbot im Sinne des Absatzes 1 steht ein entsprechendes ausländisches Verbot gleich.

§ 39
Bußgeldvorschriften

(1) Ordnungswidrig handelt, wer vorsätzlich oder leichtfertig

2. the management of Federal debt, any Federal special funds or of a Land, another member state of the European Community or a contracting state of the European Economic Area Treaty, the German Federal Bank or the central bank of another state of the European Community or European Economic Area Treaty.

(2) §§31, 32 and 34 shall not apply to transactions on a stock exchange between two enterprises providing services relating to securities. Enterprises providing services relating to securities, which transact on a stock exchange as commission agents, shall be subject to the obligations provided for in § 34. § 33 shall not apply to an enterprise providing services relating to securities which undertakes only transactions of the type specified in sentence 1.

Chapter Six

Rules relating to Criminal Provisions and Fines

§ 38

Criminal Provisions

(1) Any person who

1. acquires or disposes of an insider security contrary to the statutory prohibition under § 14 sub-paragraph 1 No. 1 or sub-paragraph 2,
2. passes on or makes available an insider fact contrary to § 14 sub-paragraph 1 No.2, or
3. recommends the acquisition or disposal of an insider security contrary to § 14 sub-paragraph 1 No.3

is liable to imprisonment of up to five years or a fine.

(2) The above shall include any act contrary to an equivalent prohibition abroad.

§ 39

Fines Provisions

(1) A person shall be guilty of a breach of regulation if he intentionally or recklessly

Wertpapierhandelsgesetz

1. entgegen

   a) § 9 Abs. 1 Satz 1, 2 oder 3 jeweils in Verbindung mit Absatz 2, auch in Verbindung mit einer Rechtsverordnung nach Absatz 3,

   b) § 15 Abs. 2 Satz 1 oder

   c) § 21 Abs. 1 Satz 1, auch in Verbindung mit § 22 Abs. 1 oder 2,

   eine Mitteilung nicht, nicht richtig, nicht vollständig, nicht in der vorgeschriebenen Form oder nicht rechtzeitig macht,

2. entgegen

   a) § 15 Abs. 1 Satz 1 in Verbindung mit Abs. 3 Satz 1 oder

   b) § 25 Abs. 1 Satz 1 in Verbindung mit Satz 2, § 25 Abs. 2 Satz 1 in Verbindung mit Satz 2 oder § 26 Abs. 1 Satz 1

   eine Veröffentlichung nicht, nicht richtig, nicht vollständig, nicht in der vorgeschriebenen Form oder nicht rechtzeitig vornimmt,

3. entgegen § 15 Abs. 3 Satz 2 eine Veröffentlichung vornimmt,

4. entgegen § 15 Abs. 3 Satz 3, auch in Verbindung mit Satz 5, oder § 25 Abs. 1 Satz 3, auch in Verbindung mit § 26 Abs. 3 Satz 2, eine Bekanntmachung nicht, nicht richtig oder nicht rechtzeitig vornimmt,

5. entgegen § 15 Abs. 4 oder § 25 Abs. 3 Satz 1, auch in Verbindung mit § 26 Abs. 2, eine Veröffentlichung oder einen Beleg nicht oder nicht rechtzeitig übersendet,

6. entgegen § 34 Abs. 1, auch in Verbindung mit einer Rechtsverordnung nach § 34 Abs. 2, eine Aufzeichnung nicht, nicht richtig oder nicht vollständig fertigt oder

7. entgegen § 34 Abs. 3 Satz 1 eine Aufzeichnung nicht oder nicht mindestens sechs Jahre aufbewahrt.

(2) Ordnungswidrig handelt, wer vorsätzlich oder fahrlässig

1. einer vollziehbaren Anordnung nach § 15 Abs. 5 Satz 1, § 16 Abs. 2, 3 Satz 1, Abs. 4 oder 5, § 29 Abs. 1, auch in Verbindung mit § 30 Abs. 3, oder § 35 Abs. 1 Satz 1 zuwiderhandelt oder

Securities Trading Act

1. fails to register or provide information, fails to do so correctly, fails to do so in the prescribed form or does so incompletely or not on time, contrary to

    a) § 9 sub-paragraph 1 sentence 1, 2 or 3, respectively, in connection with sub-paragraph 2, also in connection with a Regulation under sub-paragraph 3,

    b) § 15 sub-paragraph 2 sentence 1 or

    c) § 21 sub-paragraph 1 sentence 2, also in connection with § 22 sub-paragraph 1 or 2;

2. fails to publish, fails to do so correctly, fails to publish in the prescribed form or does so incompletely or not on time contrary to

    a) § 15 sub-paragraph 1 sentence 1 in connection with sub-paragraph 3 sentence 1 or

    b) § 25 sub-paragraph 1 sentence 1 in connection with sentence 2, § 25 sub-paragraph 2 sentence 1 in connection with sentence 2 or § 26 sub-paragraph 1 sentence 1;

3. effects publication contrary to § 15 sub-paragraph 3 sentence 2;

4. fails to give notice, fails to do so correctly, or fails to do so on time, contrary to § 15 sub-paragraph 3 sentence 3, also in connection with sentence 5, or § 25 sub-paragraph 1 sentence 3, also in connection with § 26 sub-paragraph 3 sentence 2;

5. fails to provide a copy notice on time or at all, contrary to § 15 sub-paragraph 4 or § 25 sub-paragraph 3 sentence 1, also in connection with § 26 sub-paragraph 2;

6. fails to retain records or do so correctly or completely contrary to § 34 sub-paragraph 1, also in connection with a Regulation made under § 34 sub-paragraph 2;

7. fails to retain records for a minimum of six years contrary to § 34 sub-paragraph 3 sentence 1.

(2) A person is guilty of a breach of regulation if he intentionally or negligently

1. acts in breach of any Regulation made under § 15 sub-paragraph 5 sentence 1, § 16 sub-paragraph 2, 3 sentence 1, sub-paragraphs 4 or 5, § 29 sub-paragraph 1, also in connection with § 30 sub-paragraph 3 or § 35 sub-paragraph 3 sentence 3 fails to tolerate the presence of the officials.

Wertpapierhandelsgesetz

2. ein Betreten entgegen § 15 Abs. 5 Satz 2, § 16 Abs. 3 Satz 2 oder § 35 Abs. 1 Satz 3 nicht gestattet oder entgegen § 16 Abs. 3 Satz 3 nicht duldet.

(3) Die Ordnungswidrigkeit kann in den Fällen des Absatzes 1 Nr. 2 Buchstabe a und Nr. 3 mit einer Geldbuße bis zu drei Millionen Deutsche Mark, in den Fällen des Absatzes 1 Nr. 1 Buchstabe b und c mit einer Geldbuße bis zu fünfhunderttausend Deutsche Mark, in den Fällen des Absatzes 1 Nr. 1 Buchstabe a, Nr. 2 Buchstabe b, Nr. 4 bis 7 sowie des Absatzes 2 mit einer Geldbuße bis zu einhunderttausend Deutsche Mark geahndet werden.

§ 40

Zuständige Verwaltungsbehörde

Verwaltungsbehörde im Sinne des § 36 Abs. 1 Nr. 1 des Gesetzes über Ordnungswidrigkeiten ist das Bundesaufsichtsamt für den Wertpapierhandel.

Siebter Abschnitt

Übergangsbestimmungen

§ 41

Erstmalige Mitteilungs- und Veröffentlichungspflicht

(1) Mitteilungen nach § 9 Abs. 1 müssen erstmals zu dem Zeitpunkt abgegeben werden, der durch Rechtsverordnung des Bundesministeriums der Finanzen, die nicht der Zustimmung des Bundesrates bedarf, bestimmt wird; der Zeitpunkt darf nicht nach dem 1. Januar 1996 liegen. § 9 Abs. 4 ist entsprechend anzuwenden.

(2) Wem am 1. Januar 1995 unter Berücksichtigung des § 22 Abs. 1 fünf Prozent oder mehr der Stimmrechte einer börsennotierten Gesellschaft zustehen, hat spätestens am Tag der ersten Hauptversammlung der Gesellschaft, die nach dem 1. April 1995 stattfindet, der Gesellschaft sowie dem Bundesaufsichtsamt die Höhe seines Anteils am stimmberechtigten Kapital unter Angabe seiner Anschrift schriftlich mitzuteilen, sofern nicht zu diesem Zeitpunkt bereits eine Mitteilung gemäß § 21 Abs. 1 abgegeben worden ist.

Securities Trading Act

2. fails to grant access contrary to § 15 sub-paragraph 5 sentence 2, § 16 sub-paragraph 3 sentence 2 or § 35 sub-paragraph 1 sentence 3 or contrary to § 16 sub-paragraph 3 sentence 3, fails to tolerate the presence of the officials.

(3) A breach of regulation of the kind referred to in sub-paragraph 1 No. 2 (a) and No. 3 may be punished by a fine of up to three million German Marks; a breach of regulation of the kind referred to in sub-paragraph 1 No. 1 (b) and (c) may be punished by a fine of up to five hundred thousand German Marks; a breach of regulation of the kind referred to in sub-paragraph 1 No. 1 (a), No. 2 (b), Nos. 4–7 and sub-paragraph 2 may be punished by a fine of up to one hundred thousand German Marks.

§ 40
Relevant Administrative Authority

The Federal Supervisory Authority for Securities Trading shall be the relevant administrative authority within the meaning of § 36 sub-paragraph 1 No. 1 of the Breaches of Regulation Act.

Chapter Seven
Transitional Provisions

§ 41
Providing Information and Publication of Information for the First Time

(1) Information in accordance with § 9 sub-paragraph 1 shall be provided from the time specified by Regulation of the Federal Ministry of Finance which shall not require the consent of the Bundesrat, such time may be no later than 1 January 1996. § 9 sub-paragraph 4 applies.

(2) Any person entitled to 5% or more of the voting rights in a stock exchange listed company under § 22 sub-paragraph 1 as of 1 January 1995 shall, by no later than the date of the first general meeting of the company held after 1 April 1995, notify the company concerned and the Federal Supervisory Authority in writing of the extent of his participation of voting

Wertpapierhandelsgesetz

(3) Die Gesellschaft hat Mitteilungen nach Absatz 2 innerhalb von einem Monat nach Zugang nach Maßgabe des § 25 Abs. 1 Satz 1, Abs. 2 zu veröffentlichen und dem Bundesaufsichtsamt unverzüglich einen Beleg über die Veröffentlichung zu übersenden.

(4) Auf die Pflichten nach den Absätzen 2 und 3 sind die §§ 23, 24, 25 Abs. 1 Satz 3, Abs. 3 Satz 2, Abs. 4, §§ 27 bis 30 entsprechend anzuwenden.

(5) Ordnungswidrig handelt, wer vorsätzlich oder leichtfertig

1. entgegen Absatz 2 eine Mitteilung nicht, nicht richtig, nicht vollständig, nicht in der vorgeschriebenen Form oder nicht rechtzeitig macht oder

2. entgegen Absatz 3 in Verbindung mit § 25 Abs. 1 Satz 1 oder Abs. 2 eine Veröffentlichung nicht, nicht richtig, nicht vollständig, nicht in der vorgeschriebenen Form oder nicht rechtzeitig vornimmt oder einen Beleg nicht oder nicht rechtzeitig übersendet.

(6) Die Ordnungswidrigkeit kann in den Fällen des Absatzes 5 Nr. 1 mit einer Geldbuße bis zu fünfhunderttausend Deutsche Mark und in den Fällen des Absatzes 5 Nr. 2 mit einer Geldbuße bis zu einhunderttausend Deutsche Mark geahndet werden.

Securities Trading Act

rights of the company and provide his address, unless by such date that information has been given in accordance with § 21 sub-paragraph 1.

(3) The company shall publish details of any information provided under sub-paragraph 2 in accordance with the criteria laid down by § 25 sub-paragraph 1 sentence 1 sub-paragraph 2 within 1 month of receipt thereof and shall send evidence of publication forthwith to the Federal Supervisory Authority.

(4) §§ 23, 24, 25 sub-paragraph 1 sentence 3, sub-paragraph 3 sentence 2, sub-paragraph 4, and §§ 27–30 shall apply to the obligations referred to in sub-paragraphs 2 and 3 above.

(5) A person is guilty of a breach of regulation if he intentionally or recklessy

1. fails to provide information, fails to do so correctly, does so incompletely or fails to do so in the prescribed form or on time contrary to sub-paragraph 2;

2. fails to publish, fails to do so correctly or does so incompletely, fails to publish in the prescribed form or on time or fails to provide proof of publication contrary to sub-paragraph 3 in connection with § 25 sub-paragraph 1 sentences 1 or sub-paragraph 2.

(6) A breach of regulation of the kind referred to in sub-paragraph 5 No. 1 may be punished by a fine of up to five hundred thousand German Marks; a breach of regulation of the kind referred to in sub-paragraph 5 No. 2 may be punished by a fine of up to one hundred thousand German Marks.

Börsengesetz (BörsG)

in der Fassung vom 27. Mai 1908 (RGBl. S. 215), zuletzt geändert durch Artikel 2 des Zweiten Finanzmarktförderungsgesetzes vom 26. Juli 1994 (BGBl. I, S. 1760)

Inhaltsübersicht

§

I. Allgemeine Bestimmungen über die Börsen und deren Organe

Errichtung, Aufhebung, Aufsicht	1
Auskünfte, Prüfungen	1a
Überwachung	1b
Übertragung von Befugnissen	2
Einhaltung von Vorschriften	2a
Geheimhaltung	2b
Einzelweisungen	2c
Börsenrat	3
Mitglieder des Börsenrates	3a
Börsenrat an Warenbörsen	3b
Leitung, Geschäftsführer	3c
Börsenordnung	4
Gebührenordnung	5
Benutzung von Börseneinrichtungen	6
Zulassung zur Börse	7
Teilnahme am elektronischen Börsenhandel	7a
Handhabung der Ordnung	8
Kursmakler und freie Makler	8a
Anordnungen gegenüber Maklern	8b
Börsenverbindlichkeiten der Makler	8c
Sanktionsausschuß	9
Kauf und Verkauf von Wertpapieren	10
Börsenpreise	11
Elektronisches Handelssystem	12
Aufgabegeschäft	13
Börsenschiedsgericht	28

Stock Exchange Act

in the wording of the publication of May 27, 1908 (Legal Gazette 215), last amended by Article 2 of the Second Financial Market Advancement Law of July 26, 1994 (Federal Gazette I 1760)

Table of Contents

§

I. General Provisions for Stock Exchanges and their Organs

Opening, Closing and Supervision	1
Information and Audits	1a
Supervision	1b
Delegation of Duties and Powers	2
Adherence to Provisions	2a
Confidentiality	2b
Directives	2c
Stock Exchange Council	3
Members of the Stock Exchange Council	3a
Commodities Exchange Council	3b
Management, Board of Governors	3c
Stock Exchange Order	4
Fees Order	5
Use of Stock Exchange Facilities	6
Admission to the Stock Exchange	7
Participation in Electronic Trading	7a
Maintaining Order	8
Supervision of Brokers	8a
Regulation of Brokers	8b
Limitation of Engagements of Brokers	8c
Sanctions Committee	9
Buy and Sell Orders	10
Stock Exchange Prices	11
Electronic Trading System	12
Open Transaction for an Unidentified Party	13
Arbitration Agreements	28

Börsengesetz

II. Feststellung des Börsenpreises und Maklerwesen

Feststellung des Börsenpreises 29
Kursmakler 30
Anspruch auf Berücksichtigung 31
Pflichten der Kursmakler 32
Maklertagebuch 33
Vornahme von Käufen und Verkäufen durch die Kursmakler 34
Maklergesellschaften 34a
Amtliche Feststellung des Börsenpreises 35

III. Zulassung von Wertpapieren zum Börsenhandel mit amtlicher Notierung

Zulassungsvoraussetzungen 36
Zulassungsstelle 37
Zulassungsverordnung 38
Ablehnung der Zulassung 39
Zusammenarbeit der Zulassungsstellen 40
Gegenseitige Anerkennung von Prospekten 40a
Staatsanleihen 41
Einführung 42
Aussetzung und Einstellung der amtlichen Notierung 43
Pflichten des Emittenten 44
Zwischenbericht 44b
Auskunftspflicht 44c
Pflichtversäumnisse des Emittenten 44d
Prospekthaftung 45
Umfang der Ersatzpflicht 46
Verjährung des Ersatzanspruchs 47
Umwirksamkeit von Vereinbarungen über Haftungsausschluß 48
Gerichtliche Zuständigkeit bei Ersatzansprüchen 49

IV. Terminhandel

Zulassung zum Börsenterminhandel 50
Ausschluß des Börsenterminhandels 51
Wirksamkeit des Börsentermingeschäfts 52
Verbindlichkeit von Börsentermingeschäften 53
Rückforderung von Leistungen 55

Stock Exchange Act

II. Brokers and Fixing of Prices

Fixing Exchange Prices 29
Official Brokers 30
Right to be Taken into Account in the Fixing of Official Prices 31
Obligations of Official Brokers 32
Brokers' Transaction Book 33
Purchase and Sale by Official Brokers 34
Brokers' Companies 34a
Official Determination of a Stock Exchange Price 35

III. Admission of Securities to Official Listing on Stock Exchanges

Requirements for Admission 36
Listing Board 37
Admissions Regulations 38
Refusal of Admission 39
Cooperation between Listing Boards 40
Mutual Recognition of Prospectuses 40a
Government Bonds 41
Introduction of Securities 42
Suspension and Cancellation of Official Listing 43
Obligations of the Issuer 44
Interim Report 44b
Obligation to Provide Information 44c
Failure of Issuer to Comply with Obligations 44d
Liability for Prospectuses 45
Extent of Liability for Damages 46
Limitation on Claims for Damages 47
Unfair Contract Terms 48
Jurisdiction for Claims for Damages 49

IV. Futures Trading

Admission to Futures Trading on the Stock Exchange 50
Exclusion of Futures Trading 51
Effectiveness of Stock Exchange Futures Transactions 52
Enforceability of Stock Exchange Futures Transactions 53
Claims for Recovery of Consideration 55

Börsengesetz

Aufrechnung 56
Verbindlichkeit bei Leistungsbereitschaft und Leistungswirkung 57
Einwendungen 58
Schuldanerkenntnis 59
Erteilung und Übernahme von Aufträgen – Abschlußvereinigungen ... 60
Auslandsgeschäfte 61
Verzug bei einem Warenbörsentermingeschäft 62
Beschränkung bei Börsentermingeschäften 63
Unwirksamkeit verbotener Börsentermingeschäfte 64
Vereinbarung zwecks Schulderfüllung 69
Aufträge und Vereinbarungen 70

V. Zulassung von Wertpapieren zum Börsenhandel mit nichtamtlicher Notierung

Zulassungsantrag 71
Nähere Bestimmungen in der Börsenordnung 72
Zulassungsvoraussetzungen 73
Staatsanleihen 74
Feststellung des Börsenpreises 75
Verpflichtungen des Emittenten 76
Haftung für Unternehmensbericht 77
Freiverkehr 78
Strafvorschrift 88
Verleitung zu Börsenspekulationsgeschäften 89
Ordnungswidrigkeiten 90
Geltung für Wechsel und ausländische Zahlungsmittel 96
Übergangsregelung 97

Stock Exchange Act

Set Off 56
Enforceability in Cases of Readiness and Ability to Perform 57
Objections 58
Recognition of Debt 59
Giving and Acceptance of Instructions 60
Foreign Transactions 61
Default in Relation to Commodities Futures Dealings on the Stock
Exchange 62
Restrictions on Stock Exchange Futures Transactions 63
Invalidity of Prohibited Stock Exchange Futures Transactions 64
Agreement to Settle a Debt 69
Instructions, Associations 70

V. The Admission of Securities to Stock Exchange Trading with Unofficial Listing

Application for Admission 71
Further Provisions in the Stock Exchange Order 72
Prerequisites for Admission 73
Public Bonds 74
Fixing the Stock Exchange Price 75
Obligations of Issuer 76
Liability for Report 77
Free Market 78
Manipulation of Prices 88
Inducement to Speculation on the Stock Exchange 89
Breaches of Regulations 90
Application for Bills of Exchange and Foreign Currencies 96
Transitional Provisions 97

Börsengesetz

I. Allgemeine Bestimmungen über die Börsen und deren Organe

§ 1
Errichtung, Aufhebung, Aufsicht

(1) Die Errichtung einer Börse bedarf der Genehmigung der zuständigen obersten Landesbehörde (Börsenaufsichtsbehörde). Diese ist befugt, die Aufhebung bestehender Börsen anzuordnen.

(2) Die Börsenaufsichtsbehörde übt die Aufsicht über die Börse nach den Vorschriften dieses Gesetzes aus. Ihrer Aufsicht unterliegen auch die Einrichtungen, die sich auf den Börsenverkehr beziehen. Die Aufsicht erstreckt sich auf die Einhaltung der börsenrechtlichen Vorschriften und Anordnungen sowie die ordnungsgemäße Durchführung des Handels an der Börse und der Börsengeschäftsabwicklung.

(3) Die Börsenaufsichtsbehörde kann für die Durchführung der Aufsicht an der Börse einen Staatskommissar einsetzen. Sie ist berechtigt, an den Beratungen der Börsenorgane teilzunehmen. Die Börsenorgane sind verpflichtet, die Börsenaufsichtsbehörde bei der Erfüllung ihrer Aufgabe zu unterstützen.

(4) Die Börsenaufsichtsbehörde nimmt die ihr nach diesem Gesetz zugewiesenen Aufgaben und Befugnisse nur im öffentlichen Interesse wahr.

(5) Wertpapierbörsen im Sinne dieses Gesetzes sind Börsen, an denen Wertpapiere oder Derivate im Sinne des § 2 Abs. 1 und 2 des Wertpapierhandelsgesetzes gehandelt werden.

§ 1a
Auskünfte, Prüfungen

(1) Die Börsenaufsichtsbehörde kann, soweit dies zur Erfüllung ihrer Aufgaben erforderlich ist, auch ohne besonderen Anlaß von der Börse sowie von den nach § 7 zur Teilnahme am Börsenhandel zugelassenen Unternehmen und Börsenhändlern und den Kursmaklern (Handelsteilnehmer) Auskünfte und die Vorlage von Unterlagen verlangen sowie Prüfungen vornehmen. Während der üblichen Arbeitszeit ist den Bediensteten der Börsenaufsichtsbehörde, soweit dies zur Wahrnehmung ihrer Aufgabe erforderlich ist, das Betreten der Grundstücke und Geschäftsräume der Börse und der Handelsteilnehmer zu

Stock Exchange Act

I. General Provisions for Stock Exchanges and their Organs

§ 1

Opening, Closing, and Supervision

(1) The establishment of a stock exchange requires the licence of the appropriate state authority ("Stock Exchange Supervisory Agency"). It shall have the power to close the operation of stock exchanges.

(2) The Stock Exchange Supervisory Agency shall supervise the stock exchange in accordance with the provisions of this Act. It shall supervise any facilities concerned with stock exchange business. Such supervision shall include supervision of compliance with stock exchange legal provisions and orders, as well as the proper conduct of stock exchange trading and settlement.

(3) The Stock Exchange Supervisory Agency may appoint a state commissioner responsible for the supervision of the stock exchange. It shall have the power to take part in the deliberations of stock exchange organs. Stock exchange organs shall be obliged to assist the Stock Exchange Supervisory Agency in the carrying out of its obligations.

(4) The Stock Exchange Supervisory Agency shall carry out its obligations and exercise its powers under this Act solely in the public interest.

(5) Securities stock exchanges according to this Act are stock exchanges on which securities or derivatives, as defined in § 2 sub-paragraphs 1 and 2 of the Securities Trading Act, are traded.

§ 1a

Information and Audits

(1) The Stock Exchange Supervisory Agency may, to the extent necessary to carry out its obligations under this Act, require information and documents to be provided to it at any time and without specific reason by a stock exchange or by any enterprise admitted to trade on a stock exchange under § 7, stock exchange traders or official brokers admitted to trade on a stock exchange; and to perform audits. Officers engaged by the Stock Exchange Supervisory Agency may enter stock exchange premises and those of traders during normal business hours, so far as necessary for the execution of their

Börsengesetz

gestatten. Das Betreten außerhalb dieser Zeit oder wenn die Geschäftsräume sich in einer Wohnung befinden, ist ohne Einverständnis nur zur Verhütung von dringenden Gefahren für die öffentliche Sicherheit und Ordnung zulässig und insoweit zu dulden. Das Grundrecht der Unverletzlichkeit der Wohnung (Artikel 13 des Grundgesetzes) wird insoweit eingeschränkt. Die Befugnisse nach den Sätzen 1 bis 3 stehen auch den von der Börsenaufsichtsbehörde beauftragten Personen und Einrichtungen zu, soweit sie nach diesem Gesetz tätig werden. Der zur Erteilung einer Auskunft Verpflichtete kann die Auskunft auf solche Fragen verweigern, deren Beantwortung ihn selbst oder einen der in § 383 Abs. 1 Nr. 1 bis 3 der Zivilprozeßordnung bezeichneten Angehörigen der Gefahr strafgerichtlicher Verfolgung oder eines Verfahrens nach dem Gesetz über Ordnungswidrigkeiten aussetzen würde. Der Verpflichtete ist über sein Recht zur Verweigerung der Auskunft zu belehren.

(2) Die Börsenaufsichtsbehörde kann gegenüber der Börse und den Handelsteilnehmern Anordnungen treffen, die geeignet sind, Verstöße gegen börsenrechtliche Vorschriften und Anordnungen zu unterbinden oder sonstige Mißstände zu beseitigen oder zu verhindern, welche die ordnungsmäßige Durchführung des Handels an der Börse und der Börsengeschäftsabwicklung sowie deren Überwachung beeinträchtigen können.

(3) Widerspruch und Anfechtungsklage gegen Maßnahmen nach Absatz 1 haben keine aufschiebende Wirkung.

§ 1b
Überwachung

(1) Die Wertpapierbörse hat unter Beachtung von Maßgaben der Börsenaufsichtsbehörde eine Handelsüberwachungsstelle als Börsenorgan einzurichten und zu betreiben, die den Handel an der Börse und die Börsengeschäftsabwicklung überwacht. Die Handelsüberwachungsstelle hat Daten über den Börsenhandel und die Börsengeschäftsabwicklung systematisch und lückenlos zu erfassen und auszuwerten sowie notwendige Ermittlungen durchzuführen. Die Börsenaufsichtsbehörde kann der Handelsüberwachungsstelle Weisungen erteilen und die Ermittlungen übernehmen. Die Geschäftsführung kann die Handelsüberwachungsstelle im Rahmen der Aufgaben dieser Stelle nach den Sätzen 1 und 2 mit der Durchführung von Untersuchungen beauftragen.

(2) Der Leiter der Handelsüberwachungsstelle wird auf Vorschlag der Geschäftsführung vom Börsenrat im Einvernehmen mit der Börsenauf-

Stock Exchange Act

duties. Premises may be entered outside such business hours, or where the premises are in a dwelling, without consent, only in circumstances where there is an immediate threat to public safety and order. The constitutional right of the inviolability of a person's dwelling (Article 13 of the Basic Law) is thereby restricted. These powers shall also apply to any persons retained by the Stock Exchange Supervisory Agency, where such persons are acting in accordance with this Act pursuant to sentence 1 to 3. Any person obliged to provide information may decline to answer any question where doing so would place him or any person referred to in § 383 sub-paragraph 1 Nos. 1 to 3 of the Civil Procedure Code in danger of criminal prosecution or of proceedings under the Breaches of Regulation Act. Any person obliged to provide information shall be informed of his right to remain silent.

(2) The Stock Exchange Supervisory Agency may make orders for the stock exchange and traders to prevent breaches of stock exchange provisions and orders or to counteract other irregularities likely to prejudice the proper carrying on of business on the stock exchange, the trading functions of the stock exchange, the settlement and the supervision thereof.

(3) Any objections or appeal against the measures referred to in sub-paragraph 1 shall not delay the effect of such measures.

§ 1b
Supervision

(1) The securities stock exchange shall establish and operate a trading monitoring office as an organ of the stock exchange to supervise trading on the stock exchange and stock exchange settlement, and in so doing shall respect the directions of the Stock Exchange Supervisory Agency. The trading monitoring office shall collect and evaluate data concerning trading on the stock exchange and the settlement of stock exchange business systematically and comprehensively and carry out any necessary investigations. The Stock Exchange Supervisory Agency may give directions to the trading monitoring office and take over investigations from it. The Board of Governors may order the trading monitoring office to carry out investigations within the framework of the obligations imposed on it by sentences 1 and 2.

(2) The director of the trading monitoring office shall be appointed or reappointed by the Stock Exchange Council, following nomination by the

Börsengesetz

sichtsbehörde bestellt oder wiederbestellt. Er hat der Börsenaufsichtsbehörde regelmäßig zu berichten. Die bei der Handelsüberwachungsstelle mit Überwachungsaufgaben betrauten Personen können gegen ihren Willen nur im Einvernehmen mit der Börsenaufsichtsbehörde von ihrer Tätigkeit entbunden werden. Mit Zustimmung der Börsenaufsichtsbehörde kann die Geschäftsführung diesen Personen auch andere Aufgaben übertragen. Die Zustimmung ist zu erteilen, wenn hierdurch die Erfüllung der Überwachungsaufgaben der Handelsüberwachungsstelle nicht beeinträchtigt wird.

(3) Der Handelsüberwachungsstelle stehen die Befugnisse der Börsenaufsichtsbehörde nach § 1a Abs. 1 Satz 1 bis 3 zu; § 1a Abs. 1 Satz 6 und 7, Abs. 3 gilt entsprechend.

(4) Die Handelsüberwachungsstelle kann Daten über Geschäftsabschlüsse der Geschäftsführung der Börse und der Handelsüberwachungsstelle einer anderen Wertpapierbörse übermitteln, soweit sie für die Erfüllung der Aufgaben dieser Stellen erforderlich sind.

(5) Stellt die Handelsüberwachungsstelle Tatsachen fest, welche die Annahme rechtfertigen, daß börsenrechtliche Vorschriften oder Anordnungen verletzt werden oder sonstige Mißstände vorliegen, welche die ordnungsgemäße Durchführung des Handels an der Börse oder die Börsengeschäftsabwicklung beeinträchtigen können, hat sie die Börsenaufsichtsbehörde und die Geschäftsführung unverzüglich zu unterrichten. Die Geschäftsführung kann eilbedürftige Anordnungen treffen, die geeignet sind, die ordnungsmäßige Durchführung des Handels an der Börse und der Börsengeschäftsabwicklung sicherzustellen; § 1a Abs. 3 gilt entsprechend. Die Geschäftsführung hat die Börsenaufsichtsbehörde über die getroffenen Maßnahmen unverzüglich zu unterrichten.

§ 2
Übertragung von Befugnissen

(1) Die nach Landesrecht zuständige Stelle wird ermächtigt, Aufgaben und Befugnisse der Börsenaufsichtsbehörde auf eine andere Behörde zu übertragen.

(2) Die Börsenaufsichtsbehörde kann sich bei der Durchführung ihrer Aufgaben anderer Personen und Einrichtungen bedienen.

Stock Exchange Act

board, with the agreement of the Stock Exchange Supervisory Agency. He is to report to it on a regular basis. The employment of any persons engaged by the trading monitoring office to carry out monitoring work may be terminated without their consent only with the agreement of the Stock Exchange Supervisory Agency. Subject to the agreement of the Stock Exchange Supervisory Agency, the board may assign such persons to other duties. Consent shall, however, be given where transfer will not adversely affect the monitoring activities of the trading monitoring office.

(3) The trading monitoring office shall enjoy the powers available to the Stock Exchange Supervisory Agency under § 1a sub-paragraph 1 sentences 2 to 3; § 1a sub-paragraph 1 sentences 6 and 7, sub-section 3 shall apply.

(4) The trading monitoring office may provide data on transactions carried out to the board of the stock exchange or to the trading monitoring office of another stock exchange to fulfill the obligations of such authorities.

(5) If the trading monitoring office establishes facts justifying it in assuming that stock exchange provisions or orders are being breached or other irregularities have occurred which are likely to adversely affect the proper carrying on of trading on the stock exchange or the settlement of such trading, it shall forthwith inform the Stock Exchange Supervisory Agency and the Board of Governors. The board may make emergency orders to safeguard the orderly carrying out of business on the stock exchange and the orderly development of trading; § 1a sub-paragraph 3 applies. The board shall give notice to the Stock Exchange Supervisory Agency forthwith of the measures it has taken.

§ 2

Delegation of Duties and Powers

(1) The authority responsible under state law shall have the power to delegate the duties and powers of the Stock Exchange Supervisory Agency to another authority.

(2) The Stock Exchange Supervisory Agency may engage other persons and institutions to carry out its obligations.

Börsengesetz

§ 2a

Einhaltung von Vorschriften

(1) Die Börsenaufsichtsbehörde hat darauf hinzuwirken, daß die Vorschriften des Gesetzes gegen Wettbewerbsbeschränkungen eingehalten werden. Dies gilt insbesondere für den Zugang zu Handels-, Informations- und Abwicklungssystemen und sonstigen börsenbezogenen Dienstleistungseinrichtungen sowie deren Nutzung.

(2) Die Zuständigkeit der Kartellbehörden bleibt unberührt. Die Börsenaufsichtsbehörde unterrichtet die zuständige Kartellbehörde bei Anhaltspunkten für Verstöße gegen das Gesetz gegen Wettbewerbsbeschränkungen. Diese unterrichtet die Börsenaufsichtsbehörde nach Abschluß ihrer Ermittlungen über das Ergebnis der Ermittlungen.

§ 2b

Geheimhaltung

(1) Die bei der Börsenaufsichtsbehörde oder einer Behörde, der Aufgaben und Befugnisse der Börsenaufsichtsbehörde nach § 2 Abs. 1 übertragen worden sind, Beschäftigten, die nach § 2 Abs. 2 beauftragten Personen, die Mitglieder der Börsenorgane sowie die beim Träger der Börse Beschäftigten, soweit sie für die Börse tätig sind, dürfen die ihnen bei ihrer Tätigkeit bekanntgewordenen Tatsachen, deren Geheimhaltung im Interesse der Handelsteilnehmer oder eines Dritten liegt, insbesondere Geschäfts- und Betriebsgeheimnisse sowie personenbezogene Daten, nicht unbefugt offenbaren oder verwerten, auch wenn sie nicht mehr im Dienst sind oder ihre Tätigkeit beendet ist. Dies gilt auch für andere Personen, die durch dienstliche Berichterstattung Kenntnis von den in Satz 1 bezeichneten Tatsachen erhalten. Ein unbefugtes Offenbaren oder Verwerten im Sinne des Satzes 1 liegt insbesondere nicht vor, wenn Tatsachen weitergegeben werden an

1. Strafverfolgungsbehörden oder für Straf- und Bußgeldsachen zuständige Gerichte,

2. kraft Gesetzes oder im öffentlichen Auftrag mit der Überwachung von Börsen, anderen Wertpapiermärkten und des Wertpapierhandels sowie von Kreditinstituten, Finanzinstituten oder Versicherungsunternehmen betraute Stellen sowie von diesen beauftragte Personen,

§ 2a
Adherence to Provisions

(1) The Stock Exchange Supervisory Agency shall take steps to ensure that the provisions of the Restrictions on Competition Act are adhered to. This shall apply in particular to access to trading, information and settlement systems, and to other stock exchange facilities and the use thereof.

(2) The powers of antitrust authorities shall remain unaffected by this Act. The Stock Exchange Supervisory Agency shall notify the relevant antitrust authorities of any indications of breaches of the Restrictions on Competition Act. The latter shall inform the Stock Exchange Supervisory Agency of the results of any investigations they carry out.

§ 2b
Confidentiality

(1) Persons employed by the Stock Exchange Supervisory Agency or by any authority to which the obligations and powers of the Stock Exchange Supervisory Agency have been delegated under § 2 sub-paragraph 1, persons retained under § 2 sub-paragraph 2, members of stock exchange organs and persons employed by organisations responsible for the functioning of the stock exchange, to the extent that they are acting on behalf of the stock exchange, may not make unauthorised use of or disclose information which has come to their knowledge in the course of their employment, in particular trade and business secrets as well as personal data, if it is in the interests of a trader or a third party that such information be kept secret, even after the cessation or termination of their employment. This also applies to other persons who have obtained information of the facts described in sentence 1 as a result of reporting procedures during the course of their employment. Disclosing or making use of information of the kind referred to in sentence 1 shall not be a breach where it is passed on to

1. the public prosecution authorities or courts having jurisdiction to impose criminal penalties or fines,
2. other offices which by reason of law or on behalf of the government are entrusted with the supervision of stock exchanges, other securities markets, and securities trading or credit institutions, financial institutions, insurance enterprises, or persons retained thereby

Börsengesetz

soweit diese Stellen diese Informationen zur Erfüllung ihrer Aufgaben benötigen. Für die bei diesen Stellen Beschäftigten gilt die Verschwiegenheitspflicht nach Satz 1 entsprechend.

(2) Die Vorschriften der §§ 93, 97, 105 Abs. 1, § 111 Abs. 5 in Verbindung mit § 105 Abs. 1 sowie § 116 Abs. 1 der Abgabenordnung gelten nicht für die in Absatz 1 Satz 1 oder 2 bezeichneten Personen, soweit sie zur Durchführung dieses Gesetzes tätig werden. Sie finden Anwendung, soweit die Finanzbehörden die Kenntnis für die Durchführung eines Verfahrens wegen einer Steuerstraftat sowie eines damit zusammenhängenden Besteuerungsverfahrens benötigen, an deren Verfolgung ein zwingendes öffentliches Interesse besteht, und nicht Tatsachen betroffen sind, die den in Absatz 1 Satz 1 oder 2 bezeichneten Personen durch eine Stelle eines anderen Staates im Sinne des Absatzes 1 Satz 3 Nr. 2 oder durch von dieser Stelle beauftragte Personen mitgeteilt worden sind.

§ 2c

Einzelweisungen

Das Bundesministerium der Finanzen kann im Einvernehmen mit dem Bundesministerium für Wirtschaft und nach Anhörung der Deutschen Bundesbank Einzelweisungen erteilen, die amtliche Preisfeststellung für ausländische Währungen vorübergehend zu untersagen, wenn eine erhebliche Marktstörung droht, die schwerwiegende Gefahren für die Gesamtwirtschaft oder das Publikum erwarten läßt.

§ 3

Börsenrat

(1) Die Wertpapierbörse hat einen Börsenrat zu bilden, der aus höchstens 24 Personen besteht. Im Börsenrat müssen die zur Teilnahme am Börsenhandel zugelassenen Kreditinstitute einschließlich der Kapitalanlagegesellschaften, die freien Makler und sonstigen zugelassenen Unternehmen, die Kursmakler, die Versicherungsunternehmen, deren emittierte Wertpapiere an der Börse zum Handel zugelassen sind, andere Emittenten solcher Wertpapiere und die Anleger vertreten sein. Die Zahl der Vertreter der Kreditinstitute einschließlich der Kapitalanlagegesellschaften sowie der mit den Kreditinstituten verbundenen Unternehmen darf insgesamt nicht mehr als die Hälfte der Mitglieder des Börsenrates betragen.

Stock Exchange Act

provided that such offices need such information to carry out their obligations. Persons employed by such authorities shall be subject to the duty of confidentiality referred to in sentence 1.

(2) The provisions of § 93, 97, 105 sub-paragraph 1, § 111 sub-paragraph 5 in conjunction with § 105 sub-paragraph 1, together with § 116 sub-paragraph 1 of the Taxes Order shall not apply to the persons referred to in sub-paragraph 1 sentences 1 or 2 to the extent that such persons are acting to enforce the terms of this Act. They shall apply to the extent that the tax authorities require the information for the purpose of bringing proceedings relating to a tax offence under the criminal law or for tax proceedings connected therewith, the prosecution of which is a matter of overriding public interest and where information is not involved which has been passed on to the persons referred to in sub-paragraph 1 sentences 1 or 2 by an authority of another state within the meaning of sub-paragraph 1 sentence 3 number 2 or by any persons retained by such an authority who carry out their obligations under this Act.

§ 2c

Directives

The Federal Ministry of Finance may, with the agreement of the Federal Ministry for the Economy, and after taking into account the views of the German Federal Bank, make directives temporarily prohibiting the official fixing of rates for foreign currencies in circumstances when the market is likely to be subject to significant instability or when it is likely to jeopardise the public or the economy as a whole.

§ 3

Stock Exchange Council

(1) The securities stock exchange shall establish a Stock Exchange Council consisting of up to 24 persons. Credit institutions, including capital investment companies, independent brokers and other admitted enterprises, official brokers, insurance enterprises having securities which are admitted for trading on the stock exchange, other issuers of such securities and investors shall be represented. The number of representatives of credit institutions and enterprises connected with them, including capital investment companies, shall not make up more than one half of the members of the Stock Exchange Council.

Börsengesetz

(2) Dem Börsenrat obliegt insbesondere
1. der Erlaß der Börsenordnung und der Gebührenordnung,
2. die Bestellung und Abberufung der Geschäftsführer im Benehmen mit der Börsenaufsichtsbehörde,
3. die Überwachung der Geschäftsführung,
4. der Erlaß einer Geschäftsordnung für die Geschäftsführung,
5. der Erlaß der Bedingungen für die Geschäfte an der Börse.

Die Entscheidung über die Einführung von technischen Systemen, die dem Handel oder der Abwicklung von Börsengeschäften dienen, bedarf der Zustimmung des Börsenrates. Die Börsenordnung kann für andere Maßnahmen der Geschäftsführung von grundsätzlicher Bedeutung die Zustimmung des Börsenrates vorsehen.

(3) Der Börsenrat gibt sich eine Geschäftsordnung. Er wählt aus seiner Mitte einen Vorsitzenden und mindestens einen Stellvertreter, der einer anderen Gruppe im Sinne des Absatzes 1 Satz 2 angehört als der Vorsitzende. Wahlen nach Satz 2 sind geheim; andere Abstimmungen sind auf Antrag eines Viertels der Mitglieder geheim durchzuführen.

(4) Setzt der Börsenrat zur Vorbereitung seiner Beschlüsse Ausschüsse ein, hat er bei der Zusammensetzung der Ausschüsse dafür zu sorgen, daß Angehörige der Gruppen im Sinne des Absatzes 1 Satz 2, deren Belange durch die Beschlüsse berührt werden können, angemessen vertreten sind.

(5) Mit der Genehmigung einer neuen Börse bestellt die Börsenaufsichtsbehörde einen vorläufigen Börsenrat höchstens für die Dauer eines Jahres.

§ 3a

Mitglieder des Börsenrates

(1) Die Mitglieder des Börsenrates werden für die Dauer von drei Jahren von den in § 3 Abs. 1 Satz 2 genannten Gruppen jeweils aus ihrer Mitte gewählt; der Vertreter der Anleger wird von den übrigen Mitgliedern des Börsenrates hinzugewählt.

Stock Exchange Act

(2) The Stock Exchange Council shall be responsible in particular for
1. making stock exchange orders and fees orders,
2. the appointment and removal of the Governors in consultation with the Stock Exchange Supervisory Agency,
3. the supervision of the Board of Governors,
4. the making of standing orders for the Board of Governors,
5. the laying down of conditions applying to trading on the stock exchange.

Decisions relating to the introduction of technical systems for trading or the settlement of business on the stock exchange shall require the approval of the Stock Exchange Council. The Stock Exchange Order may provide that the Board of Governors require the consent of the Stock Exchange Council before it takes any other measures of fundamental importance.

(3) The Stock Exchange Council shall formulate its own standing orders. It shall elect from its midst a chairman and at least one vice-chairman who shall be a member of a group, within the meaning of sub-paragraph 1 sentence 2, to which the chairman does not belong. Voting pursuant to sentence 2 by the Stock Exchange Council shall be by secret ballot; any other matters requiring a vote shall be decided by secret ballot if one quarter of members so require.

(4) If the Stock Exchange Council establishes a committee to consider the passing of any resolution, it shall ensure that, in respect to the composition of such committee, members of the groups referred to in sub-paragraph 1 sentence 2, whose interests are likely to be affected by the decisions of such committee, shall be adequately represented.

(5) Where a new stock exchange is licensed to operate, the Stock Exchange Supervisory Agency shall establish a temporary Stock Exchange Council for a maximum period of one year.

§ 3a
Members of the Stock Exchange Council

(1) The members of the Stock Exchange Council shall be elected for a period of three years from the groups referred to in § 3 sub-paragraph 1 sentence 2; investors' representatives shall be co-opted by the other members of the Stock Exchange Council.

Börsengesetz

(2) Unternehmen, die mehr als einer der in § 3 Abs. 1 Satz 2 genannten Gruppen angehören, dürfen nur in einer Gruppe wählen. Verbundene Unternehmen dürfen im Börsenrat nur mit einem Mitglied vertreten sein.

(3) Das Nähere über die Aufteilung in Gruppen, die Ausübung des Wahlrechts und die Wählbarkeit, die Durchführung der Wahl und die vorzeitige Beendigung der Mitgliedschaft im Börsenrat wird durch Rechtsverordnung der Landesregierung nach Anhörung des Börsenrates bestimmt. Die Landesregierung kann diese Ermächtigung durch Rechtsverordnung auf die Börsenaufsichtsbehörde übertragen. Die Rechtsverordnung muß sicherstellen, daß alle in § 3 Abs. 1 Satz 2 genannten Gruppen angemessen vertreten sind. Die Bereiche der privaten, öffentlichen und genossenschaftlichen Kreditinstitute sowie der Kapitalanlagegesellschaften müssen vertreten sein, soweit dies nach Absatz 2 Satz 2 zulässig ist; die Rechtsverordnung kann die Bildung von Untergruppen vorsehen. Die Kursmakler sind mit mindestens zwei Mitgliedern, sofern keine Kursmaklerkammer besteht mit mindestens einem Mitglied, und die freien Makler mit mindestens einem Mitglied im Börsenrat zu berücksichtigen. Die Rechtsverordnung kann für Organe des Handelsstandes ein Entsendungsrecht vorsehen.

§ 3b
Börsenrat an Warenbörsen

Auf Warenbörsen sind die Vorschriften der §§ 3 und 3a über den Börsenrat mit folgender Maßgabe anzuwenden:

1. Abweichend von § 3 Abs. 1 Satz 2 müssen die zur Teilnahme am Börsenhandel zugelassenen Unternehmen und in § 7 Abs. 2 Satz 2 genannten Personen sowie die Kursmakler im Börsenrat vertreten sein;
2. der Börsenrat wählt aus seiner Mitte einen Vorsitzenden;
3. die Rechtsverordnung nach § 3a Abs. 3 muß sicherstellen, daß alle wirtschaftlichen Gruppen der in Nummer 1 genannten Unternehmen und Personen sowie die Kursmakler angemessen vertreten sind.

§ 3c
Leitung, Geschäftsführer

(1) Die Leitung der Börse obliegt der Geschäftsführung in eigener Verantwortung. Sie kann aus einer oder mehreren Personen bestehen. Die

Stock Exchange Act

(2) Enterprises which belong to more than one of the groups referred to in § 3 sub-paragraph 1 sentence 2 may only vote in one group. Connected enterprises may only have one representative on the Stock Exchange Council.

(3) Detailed provisions concerning the division between groups, the exercise of voting rights, eligibility to stand for election, the conduct of elections and the termination of Stock Exchange Council membership before the end of an electoral period, shall be laid down by Regulation by the Land government after consultation with the Stock Exchange Council. The Land government may delegate this power by Regulations to the Stock Exchange Supervisory Agency. Any Regulations must ensure that all the groups referred to in § 3 sub-paragraph 1 sentence 2 be adequately represented. Private, public and cooperative credit institutions, including capital investment companies, shall be represented to the extent permitted by sub-paragraph 2 sentence 2; the Regulations may provide for the formation of sub-groups. Official brokers shall be represented by a minimum of two members, when there is no brokers' chambers the official brokers shall be represented by one member, and independent brokers shall have a minimum of one representative on the Stock Exchange Council. The Regulation may give representatives of trader organisations the right to send representatives.

§ 3b
Commodities Exchange Council

The provisions of §§ 3 and 3a concerning the Stock Exchange Council shall apply to commodities exchanges with the following provisos:

1. In distinction from the provisions of § 3 sub-paragraph 1 sentence 2, enterprises admitted to trade on the commodities exchange, the persons referred to in § 7 sub-paragraph 2 sentence 2, and official brokers shall be represented on the Commodities Exchange Council;
2. The Commodities Exchange Council shall elect a chairman from its midst;
3. Any Regulation passed under § 3a sub-paragraph 3 must ensure that each commercial group of enterprises of the kind referred to in number 1, as well as official brokers, be adequately represented.

§ 3c
Management, Board of Governors

(1) The management of any stock exchange shall be the responsibility of its governors. The board may consist of one or more persons. The governors

Börsengesetz

Geschäftsführer werden für höchstens fünf Jahre bestellt; die wiederholte Besetzung ist zulässig.

(2) Die Geschäftsführer vertreten die Börse gerichtlich und außergerichtlich, soweit nicht der Träger der Börse zuständig ist. Das Nähere über die Vertretungsbefugnis der Geschäftsführer regelt die Börsenordnung.

§ 4
Börsenordnung

(1) Der Börsenrat erläßt die Börsenordnung als Satzung. Sofern eine öffentlich-rechtliche Körperschaft Träger der Börse ist, ist die Börsenordnung im Einvernehmen mit ihr zu erlassen.

(2) Die Börsenordnung soll sicherstellen, daß die Börse die ihr obliegenden Aufgaben erfüllen kann und dabei den Interessen des Publikums und des Handels gerecht wird. Sie muß Bestimmungen enthalten über

1. den Geschäftszweig der Börse;
2. die Organisation der Börse;
3. die Veröffentlichung der Preise und Kurse sowie der ihnen zugrundeliegenden Umsätze und die Berechtigung der Geschäftsführung, diese zu veröffentlichen.

(3) Bei Wertpapierbörsen muß die Börsenordnung zusätzlich Bestimmungen enthalten über

1. die Zusammensetzung und die Wahl der Mitglieder der Zulassungsstelle;
2. die Bedeutung der Kurszusätze und -hinweise.

(4) Die Börsenordnung bedarf der Genehmigung durch die Börsenaufsichtsbehörde. Diese kann die Aufnahme bestimmter Vorschriften in die Börsenordnung verlangen, wenn und soweit sie zur Erfüllung der der Börse oder der Börsenaufsichtsbehörde obliegenden gesetzlichen Aufgaben notwendig sind.

(5) In verwaltungsgerichtlichen Verfahren kann die Börse unter ihrem Namen klagen und verklagt werden.

Stock Exchange Act

shall be appointed for up to 5 years; re-appointment shall be permitted.

(2) The Board of Governors shall represent the stock exchange for both court and non-court purposes where there are no other bodies responsible. Detailed provisions concerning the power of the Board of Governors to represent the stock exchange shall be regulated by the Stock Exchange Order.

§ 4
Stock Exchange Order

(1) The Stock Exchange Council shall pass a Stock Exchange Order in the form of a charter. If a stock exchange is organised by a public corporate body, the Stock Exchange Order shall be passed by agreement therewith.

(2) The Stock Exchange Order shall ensure that the stock exchange is able to fulfil the duties imposed on it and is able to properly safeguard the interests of the public and of trading. It is to include provisions concerning

1. the principle business activity of the stock exchange;
2. the organisation of the stock exchange;
3. the publication of prices and rates, as well as any underlying turnover and the right of the Board of Governors to publish them.

(3) In the case of stock exchanges for securities, the Stock Exchange Order shall contain additional provisions concerning

1. the composition and election of members of the Listing Board;
2. the meaning of the addenda and the notices to rates;

(4) The Stock Exchange Order requires the approval of the Stock Exchange Supervisory Agency. The latter may demand the inclusion of specific provisions in the Stock Exchange Order to ensure compliance with the obligations imposed by law on the stock exchange or the Stock Exchange Supervisory Agency as necessary.

(5) In administrative court proceedings the stock exchange may sue and be sued in its own name.

Börsengesetz

§ 5
Gebührenordnung

(1) Die Gebührenordnung kann die Erhebung von Gebühren und die Erstattung von Auslagen vorsehen für

1. die Zulassung zur Teilnahme am Börsenhandel und die Teilnahme am Börsenhandel in einem elektronischen Handelssystem,
2. die Zulassung zum Besuch der Börse ohne das Recht zur Teilnahme am Handel,
3. die Zulassung von Wertpapieren zum Börsenhandel,
4. die Einführung von Wertpapieren an der Börse,
5. die Prüfung der Druckausstattung von Wertpapieren,
6. die Ablegung der Börsenhändlerprüfung.

Sofern eine öffentlich-rechtliche Körperschaft Träger der Börse ist, ist zum Erlaß der Vorschriften über Gebühren nach Satz 1 Nr. 1 und 2 das Einvernehmen mit ihr erforderlich.

(2) Die Gebührenordnung bedarf der Genehmigung durch die Börsenaufsichtsbehörde. Die Genehmigung gilt als erteilt, wenn die Gebührenordnung nicht innerhalb von sechs Wochen nach Zugang bei der Börsenaufsichtsbehörde von dieser gegenüber der Börse beanstandet wird.

§ 6
Benutzung von Börseneinrichtungen

Die Börsenordnung kann für einen anderen als den nach § 4 Absatz 2 zu Nr. 1 bezeichnenden Geschäftszweig, sofern dies nicht mit besonderen Bestimmungen dieses Gesetzes (§ 51) im Widerspruche steht, die Benutzung von Börseneinrichtungen zulassen. Ein Anspruch auf die Benutzung erwächst in diesem Falle für die Beteiligten nicht.

§ 7
Zulassung zur Börse

(1) Zum Besuch der Börse und zur Teilnahme am Börsenhandel ist eine Zulassung durch die Geschäftsführung erforderlich. Zum Börsenhandel gehören auch Geschäfte über zugelassene Gegenstände, die durch Übermittlung von Willenserklärungen durch elektronische Datenübertragung börsenmäßig zustande kommen.

§ 5
Fees Order

(1) The Fees Order shall regulate the levying of fees and the reimbursement of expenses relating to:

1. admission to trading on the stock exchange and admission to trading on the stock exchange by electronic trading system,
2. admission to attend the stock exchange without the right to take part in trading,
3. the admission of securities to trading on the stock exchange,
4. the introduction of securities to the stock exchange,
5. checking the printing standard of securities,
6. the stock exchange dealers' examination.

If a public corporate body is responsible for the organisation of a stock exchange, the passing of orders in respect to fees under sentence 1 Nos. 1 and 2 shall require its consent.

(2) The fees order requires the approval of the Stock Exchange Supervisory Agency. Approval shall be deemed to have been given if no objection has been made to the Fees Order within six weeks of its delivery to the Stock Exchange Supervisory Agency.

§ 6
Use of Stock Exchange Facilities

The Stock Exchange Order may permit the use of stock exchange facilities by a line of business other than that designated under § 4 sub-paragraph 2 No.1 where doing so does not contravene specific provisions of this Act (§51). This shall not give rise to any right of use for the persons concerned.

§ 7
Admission to the Stock Exchange

(1) The consent of the Board of Governors shall be required to attend and to be admitted to trading on a stock exchange. Trading on a stock exchange includes the trading in admitted items based on electronically transmitted declarations of intention.

Börsengesetz

(2) Zur Teilnahme am Börsenhandel darf nur zugelassen werden, wer gewerbsmäßig bei börsenmäßig handelbaren Gegenständen

1. die Anschaffung und Veräußerung für eigene Rechnung betreibt oder
2. die Anschaffung und Veräußerung im eigenen Namen für fremde Rechnung betreibt oder
3. die Vermittlung von Verträgen über die Anschaffung und Veräußerung übernimmt

und dessen Gewerbebetrieb nach Art und Umfang einen in kaufmännischer Weise eingerichteten Geschäftsbetrieb erfordert. An Warenbörsen können auch Landwirte und Personen zugelassen werden, deren Gewerbebetrieb nach Art und Umfang einen in kaufmännischer Weise eingerichteten Geschäftsbetrieb nicht erfordert.

(3) Die Zulassung von Personen ohne das Recht zur Teilnahme am Handel regelt die Börsenordnung.

(4) Die Zulassung eines Unternehmens zur Teilnahme am Börsenhandel nach Absatz 2 Satz 1 ist zu erteilen, wenn

1. bei Unternehmen, die in der Rechtsform des Einzelkaufmanns betrieben werden, der Geschäftsinhaber, bei anderen Unternehmen die Personen, die nach Gesetz, Satzung oder Gesellschaftsvertrag mit der Führung der Geschäfte des Antragstellers betraut und zu seiner Vertretung ermächtigt sind, zuverlässig sind und zumindest eine dieser Personen die für das börsenmäßige Wertpapier- oder Warengeschäft notwendige berufliche Eignung hat,
2. die ordnungsmäßige Abwicklung der Geschäfte am Börsenplatz sichergestellt ist,
3. der Antragsteller, sofern er kein Kreditinstitut ist, nach Maßgabe des Absatzes 4a Sicherheit leistet, um die Verpflichtungen aus den Geschäften im Sinne des Absatzes 2 Satz 1, die an der Börse, in einem an der Börse zugelassenen elektronischen Handelssystem und außerhalb der Börse abgeschlossen und über die Börsendatenverarbeitung abgerechnet werden, jederzeit erfüllen zu können, und die zur Absicherung von Börsenverbindlichkeiten, insbesondere der Risiken aus Aufgabegeschäften und der Kursdifferenzen für den jeweiligen Abrechnungszeitraum, dient,
4. der Antragsteller, sofern er kein Kreditinstitut ist, ein Eigenkapital von mindestens 100 000 Deutsche Mark nachweist; als Eigenkapital sind das

(2) Only persons carrying on business in instruments capable of being traded on a stock exchange

1. who buy and sell for their own account or
2. who buy and sell in their own name for the account of others or
3. who buy and sell as intermediaries

and the scope and volume of whose business requires a commercially organised business operation, may be admitted to trade on a stock exchange. Farmers and persons whose kind and scope of trade does not require the existence of commercially established businesses, may also be admitted to the stock exchange.

(3) The admission of persons without the right to trade shall be governed by the Stock Exchange Order.

(4) An enterprise shall be admitted to trade on the stock exchange in accordance with sub-paragraph 2 sentence 1 if

1. the owner, for an enterprise carrying on business under the legal form of a sole trader, or in the case of some other concern, the person who in accordance with the law, the memorandum and articles, is entrusted with the management of the applicant, and is entitled to represent the enterprise, is trustworthy and at least one of the persons concerned has the necessary professional background for trading on the stock exchange in securities or commodities,
2. steps have been taken to ensure proper business transaction on the stock exchange,
3. the applicant, save where it is a credit institution, has provided collateral in accordance with the provisions of sub-paragraph 4a so as to be able to fulfil at any time any obligations arising out of dealings according to sub-paragraph 2 sentence 1 which have been concluded on the stock exchange or by means of an admitted electronic dealing system or off the stock exchange and have been settled by means of the stock exchange computerised settlement system, which is sufficient to guarantee stock exchange obligations, in particular risks arising out of transactions for an undisclosed party or differences in rate for the relevant settlement period,
4. the applicant, except where it is a credit institution, can provide evidence of a capital of a minimum of 100,000 German Marks; capital shall mean

Börsengesetz

eingezahlte Kapital und die Rücklagen nach Abzug der Entnahmen des Inhabers oder der persönlich haftenden Gesellschafter und der diesen gewährten Kredite sowie eines Schuldenüberhanges beim freien Vermögen des Inhabers anzusehen,

5. bei dem Antragsteller, sofern er kein Kreditinstitut ist, keine Tatsachen die Annahme rechtfertigen, daß er unter Berücksichtigung des nachgewiesenen Eigenkapitals nicht die für eine ordnungsmäßige Teilnahme am Börsenhandel erforderliche wirtschaftliche Leistungsfähigkeit hat.

(4a) Die Höhe der Sicherheit nach Absatz 4 Nr. 3 bestimmt sich nach Art und Umfang der erstrebten oder ausgeübten Geschäftstätigkeit und nach der Zahl der für das antragstellende Unternehmen zuzulassenden natürlichen Personen, die nach Absatz 4b berechtigt sind, an der Börse für das Unternehmen Geschäfte abzuschließen. Es dürfen höchstens 500 000 Deutsche Mark, im Falle des Absatzes 2 Satz 1 Nr. 3 höchstens 100 000 Deutsche Mark als Sicherheit gefordert werden; der Antragsteller kann höhere Sicherheiten anbieten. Die Sicherheit ist nach Wahl des Antragstellers durch die Garantieerklärung eines Kreditinstituts, durch eine Kautionsversicherung oder durch Zahlung an die Börse zu leisten. Einer Sicherheitsleistung bedarf es nicht, wenn die an der Börse abgeschlossenen Geschäfte des Antragstellers aufgrund eines in der Börsenordnung geregelten Systems zur Sicherung der Erfüllung der Börsengeschäfte durch den Eintritt eines Kreditinstituts in diese Geschäfte nur zu einer Verbindlichkeit des Antragstellers gegenüber dem eintretenden Kreditinstitut führen können.

(4b) Personen, die berechtigt sein sollen, für ein zugelassenes Unternehmen an der Börse zu handeln (Börsenhändler), sind zuzulassen, wenn sie zuverlässig sind und die hierfür notwendige berufliche Eignung haben.

(5) Die berufliche Eignung im Sinne des Absatzes 4 Nr. 1 ist regelmäßig anzunehmen, wenn eine Berufsausbildung nachgewiesen wird, die zum börsenmäßigen Wertpapier- oder Warengeschäft befähigt. Die berufliche Eignung im Sinne des Absatzes 4b ist anzunehmen, wenn die erforderlichen fachlichen Kenntnisse und Erfahrungen nachgewiesen werden, die zum Handel an der Börse befähigen. Der Nachweis über die erforderlichen fachlichen Kenntnisse wird insbesondere durch die Ablegung einer Prüfung vor der Prüfungskommission einer Börse erbracht. Das Nähere über das Prüfungsverfahren regelt eine vom Börsenrat zu erlassende Prüfungsordnung, die der Genehmigung durch die Börsenaufsichtsbehörde bedarf.

(6) Das Nähere darüber, wie die in Absätzen 4 bis 5 genannten Voraussetzungen nachzuweisen sind, bestimmt die Börsenordnung.

Stock Exchange Act

paid up capital and reserves after deducting the drawings of any owner or of any personally liable partner, any credit given in favour of them, and any excess of liabilities over assets in the personal assets of the owner,

5. the applicant, except where it is a credit institution, gives no grounds for supposing that, in respect to its capital, it does not have the financial capacity to enable proper participation in stock exchange trading.

(4a) The amount of collateral under sub-paragraph 4 number 3 shall be determined by reference to the type and volume of business carried on or intended to be carried on and in accordance with the number of natural persons who are to be allowed to conduct business on the stock exchange on behalf of the applicant according to sub-paragraph 4b. It shall be a maximum of 500,000 German Marks, or in a case falling under sub-paragraph 2 sentence 1 No. 3, a maximum of 100,000 German Marks; the applicant may offer higher security. Collateral may be given, at the option of the applicant, in the form of a declaration of guarantee from a credit institution or in the form of an insurance bond or by payment to the Stock Exchange. Collateral in accordance with sub-paragraph 4 sentence 1 No. 3 shall not be required if transactions concluded on the stock exchange by the applicant under a system regulated under the Stock Exchange Order for the purpose of ensuring compliance with stock exchange obligations by the intervention of a credit institution in such business could only give rise to an obligation on the part of the applicant in favour of the intervening credit institution.

(4b) Persons who are to be authorised to conduct business ("stock exchange dealers") on behalf of an admitted enterprise shall be admitted if they are trustworthy and have the appropriate professional experience.

(5) A person shall be deemed to have appropriate professional experience within the meaning of sub-paragraph 4b if he can demonstrate professional training qualifying him to deal in securities or commodities on the exchange. A person shall be deemed to have the appropriate professional experience within the meaning of sub-paragraph 4b if he can demonstrate specialist knowledge and experience which qualifies him to trade on the stock exchange. Relevant specialist knowledge may be demonstrated by passing an examination set by the examinations committee of a stock exchange. Detailed examinations regulations shall be specified in an Examinations Order made by the Stock Exchange Council with the approval of the Stock Exchange Supervisory Agency.

(6) Detailed regulations as to how compliance with the provisions of sub-paragraphs 4 to 5 is to be demonstrated shall be made in the Stock Exchange Order.

Börsengesetz

(7) Unbeschadet der allgemeinen Vorschriften über die Rücknahme und den Widerruf von Verwaltungsakten können freie Makler auf die Tätigkeit als Vermittler beschränkt werden, wenn die geleistete Sicherheit nicht mehr den Voraussetzungen nach Absatz 4 Nr. 3 und Absatz 4a entspricht.

(8) Besteht der begründete Verdacht, daß eine der in den Absätzen 2, 4 bis 4b bezeichneten Voraussetzungen nicht vorgelegen hat oder nachträglich weggefallen ist, so kann das Ruhen der Zulassung längstens für die Dauer von sechs Monaten angeordnet werden. Das Ruhen der Zulassung kann auch für die Dauer des Verzuges mit der Zahlung der nach § 5 Abs. 1 Satz 1 Nr. 1 und 2 festgesetzten Gebühren angeordnet werden. Das Recht einer nach Absatz 4b zugelassenen Person zum Abschluß von Börsengeschäften ruht für die Dauer des Wegfalls der Zulassung des Unternehmens, für das sie Geschäfte an der Börse abschließt.

(9) Haben sich in einem Verfahren vor dem Sanktionsausschuß Tatsachen ergeben, welche die Rücknahme oder den Widerruf der Zulassung rechtfertigen, so ist das Verfahren an die Geschäftsführung abzugeben. Sie ist berechtigt, in jeder Lage des Verfahrens von dem Sanktionsausschuß Berichte zu verlangen und das Verfahren an sich zu ziehen. Hat die Geschäftsführung das Verfahren übernommen und erweist sich, daß die Zulassung nicht zurückzunehmen oder zu widerrufen ist, so verweist sie das Verfahren an den Sanktionsausschuß zurück.

§ 7a
Teilnahme am elektronischen Börsenhandel

Für die Teilnahme am Börsenhandel in einem elektronischen Handelssystem an einer Wertpapierbörse genügt die Zulassung des Unternehmens nach § 7 an einer Wertpapierbörse zum Börsenhandel, wenn das Unternehmen das Regelwerk für das elektronische Handelssystem anerkennt.

§ 8
Handhabung der Ordnung

(1) Die Börsenaufsichtsbehörde ist befugt, zur Aufrechterhaltung der Ordnung und für den Geschäftsverkehr an der Börse Anordnungen zu erlassen.

(2) Die Aufrechterhaltung der Ordnung in den Börsenräumen obliegt der Geschäftsführung. Sie ist befugt, Personen, welche die Ordnung oder den Geschäftsverkehr an der Börse stören, aus den Börsenräumen zu entfernen.

Stock Exchange Act

(7) Without prejudice to the general provisions concerning the withdrawal and revocation of administrative acts, independent brokers may be restricted to acting as intermediary brokers if they fail to provide collateral in accordance with the provisions of sub-paragraph 4 No. 3 and sub-paragraph 4a.

(8) If there is good reason to suppose that compliance with one of the requirements of sub-paragraphs 2, 4 to 4b does not obtain or subsequently ceased to obtain, admission may be suspended for up to six months. Suspension of admission may also be ordered for the duration of non-compliance with payment of fees in accordance with § 5 sub-paragraph 1 sentence 1 Nos. 1 and 2. The right of a person admitted in accordance with sub-paragraph 4b to do business on a stock exchange shall be suspended for the duration of the suspension of admission of any enterprise on behalf of which he does business on the stock exchange.

(9) If matters arise in proceedings before a sanctions committee that justify the withdrawal or revocation of admission, the proceedings shall be passed to the Board of Governors. The Board of Governors shall have the right, at any stage in the proceedings before a sanctions committee, to require that reports be made to it or to take over the proceedings itself. If it takes over the proceedings and it appears that admission should not be withdrawn or revoked, it should remit the proceedings to the sanctions committee.

§ 7a
Participation in Electronic Trading

In order to make use of an electronic trading system for stock exchange trading in securities, admission to a securities stock exchange in accordance with § 7 sub-paragraph 1 shall suffice, provided that the user accepts the terms of the regulations applicable to the electronic trading system.

§ 8
Maintaining Order

(1) The Stock Exchange Supervisory Agency shall be empowered to make regulations to maintain order and carry on business on the stock exchange.

(2) The Board of Governors shall be responsible for maintaining order on stock exchange premises. It shall have the power to remove from the stock exchange any person who is interfering with good order or the orderly carrying on of business on the stock exchange.

Börsengesetz

(3) Finden sich an der Börse Personen zu Zwecken ein, welche mit der Ordnung oder dem Geschäftsverkehr an derselben unvereinbar sind, so ist ihnen der Zutritt zu untersagen.

§ 8a

Kursmakler und freie Makler

(1) Kursmakler und freie Makler, die zur Teilnahme am Börsenhandel zugelassen sind, unterliegen der Aufsicht der Börsenaufsichtsbehörde, soweit in diesem Gesetz nichts anderes bestimmt ist. Die Aufsicht umfaßt sowohl die börslichen als auch die außerbörslichen Geschäfte im Rahmen des Handelsgewerbes. Sie bezieht sich auf die Einhaltung der börsenrechtlichen Vorschriften und Anordnungen.

(2) Der Makler hat der Börsenaufsichtsbehörde jeweils vier Monate nach Ablauf des Geschäftsjahres für das vergangene Geschäftsjahr einen Jahresabschluß einschließlich Anhang und einen Lagebericht mit dem Bestätigungsvermerk eines Wirtschaftsprüfers oder einer Wirtschaftsprüfungsgesellschaft und den dazugehörigen Prüfungsbericht vorzulegen. Die Börsenaufsichtsbehörde kann dem Makler aufgeben, einen anderen Wirtschaftsprüfer oder eine andere Wirtschaftsprüfungsgesellschaft mit der Prüfung für das folgende Geschäftsjahr zu beauftragen.

(3) Der Makler hat ferner innerhalb von vier Wochen nach Ende eines jeden Kalendervierteljahres einen Vermögensstatus auf das Ende dieses Kalendervierteljahres und eine Erfolgsrechnung vorzulegen, die den Zeitraum seit dem Ende des letzten Geschäftsjahres umfaßt.

(4) Die Prüfung der wirtschaftlichen Leistungsfähigkeit des Maklers bezieht sich auf die Feststellung von Tatsachen, die Zweifel an dieser Leistungsfähigkeit begründen. Die Börsenaufsichtsbehörde kann mit der Durchführung dieser Prüfung ganz oder teilweise einen Wirtschaftsprüfer oder eine Wirtschaftsprüfungsgesellschaft beauftragen.

§ 8b

Anordnungen gegenüber Maklern

(1) Der Börsenaufsichtsbehörde und den von ihr beauftragten Personen und Einrichtungen stehen die Befugnisse nach § 1a Abs. 1 Satz 1 bis 3 zu; § 1a Abs. 1 Satz 6 und 7 ist anzuwenden. Die Börsenaufsichtsbehörde kann, soweit dies zur Erfüllung ihrer Aufgaben nach § 8a erforderlich ist,

Stock Exchange Act

(3) Entrance to the Stock Exchange may be refused to persons whose intentions are inconsistent with maintaining good order and proper carrying on of business on the stock exchange.

§ 8a
Supervision of Brokers

(1) Official brokers and independent brokers admitted to trade on the stock exchange are subject to the supervision of the Stock Exchange Supervisory Agency except as otherwise provided for in this Act. Supervision shall include the supervision of trading both on and off the stock exchange, if it is carried on in the course of commercial business. In particular, it shall extend to compliance with stock exchange regulations and orders.

(2) A broker shall be obliged to submit to the Stock Exchange Supervisory Agency four months after the end of his financial year accounts for the last financial year, including any appendices and financial reports, certified by an auditor or a firm of auditors, together with the auditors' report. The Stock Exchange Supervisory Agency may require a broker to engage an alternative auditor or an alternative firm of auditors for the following financial year.

(3) Further, within four weeks of each calendar quarter, a broker shall be obliged to submit a statement of his assets as of the end of the quarter and profit and loss accounts covering the period since the end of the last financial year.

(4) Auditing the financial capacity of a broker shall include establishing any facts giving rise to doubts concerning his financial viability. The Stock Exchange Supervisory Agency may engage an auditor or a firm of auditors to carry out a partial or complete audit.

§ 8b
Regulation of Brokers

(1) The Stock Exchange Supervisory Agency and any persons or institutions engaged by it shall have the powers referred to in § 1a sub-paragraph 1 sentences 1 to 3; § 1a sub-paragraph 1 sentences 6 and 7 apply. The Stock Exchange Supervisory Agency may, to the extent necessary to enable it to carry out its obligations under § 8a,

Börsengesetz

1. Anordnungen gegenüber Maklern über das Führen von Büchern und das Fertigen von Aufzeichnungen, über eine weitergehende Gliederung des Jahresabschlusses sowie über die Aufstellung und den Inhalt des Vermögensstatus und der Erfolgsrechnung erlassen,

2. von den Maklern, die ihr Unternehmen in der Rechtsform des Einzelkaufmanns betreiben, Auskunft und Nachweise über ihre privaten Vermögensverhältnisse verlangen.

(2) Stellt die Börsenaufsichtsbehörde Tatsachen fest, welche die Rücknahme oder den Widerruf der Zulassung oder der Bestellung des Maklers oder andere Maßnahmen rechtfertigen können, hat sie die Geschäftsführung zu unterrichten.

(3) Widerspruch und Anfechtungsklage gegen Maßnahmen nach Absatz 1 Nr. 2 haben keine aufschiebende Wirkung.

§ 8c

Börsenverbindlichkeiten der Makler

(1) Die Börsenordnung kann Regelungen zur Begrenzung und Überwachung der Börsenverbindlichkeiten der Makler vorsehen.

(2) Die Handelsüberwachungsstelle hat die nach § 7 Abs. 4 Nr. 3, Abs. 4a zu leistenden Sicherheiten zu überwachen. Ihr stehen die Befugnisse der Börsenaufsichtsbehörde nach § 1a Abs. 1 zu. Sie kann insbesondere von der jeweiligen Abrechnungsstelle die Liste der offenen Aufgabegeschäfte und die Mitteilung negativer Kursdifferenzen verlangen.

(3) Stellt die Handelsüberwachungsstelle fest, daß der Sicherheitsrahmen überschritten ist, hat die Geschäftsführung Anordnungen zu treffen, die geeignet sind, die Erfüllung der Verpflichtungen aus den börslichen und außerbörslichen Geschäften nach § 7 Abs. 4 Nr. 3 sicherzustellen. Sie kann insbesondere anordnen, daß der Makler unverzüglich weitere Sicherheiten zu leisten oder seine offenen Geschäfte zu erfüllen hat, oder ihn mit sofortiger Wirkung ganz oder teilweise vom Börsenhandel vorläufig ausschließen. Die Geschäftsführung hat die Börsenaufsichtsbehörde über die Überschreitung des Sicherheitsrahmens und die getroffenen Anordnungen unverzüglich zu unterrichten.

(4) Widerspruch und Anfechtungsklage gegen Maßnahmen nach den Absätzen 2 und 3 haben keine aufschiebende Wirkung.

Stock Exchange Act

1. make orders for brokers concerning bookkeeping, the maintenance of records, the breakdown of categories in the annual accounts, the presentation and content of capital statements and profit and loss accounts,

2. require brokers who carry on business as sole traders to provide information relating to and evidence of their personal financial circumstances.

(2) If the Stock Exchange Supervisory Agency discovers facts justifying the withdrawal or revocation of admission of a broker or the taking of other measures, it shall report the same to the Board of Governors.

(3) Any objections or appeal against the measures referred to in paragraph 1 No. 2 shall not delay the effect of such measures.

§ 8c
Limitation of Engagements of Brokers

(1) The Stock Exchange Order can provide regulations for the purpose of limiting and monitoring obligations undertaken on the stock exchange by brokers.

(2) The supervision of the giving of collateral in accordance with § 7 sub-paragraph 4 No. 3, and sub-paragraph 4a, shall be the responsibility of the trading monitoring office. It shall have the powers of the Stock Exchange Supervisory Agency referred to in § 1a sub-paragraph 1. In particular, it may require the relevant settlement office to provide a list of open transactions for unidentified parties and negative differences in rates.

(3) If the trading monitoring office establishes that any collateral limits have been exceeded, the board shall take measures to ensure compliance with any obligations relating to the business on or off the stock exchange in accordance with § 7 sub-paragraph 4 No. 3. In particular, it may order a broker forthwith to provide further security or to complete any open transactions, or it may provisionally exclude him with immediate effect wholly or in part from trading on the stock exchange. The board shall notify the Stock Exchange Supervisory Agency forthwith of the fact that a collateral limit has been exceeded and of the measures it has taken.

(4) Any objections or appeals against the measures referred to in sub-paragraphs 2 and 3 shall not delay the effect of such measures.

Börsengesetz

§ 9

Sanktionsausschuß

(1) Die Landesregierung wird ermächtigt, durch Rechtsverordnung Vorschriften über die Errichtung eines Sanktionsausschusses, seine Zusammensetzung, sein Verfahren einschließlich der Beweisaufnahme und der Kosten sowie die Mitwirkung der Börsenaufsichtsbehörde zu erlassen. Die Vorschriften können vorsehen, daß der Sanktionsausschuß Zeugen und Sachverständige, die freiwillig vor ihm erscheinen, ohne Beeidigung vernehmen und das Amtsgericht um die Durchführung einer Beweisaufnahme, die er nicht vornehmen kann, ersuchen darf. Die Landesregierung kann die Ermächtigung nach Satz 1 durch Rechtsverordnung auf die Börsenaufsichtsbehörde übertragen.

(2) Der Sanktionsausschuß kann einen Handelsteilnehmer mit Verweis, mit Ordnungsgeld bis zu fünfzigtausend Deutschen Mark oder mit Ausschluß von der Börse bis zu 30 Sitzungstagen belegen, wenn der Handelsteilnehmer vorsätzlich oder leichtfertig

1. gegen börsenrechtliche Vorschriften oder Anordnungen verstößt, die eine ordnungsmäßige Durchführung des Handels an der Börse oder der Börsengeschäftsabwicklung sicherstellen sollen, oder

2. im Zusammenhang mit seiner Tätigkeit den Anspruch auf kaufmännisches Vertrauen oder die Ehre eines anderen Handelsteilnehmers verletzt.

Handelt es sich bei dem Handelsteilnehmer um einen Kursmakler oder einen Kursmaklerstellvertreter, ist an Stelle des Sanktionsausschusses die Börsenaufsichtsbehörde für die Entscheidung zuständig.

(3) In Streitigkeiten wegen der Entscheidungen des Sanktionsausschusses oder der Börsenaufsichtsbehörde nach Absatz 2 ist der Verwaltungsrechtsweg gegeben. Vor Erhebung einer Klage bedarf es keiner Nachprüfung in einem Vorverfahren.

§ 10

Kauf und Verkauf von Wertpapieren

(1) Aufträge für den Kauf und Verkauf von Wertpapieren, die zum Handel an einer inländischen Wertpapierbörse zugelassen oder in den Freiverkehr einbezogen sind, sind über den Handel an der Börse auszuführen, es sei denn, der Auftraggeber erteilt für den Einzelfall oder für eine unbestimmte Zahl von Fällen ausdrücklich eine andere Weisung. Der Auftraggeber

Stock Exchange Act

§ 9
Sanctions Committee

(1) The Land government has the power to make regulations providing for the setting up of a sanctions committee, its composition, its proceedings including the taking of evidence; cost matters; its cooperation with the Stock Exchange Supervisory Agency. Such provisions may provide that the sanctions committee be entitled to hear evidence other than on oath from witnesses and experts who appear voluntarily before it and it may seek the assistance of the county court to obtain evidence which it cannot obtain itself. The Land government may delegate its powers under sentence 1 to the Stock Exchange Supervisory Agency.

(2) The sanctions committee may impose on a trader a reprimand, a fine of up to 50,000 German Marks, or suspension from the stock exchange for up to thirty business days if he intentionally or recklessly

1. breaches stock exchange orders or regulations made to ensure orderly carrying on of business on the stock exchange or the settlement of transactions or
2. in connection with his activity impugns the business integrity or honesty of another trader.

If the trader concerned is an official broker or a deputy official broker, then the Stock Exchange Supervisory Agency shall have jurisdiction in place of the sanctions committee.

(3) Disputes arising out of decisions of the sanctions committee or the Stock Exchange Supervisory Agency under sub-paragraph 2 shall be subject to administrative proceedings. No preliminary hearing is necessary to institute an action.

§ 10
Buy and Sell Orders

(1) Orders for the buying and selling of securities admitted to trading on a domestic stock exchange or included in the free market, shall be performed by trading on the stock exchange, unless a client gives other specific instructions for an individual transaction or for an indeterminate number of transac-

Börsengesetz

bestimmt den Ausführungsplatz und darüber, ob der Auftrag im Präsenzhandel oder im elektronischen Handel auszuführen ist.

(2) Trifft der Auftraggeber keine Bestimmung nach Absatz 1 Satz 2, ist der Auftrag im Präsenzhandel auszuführen, es sei denn, das Interesse des Auftraggebers gebietet eine andere Ausführungsart; über den Ausführungsplatz entscheidet der Auftragnehmer unter Wahrung der Interessen des Auftraggebers.

(3) Die Absätze 1 und 2 sind auf festverzinsliche Schuldverschreibungen, die Gegenstand einer Emission sind, deren Gesamtnennbetrag weniger als zwei Milliarden Deutsche Mark beträgt, nicht anzuwenden.

§ 11
Börsenpreise

(1) Preise für Wertpapiere, die während der Börsenzeit an einer Wertpapierbörse im amtlichen Handel oder im geregelten Markt, oder Preise, die an einer Warenbörse festgestellt werden, sind Börsenpreise. Börsenpreise sind auch Preise, die sich für Wertpapiere, die zum Handel zugelassen sind, oder Waren in einem an einer Börse durch die Börsenordnung geregelten elektronischen Handelssystem oder an Börsen bilden, an denen nur ein elektronischer Handel stattfindet.

(2) Börsenpreise müssen ordnungsmäßig zustande kommen. Insbesondere müssen den Handelsteilnehmern Angebote zugänglich und die Annahme der Angebote möglich sein. Vor der Feststellung eines Börsenpreises muß den Handelsteilnehmern die aus Angebot und Nachfrage ermittelte Preisspanne zur Kenntnis gegeben werden. Die Sätze 2 und 3 gelten nicht für Angebote, die zur Feststellung des Eröffnungs-, Einheits- oder Schlußkurses führen. Die Börsenpreise und die ihnen zugrundeliegenden Umsätze sind den Handelsteilnehmern unverzüglich bekanntzumachen. Das Nähere regelt die Börsenordnung. Die Börsenordnung kann auch festlegen, daß vor Feststellung eines Börsenpreises den Handelsteilnehmern zusätzlich der Preis des am höchsten limitierten Kaufauftrages und des am niedrigsten limitierten Verkaufsauftrages zur Kenntnis gegeben werden muß.

(3) Geschäfte, die zu Börsenpreisen geführt haben, sind bei der Eingabe in das Geschäftsabwicklungssystem der Börse besonders zu kennzeichnen.

tions. The client stipulates the place of performance and whether the contract is to be carried out on the floor or by electronic trading.

(2) If a client fails to make any stipulation, in accordance with sub-paragraph 1 sentence 2, the contract shall be performed on the floor unless the interests of the customer dictate another method; a person accepting business from a client shall decide the place of performance in regard to the client's interests.

(3) Sub-paragraphs 1 and 2 shall not apply to fixed interest bonds which are the subject of an issue the total face value of which is less than two thousand million German Marks.

§ 11
Stock Exchange Prices

(1) Prices for securities which are fixed on a securities exchange during trading hours in official trading or in a regulated market or on a commodities exchange, are stock exchange prices. Stock exchange prices shall also include prices for securities or commodities admitted to trading on a stock exchange which are fixed on an electronic trading system regulated on a stock exchange by the Stock Exchange Order or on stock exchanges on which there is only electronic trading.

(2) Stock exchange prices must be properly arrived at. In particular, offers must be available to and capable of acceptance by all traders. Before a stock exchange price is fixed, the price margin arrived at on the basis of offer and demand has to be made known to traders. Sentences 2 and 3 shall not apply to offers leading to the fixing of an opening rate, standard rate or closing rate. Stock exchange prices and the underlying turnover on which they are based shall be made known forthwith to traders. Detailed regulations shall be made in the Stock Exchange Order. The Stock Exchange Order may also provide that traders be notified of the prices of the highest purchase offer and the lowest sale offer.

(3) Securities dealings which have given rise to stock exchange prices shall be specifically designated when entered in the settlement system.

Börsengesetz

§ 12
Elektronisches Handelssystem

(1) In einem elektronischen Handelssystem nach § 11 Abs. 1 Satz 2 können Wertpapiere gehandelt werden, wenn eine der Börsen, an der diese Wertpapiere zum Handel zugelassen sind und in deren Börsenordnung das elektronische Handelssystem geregelt ist, dem zugestimmt hat. In einem elektronischen Handelssystem können auch Wertpapiere gehandelt werden, die ausschließlich in den Freiverkehr einbezogen sind; Satz 1 gilt entsprechend.

(2) Die näheren Bestimmungen für den Handel in einem elektronischen Handelssystem sind in der Börsenordnung zu treffen. Die Börsenordnung muß insbesondere Bestimmungen enthalten über die Bildung des Börsenpreises und die Einbeziehung von Wertpapieren in das elektronische Handelssystem. Die Geschäftsführung hat den Emittenten über die Einbeziehung von Wertpapieren in das elektronische Handelssystem zu unterrichten.

§ 13
Aufgabegeschäft

Ein Makler, der während der Börsenzeit im amtlichen Handel oder im geregelten Markt in einem ihm zugewiesenen Wertpapier den Auftrag eines an dieser Wertpapierbörse zur Teilnahme am Börsenhandel zugelassenen Kreditinstituts nicht in angemessener Zeit ganz oder teilweise ausführen kann und daher ein Aufgabegeschäft tätigt, darf am selben Börsentag an einer anderen Wertpapierbörse einen Makler, dem dieses Wertpapier ebenfalls zugewiesen ist, damit beauftragen, ein zur Teilnahme am Handel an der anderen Börse zugelassenes Kreditinstitut innerhalb der an der Börse des beauftragenden Maklers geltenden Fristen zur Schließung des Aufgabegeschäftes zu benennen. Das Aufgabegeschäft des beauftragten Maklers ist der Börse dieses Maklers, das Deckungsgeschäft der Börse des beauftragten Maklers zuzurechnen. Für das zwischen den Kreditinstituten zustandegekommene Wertpapiergeschäft gelten die Bedingungen für die Geschäfte an der Börse des Verkäufers, es sei denn, in den Bedingungen für die Geschäfte an der Börse aller Wertpapierbörsen, an denen nicht nur Derivate im Sinne des § 2 Abs. 2 des Wertpapierhandelsgesetzes gehandelt werden, ist einheitlich etwas anderes bestimmt. Das Nähere regelt die Börsenordnung.

Stock Exchange Act

§ 12
Electronic Trading System

(1) Securities may be traded by means of electronic trading systems in accordance with § 11 sub-paragraph 1 sentence 2, if one of the stock exchanges to which such securities have been admitted to trading and under the terms of the Stock Exchange Order which regulates the electronic trading system, consent thereto. Securities which are included exclusively on the free market may also be traded on an electronic trading system; sentence 1 applies.

(2) Specific regulations for trading on an electronic trading system shall be provided in the Stock Exchange Order. The Stock Exchange Order shall contain in particular provisions concerning the fixing of the stock exchange price and the inclusion of securities in the electronic trading system. The Board of Governors shall notify the issuer of the inclusion of securities in the electronic trading system.

§ 13
Open Transaction for an Unidentified Party

A broker who, in the course of official trading or on a regulated market in relation to any securities assigned to him, is unable to complete on time during stock exchange business hours a transaction on behalf of a credit institution admitted to the stock exchange for dealing, and as a result engages in an open transaction for an unidentified party, may on the same day instruct a broker on another stock exchange to whom the security has also been assigned to nominate a credit institution admitted to trade at that other stock exchange to complete the transaction within the time allowed for the instructing broker. The open transaction of the instructing broker shall be deemed to be a transaction on the stock exchange of the latter broker, and the covering transaction shall be deemed to be a transaction on the stock exchange of the instructed broker. The securities transaction between the credit institutions shall be governed by the conditions applying to transactions on the stock exchange of the seller unless the conditions which apply to transactions on all stock exchanges, on which not only derivatives in the sense of §2 sub-paragraph 2 are traded, uniformly dictate otherwise. Detailed provisions may be made in the Stock Exchange Order.

Börsengesetz

§§ 14–27

[aufgehoben]

§ 28

Börsenschiedsgericht

Eine Vereinbarung, durch welche die Beteiligten sich der Entscheidung eines Börsenschiedsgerichts unterwerfen, ist nur verbindlich, wenn beide Teile zu den Personen gehören, die nach § 53 Abs. 1 Börsentermingeschäfte abschließen können, oder wenn die Unterwerfung unter das Schiedsgericht nach Entstehung des Streitfalls erfolgt.

II. Maklerwesen und Feststellung des Börsenpreises

§ 29

Feststellung des Börsenpreises

(1) Bei Wertpapieren, deren Börsenpreis amtlich festgestellt wird, erfolgt diese Feststellung durch Kursmakler. Bei Waren, deren Börsenpreis amtlich festgestellt wird, erfolgt diese Feststellung durch die Geschäftsführung, soweit die Börsenordnung nicht die Mitwirkung von Vertretern anderer Berufszweige vorschreibt.

(2) Bei der amtlichen Feststellung des Börsenpreises von Wertpapieren dürfen nur Vertreter der Börsenaufsichtsbehörde und der Handelsüberwachungsstelle, bei der amtlichen Feststellung des Börsenpreises von Waren darüber hinaus nur die Vertreter der beteiligten Berufszweige, deren Mitwirkung die Börsenordnung vorschreibt, anwesend sein.

(3) Als Börsenpreis ist derjenige Preis amtlich festzustellen, welcher der wirklichen Geschäftslage des Handels an der Börse entspricht. Der Kursmakler hat alle zum Zeitpunkt der Feststellung vorliegenden Aufträge bei ihrer Ausführung unter Beachtung der an der Börse bestehenden besonderen Regelungen gleichzubehandeln.

(4) Der Börsenrat kann beschließen, daß bestimmte Wertpapiere in ausländischer Währung oder in einer Rechnungseinheit notiert werden.

Stock Exchange Act

§§ 14–27

[repealed]

§ 28
Arbitration Agreements

An agreement whereby the parties submit themselves to stock exchange arbitration shall be binding only if both parties belong to the category of persons who are entitled to transact stock exchange futures business in accordance with § 53, sub-paragraph 1, or where the parties have agreed to submit to arbitration after a dispute has arisen.

II. Brokers and Fixing of Prices

§ 29
Fixing Exchange Prices

(1) In the case of securities, the stock exchange price of which is officially fixed, official fixing of the stock exchange price shall be undertaken by an official broker. In the case of commodities, the exchange price of which is officially fixed, fixing shall be undertaken by the Board of Governors except where the Stock Exchange Order prescribes the involvement of representatives of other relevant professions.

(2) When the official stock exchange price of securities is being fixed, only representatives of the Stock Exchange Supervisory Agency and the trading monitoring office may be present, and when fixing the official stock exchange price of commodities, in addition to the aforementioned, only representatives of those relevant professions whose involvement is provided for by the Stock Exchange Order.

(3) The stock exchange price shall be the price that truly represents the trading situation on the stock exchange. The official broker concerned shall attach equal weight to all orders available at the time of the official rate fixing, subject to any particular regulations existing on the stock exchange.

(4) The Stock Exchange Council may resolve that certain securities be quoted in foreign currencies or in a unit of account.

Börsengesetz

§ 30

Kursmakler

(1) An den Börsen, an denen Börsenpreise amtlich festgestellt werden, sind Kursmakler zu bestellen. Die Kursmakler haben an den Wertpapierbörsen die Börsenpreise amtlich festzustellen, an den Warenbörsen bei der amtlichen Feststellung mitzuwirken. Die Börsenaufsichtsbehörde bestellt und entläßt die Kursmakler nach Anhörung der Kursmaklerkammer und der Geschäftsführung. Die Kursmakler haben vor Antritt ihrer Stellung den Eid zu leisten, daß sie die ihnen obliegenden Pflichten getreu erfüllen werden.

(2) Zum Kursmakler kann bestellt werden, wer

1. die für die Tätigkeit notwendige Zuverlässigkeit und berufliche Eignung hat,

2. Sicherheit nach § 32 Abs. 6 leistet und

3. Eigenkapital nach § 7 Abs. 4 Nr. 4 nachweist.

Ein Bewerber kann nicht bestellt werden, wenn Tatsachen die Annahme rechtfertigen, daß er unter Berücksichtigung des nachgewiesenen Eigenkapitals nicht die für die Teilnahme am Börsenhandel erforderliche wirtschaftliche Leistungsfähigkeit hat. Ist der Bewerber an einer Gesellschaft im Sinne des § 34a beteiligt, sind die Voraussetzungen nach Satz 1 Nr. 2 und 3 von der Gesellschaft zu erfüllen.

(3) Der Kursmakler scheidet mit Ablauf des Kalenderjahres, in dem er das 65. Lebensjahr vollendet, aus seinem Amt aus.

(4) Die Börsenaufsichtsbehörde hat einen Kursmakler zu entlassen, wenn

1. er die Entlassung beantragt,

2. die Voraussetzungen für die Bestellung weggefallen sind oder sich herausstellt, daß diese Voraussetzungen zu Unrecht als vorhanden angenommen wurden,

3. er sich weigert, den vorgeschriebenen Eid zu leisten,

4. er die Fähigkeit zur Bekleidung öffentlicher Ämter verloren hat,

5. er durch gerichtliche Anordnung in der Verfügung über sein Vermögen beschränkt ist,

6. er infolge eines körperlichen oder geistigen Gebrechens oder wegen einer Sucht nicht nur vorübergehend zur ordnungsmäßigen Ausübung seines Amtes unfähig ist oder

§ 30
Official Brokers

(1) Official brokers shall be appointed for stock exchanges on which official stock exchange prices are fixed. They shall fix official stock exchange prices for securities on securities exchanges, and shall assist in fixing the official exchange prices for commodities. The Stock Exchange Supervisory Agency shall appoint or dismiss official brokers, upon hearing the chamber of official brokers and the Board of Governors. Official brokers shall, before taking office, take an oath that they will faithfully carry out their duties.

(2) A person may be appointed an official broker if

1. he is trustworthy and has the appropriate professional qualifications,
2. he has given collateral in accordance with § 32 sub-paragraph 6, and
3. he has demonstrated that he has the personal capital required under § 7 sub-paragraph 4 No. 4.

An applicant shall not be appointed if his personal capital situation gives reason to suppose that he does not have the requisite financial capacity to enable him to properly carry on business on the stock exchange. If an applicant is a member of a corporation within the meaning of § 34a, the requirements of sentence 1 Nos. 2 and 3 must be met by such corporation.

(3) An official broker shall retire from office at the end of the calendar year following his 65th birthday.

(4) The Stock Exchange Supervisory Agency shall dismiss an official broker if

1. he applies therefor,
2. he is no longer able to meet the requirements for holding office or it emerges that such requirements were not met,
3. he refuses to take the prescribed oath,
4. he loses the capacity to hold public office,
5. his control over his assets is restricted by court order,
6. by reason of mental or physical infirmity or by reason of some addiction, other than only temporary, he is unable to properly carry out his duties, or

Börsengesetz

7. er sich einer groben Verletzung seiner Pflichten schuldig gemacht hat.

In dringenden Fällen kann die Börsenaufsichtsbehörde einem Kursmakler auch ohne Anhörung nach Absatz 1 Satz 3 die Ausübung seines Amtes mit sofortiger Wirkung vorläufig untersagen; Widerspruch und Anfechtungsklage haben keine aufschiebende Wirkung.

(5) Die Börsenaufsichtsbehörde kann Kursmaklerstellvertreter bestellen, die in Fällen einer vorübergehenden Abwesenheit des Kursmaklers dessen Amt ausüben; Absatz 1 Satz 3 und 4 ist entsprechend anzuwenden. Zum Kursmaklerstellvertreter kann nur bestellt werden, wer Angestellter eines Kursmaklers, einer Gesellschaft im Sinne des § 34a oder einer Kursmaklerkammer ist und die Voraussetzungen des Absatzes 2 Nr. 1 erfüllt. Die Bestellung kann befristet erfolgen. Die Vorschriften des Absatzes 4 sind entsprechend anzuwenden.

(6) Eine Kursmaklerkammer ist bei jeder Börse zu bilden, an der mindestens acht Kursmakler bestellt sind. Sie ist von der Geschäftsführung vor der Verteilung der Geschäfte unter die einzelnen Kursmakler zu hören.

(7) Die Landesregierung wird ermächtigt, durch Rechtsverordnung die näheren Bestimmungen über die Rechte und Pflichten der Kursmakler und der Kursmaklerstellvertreter, das Verfahren ihrer Bestellung und Entlassung, die Organisation der Kursmaklerkammer und ihr Verhältnis zu den anderen Börsenorganen zu erlassen; die Landesregierung kann die Ermächtigung durch Rechtsverordnung auf die Börsenaufsichtsbehörde übertragen.

(8) Die Landesregierung wird ermächtigt, durch Rechtsverordnung nach Anhörung der Kursmaklerkammer und der Geschäftsführung eine Gebührenordnung für die Tätigkeit der Kursmakler zu erlassen. Die Festsetzung hat bei Aktien und Optionsscheinen auf der Grundlage des Kurswertes, bei festverzinslichen Wertpapieren auf der Grundlage des Nennbetrages der Geschäfte zu erfolgen. Bei der Bemessung der Höhe der Gebühren sind das Wagnis und die Beschränkungen der sonstigen gewerblichen Tätigkeit der Kursmakler nach § 32 Abs. 5 zu berücksichtigen. Neben den Gebühren darf die Erstattung von Auslagen, die durch die gebührenpflichtige Tätigkeit entstehen, nicht vorgesehen werden. Die Landesregierung kann die Ermächtigung nach Satz 1 durch Rechtsverordnung auf die Börsenaufsichtsbehörde übertragen.

Stock Exchange Act

7. he is guilty of a gross breach of his obligations.

In urgent cases the Stock Exchange Supervisory Agency may temporarily prohibit an official trader from exercising his office with immediate effect and without seeking the views of the chamber or the board in accordance with sub-paragraph 1 sentence 3; any objection or appeal shall not delay the enforcement.

(5) The Stock Exchange Supervisory Agency may appoint deputy official brokers to hold office during the temporary absence of an official broker; sub-paragraph 1 sentences 3 and 4 shall apply. A person may only be appointed as a deputy official broker if he is employed by an official broker or by a corporation within the meaning of § 34a or by a chamber of official brokers and provided that the requirements of sub-paragraph 2 No.1 are complied with. Such appointment may be for a limited period of time. The provisions of sub-paragraph 4 apply.

(6) A chamber of official brokers shall be formed on every stock exchange whith at least eight appointed official brokers. The Board of Governors is to hear it before deciding on the distribution of business among individual official brokers.

(7) The Land government is empowered to make Orders to deal with the particularities of the rights and duties of official brokers and their deputies, the procedure for their appointment and dismissal, the organisation of the chamber of official brokers and its relationship with other stock exchange organisations; the Land government may by Regulations delegate its power to the Stock Exchange Supervisory Agency.

(8) The Land government has the power, after hearing the chamber of official brokers and the Board of Governors, to make regulations providing for a Fees Order relating to the work of official brokers. Such fees shall be determined in the case of shares and options certificates on the basis of the market rate, and in the case of fixed interest rate securities on the basis of the nominal value of the transactions. In assessing the amount of fees, the risk and restrictions on other business activities of official brokers arising out of § 32 sub-paragraph 5 are to be taken into account. No provision shall be made for the reimbursement of expenses over and above the said fees. The state government shall have the power to delegate by regulation its powers under sentence 1 to the Stock Exchange Supervisory Agency.

Börsengesetz

§ 31
Anspruch auf Berücksichtigung

Bei Geschäften in Waren oder Wertpapieren kann ein Anspruch auf Berücksichtigung bei der amtlichen Feststellung des Börsenpreises nur erhoben werden, wenn sie durch Vermittlung eines Kursmaklers abgeschlossen sind. Die Berechtigung des Kursmaklers, im Falle des § 29 Abs. 1 Satz 2 die Berechtigung der Geschäftsführung, auch andere Geschäfte zu berücksichtigen, bleibt hierdurch unberührt.

§ 32
Pflichten der Kursmakler

(1) Die Kursmakler müssen, solange sie die Tätigkeit als Kursmakler ausüben, die Vermittlung von Börsengeschäften in den Waren oder Wertpapieren betreiben, für die sie bei der amtlichen Feststellung der Börsenpreise mitwirken oder für die ihnen diese Feststellung selbst übertragen ist. Die Kursmakler dürfen während des Präsenzhandels an der Börse nur in den ihnen zugewiesenen Waren oder Wertpapieren handeln.

(2) Der Kursmakler darf bei Wertpapieren oder Waren, für die nur Einheitskurse festgesetzt werden, oder bei der Feststellung sonstiger gerechneter Kurse Handelsgeschäfte für eigene Rechnung oder im eigenen Namen nur abschließen oder eine Bürgschaft oder Garantie für die von ihm vermittelten Geschäfte nur übernehmen (Eigengeschäfte), soweit dies zur Ausführung der ihm erteilten Aufträge nötig ist. Aufgabegeschäfte unterliegen der gleichen Beschränkung. Der Kursmakler darf Eigen- und Aufgabegeschäfte auch beim Fehlen marktnah limitierter Aufträge, bei unausgeglichener Marktlage oder beim Vorliegen unlimitierter Aufträge, die nur zu nicht marktgerechten Kursen zu vermitteln wären, tätigen. Eigen- und Aufgabegeschäfte dürfen nicht tendenzverstärkend wirken. Die Wirksamkeit der Geschäfte wird durch einen Verstoß gegen die Sätze 1 bis 4 nicht berührt.

(3) Eigenbestände und offene Lieferverpflichtungen des Kursmaklers, die sich aus zulässigen Eigen- und Aufgabegeschäften ergeben, dürfen durch Gegengeschäfte ausgeglichen werden.

(4) Alle Eigen- und Aufgabegeschäfte des Kursmaklers sind gesondert zu kennzeichnen.

Stock Exchange Act

§ 31
Right to be Taken into Account in the Fixing of Official Prices

In the case of transactions in commodities or securities, a right to be taken into account in fixing the official exchange price may only be raised if such transactions have taken place using an official broker as intermediary. The right of an official broker, or in a case under § 29 sub-paragraph 1 sentence 2, the right of the board to take other transactions into account is not affected hereby.

§ 32
Obligations of Official Brokers

(1) Official brokers, when acting in their official capacity, must provide their intermediary services in relation to exchange transactions in commodities or securities for which they assist in the official fixing of Stock Exchange prices or for which they themselves are assigned the fixing. Official brokers may only trade in commodities or securities assigned to them during floor trading hours.

(2) An official broker may undertake dealings on his own account or in his own name or stand surety or give guarantees in deals conducted by him as intermediary in relation to the securities or commodities for which only standard rates are fixed or where other rates are fixed under the same way of calculation only to the extent that is necessary to complete orders given to him. Open transactions for unidentified parties are subject to the same restriction. An official broker may complete own account transactions and open transactions for unidentified parties also where there are no orders the limits of which are compatible with the market situation or where the market situation is out of balance or where there are orders without limits which cannot be transacted at a fair market price. Own account transactions and open transactions for unidentified parties may not be performed if they strengthen a market trend. The validity of any transaction shall not be affected by any breach of the provisions of sentences 1 to 4.

(3) Own holdings and open delivery obligations of an official broker which arise from permissible own account transactions and open transactions for unidentified parties may be settled by way of set-off transactions.

(4) All own account transactions and open transactions for unidentified parties of an official broker shall be separately designated.

Börsengesetz

(5) Der Kursmakler darf, soweit nicht Ausnahmen zugelassen werden, kein sonstiges Handelsgewerbe betreiben, auch nicht an einem solchen als Kommanditist oder stiller Gesellschafter beteiligt sein; ebensowenig darf er zu einem Kaufmann in dem Verhältnis eines gesetzlichen Vertreters, Prokuristen oder Angestellten stehen.

(6) Die Vorschriften des § 7 Abs. 4 Nr. 3, Abs. 4a und 6 über die Sicherheitsleistung sind auf die Kursmakler entsprechend anzuwenden.

§ 33
Maklertagebuch

(1) Der Kursmakler hat ein Tagebuch zu führen, dessen Seiten börsentäglich zu numerieren und mit einem Abschlußvermerk zu versehen sind.

(2) Wenn der Kursmakler stirbt oder aus dem Amt scheidet, ist sein Tagebuch bei der Kursmaklerkammer, wenn eine solche nicht vorhanden ist, bei der Börsenaufsichtsbehörde niederzulegen.

§ 34
Vornahme von Käufen und Verkäufen durch die Kursmakler

Die Kursmakler sind zur Vornahme von Verkäufen und Käufen befugt, die durch einen dazu öffentlich ermächtigten Handelsmakler zu bewirken sind.

§ 34a
Maklergesellschaften

(1) Der Kursmakler darf seine börslichen und außerbörslichen Wertpapiergeschäfte außer als Einzelkaufmann in der Rechtsform einer Aktiengesellschaft oder einer Gesellschaft mit beschränkter Haftung betreiben, wenn

1. die Mehrheit der Aktien oder der Geschäftsanteile der Gesellschaft und der Stimmrechte einem oder mehreren Kursmaklern zusteht,
2. die Aktien der Gesellschaft auf Namen lauten,
3. die Übertragung von Aktien oder Geschäftsanteilen der Gesellschaft an die Zustimmung der Gesellschaft gebunden ist,
4. die beteiligten Kursmakler die gesetzlichen Vertreter der Gesellschaft sind,

Stock Exchange Act

(5) An official broker shall not, except where exceptions are permitted, engage in any other commercial business, even as a limited or silent partner; neither shall he be permitted to act on behalf of a merchant as a legal representative, *Procurist* or employee.

(6) The provisions of § 7 sub-paragraph 4 No. 3, sub-paragraph 4a and 6 concerning the giving of collateral shall apply to official brokers.

§ 33
Brokers' Transaction Book

(1) Official brokers shall keep a journal the pages of which shall be numbered consecutively beginning afresh for each consecutive stock exchange business day and which shall bear a closing note.

(2) If an official broker dies or vacates office, his journal shall be deposited with the chamber of official brokers, or if there is none, with the Stock Exchange Supervisory Agency.

§ 34
Purchase and Sale by Official Brokers

Official brokers are entitled to make sales and purchases which must be effected by a publicly authorised trading broker.

§ 34a
Brokers' Companies

(1) An official broker may carry on business related to securities on or off the stock exchange, apart from doing so as a sole trader, in the legal form of a joint stock company or limited company, if

1. the majority of shares in the joint stock company or of interest in the limited company and the majority of voting rights are attributable to one or more official brokers;
2. the shares in the company are personal shares;
3. any transfer of shares or holding in the company requires the consent of the company;
4. the official brokers holding shares are legal representatives of the company;

Börsengesetz

5. an der Gesellschaft keine Unternehmen, die den Wertpapierhandel gewerbsmäßig betreiben, Finanzinstitute im Sinne des § 1 Abs. 3 des Gesetzes über das Kreditwesen, Versicherungsunternehmen oder mit diesen Unternehmen oder Instituten verbundene Unternehmen beteiligt sind,

6. die Gesellschaft nicht an Unternehmen im Sinne der Nummer 5 beteiligt ist,

7. eine Beeinträchtigung der Amtspflichten des Kursmaklers nicht zu befürchten ist, insbesondere der Kursmakler sein Amt weisungsfrei, eigenverantwortlich und persönlich ausübt,

8. die Vertretung des Kursmaklers bei Abwesenheit sichergestellt ist,

9. die Gesellschaft für jeden beteiligten Kursmakler Eigenkapital nach § 7 Abs. 4 Nr. 4 nachgewiesen hat,

10. die Gesellschaft für jeden beteiligten Kursmakler Sicherheit nach Maßgabe des § 32 Abs. 6 in Verbindung mit § 7 Abs. 4 Nr. 3, Abs. 4a und 6 geleistet hat,

11. keine Tatsachen die Annahme rechtfertigen, daß die Gesellschaft unter Berücksichtigung des nachgewiesenen Eigenkapitals nicht die für die Teilnahme am Börsenhandel erforderliche wirtschaftliche Leistungsfähigkeit hat.

(2) Die Satzung oder der Gesellschaftsvertrag sowie deren Änderungen bedürfen der Genehmigung der Börsenaufsichtsbehörde.

(3) Die §§ 8a bis 8c sind entsprechend anzuwenden.

(4) Die Börsenaufsichtsbehörde untersagt eine Beteiligung an der Gesellschaft, wenn die Voraussetzungen des Absatzes 1 nicht erfüllt sind.

(5) Die Gesellschaft darf während des Präsenzhandels an der Börse in den Wertpapieren handeln, die nicht den an ihr beteiligten Kursmaklern zugewiesen sind, wenn sie hierzu nach § 7 zugelassen ist.

§ 35
Amtliche Feststellung des Börsenpreises

(1) Der Bundesrat ist befugt:

1. eine von den Vorschriften in § 29 Absatz 1 und 2 und in den §§ 30 und 31 abweichende amtliche Feststellung des Börsenpreises von Waren oder Wertpapieren für einzelne Börsen zuzulassen;

Stock Exchange Act

5. there are no enterprises trading on a commercial basis in securities, financial institutions within the meaning of § 1 sub-paragraph 3 of the Banking Act, insurance enterprises or institutions connected with such concerns holding shares in the company;
6. the company has no holdings in any enterprises within the meaning of No. 5;
7. there is no likelihood of interference with the official duties of the official broker and in particular his ability to carry out his duties free from influence, on his own authority and in person;
8. steps have been taken to ensure that the official broker can be represented in his absence;
9. the company has demonstrated for each official broker that it has sufficient capital in accordance with § 7 sub-paragraph 4 No. 4;
10. the company has, for each official broker, provided collateral in accordance with the provisions of § 32 paragraph 6 and § 7 sub-paragraph 4 No. 3 and sub-paragraph 4a and 6;
11. there are no matters which could give rise to the presumption that the company, regarding its proven capital, does not have the necessary economic and financial capacity to properly carry on trading on the stock exchange.

(2) The memorandum and articles of association, together with any amendments thereof, shall require the consent of the Stock Exchange Supervisory Agency.

(3) §§ 8a to 8c shall apply.

(4) The Stock Exchange Supervisory Agency shall prohibit any person from taking a participation in the company where the requirements of sub-paragraph 1 have not been complied with.

(5) A company may trade in securities which have not been assigned to an official broker during floor trading hours on the stock exchange if it is permitted to do so under § 7.

§ 35

Official Determination of a Stock Exchange Price

(1) The Bundesrat has the power:
1. to permit an official stock exchange price of commodities or securities to be fixed on individual stock exchanges which vary from that fixed in accordance with § 29 sub-paragraphs 1 and 2 and §§ 30 and 31;

Börsengesetz

2. eine amtliche Feststellung des Börsenpreises bestimmter Waren allgemein oder für einzelne Börsen vorzuschreiben;

3. Bestimmungen zu erlassen, um eine Einheitlichkeit der Grundsätze über die den Feststellungen von Warenpreisen zugrunde zu legenden Mengen und über die für die Feststellung der Preise von Wertpapieren maßgebenden Gebräuche herbeizuführen.

(2) Die Befugnis der Landesregierung zu Anordnungen der in Absatz 1 bezeichneten Art wird hierdurch nicht berührt, soweit der Reichsrat oder die Reichsregierung keine Anordnungen getroffen hat; zu Anordnungen der in Absatz 1 Nr. 1 bezeichneten Art bedarf jedoch die Landesregierung der Zustimmung der Reichsregierung. Die Anordnungen sind der Reichsregierung zur Kenntnisnahme mitzuteilen.

III. Zulassung von Wertpapieren zum Börsenhandel mit amtlicher Notierung

§ 36
Zulassungsvoraussetzungen

(1) Wertpapiere, die mit amtlicher Feststellung des Börsenpreises (amtliche Notierung) an der Börse gehandelt werden sollen, bedürfen der Zulassung, soweit nicht in § 41 oder in anderen Gesetzen etwas anderes bestimmt ist.

(2) Die Zulassung ist vom Emittenten der Wertpapiere zusammen mit einem Kreditinstitut zu beantragen, das an einer inländischen Börse mit dem Recht zur Teilnahme am Handel zugelassen ist; ist der Emittent ein solches Kreditinstitut, so kann er den Antrag allein stellen.

(3) Wertpapiere sind zuzulassen, wenn

1. der Emittent und die Wertpapiere den Bestimmungen entsprechen, die zum Schutz des Publikums und für einen ordnungsgemäßen Börsenhandel gemäß § 38 erlassen worden sind,

2. dem Antrag ein Prospekt zur Veröffentlichung beigefügt ist, der gemäß § 38 die erforderlichen Angaben enthält, um dem Publikum ein zutreffendes Urteil über den Emittenten und die Wertpapiere zu ermöglichen, soweit nicht gemäß § 38 Abs. 2 von der Veröffentlichung eines Prospekts abgesehen werden kann, und

Stock Exchange Act

2. to prescribe the manner of fixing an official exchange price for specific commodities either generally or in relation to individual exchanges;
3. to make rules so as to ensure uniformity of the basis on which prices are fixed by reference to quantities of commodities and the standard practices to be adopted in fixing the prices of securities.

(2) The power of a Land government to make regulations in accordance with sub-paragraph 1 shall not be affected thereby to the extent that the *Reichsrat* or *Reichsregierung* have not passed any regulations; however, regulations of the *Landesregierung* of the type described in sub-paragraph 1 No. 1 require the consent of the *Reichsregierung*. All regulations made shall be notified to the *Reichsregierung*.

III. Admission of Securities to Official Listing on Stock Exchanges

§ 36
Requirements for Admission

(1) Securities which are intended to be the subject of trading on the stock exchange on the basis of an official fixing of the stock exchange price (official listing) shall require admission except as provided for in § 41 or in other legislation.

(2) Admission shall be applied for by the issuer of the security in combination with a credit institution which is admitted to trade on a domestic stock exchange; where the issuer is itself a credit institution it may make the application alone.

(3) Securities are to be admitted if

1. the issuer and securities comply with the provisions under § 38 regarding the protection of the public and proper stock exchange trading,
2. the application is accompanied by a prospectus ready for publication containing the information required under § 38 so as to enable the public to evaluate properly both the issuer and the securities concerned unless publication of a prospectus is dispensed with under § 38 sub-paragraph 2, and

175

Börsengesetz

3. keine Umstände bekannt sind, die bei Zulassung der Wertpapiere zu einer Übervorteilung des Publikums oder einer Schädigung erheblicher allgemeiner Interessen führen.

(4) Der Prospekt ist zu veröffentlichen
1. durch Abdruck in den Börsenpflichtblättern (§ 37 Abs. 4), in denen der Zulassungsantrag veröffentlicht ist, oder
2. durch Bereithalten zur kostenlosen Ausgabe bei den im Prospekt benannten Zahlstellen und bei der Zulassungsstelle; in den Börsenpflichtblättern, in denen der Zulassungsantrag veröffentlicht ist, ist bekanntzumachen, bei welchen Stellen der Prospekt bereitgehalten wird.

Außerdem ist im Bundesanzeiger der Prospekt oder ein Hinweis darauf bekanntzumachen, wo der Prospekt veröffentlicht und für das Publikum zu erhalten ist. Die Zulassungsstelle hat dem Emittenten auf Verlangen eine Bescheinigung über die Billigung des Prospekts auszustellen; etwaige Befreiungen im Hinblick auf einzelne Angaben oder Abweichungen von den im Regelfall vorgeschriebenen Angaben sind mit Begründung anzugeben. Beantragt der Emittent die Zulassung der Wertpapiere auch an Börsen anderer Mitgliedstaaten der Europäischen Wirtschaftsgemeinschaft oder anderer Vertragsstaaten des Abkommens über den Europäischen Wirtschaftsraum, so hat er den zuständigen Stellen dieser Staaten den Entwurf des Prospekts, den er in diesen Staaten verwenden will, zu übermitteln.

(5) Der Antrag auf Zulassung der Wertpapiere kann trotz Erfüllung der Voraussetzungen des Absatzes 3 abgelehnt werden, wenn der Emittent seine Pflichten aus der Zulassung zur amtlichen Notierung an einer anderen inländischen Börse oder an einer Börse in einem anderen Mitgliedstaat der Europäischen Wirtschaftsgemeinschaft oder in einem anderen Vertragsstaat des Abkommens über den Europäischen Wirtschaftsraum nicht erfüllt.

§ 37

Zulassungsstelle

(1) Über die Zulassung entscheidet die Zulassungsstelle. Die Zulassungsstelle trifft, soweit nicht die Geschäftsführung zuständig ist, die zum Schutz des Publikums und für einen ordnungsgemäßen Börsenhandel erforderlichen Maßnahmen und überwacht die Einhaltung der Pflichten, die sich aus der Zulassung für den Emittenten und für das antragsstellende Kreditinstitut ergeben.

Stock Exchange Act

3. there are no circumstances which, if the securities are admitted, will have as a consequence the deception of the public or damage to the general public interest.

(4) The prospectus is to be published

1. by being printed in the authorised journals for the publication of mandatory stock exchange announcements (authorised journal) (§ 37 sub-paragraph 4) in which the application for admission is published, or
2. by making it available free of charge at the paying offices referred to in the prospectus and at the offices of the Listing Board; details of all offices where the prospectus is available is to be given in the authorised journals in which the application for admission is published.

Further, the prospectus shall be published in the Federal Gazette, or notice of where it has been published and is available for the public. The Listing Board shall, if requested, provide to the issuer a certificate of approval of the prospectus; any exemptions granted for specific items of information and any deviations from the norms prescribed for the provision of information are to be given and the reasons provided therefor. If the issuer applies for admission of securities to other stock exchanges of member states of the European Community or another contracting state of the European Economic Area Treaty, the issuer is to provide to the relevant authorities of such states a draft of the prospectus to be used in those states.

(5) Notwithstanding compliance with the provisions of sub-paragraph 3, an application for admission of securities may be refused if the issuer has not complied with his obligations arising out of admission to official listing on another domestic stock exchange or on a stock exchange in another member state of the European Community or another contracting state of the European Economic Area Treaty.

§ 37

Listing Board

(1) The Listing Board shall decide any application for admission. The Listing Board shall, except where the Board of Governors has power, take such measures as are appropriate to ensure public protection and the proper conduct of trading on the stock exchange and shall monitor compliance with the obligations which arise out of admission on the part of the issuer and the credit institution which has made the application.

Börsengesetz

(2) Mindestens die Hälfte der Mitglieder der Zulassungsstelle müssen Personen sein, die sich nicht berufsmäßig am Börsenhandel mit Wertpapieren beteiligen.

(3) Die Börsenordnung kann vorsehen, daß Entscheidungen der Zulassungsstelle von aus ihrer Mitte gebildeten Ausschüssen getroffen werden, die aus mindestens fünf Mitgliedern bestehen; Absatz 2 gilt entsprechend.

(4) Die Zulassungsstelle bestimmt mindestens drei inländische Zeitungen zu Bekanntmachungsblättern für vorgeschriebene Veröffentlichungen (Börsenpflichtblätter); mindestens zwei dieser Zeitungen müssen Tageszeitungen mit überregionaler Verbreitung im Inland sein (überregionale Börsenpflichtblätter). Die Bestimmung kann zeitlich begrenzt werden; sie ist durch Börsenbekanntmachung zu veröffentlichen.

§ 38

Zulassungsverordnung

(1) Die Bundesregierung wird ermächtigt, durch Rechtsverordnung mit Zustimmung des Bundesrates die zum Schutz des Publikums und für einen ordnungsgemäßen Börsenhandel erforderlichen Vorschriften zu erlassen über

1. die Voraussetzungen der Zulassung, insbesondere

    a) die Anforderungen an den Emittenten im Hinblick auf seine Rechtsgrundlage, seine Größe und die Dauer seines Bestehens;

    b) die Anforderungen an die zuzulassenden Wertpapiere im Hinblick auf ihre Rechtsgrundlage, Handelbarkeit, Stückelung und Druckausstattung;

    c) den Mindestbetrag der Emission;

    d) das Erfordernis, den Zulassungsantrag auf alle Aktien derselben Gattung oder auf alle Schuldverschreibungen derselben Emission zu erstrecken;

2. den Inhalt des Prospekts, insbesondere die zuzulassenden Wertpapiere und den Emittenten, dessen Kapital, Geschäftstätigkeit, Vermögens-, Finanz- und Ertragslage, Geschäftsführungs- und Aufsichtsorgane und dessen Geschäftsgang und Geschäftsaussichten sowie die Personen oder Gesellschaften, welche die Verantwortung für den Inhalt des Prospekts übernehmen;

3. den Zeitpunkt der Veröffentlichung des Prospekts;

Stock Exchange Act

(2) At least one half of the members of the Listing Board must be persons who are not professionally engaged in stock exchange securities dealings.

(3) The stock exchange order may provide for the Listing Board to delegate its powers to committees consisting of at least 5 of its members; subparagraph 2 shall apply accordingly.

(4) The Listing Board shall designate a minimum of three domestic newspapers as official gazettes for the purpose of prescribed publication ("authorised journals"); at least two of such newspapers shall be daily newspapers having a domestic national circulation ("national authorised journal"). Such designation may be for a limited period of time; notification thereof shall be made by announcement on the stock exchange.

§ 38
Admissions Regulations

(1) The Federal Government has the power to make regulations, with the approval of the Bundesrat, for the purpose of public protection and to ensure the proper conduct of business on the stock exchange in respect to

1. the requirements for admission, in particular

    a) the requirements to be complied with by the issuer in respect to its legal basis, size, and duration of its existence;

    b) the requirements in relation to the securities to be admitted, their legal basis, negotiability, denomination and printed form;

    c) the minimum amount of the issue;

    d) any requirement that the application should extend to include all shares of the same class or all bonds forming part of the same issue;

2. the contents of the prospectus, and in particular the securities to be admitted and the issuer, its capital, the nature of its business, its net worth, financial position and results, its management and supervisory bodies, its conduct of business and business prospects together with persons or corporations responsible for the contents of the prospectus;

3. the time of publication of the prospectus;

Börsengesetz

4. das Zulassungsverfahren.

(2) In die Rechtsverordnung können auch Vorschriften aufgenommen werden über Ausnahmen, in denen von der Veröffentlichung eines Prospekts ganz oder teilweise oder von der Aufnahme einzelner Angaben in den Prospekt abgesehen werden kann,

1. wenn beim Emittenten, bei den zuzulassenden Wertpapieren, bei ihrer Ausgabe oder beim Kreis der mit der Wertpapierausgabe angesprochenen Anleger besondere Umstände vorliegen und den Interessen des Publikums durch eine anderweitige Unterrichtung ausreichend Rechnung getragen ist,

2. mit Rücksicht auf die geringe Bedeutung einzelner Angaben oder

3. im Hinblick auf das öffentliche Interesse oder einen beim Emittenten zu befürchtenden erheblichen Schaden.

§ 39
Ablehnung der Zulassung

(1) Lehnt die Zulassungsstelle einen Zulassungsantrag ab, so hat sie dies den anderen Zulassungsstellen unter Angabe der Gründe für die Ablehnung mitzuteilen.

(2) Wertpapiere, deren Zulassung von einer anderen Zulassungsstelle abgelehnt worden ist, dürfen nur mit Zustimmung dieser Zulassungsstelle zugelassen werden. Die Zustimmung ist zu erteilen, wenn die Ablehnung aus Rücksicht auf örtliche Verhältnisse geschah oder wenn die Gründe, die einer Zulassung entgegenstanden, weggefallen sind.

(3) Wird ein Zulassungsantrag an mehreren inländischen Börsen gestellt, so dürfen die Wertpapiere nur mit Zustimmung aller Zulassungsstellen, die über den Antrag zu entscheiden haben, zugelassen werden. Die Zustimmung darf nicht aus Rücksicht auf örtliche Verhältnisse verweigert werden.

(4) Sind Wertpapiere eines Emittenten mit Sitz im Inland an einer inländischen Börse zugelassen, so ist, sofern der Emittent nicht von der Pflicht zur Veröffentlichung eines Prospekts befreit worden ist, der Prospekt von den Zulassungsstellen der anderen inländischen Börsen als den Anforderungen des § 36 Abs. 3 Nr. 2 entsprechend anzuerkennen, wenn der Zulassungsantrag innerhalb von sechs Monaten nach der Zulassung gestellt wird. Sind seit der Veröffentlichung des Prospekts Veränderungen bei Umständen eingetreten, die für die Beurteilung des Emittenten oder der zuzulassenden Wertpa-

Stock Exchange Act

4. the admissions procedure.

(2) The Regulation may also contain provisions concerning exceptional cases in which publication of a prospectus may be dispensed with in whole or part or the publication of specific items of information may be dispensed with

1. if there are special circumstances in respect to the issuer, the securities to be admitted, the issue itself or the class of investors to whom the issue is to be directed, and the public interest has been safeguarded by the provision of information in another form,
2. regarding the negligible importance of individual items of information or
3. regarding the public interest or the damage likely to be suffered on the part of the issuer.

§ 39

Refusal of Admission

(1) If the Listing Board rejects an application for admission, it shall notify the other Listing Boards and provide them with the reasons for refusal.

(2) Any securities which have been refused admission by another Listing Board may only be admitted with the consent of such Listing Board. Consent shall be given if refusal was based on local considerations or if the reasons that gave rise to the refusal of admission no longer apply.

(3) Where application for admission is made to a number of domestic stock exchanges, securities may only be admitted with the consent of all the admissions authorities deciding the application. Admission may not be refused out of local considerations.

(4) If securities issued by a domestic issuer are admitted to a domestic stock exchange, any prospectus recognised by the Listing Boards of other domestic stock exchanges as complying with the requirements of § 36 subparagraph 3 No.2 shall be recognised, provided that the issuer has not been exempted from the obligation to publish a prospectus and provided that the application for admission is made within six months of the prior admission. If, since publication of the prospectus, there has been a change of circumstances which could be of importance in evaluating the issuer or the securities to be admitted, such changes of circumstances shall be contained in the prospectus to be published or in an appendix to the prospectus to be pub-

Börsengesetz

piere von wesentlicher Bedeutung sind, so sind die Veränderungen entweder in den zu veröffentlichenden Prospekt aufzunehmen oder in einem Nachtrag zum Prospekt zu veröffentlichen; auf diesen Nachtrag sind die Vorschriften über den Prospekt und dessen Veröffentlichung entsprechend anzuwenden.

§ 40
Zusammenarbeit der Zulassungsstellen

(1) Die Zulassungsstellen arbeiten untereinander und mit den entsprechenden Stellen oder Börsen in den anderen Mitgliedstaaten der Europäischen Wirtschaftsgemeinschaft oder den anderen Vertragsstaaten des Abkommens über den Europäischen Wirtschaftsraum im Rahmen ihrer Aufgaben und Befugnisse zusammen und übermitteln sich gegenseitig die hierfür erforderlichen Angaben, soweit die Amtsverschwiegenheit gewährleistet ist; insoweit unterliegen die Mitglieder der Zulassungsstellen und die für die Zulassungsstellen tätigen Personen nicht der Pflicht zur Geheimhaltung.

(2) Beantragt ein Emittent mit Sitz in einem anderen Mitgliedstaat der Europäischen Wirtschaftsgemeinschaft oder in einem anderen Vertragsstaat des Abkommens über den Europäischen Wirtschaftsraum, dessen Aktien zur amtlichen Notierung in diesem Mitgliedstaat oder Vertragsstaat zugelassen sind, die Zulassung von Wertpapieren, mit denen Bezugsrechte für diese Aktien verbunden sind, so hat die Zulassungsstelle vor ihrer Entscheidung eine Stellungnahme der zuständigen Stelle des anderen Mitgliedstaates oder Vertragsstaates einzuholen.

(3) Wird die Zulassung für Wertpapiere beantragt, die seit weniger als sechs Monaten in einem anderen Mitgliedstaat der Europäischen Wirtschaftsgemeinschaft oder in einem anderen Vertragsstaat des Abkommens über den Europäischen Wirtschaftsraum amtlich notiert werden, so kann die Zulassungsstelle den Emittenten davon befreien, einen neuen Prospekt zu erstellen, wenn der vorhandene auf den neuesten Stand gebracht und entsprechend den Vorschriften im Geltungsbereich dieses Gesetzes ergänzt und veröffentlicht wird.

§ 40a
Gegenseitige Anerkennung von Prospekten

(1) Stellt ein Emittent mit Sitz in einem anderen Mitgliedstaat der Europäischen Wirtschaftsgemeinschaft oder in einem anderen Vertragsstaat des Abkommens über den Europäischen Wirtschaftsraum einen Zulassungs-

lished; the provisions in relation to prospectuses generally and the publication thereof shall apply to such an appendix.

§ 40
Cooperation between Listing Boards

(1) The Listing Boards will cooperate with one another and with their corresponding authorities at stock exchanges in other member states of the European Community or another contracting state of the European Economic Area Treaty within the scope of their duties and powers and shall provide one another with the required information, provided confidentiality is guaranteed; in this respect, the members of admissions authorities and persons employed by them shall not be subject to secrecy obligations.

(2) If an issuer, having its principal place of business in another member state of the European Community or another contracting state of the European Economic Area Treaty, and having shares admitted to official listing in that member state or contracting state, applies for the admission of securities for which there are subscription rights for the shares, the Listing Board shall consult the relevant authority of the other member state or contracting state before reaching a decision as to admission.

(3) If an application is made for admission for securities which have been officially quoted in another member state of the European Community or another contracting state of the European Economic Area Treaty for less than six months, the Listing Board may waive the requirement for the issuer to prepare a new prospectus if the available prospectus is brought up to date and amended and published in accordance with the provisions in force in the area of application of this Act.

§ 40a
Mutual Recognition of Prospectuses

(1) If an issuer, whose principal place of business is in another member state of the European Community or another contracting state of the European Economic Area Treaty, applies for admission simultaneously or almost simultaneously for the same securities to a stock exchange in that state as well to a domestic stock exchange, the Listing Board, subject to sub-para-

Börsengesetz

antrag für dieselben Wertpapiere gleichzeitig oder annähernd gleichzeitig sowohl bei einer Börse in diesem Staat als auch bei einer inländischen Börse, so hat die Zulassungsstelle vorbehaltlich des Absatzes 2 den von der zuständigen Stelle des anderen Staates gebilligten Prospekt als den Anforderungen des § 36 Abs. 3 Nr. 2 entsprechend anzuerkennen, sofern der Zulassungsstelle eine Übersetzung des Prospekts in die deutsche Sprache sowie eine Bescheinigung der entsprechenden Stelle des anderen Staates gemäß § 36 Abs. 4 Satz 3 über die Billigung des Prospekts vorliegt. Die Zulassungsstelle kann jedoch vom Emittenten verlangen, daß in den Prospekt besondere Angaben für den inländischen Markt, insbesondere über die Zahl- und Hinterlegungsstellen, die Art und Form der nach diesem Gesetz und der Börsenzulassungs-Verordnung vorgeschriebenen Veröffentlichungen sowie die steuerliche Behandlung der Erträge im Inland aufgenommen werden.

(2) Hat die zuständige Stelle des anderen Staates den Emittenten von einzelnen Angaben im Prospekt befreit oder Abweichungen von den im Regelfall vorgeschriebenen Angaben zugelassen, so anerkennt die Zulassungsstelle den Prospekt nach Absatz 1 Satz 1 nur, wenn

1. die Befreiung oder Abweichung nach diesem Gesetz oder aufgrund dieses Gesetzes zulässig ist,

2. im Inland dieselben Bedingungen bestehen, welche die Befreiungen rechtfertigen und

3. die Befreiung oder Abweichung an keine weitere Bedingung gebunden ist, welche die Zulassungsstelle veranlassen würde, die Befreiung oder Abweichung abzulehnen.

(3) Die Absätze 1 und 2 sind entsprechend anzuwenden, wenn der Prospekt von der zuständigen Stelle des anderen Staates anläßlich eines öffentlichen Angebots der zuzulassenden Wertpapiere gebilligt worden ist und der Zulassungsantrag innerhalb von drei Monaten nach dieser Billigung gestellt wird.

(4) Stellt ein Emittent mit Sitz außerhalb des Geltungsbereichs dieses Gesetzes einen Zulassungsantrag sowohl bei einer Börse in einem anderen Mitgliedstaat der Europäischen Wirtschaftsgemeinschaft oder in einem anderen Vertragsstaat des Abkommens über den Europäischen Wirtschaftsraum, der nicht der Sitzstaat ist, als auch bei einer inländischen Börse, so sind die Vorschriften der Absätze 1 bis 3 entsprechend anzuwenden, wenn der Emittent bestimmt, daß der Prospekt von der zuständigen Stelle des anderen Mitgliedstaates oder Vertragsstaates des Abkommens über den Europäischen Wirtschaftsraum gebilligt werden soll. § 39 Abs. 4 Satz 2 ist entsprechend anzuwenden.

graph 2, shall recognise any prospectus approved by the relevant authority of the other states as complying with the requirements of § 36 sub-paragraph 3 No. 2, provided that a translation of the prospectus into the German language and a certificate from the relevant authority of the other state, in accordance with § 36 sub-paragraph 4 sentence 3, are provided to the Listing Board. The Listing Board may, however, require the issuer to include in the prospectus particular items of information for the domestic market, in particular in relation to the paying agent and depository agents, the nature and form of any publications required by this Act and by the stock exchange admissions Regulation and the treatment of income for tax purposes in Germany.

(2) If the relevant authority of the other state exempts the issuer from providing individual items of information in the prospectus or permits any deviation from the normal provisions concerning the information to be provided, the Listing Board shall recognise a prospectus in accordance with sub-paragraph 1 sentence 2 only if

1. such exemption or deviation is permitted in accordance with or on the basis of this Law,
2. the same conditions which justify the exemptions obtain in Germany, and
3. the exemption or deviation is not connected with any other condition which would cause the Listing Board to refuse the exemption or deviation.

(3) Sub-Paragraphs 1 and 2 shall apply if the prospectus has been approved by the relevant authority of another state in connection with a public offer of the securities to be admitted and admission has been applied for within three months of such approval.

(4) If an issuer, having its principal place of business outside the area of application of this Act, makes an application for admission to a stock exchange in another member state of the European Community or another contracting state of the European Economic Area Treaty (not being the state where it has its principal place of business) and at the same time to a domestic stock exchange, the provisions of sub-paragraphs 1 to 3 shall apply if the issuer stipulates that the prospectus be approved by the relevant authority of the other member state or contracting state of the European Economic Area Treaty. § 39, sub-paragraph 4, sentence 2 shall apply accordingly.

Börsengesetz

§ 41
Staatsanleihen

Schuldverschreibungen des Bundes, seiner Sondervermögen oder eines Bundeslandes, auch soweit sie in das Bundesschuldbuch oder in die Schuldbücher der Bundesländer eingetragen sind, sowie Schuldverschreibungen, die von einem anderen Mitgliedstaat der Europäischen Wirtschaftsgemeinschaft oder von einem anderen Vertragsstaat des Abkommens über den Europäischen Wirtschaftsraum ausgegeben werden, sind an jeder inländischen Börse zur amtlichen Notierung zugelassen.

§ 42
Einführung

(1) Für die Aufnahme der ersten amtlichen Notierung der zugelassenen Wertpapiere an der Börse (Einführung) hat ein Kreditinstitut, das an dieser Börse mit dem Recht zur Teilnahme am Handel zugelassen ist, im Auftrag des Emittenten der Geschäftsführung den Zeitpunkt für die Einführung und die Merkmale der einzuführenden Wertpapiere mitzuteilen; ist der Emittent ein solches Kreditinstitut, so kann er dies selbst mitteilen.

(2) Wertpapiere, die zur öffentlichen Zeichnung aufgelegt werden, dürfen erst nach beendeter Zuteilung eingeführt werden.

(3) Die Bundesregierung wird ermächtigt, durch Rechtsverordnung mit Zustimmung des Bundesrates zum Schutz des Publikums den Zeitpunkt zu bestimmen, zu dem die Wertpapiere frühestens eingeführt werden dürfen.

(4) Werden die Wertpapiere nicht innerhalb von drei Monaten nach Veröffentlichung der Zulassungsentscheidung eingeführt, erlischt ihre Zulassung. Die Zulassungsstelle kann die Frist auf Antrag angemessen verlängern, wenn ein berechtigtes Interesse des Emittenten der zugelassenen Wertpapiere an der Verlängerung dargetan wird.

§ 43
Aussetzung und Einstellung der amtlichen Notierung

(1) Die Geschäftsführung kann die amtliche Notierung zugelassener Wertpapiere

1. aussetzen, wenn ein ordnungsgemäßer Börsenhandel zeitweilig gefährdet oder wenn dies zum Schutz des Publikums geboten erscheint;

Stock Exchange Act

§ 41
Government Bonds

Bonds issued by the Federal Government, its special funds or a Land, including those registered in the Federal debt register or in the debt registers of Länder, as well as bonds issued by another member state of the European Community or another contracting state of the European Economic Area Treaty, shall be admitted to official listing on any domestic stock exchange.

§ 42
Introduction of Securities

(1) For the purpose of the first official listing of securities admitted to the stock exchange (introduction), a credit institution admitted to trade on the stock exchange shall, on behalf of the issuer, inform the Board of Governors of the stock exchange of the time of the introduction and inform it of the characteristics of the securities to be introduced; if the issuer is itself a credit institution, it may provide that information itself.

(2) Securities offered for public subscription may only be introduced after allotment is completed.

(3) The Federal Government shall have the power to make regulations with the consent of the Bundesrat, stipulating the earliest time when securities may be introduced, to protect the public.

(4) If securities are not introduced within three months of publication of the admissions decision, such admission shall lapse. The admission authority may, on application, grant a time extension if the issuer of the admitted securities can justify its so doing.

§ 43
Suspension and Cancellation of Official Listing

(1) The Board of Governors may

1. suspend the official listing of admitted securities if there is a temporary threat to the orderly conduct of business on the stock exchange

Börsengesetz

2. einstellen, wenn ein ordnungsgemäßer Börsenhandel für die Wertpapiere nicht mehr gewährleistet erscheint.

(2) Widerspruch und Anfechtungsklage gegen die Aussetzung der amtlichen Notierung haben keine aufschiebende Wirkung.

(3) Die Zulassungsstelle kann die Zulassung zur amtlichen Notierung außer nach den Vorschriften der Verwaltungsverfahrensgesetze und nach § 44d Satz 2 widerrufen, wenn ein ordnungsgemäßer Börsenhandel auf Dauer nicht mehr gewährleistet ist und die Geschäftsführung die amtliche Notierung eingestellt hat.

§ 44

Pflichten des Emittenten

(1) Der Emittent der zugelassenen Wertpapiere ist verpflichtet,

1. die Inhaber der zugelassenen Wertpapiere unter gleichen Voraussetzungen gleich zu behandeln; dies gilt nicht für vorzeitige Rücknahmeangebote, die der Emittent zugelassener Schuldverschreibungen im berechtigen Interesse bestimmter Gruppen von Inhabern der Schuldverschreibungen abgibt;

2. für die gesamte Dauer der Zulassung der Wertpapiere mindestens eine Zahl- und Hinterlegungsstelle, bei zugelassenen Schuldverschreibungen nur Zahlstelle, am Börsenplatz zu benennen, bei der alle erforderlichen Maßnahmen hinsichtlich der Wertpapiere, im Falle der Vorlegung der Wertpapierurkunde bei dieser Stelle kostenfrei, bewirkt werden können;

3. das Publikum und die Zulassungsstelle über den Emittenten und die zugelassenen Wertpapiere angemessen zu unterrichten;

4. im Falle zugelassener Aktien für später ausgegebene Aktien derselben Gattung die Zulassung zur amtlichen Notierung zu beantragen.

(2) Die Bundesregierung wird ermächtigt, durch Rechtsverordnung mit Zustimmung des Bundesrates Vorschriften zu erlassen über Art, Umfang und Form der nach Absatz 1 Nr. 3 vorgenommenen Veröffentlichungen und Mitteilungen sowie darüber, wann und unter welchen Voraussetzungen die Verpflichtung nach Absatz 1 Nr. 4 eintritt.

§ 44a

[aufgehoben]

2. discontinue the official listing of admitted securities if there is a threat to the orderly conduct of business on the stock exchange or if it appears necessary to protect the public;

(2) Any objection or appeal against suspension of the official listing shall not prevent such suspension taking effect.

(3) The Listing Board may, for a prolonged period, revoke admission to an official listing for reasons other than those provided for in the administrative procedures legislation and under § 44d sentence 2 if there is a threat to the orderly conduct of business on the stock exchange and the Board of Governors has officially suspended quotation.

§ 44
Obligations of the Issuer

(1) An issuer of admitted securities is obliged

1. to treat all bearers of admitted securities equally if the prerequisites are the same; this shall not apply to offers for repayment prior to maturity made by an issuer of admitted bonds in the legitimate interests of particular classes of bondholders;
2. to nominate at least one payment and deposit office, or in the case of admitted bonds, a payment office only, in a city where there is a stock exchange, for the duration of the admission of the securities, where all necessary measures in respect to the securities can be taken, without charge, upon producing the securities certificate;
3. to give adequate information to the public and to the Listing Board about the issuer and the admitted securities;
4. in the case of admitted shares, to apply for admission to listing to later issues of the same class.

(2) The Federal Government shall have the power to make regulations, with the consent of the Bundesrat, about the nature, state and form of publications and notifications in accordance with sub-paragraph 1 No. 3, as well as when and subject to what conditions an obligation under sub-paragraph 1 No. 4 arises.

§ 44a
[repealed]

Börsengesetz

§ 44b

Zwischenbericht

(1) Der Emittent zugelassener Aktien ist verpflichtet, innerhalb des Geschäftsjahrs regelmäßig mindestens einen Zwischenbericht zu veröffentlichen, der anhand von Zahlenangaben und Erläuterungen ein den tatsächlichen Verhältnissen entsprechendes Bild der Finanzlage und des allgemeinen Geschäftsgangs des Emittenten im Berichtszeitraum vermittelt; dies gilt auch, wenn nicht die Aktien, sondern sie vertretende Zertifikate zur amtlichen Notierung zugelassen sind.

(2) Die Bundesregierung wird ermächtigt, durch Rechtsverordnung mit Zustimmung des Bundesrates zum Schutz des Publikums Vorschriften über den Inhalt des Zwischenberichts, insbesondere über die aufzunehmenden Zahlenangaben und Erläuterungen sowie über den Zeitpunkt und die Form seiner Veröffentlichung zu erlassen. Die Rechtsverordnung kann vorsehen, daß in Ausnahmefällen von der Aufnahme einzelner Angaben in den Zwischenbericht abgesehen werden kann, insbesondere im Hinblick auf die Gefährdung öffentlicher Interessen oder einen beim Emittenten zu befürchtenden erheblichen Schaden.

§ 44c

Auskunftspflicht

(1) Der Emittent der zugelassenen Wertpapiere sowie das antragstellende und das einführende Kreditinstitut sind verpflichtet, aus ihrem Bereich alle Auskünfte zu erteilen, die für die Zulassungsstelle oder die Geschäftsführung zur ordnungsgemäßen Erfüllung ihrer Aufgaben erforderlich sind.

(2) Die Zulassungsstelle kann verlangen, daß der Emittent der zugelassenen Wertpapiere in angemessener Form und Frist bestimmte Auskünfte veröffentlicht, wenn dies zum Schutz des Publikums oder für einen ordnungsgemäßen Börsenhandel erforderlich ist. Kommt der Emittent dem Verlangen der Zulassungsstelle nicht nach, kann die Zulassungsstelle nach Anhörung des Emittenten auf dessen Kosten diese Auskünfte selbst veröffentlichen.

§ 44d

Pflichtversäumnisse des Emittenten

Erfüllt der Emittent der zugelassenen Wertpapiere seine Pflichten aus der Zulassung nicht, so kann die Zulassungsstelle diese Tatsache durch Börsen-

Stock Exchange Act

§ 44b
Interim Report

(1) An issuer of admitted shares shall be obliged to publish at regular intervals at least one interim report in the course of each financial year, providing financial information and explanations so as to give an accurate picture of the financial position and the general conduct of the business of the issuer; this shall also apply where certificates representing shares are admitted to official listing rather than shares themselves.

(2) The Federal Government shall have the power, with the consent of the Bundesrat, to make regulations for the protection of the public concerning the contents of interim reports and in particular concerning the figures and explanations to be given and the time and form of publication. Such regulations may provide, in exceptional cases, for exemption from the inclusion of certain individual items of information, in particular with respect to any danger to the public interest or the likelihood of substantial damage to the issuer.

§ 44c
Obligation to Provide Information

(1) An issuer of admitted securities, together with any credit institution applying for the admission of securities or introducing securities, shall be obliged to furnish all information from their commercial sphere required by the Listing Board or the Board of Governors of the stock exchange for the purpose of fulfilling the latter's obligations.

(2) The admissions authorities may require an issuer of admitted securities to publish certain information in a particular form and within a reasonable period if necessary for the protection of the public or to ensure orderly business activity on the stock exchange. If an issuer fails to comply with a requirement of an issuing authority, the issuing authority may, after hearing representations from the issuer, publish such information itself at the issuers' expense.

§ 44d
Failure of Issuer to Comply with Obligations

If an issuer of admitted securities fails to comply with its obligations arising from admission, the Listing Board may publish details of the breach by

Börsengesetz

bekanntmachung veröffentlichen. Die Zulassungsstelle kann die Zulassung zur amtlichen Notierung widerrufen, wenn der Emittent auch nach einer ihm gesetzten angemessenen Frist diese Pflichten nicht erfüllt.

§ 45
Prospekthaftung

(1) Sind in einem Prospekt, auf Grund dessen Wertpapiere zum Börsenhandel zugelassen sind, Angaben, welche für die Beurteilung des Wertes erheblich sind, unrichtig, so haften diejenigen, welche den Prospekt erlassen haben, sowie diejenigen, von denen der Erlaß des Prospekts ausgeht, wenn sie die Unrichtigkeit gekannt haben oder ohne grobes Verschulden hätten kennen müssen, als Gesamtschuldner jedem Besitzer eines solchen Wertpapiers für den Schaden, welcher demselben aus der von den gemachten Angaben abweichenden Sachlage erwächst. Das gleiche gilt, wenn der Prospekt infolge der Fortlassung wesentlicher Tatsachen unvollständig ist und diese Unvollständigkeit auf böslichem Verschweigen oder auf der böslichen Unterlassung einer ausreichenden Prüfung seitens derjenigen, welche den Prospekt erlassen haben, oder derjenigen, von denen der Erlaß des Prospekts ausgeht, beruht.

(2) Die Ersatzpflicht wird dadurch nicht ausgeschlossen, daß der Prospekt die Angaben als von einem Dritten herrührend bezeichnet.

§ 46
Umfang der Ersatzpflicht

(1) Die Ersatzpflicht erstreckt sich nur auf diejenigen Stücke, welche auf Grund des Prospekts zugelassen und von dem Besitzer auf Grund eines im Inland abgeschlossenen Geschäfts erworben sind.

(2) Der Ersatzpflichtige kann der Ersatzpflicht dadurch genügen, daß er das Wertpapier gegen Erstattung des von dem Besitzer nachgewiesenen Erwerbspreises oder desjenigen Kurswerts übernimmt, den die Wertpapiere zur Zeit der Einführung hatten.

(3) Die Ersatzpflicht ist ausgeschlossen, wenn der Besitzer des Papiers die Unrichtigkeit oder Unvollständigkeit der Angaben des Prospekts bei dem Erwerbe kannte. Gleiches gilt, wenn der Besitzer des Papiers bei dem Erwerbe die Unrichtigkeit der Angaben des Prospekts bei Anwendung derjenigen Sorgfalt, welche er in eigenen Angelegenheiten beobachtet, kennen mußte, es sei denn, daß die Ersatzpflicht durch bösliches Verhalten begründet ist.

means of a stock exchange announcement. The Listing Board may revoke admission to official listing if an issuer fails to comply with its obligations after a set reasonable period.

§ 45

Liability for Prospectuses

(1) If a prospectus, on the basis of which securities have been admitted to trading on a stock exchange, contains incorrect information which is material for the evaluation of the securities, the person who issued the prospectus, together with such persons at whose bidding the prospectus was issued, shall be liable on a joint and several basis to the bearer of such securities for any damages arising from any discrepancy in the statements made, if they recognised the inconsistencies or without gross negligence should have recognised the inconsistencies. The same shall apply if a prospectus is incomplete as a result of the omission of material facts resulting from malicious concealment or a malicious failure to sufficiently examine on the part of those issuing the prospectus or those on whose authority the prospectus was issued.

(2) Such liability may not be excluded by indicating in the prospectus that information has been provided by a third party.

§ 46

Extent of Liability for Damages

(1) Liability for damages shall extend only to securities which were admitted on the basis of the prospectus and purchased by a holder in the course of a transaction which took place in Germany.

(2) Any person obliged to pay damages may satisfy his liability for damages by purchasing the securities at the holder's substantiated purchase price or at the official rate applicable at the time the securities were introduced.

(3) There shall be no liability for damages if the holder of the securities, upon acquisition, was aware of the inaccuracy or incomplete nature of the information in the prospectus. The same applies to the holder of the securities, if at the time of purchase he ought to have been aware of inaccuracies in the prospectus, by exercising the level of care which he would observe in his own affairs, unless the damages liability is based on malicious conduct.

Börsengesetz

§ 47
Verjährung des Ersatzanspruchs

Der Ersatzanspruch verjährt in fünf Jahren seit der Zulassung der Wertpapiere.

§ 48
Unwirksamkeit von Vereinbarungen über Haftungsausschluß

(1) Eine Vereinbarung, durch welche die nach den §§ 45 bis 47 begründete Haftung ermäßigt oder erlassen wird, ist unwirksam.

(2) Weitergehende Ansprüche, welche nach den Vorschriften des bürgerlichen Rechtes auf Grund von Verträgen erhoben werden können, bleiben unberührt.

§ 49
Gerichtliche Zuständigkeit bei Ersatzansprüchen

Für die Entscheidung der Ansprüche aus den §§ 45 bis 48 ist ohne Rücksicht auf den Wert des Streitgegenstandes ausschließlich das Landgericht des Ortes zuständig, an dessen Börse die Einführung des Wertpapiers erfolgte. Besteht an diesem Landgericht eine Kammer für Handelssachen, so gehört der Rechtsstreit vor diese. Die Revision sowie die Beschwerde gegen Entscheidungen des Oberlandesgerichts geht an den Bundesgerichtshof.

IV. Terminhandel

§ 50
Zulassung zum Börsenterminhandel

(1) Börsentermingeschäfte bedürfen, soweit sie an der Börse abgeschlossen werden (Börsenterminhandel), der Zulassung durch die Geschäftsführung nach näherer Bestimmung der Börsenordnung. Zu den Börsentermingeschäften gehören auch Geschäfte, die wirtschaftlich gleichen Zwecken dienen, auch wenn sie nicht auf Erfüllung ausgerichtet sind.

(2) Vor der Zulassung nach Absatz 1 hat der Börsenrat die Geschäftsbedingungen für den Börsenterminhandel festzusetzen.

Stock Exchange Act

§ 47
Limitation on Claims for Damages

A claim for damages shall be statute-barred after 5 years from the date of the admission of the securities.

§ 48
Unfair Contract Terms

(1) Any agreement purporting to restrict or exclude liability under §§ 45 to 47 shall be null and void.

(2) Any civil claims arising contractually remain unaffected.

§ 49
Jurisdiction for Claims for Damages

The district court having jurisdiction over the place of business of the stock exchange where the securities were introduced shall have exclusive jurisdiction for claims under §§ 45 to 48 regardless of their value. If a regional court has a commercial division, the commercial division of the court shall have jurisdiction over the dispute. Any appeal against or objection to any decision of the court of appeal shall be decided by the Supreme Court.

IV. Futures Trading

§ 50
Admission to Futures Trading on the Stock Exchange

(1) Futures transactions undertaken on a stock exchange (stock exchange futures trading) shall require admission by the Board of Governors in accordance with the provisions of the stock exchange order. Stock exchange futures business shall include transactions having the same financial purpose, even if delivery is not contemplated.

(2) Prior to admission in accordance with sub-paragraph 1, the Stock Exchange Council will stipulate business terms and conditions for futures trading on the stock exchange.

Börsengesetz

(3) Die Geschäftsführung hat vor der Zulassung von Waren zum Börsenterminhandel in jedem einzelnen Falle Vertreter der beteiligten Wirtschaftskreise gutachtlich zu hören.

(4) Die Zulassung von Wertpapieren zum Börsenterminhandel darf nur erfolgen, wenn die Gesamtsumme der Stücke, in denen der Börsenterminhandel stattfinden soll, sich nach ihrem Nennwerte mindestens auf zehn Millionen Deutsche Mark beläuft.

(5) Anteile einer inländischen Erwerbsgesellschaft dürfen nur mit Zustimmung der Gesellschaft zum Börsenterminhandel zugelassen werden. Eine erfolgte Zulassung ist auf Verlangen der Gesellschaft spätestens nach Ablauf eines Jahres von dem Tage an gerechnet, an welchem das Verlangen der Geschäftsführung gegenüber erklärt worden ist, zurückzunehmen.

(6) Wird bei Börsentermingeschäften ein Börsenpreis amtlich festgestellt, so sind die Vorschriften des II. Abschnitts entsprechend anzuwenden.

§ 51
Ausschluß des Börsenterminhandels

(1) Soweit Börsentermingeschäfte in bestimmten Waren oder Wertpapieren verboten sind oder die Zulassung zum Börsenterminhandel endgültig verweigert oder zurückgenommen worden ist, ist der Börsenterminhandel von der Benutzung der Börseneinrichtungen und der Vermittlung durch die Kursmakler ausgeschlossen. Findet an einer Börse ein Börsenterminhandel nach Geschäftsbedingungen statt, die von den festgesetzten Geschäftsbedingungen (§ 50 Absatz 2) abweichen, oder findet ein Börsenterminhandel in solchen Waren oder Wertpapieren statt, die zum Börsenterminhandel nicht zugelassen sind, so ist er durch Anordnung der Geschäftsführung von der Benutzung der Börseneinrichtungen und der Vermittlung durch die Kursmakler auszuschließen. Die Geschäftsführung kann den Erlaß der Anordnung aussetzen, wenn Verhandlungen wegen Zulassung der Waren oder Wertpapiere zum Börsenterminhandel schweben. Die Aussetzung darf höchstens auf ein Jahr erfolgen.

(2) Soweit der Börsenterminhandel auf Grund des Absatzes 1 von der Benutzung der Börseneinrichtungen und der Vermittlung durch die Kursmakler ausgeschlossen ist, dürfen für Börsentermingeschäfte, sofern sie im Inland abgeschlossen sind, Preislisten (Kurszettel) nicht veröffentlicht oder in mechanisch hergestellter Vervielfältigung verbreitet werden.

Stock Exchange Act

(3) Prior to the admission of commodities for exchange dealing, the Board of Governors shall in each case take advice from representatives of the business circles concerned.

(4) Securities shall only be admitted to trading on the stock exchange if the sum total of the stock in which trading is to take place amounts to at least DM 10 million, based on nominal value.

(5) Shares in a domestic company shall only be admitted for the purpose of futures trading on a stock exchange with the approval of that company. At the request of the company, any admission which has been granted shall be withdrawn at the latest after one year, commencing the day of the request to the Board of Governors.

(6) If an official stock exchange price is determined for futures business, the provisions of chapter II shall apply.

§ 51

Exclusion of Futures Trading

(1) If futures transactions in specific commodities or securities are prohibited or admission has been definitely refused or withdrawn, such futures trading shall be excluded from the use of stock exchange facilities and shall not be traded via official brokers as intermediaries. If, on a stock exchange, futures are traded in accordance with terms and conditions which differ from those stipulated (§ 50 sub-paragraph 2) or if futures in such commodities or securities are traded without being admitted to trading on the stock exchange, they shall be excluded from using stock exchange facilities and from trading via official brokers as intermediaries, by order of the Board of Governors. The Board of Governors may suspend such an order if negotiations are pending for the admission of the commodities or securities. Suspension may not exceed one year.

(2) If trading in futures has been excluded from the use of stock exchange facilities and from trading via official brokers as intermediaries pursuant to sub-paragraph 1, price lists (quotation sheets) for such futures dealings, to the extent that they are being conducted in Germany, are not be to published or distributed in mechanically copied form.

Börsengesetz

§ 52
Wirksamkeit des Börsentermingeschäfts

Ein Börsentermingeschäft, das nicht gegen ein durch dieses Gesetz oder aufgrund des § 63 erlassenes Verbot verstößt, ist nur nach Maßgabe der §§ 53 bis 56 wirksam.

§ 53
Verbindlichkeit von Börsentermingeschäften

(1) Ein Börsentermingeschäft ist verbindlich, wenn auf beiden Seiten als Vertragschließende Kaufleute beteiligt sind, die

1. in das Handelsregister oder Genossenschaftsregister eingetragen sind oder

2. nach § 36 des Handelsgesetzbuchs, im Falle einer juristischen Person des öffentlichen Rechts nach der für sie maßgebenden gesetzlichen Regelung, nicht eingetragen zu werden brauchen oder

3. nicht eingetragen werden, weil sie ihren Sitz oder ihre Hauptniederlassung außerhalb des Geltungsbereichs dieses Gesetzes haben.

Als Kaufleute im Sinne dieser Vorschrift gelten auch Personen, die zur Zeit des Geschäftsabschlusses oder früher gewerbsmäßig oder berufsmäßig Börsentermingeschäfte betrieben haben oder zur Teilnahme am Börsenhandel dauernd zugelassen waren.

(2) Ist nur einer der beiden Vertragsteile Kaufmann im Sinne des Absatzes 1, so ist das Geschäft verbindlich, wenn der Kaufmann einer gesetzlichen Banken- oder Börsenaufsicht untersteht und den anderen Teil vor Geschäftsabschluß schriftlich darüber informiert, daß

– die aus Börsentermingeschäften erworbenen befristeten Rechte verfallen oder eine Wertminderung erleiden können;

– das Verlustrisiko nicht bestimmbar sein und auch über etwaige geleistete Sicherheiten hinausgehen kann;

– Geschäfte, mit denen die Risiken aus eingegangenen Börsentermingeschäften ausgeschlossen oder eingeschränkt werden sollen, möglicherweise nicht oder nur zu einem verlustbringenden Marktpreis getätigt werden können;

– sich das Verlustrisiko erhöht, wenn

Stock Exchange Act

§ 52
Effectiveness of Stock Exchange Futures Transactions
A stock exchange futures transaction which is not contrary to any prohibition provided for in this Act or under § 63 shall be valid only subject to the terms set out in §§ 53 to 56.

§ 53
Enforceability of Stock Exchange Futures Transactions
(1) A stock exchange futures transaction shall be binding if the parties to the transaction are commercial merchants who

1. are registered in a commercial register or register of cooperatives or
2. under § 36 of the Commercial Code, or in the case of a legal person under public law in accordance with the relevant legal provisions are not subject to any requirement to register or
3. are not registered because they have their principal place of business outside the area of applicability of this Act

For the purpose of this provision, persons who at the time of the transaction or prior thereto have traded commercially or professionally in stock exchange futures or have been admitted to engage professionally in stock exchange trading, shall be deemed to be commercial merchants.

(2) If only one of two parties to a transaction is a commercial merchant within the meaning of sub-paragraph 1, the transaction shall be binding if the commercial merchant was subject to statutory banking or stock exchange supervision, and prior to the transaction informed the other party in writing that

– rights acquired by reason of stock exchange futures transactions subject to time limits may lapse or lose value;
– the risk of loss may be indeterminable and may exceed the value of any guarantees or collateral which might have been furnished;
– transactions intended to exclude or limit risks of stock exchange futures transactions may possibly not be effected or only at a price which will result in a loss;
– the risk of loss is greater if

Börsengesetz

zur Erfüllung von Verpflichtungen aus Börsentermingeschäften Kredit in Anspruch genommen wird oder

die Verpflichtung aus Börsentermingeschäften oder die hieraus zu beanspruchende Gegenleistung auf ausländische Währung oder eine Rechnungseinheit lautet.

Bei Börsentermingeschäften in Waren muß der Kaufmann den anderen Teil vor Geschäftsabschluß schriftlich über die speziellen Risiken von Warentermingeschäften informieren. Die Unterrichtungsschrift darf nur Informationen über die Börsentermingeschäfte und ihre Risiken enthalten und ist vom anderen Teil zu unterschreiben. Der Zeitpunkt der Unterrichtung darf nicht länger als drei Jahre zurückliegen; nach der ersten Unterrichtung ist sie jedoch vor dem Ablauf von zwölf Monaten, frühestens aber nach dem Ablauf von zehn Monaten zu wiederholen. Ist streitig, ob oder zu welchem Zeitpunkt der Kaufmann den anderen Teil unterrichtet hat, so trifft den Kaufmann die Beweislast.

§ 54

[aufgehoben]

§ 55

Rückforderung von Leistungen

Das auf Grund des Geschäfts Geleistete kann nicht deshalb zurückgefordert werden, weil für den Leistenden nach §§ 52 und 53 eine Verbindlichkeit nicht bestanden hat.

§ 56

Aufrechnung

Gegen Forderungen aus Börsentermingeschäften ist eine Aufrechnung auf Grund anderer Börsentermingeschäfte auch dann zulässig, wenn diese Geschäfte nach den §§ 52 und 53 für den Aufrechnenden eine Forderung nicht begründen.

§ 57

Verbindlichkeit bei Leistungsbereitschaft und Leistungswirkung

Ein nicht verbotenes Börsentermingeschäft gilt als von Anfang an verbindlich, wenn der eine Teil bei oder nach dem Eintritte der Fälligkeit sich

Stock Exchange Act

– credits are taken to comply with obligations arising from a futures transaction or if an obligation resulting from a futures transaction or the consideration thereof is in a foreign currency or units of account.

In the case of stock exchange commodities futures, a merchant must inform the other party to the transaction in writing, before the transaction is completed, of the special risks of commodities futures transactions. The written warning may contain only information on stock exchange futures dealings and the risks attached thereto and shall be countersigned by the other party. The date thereof shall not be more than three years; however, after writing for the first time, the warning shall be renewed before the expiry of twelve months, but at the earliest after the expiry of ten months. If a dispute arises whether or when the commercial merchant presented the written warning to the other party, the burden of proof rests with the commercial merchant.

§ 54

[repealed]

§ 55

Claims for Recovery of Consideration

Any consideration provided by reason of a transaction may not be reclaimed by reason of a claim under §§ 52 and 53 that no obligation has arisen.

§ 56

Set Off

Claims arising out of one stock exchange futures transaction may be the subject of a set off against another stock exchange futures transaction even if the transactions do not give rise to a claim under §§ 52 and 53 on the part of the party wishing to raise the set off.

§ 57

Enforceability in Cases of Readiness and Ability to Perform

Any futures transaction which is not prohibited shall be deemed to be valid and enforceable ab initio if one party agrees with the other party when per-

Börsengesetz

dem anderen Teile gegenüber mit der Bewirkung der vereinbarten Leistung einverstanden erklärt und der andere Teil diese Leistung an ihn bewirkt hat.

§ 58
Einwendungen

Gegen Ansprüche aus Börsentermingeschäften kann von demjenigen, für den das Geschäft nach den §§ 53 und 57 verbindlich ist, ein Einwand aus den §§ 762 und 764 des Bürgerlichen Gesetzbuches nicht erhoben werden. Soweit gegen die bezeichneten Ansprüche ein solcher Einwand zulässig bleibt, ist § 56 entsprechend anzuwenden.

§ 59
Schuldanerkenntnis

Die Vorschriften der §§ 52 bis 58 gelten auch für eine Vereinbarung, durch die der eine Teil zum Zwecke der Erfüllung einer Schuld aus einem nicht verbotenen Börsentermingeschäft dem anderen Teil gegenüber eine Verbindlichkeit eingeht, insbesondere für ein Schuldanerkenntnis.

§ 60
Erteilung und Übernahme von Aufträgen – Abschlußvereinigungen

Die Vorschriften der §§ 52 bis 59 finden auch Anwendung auf die Erteilung und Übernahme von Aufträgen sowie auf die Vereinigung zum Zwecke des Abschlusses von nicht verbotenen Börsentermingeschäften.

§ 61
Auslandsgeschäfte

Aus einem Börsentermingeschäft können ohne Rücksicht auf das darauf anzuwendende Recht keine weitergehenden Ansprüche, als nach deutschem Recht begründet sind, gegen eine Person geltend gemacht werden,
1. für die das Geschäft nach § 53 nicht verbindlich ist,
2. die ihren gewöhnlichen Aufenthalt zur Zeit des Geschäftsabschlusses im Inland hat und
3. die im Inland die für den Abschluß des Geschäfts erforderliche Willenserklärung abgegeben hat.

formance is due or thereafter agrees to accept performance as contracted and provided that the other party has performed his obligations.

§ 58
Objections

Objections in accordance with §§ 762 and 764 of the Civil Code may not be raised against claims resulting from stock exchange futures transactions by a person who, under the terms of §§ 53 and 57, is bound by the transaction. Where an objection against claims of this kind remains permitted, § 56 shall apply.

§ 59
Recognition of Debt

The provisions of §§ 52 to 58 shall apply to any agreement whereby one party incurs an obligation to another party for the purpose of settling a debt arising out of a stock exchange futures transaction which is not prohibited, in particular to any recognition of debt.

§ 60
Giving and Acceptance of Instructions

The provisions of §§ 52 to 59 shall apply to the giving and acceptance of instructions as well as to an association for the purpose of concluding stock exchange futures transactions which are not prohibited.

§ 61
Foreign Transactions

Irrespective of the law applicable to a futures transaction, no claim may be made arising out of a stock exchange futures transaction except as provided for under German law against any person

1. for whom a transaction is not enforceable under § 53,
2. whose ordinary residence was Germany at the time of the conclusion of the transaction and
3. who made in Germany the declaration of intent necessary to conclude the transaction.

Börsengesetz

§ 62
Verzug bei einem Warenbörsentermingeschäft

(1) Bei einem Börsentermingeschäft in Waren kommt der Verkäufer, der nach erfolgter Kündigung eine nicht vertragsmäßige Ware liefert, in Verzug, auch wenn die Lieferungsfrist noch nicht abgelaufen ist.

(2) Eine entgegenstehende Vereinbarung ist nichtig.

§ 63
Beschränkung bei Börsentermingeschäften

Der Bundesminister der Finanzen kann durch Rechtsverordnung mit Zustimmung des Bundesrates Börsentermingeschäfte verbieten oder beschränken oder die Zulässigkeit von Bedingungen abhängig machen, soweit dies zum Schutz des Publikums geboten ist.

§ 64
Unwirksamkeit verbotener Börsentermingeschäfte

(1) Durch ein nach § 63 verbotenes Börsentermingeschäft wird eine Verbindlichkeit nicht begründet. Die Unwirksamkeit erstreckt sich auch auf die Bestellung einer Sicherheit.

(2) Das auf Grund des Geschäfts Geleistete kann nicht deshalb zurückgefordert werden, weil nach Absatz 1 Satz 1 eine Verbindlichkeit nicht bestanden hat.

§§ 65 – 68
[aufgehoben]

§ 69
Vereinbarung zwecks Schulderfüllung

§ 64 gilt auch für eine Vereinbarung, durch die der eine Teil zum Zwecke der Erfüllung einer Schuld aus einem verbotenen Termingeschäft dem anderen Teil gegenüber eine Verbindlichkeit eingeht, insbesondere für ein Schuldanerkenntnis.

Stock Exchange Act

§ 62
Default in Relation to Commodities Futures Dealings on the Stock Exchange

(1) In a stock exchange futures transaction in commoditiés, a vendor who delivers goods which are not in accordance with contract after notice has been given shall be deemed to be in default even if the time for delivery has not yet expired.

(2) Any agreement to the contrary shall be null and void.

§ 63
Restrictions on Stock Exchange Futures Transactions

The Federal Minster of Finance may, by regulation, with the approval of the Bundesrat, prohibit or restrict stock exchange futures transactions or make them subject to conditions to the extent necessary to protect the public.

§ 64
Invalidity of Prohibited Stock Exchange Futures Transactions

(1) A stock exchange futures transaction which is prohibited under § 63 cannot give rise to any obligations. The invalidity of such a transaction shall also invalidate the effect of any collateral given.

(2) Any consideration given by reason of such a transaction may not be reclaimed, because under sub-paragraph 1 sentence 1 no obligation has arisen.

§ 65 to 68
[repealed]

§ 69
Agreement to Settle a Debt

§ 64 shall also apply to any agreement whereby one party incurs an obligation to another for the purpose of settling a debt arising out of a prohibited stock exchange futures transaction, in particular to any recognition of debt.

Börsengesetz

§ 70
Aufträge und Vereinigungen

Auf die Erteilung und Übernahme von Aufträgen sowie auf die Vereinigung zum Zwecke des Abschlusses von verbotenen Börsentermingeschäften ist § 64 anzuwenden.

V. Zulassung von Wertpapieren zum Börsenhandel mit nichtamtlicher Notierung

§ 71
Zulassungsantrag

(1) Wertpapiere können zum Börsenhandel mit nichtamtlicher Notierung (geregelter Markt) zugelassen werden, wenn sie an dieser Börse nicht zur amtlichen Notierung zugelassen sind. § 74 bleibt unberührt.

(2) Die Zulassung ist vom Emittenten der Wertpapiere zusammen mit einem Kreditinstitut zu beantragen, das an einer inländischen Börse mit dem Recht zur Teilnahme am Handel zugelassen ist. Ist der Emittent ein Kreditinstitut, so kann er den Antrag allein stellen. Die Börsenordnung muß Bestimmungen enthalten, nach denen die Geschäftsführung anderen Unternehmen als den in Satz 1 genannten Kreditinstituten auf Antrag gestatten kann, die Zulassung der Wertpapiere zusammen mit dem Emittenten zu beantragen; dabei ist insbesondere darauf abzustellen, daß diese Unternehmen die fachliche Eignung und Zuverlässigkeit besitzen, die für die Beurteilung des Emittenten sowie für die Gewährleistung eines ordnungsgemäßen Börsenhandels und eines hinreichenden Schutzes des Publikums notwendig sind, und über die für diese Tätigkeit erforderlichen ausreichenden Mittel verfügen.

(3) Über die Zulassung entscheidet der Zulassungsausschuß.

§ 72
Nähere Bestimmungen in der Börsenordnung

(1) Die näheren Bestimmungen für den geregelten Markt sind in der Börsenordnung zu treffen.

§ 70
Instructions, Associations

§ 64 shall apply to giving and accepting instructions and to any association for the purpose of concluding a prohibited stock exchange futures transaction.

V. The Admission of Securities to Stock Exchange Trading with Unofficial Listing

§ 71
Application for Admission

(1) Securities may be admitted to trading on the stock exchange with unofficial listing (the regulated market) if they are not admitted to official listing on the stock exchange. The provisions of § 74 shall not be thereby affected.

(2) Admission shall be applied for by the issuer of the securities in conjunction with a credit institution admitted to trading on a domestic stock exchange. If the issuer is a credit institution, it may make the application alone. The stock exchange order must contain provisions in accordance with which the Board of Governors may, on application, permit enterprises other than credit institutions mentioned in sentence 1 to apply for the admission of securities, in conjunction with the issuer; in so doing it shall ensure that such enterprises possess the necessary professional experience and trustworthiness necessary to evaluate the issuer and to ensure orderly business activity on the stock exchange, as well as adequate protection for the public, and the requisite resources.

(3) The listing committee shall decide applications for admission.

§ 72
Further Provisions in the Stock Exchange Order

(1) Detailed provisions for the regulated market are to be made in the stock exchange order.

Börsengesetz

(2) Die Börsenordnung muß insbesondere Bestimmungen enthalten über
1. die nach § 73 Abs. 1 Nr. 1 und 2 notwendigen Anforderungen und Angaben sowie über den Zeitpunkt und die Form der Veröffentlichung;
2. die Zusammensetzung und die Wahl der Mitglieder des Zulassungsausschusses;
3. das Zulassungsverfahren;
4. die Feststellung und die Veröffentlichung des Börsenpreises.

§ 73
Zulassungsvoraussetzungen

(1) Wertpapiere sind zum geregelten Markt zuzulassen, wenn
1. der Emittent und die Wertpapiere den Anforderungen entsprechen, die für einen ordnungsgemäßen Börsenhandel notwendig sind,
2. dem Antrag ein vom Emittenten unterschriebener Unternehmensbericht zur Veröffentlichung beigefügt ist, der Angaben über den Emittenten und die Wertpapiere enthält, die für die Anlageentscheidungen des Publikums von wesentlicher Bedeutung sind; insbesondere sind Angaben über die Entwicklung des Unternehmens, die laufende Geschäftslage und die Geschäftsaussichten sowie der letzte veröffentlichte Jahresabschluß aufzunehmen, und
3. keine Umstände bekannt sind, die bei Zulassung der Wertpapiere zu einer Übervorteilung des Publikums oder einer Schädigung erheblicher allgemeiner Interessen führen.

(2) Absatz 1 Nr. 2 gilt nicht für Emittenten, von denen Aktien oder Schuldverschreibungen an einer inländischen Börse zur amtlichen Notierung oder zum geregelten Markt zugelassen sind, wenn seit der letzten Veröffentlichung des Unternehmensberichts oder des für die Zulassung zur amtlichen Notierung erforderlichen Prospekts im Falle eines Antrags auf Zulassung von Schuldverschreibungen weniger als drei Jahre, im Falle eines Antrags auf Zulassung von sonstigen Wertpapieren weniger als sechs Monate vergangen sind.

(3) Die Börsenordnung kann regeln, unter welchen Voraussetzungen von dem Unternehmensbericht abgesehen werden kann, wenn das Publikum auf andere Weise ausreichend unterrichtet wird.

Stock Exchange Act

(2) In particular, the stock exchange order is to contain provisions concerning

1. the requirements and information to be provided under § 73 sub-paragraph 1 Nos. 1 and 2 and the date and form of publication;
2. the election of members and composition of the listing committee;
3. the admissions procedures;
4. the determination and publication of the stock exchange price.

§ 73
Prerequisites for Admission

(1) Securities shall be admitted to the regulated market if

1. the issuer and the securities comply with the requirements for orderly trading on the stock exchange,
2. the application is accompanied by a business report for publication signed by the issuer containing information regarding the issuer and the securities which is of essential importance to the investment decisions of the public; it shall contain in particular information regarding the development of the issuer, its current business position and future prospects, together with the last published annual accounts,
3. there are no known circumstances which, in the event of the admission of the securities, could lead to the public being cheated or could give rise to substantial public damage.

(2) Sub-paragraph 1 No. 2 shall not apply to issuers whose shares or bonds are admitted to official listing or on the regulated market of a domestic stock exchange, provided that since the last publication of a business report or prospectus required for admission to official listing, in the case of an application for the admission of bonds, less than 3 years have elapsed, in the case of an application for admission of other securities, less than 6 months have elapsed.

(3) The stock exchange order may provide for circumstances where a report may be dispensed with, provided sufficient information is available to the public by other means.

Börsengesetz

§ 74
Staatsanleihen

Schuldverschreibungen des Bundes, seiner Sondervermögen oder eines Bundeslandes, auch soweit sie in das Bundesschuldbuch oder in die Schuldbücher der Bundesländer eingetragen sind, sowie Schuldverschreibungen, die von einem anderen Mitgliedstaat der Europäischen Wirtschaftsgemeinschaft oder von einem anderen Vertragsstaat des Abkommens über den Europäischen Wirtschaftsraum ausgegeben werden, sind an jeder inländischen Börse, an der die Schuldverschreibungen nicht eingeführt (§ 42) sind, zum geregelten Markt zugelassen.

§ 75
Feststellung des Börsenpreises

(1) Für die Feststellung des Börsenpreises im geregelten Markt bestimmt die Geschäftsführung einen oder mehrere Makler. § 29 Abs. 3 und 4 gilt entsprechend.

(2) Für Wertpapiere, die zur öffentlichen Zeichnung aufgelegt werden, ist eine Feststellung des Börsenpreises vor beendeter Zuteilung an die Zeichner nicht zulässig.

(3) Für die Aussetzung und die Einstellung der Feststellung des Börsenpreises gilt § 43 entsprechend.

§ 76
Verpflichtungen des Emittenten

Die Bestimmungen des § 44 Abs. 1 Nr. 1 und 2 und § 44c Abs. 1 über die Verpflichtungen des Emittenten gelten für den geregelten Markt entsprechend.

§ 77
Haftung für Unternehmensbericht

Sind Angaben im Unternehmensbericht unrichtig oder unvollständig, so gelten die Vorschriften der §§ 45 bis 49 entsprechend.

Stock Exchange Act

§ 74
Public Bonds

Bonds issued by the Federal Government, its special funds, or a Land, including those registered in the federal debt register or the debt registers of Länder, as well as bonds issued by another member state of the European Community or another contracting state of the European Economic Area Treaty are to be admitted to the regulated market on any domestic stock exchange to which the bonds have not been introduced (§42).

§ 75
Fixing the Stock Exchange Price

(1) The Board of Governors shall appoint one or more brokers to determine the stock exchange price on the regulated market. § 29 sub-paragraphs 3 and 4 shall apply.

(2) In the case of securities issued for public subscription, a stock exchange price shall not be determined before final allotment to subscribers.

(3) § 43 shall apply to the suspension or discontinuance of fixing of a stock exchange price.

§ 76
Obligations of Issuer

The provisions of § 44 sub-paragraph 1 Nos. 1 and 2 and § 44c sub-paragraph 1, relating to the obligations of the issuer, apply to the regulated market as well.

§ 77
Liability for Report

If incorrect or incomplete information is given in the business report, the provisions of §§ 45 to 49 shall apply.

Börsengesetz

§ 78
Freiverkehr

(1) Für Wertpapiere, die weder zum amtlichen Handel noch zum geregelten Markt zugelassen sind, kann die Börse einen Freiverkehr zulassen, wenn durch Handelsrichtlinien eine ordnungsmäßige Durchführung des Handels und der Geschäftsabwicklung gewährleistet erscheint.

(2) Preise für Wertpapiere, die während der Börsenzeit an einer Wertpapierbörse im Freiverkehr ermittelt werden, sind Börsenpreise. Börsenpreise sind auch Preise, die sich für die im Freiverkehr gehandelten Wertpapiere in einem an einer Börse durch die Börsenordnung geregelten elektronischen Handelssystem oder an Börsen bilden, an denen nur ein elektronischer Handel stattfindet. Die Börsenpreise müssen die Anforderungen nach § 11 Abs. 2 erfüllen.

§§ 79 – 87
[aufgehoben]

§ 88
Strafvorschrift

Wer zur Einwirkung auf den Börsen- oder Marktpreis von Wertpapieren, Bezugsrechten, ausländischen Zahlungsmitteln, Waren, Anteilen, die eine Beteiligung am Ergebnis eines Unternehmens gewähren sollen, oder von Derivaten im Sinne des § 2 Abs. 2 des Wertpapierhandelsgesetzes

1. unrichtige Angaben über Umstände macht, die für die Bewertung der Wertpapiere, Bezugsrechte, ausländischen Zahlungsmittel, Waren, Anteile oder Derivate erheblich sind, oder solche Umstände entgegen bestehenden Rechtsvorschriften verschweigt oder
2. sonstige auf Täuschung berechnete Mittel anwendet,

wird mit Freiheitsstrafe bis zu drei Jahren oder mit Geldstrafe bestraft.

§ 89
Verleitung zu Börsenspekulationsgeschäften

(1) Wer gewerbsmäßig andere unter Ausnutzung ihrer Unerfahrenheit in Börsenspekulationsgeschäften zu solchen Geschäften oder zur unmittelba-

Stock Exchange Act

§ 78
Free Market

(1) The stock exchange may allow free market trading in securities which are neither admitted to official trading nor admitted to the regulated market provided that there are trading guidelines in force to ensure that trading and settlement are orderly carried out.

(2) Stock exchange prices shall also include prices arrived at during regular trading hours for securities traded on the free market. Stock exchange prices are also prices for securities traded on the free market established by means of an electronic trading system regulated under the terms of the Stock Exchange Order or on a stock exchange where there is only electronic trading. Such stock exchange prices are to comply with the provisions of § 11 sub-paragraph 2.

§ 79 – 87
[repealed]

§ 88
Manipulation of Prices

Any person who, with the purpose of affecting the stock exchange or market price of securities, subscription rights, foreign exchange, commodities, interests which allow a right to participate in the profits of an enterprise, or derivatives within the meaning of § 2 sub-paragraph 2 of the Securities Trading Act

1. gives false information concerning matters materially affecting the valuation of securities, subscription rights, foreign exchange, commodities, interests or derivatives, or conceals such information contrary to the provisions of the law or
2. uses other means for the purposes of deception,

shall be liable to imprisonment for up to three years or a fine.

§ 89
Inducement to Speculation on the Stock Exchange

(1) Any person who, in the course of business, induces others by exploiting their lack of experience to engage in speculative stock exchange business

Börsengesetz

ren oder mittelbaren Beteiligung an solchen Geschäften verleitet, wird mit Freiheitsstrafe bis zu drei Jahren oder mit Geldstrafe bestraft.

(2) Börsenspekulationsgeschäfte im Sinne des Abs. 1 sind insbesondere

1. An- oder Verkaufsgeschäfte mit aufgeschobener Lieferzeit, auch wenn sie außerhalb einer inländischen oder ausländischen Börse abgeschlossen werden,

2. Optionen auf solche Geschäfte,

die darauf gerichtet sind, aus dem Unterschied zwischen dem für die Lieferzeit festgelegten Preis und dem zur Lieferzeit vorhandenen Börsen- oder Marktpreis einen Gewinn zu erzielen.

§ 90

Ordnungswidrigkeiten

(1) Ordnungswidrig handelt, wer vorsätzlich oder leichtfertig

1. einer vollziehbaren Anordnung nach § 1a Abs. 1 Satz 1 oder § 8b Abs. 1 Satz 2 Nr. 2 zuwiderhandelt,

2. ein Betreten entgegen § 1a Abs. 1 Satz 2, auch in Verbindung mit Satz 5, nicht gestattet oder entgegen § 1a Abs. 1 Satz 3, auch in Verbindung mit Satz 5, nicht duldet,

3. entgegen § 8a Abs. 2 Satz 1 oder Abs. 3 einen Jahresabschluß, einen Prüfungsbericht, einen Vermögensstatus oder eine Erfolgsrechnung nicht, nicht vollständig oder nicht rechtzeitig vorlegt,

4. entgegen § 44 Abs. 1 Nr. 2, auch in Verbindung mit § 76, eine Zahl- und Hinterlegungsstelle oder eine Zahlstelle am Börsenplatz nicht benennt,

5. entgegen § 44b Abs. 1, auch in Verbindung mit einer Rechtsverordnung nach § 44b Abs. 2, einen Zwischenbericht nicht, nicht richtig, nicht vollständig, nicht in der vorgeschriebenen Form oder nicht rechtzeitig veröffentlicht oder

6. entgegen § 44c Abs. 1, auch in Verbindung mit § 76, eine Auskunft nicht, nicht richtig oder nicht vollständig erteilt.

(2) Ordnungswidrig handelt auch, wer vorsätzlich oder leichtfertig einer Rechtsverordnung nach

Stock Exchange Act

or to participate directly or indirectly in such business, shall be liable to imprisonment for up to three years or a fine.

(2) Speculative business on the stock exchange within the meaning of sub-paragraph 1 shall include in particular

1. purchase or sales transactions with deferred delivery dates even where such transactions are contracted outside a domestic or foreign stock exchange;
2. options on such transactions,

where such transactions have as their object the making of a profit on the difference between the price agreed for delivery and the actual stock exchange or market price at the time of delivery.

§ 90
Breaches of Regulations

(1) A person who intentionally or recklessly

1. acts in breach of an enforceable order under § 1a sub-paragraph 1 sentence 2 or § 8b sub-paragraph 1 sentence 2 No.2, or
2. contrary to § 1a sub-paragraph 1 sentence 2, also in conjunction with sentence 5 does not allow entry or contrary to paragraph 1a sub-paragraph 1 sentence 3 also in conjunction with sentence 5 does not tolerate entry or
3. contrary to § 8a sub-paragraph 2 sentence 1 or sub-paragraph 3, fails to provide annual accounts, auditors' reports, status reports, or profit and loss statement, either completely or on time,
4. contrary to § 44 sub-paragraph 1 No. 2 and § 76 fails to nominate a payment and deposit office or a payment office in the city of the stock exchange,
5. contrary to § 44b sub-paragraph 1 also in conjunction with a regulation under § 44b sub-paragraph 2 fails to publish an interim report or not correctly, not completely, not in the prescribed form or not on time or
6. contrary to § 44c sub-paragraph 1, and § 76, provides incorrect or incomplete information or fails to provide information at all

shall be guilty of a breach of regulation.

(2) In addition, a person who, whether intentionally or recklessly, acts contrary to a regulation passed under

Börsengesetz

1. § 38 Abs. 1 Nr. 3 oder
2. § 44 Abs. 2

zuwiderhandelt, soweit sie für einen bestimmten Tatbestand auf diese Bußgeldvorschrift verweist.

(3) Ordnungswidrig handelt ferner, wer entgegen § 51 Abs. 2 Preislisten (Kurszettel) veröffentlicht oder in mechanisch hergestellter Vervielfältigung verbreitet.

(4) Die Ordnungswidrigkeit kann in den Fällen des Absatzes 1 Nr. 1 bis 4 und 6, des Absatzes 2 Nr. 2 und des Absatzes 3 mit einer Geldbuße bis zu fünfzigtausend Deutsche Mark, in den Fällen des Absatzes 1 Nr. 5 und des Absatzes 2 Nr. 1 mit einer Geldbuße bis zu einhunderttausend Deutsche Mark geahndet werden.

§§ 91 – 95

[aufgehoben]

§ 96
Geltung für Wechsel und ausländische Zahlungsmittel

(1) Die in dem II. Abschnitt bezüglich der Wertpapiere getroffenen Bestimmungen gelten auch für Wechsel und ausländische Zahlungsmittel.

(2) Als Zahlungsmittel im Sinne des ersten Absatzes gelten außer Geldsorten, Papiergeld, Banknoten und dergleichen auch Auszahlungen, Anweisungen und Schecks.

§ 97
Übergangsregelung

(1) Der bei Inkrafttreten des Artikels 2 des Zweiten Finanzmarktförderungsgesetzes im Amt befindliche Börsenvorstand übernimmt die Aufgaben des Börsenrates. Seine Amtsdauer endet mit der Wahl des neuen Börsenrates, spätestens jedoch zwölf Monate nach Inkrafttreten des Artikels 2 des Zweiten Finanzmarktförderungsgesetzes.

(2) Die zur Teilnahme am Börsenhandel zugelassenen Unternehmen, die keine Kreditinstitute sind, haben innerhalb von zwölf Monaten nach Inkrafttreten des § 7 Abs. 4 Nr. 4 die Kapitalanforderungen nach dieser Vorschrift zu erfüllen.

Stock Exchange Act

1. § 38 sub-paragraph 1 No. 3 or
2. § 44 sub-paragraph 2

shall be guilty of a breach of regulation to the extent that such regulation provides for a fine in respect to any specific offence.

(3) Furthermore, a person who publishes price lists ("quotation sheets") or makes them available in mechanically-reproduced form contrary to § 51 sub-paragraph 2 shall be guilty of a breach of regulation.

(4) A breach of regulation, in the cases provided for in sub-paragraph 1 Nos. 1 to 4 and 6, sub-paragraph 2 No. 2 and sub-paragraph 3, may be punished with fines of up to fifty thousand German Marks and in the cases provided for under sub-paragraph 1 No. 5 and sub-paragraph 2 No. 1 with fines of up to one hundred thousand German Marks.

§ 91–95

[repealed]

§ 96

Application for Bills of Exchange and Foreign Currencies

(1) The provisions relating to securities in chapter 2 shall also apply to bills of exchange and foreign currencies.

(2) Foreign currency within the meaning of sub-paragraph 1 shall include, in addition to cash, paper money, bank notes and the like, payment orders, transfers and cheques.

§ 97

Transitional Provisions

(1) Any stock exchange board in office at the time of the coming into force of Article 2 of the Second Financial Market Advancement Law shall undertake the duties of the Stock Exchange Council. Its period of office shall terminate upon the election of a new Stock Exchange Council and in any event within 12 months of entering into force of article 2 of the aforesaid Act.

(2) Any enterprises admitted to trading on the stock exchange which are not credit institutions shall, within twelve months of § 7 sub-paragraph 4 No. 4 coming into force, comply with the capital requirements provided for therein.

Verordnung über die Zulassung von Wertpapieren zur amtlichen Notierung an einer Wertpapierbörse (Börsenzulassungs-Verordnung – BörsZulV)

vom 15. April 1987 (BGBl. I, S. 1234), zuletzt geändert durch Artikel 16 des Zweiten Finanzmarktförderungsgesetzes vom 26. Juli 1994 (BGBl. I, S. 1783)

Inhaltsübersicht

Erstes Kapitel **Zulassung von Wertpapieren zur amtlichen Notierung** §

Erster Abschnitt

Zulassungsvoraussetzungen

Rechtsgrundlage des Emittenten 1
Mindestbetrag der Wertpapiere 2
Dauer des Bestehens des Emittenten 3
Rechtsgrundlage der Wertpapiere 4
Handelbarkeit der Wertpapiere 5
Stückelung der Wertpapiere 6
Zulassung von Wertpapieren einer Gattung oder einer Emission 7
Druckausstattung der Wertpapiere 8
Streuung der Aktien 9
Emittenten aus Drittstaaten 10
Zulassung von Wertpapieren mit Umtausch- oder Bezugsrecht 11
Zulassung von Zertifikaten, die Aktien vertreten 12

Zweiter Abschnitt

Prospekt (§ 36 Abs. 3 Nr. 2 des Börsengesetzes)

Erster Unterabschnitt
Prospektinhalt

Allgemeine Grundsätze 13
Angaben über Personen oder Gesellschaften, die für den Inhalt des Prospekts die Verantwortung übernehmen 14
Allgemeine Angaben über die Wertpapiere 15

Regulation concerning the Admission of Securities to Official Listing on a Stock Exchange
(Stock Exchange Admissions Regulation)

of April 15, 1987 (Federal Gazette I 1234)
last amended by Article 16 of the Second Financial Market Advancement
Law of July 26, 1994 (Federal Gazette I 1783)

Table of Contents

		§
Chapter One	**Admission of Securities to Official Listing**	

Part One

Conditions for Admission

The Legal Basis of the Issuer 1
Minimum Value of Securities 2
Duration of Existence of the Issuer 3
Legal Basis of Securities 4
Negotiability of Securities 5
Denomination of Securities 6
Admission of Securities of
one Class or one Issue 7
Printing of Securities 8
Distribution of Shares 9
Issuers from Non-EEC States 10
Admission of Securities with Conversion
or Subscription Rights 11
Admission of Certificates Representing Shares 12

Part Two

Prospectus (§ 36 Part 3 No. 2 of the Stock Exchange Act)

Sub-Part One
Contents of the Prospectus

General Provisions 13
Information on Persons or Companies Responsible
for the Contents of the Prospectus 14
General Information about the Securities 15

Börsenzul. Verordnung

Besondere Angaben über Aktien 16
Besondere Angaben über andere Wertpapiere
als Aktien 17
Allgemeine Angaben über den Emittenten 18
Angaben über das Kapital des Emittenten 19
Angaben über die Geschäftstätigkeit des Emittenten 20
Angaben über die Vermögens-, Finanz- und
Ertragslage des Emittenten 21
Angaben aus der Rechnungslegung des Emittenten .. 22
Aufstellung über die Herkunft und Verwendung
der Mittel 23
Angaben über Beteiligungsunternehmen 24
Angabe von Ergebnis und Dividende je Aktie 25
Aufnahme von Konzernabschlüssen 26
Angabe der Verbindlichkeiten des Emittenten der
zuzulassenden Schuldverschreibungen 27
Angaben über Geschäftsführungs- und
Aufsichtsorgane des Emittenten 28
Angaben über den jüngsten Geschäftsgang und die
Geschäftsaussichten des Emittenten 29
Angaben über die Prüfung der Jahresabschlüsse
des Emittenten und anderer Angaben im Prospekt .. 30
Angaben über Zertifikate, die Aktien vertreten 31
Angaben über den Emittenten der Zertifikate,
die Aktien vertreten 32

Zweiter Unterabschnitt
Prospektinhalt in Sonderfällen

Aktien auf Grund von Bezugsrechten 33
Wertpapiere von Emittenten börsennotierter
Wertpapiere 34
Wertpapiere mit Umtausch- oder Bezugsrecht
auf Aktien 35
Wertpapiere außer Aktien auf Grund von
Bezugsrechten 36
Bank- oder Versicherungsgeschäfte betreibende
Emittenten 37
Von Kreditinstituten dauernd oder wiederholt
ausgegebene Schuldverschreibungen 38

Admissions Regulation

Specific Information concerning Shares 16
Specific Information concerning Securities
other than Shares............................... 17
General Information about the Issuer................ 18
Information concerning the Capital of the Issuer....... 19
Information concerning the Business Activities
of the Issuer.................................... 20
Information about Net Worth, Financial Position
and Results of the Issuer.......................... 21
Information about the Accounting Principles
of the Issuer.................................... 22
Information about the Source and Applicaton
of Funds 23
Information about Subsidiaries or Affiliates 24
Information concerning Earnings and Dividends
per Share....................................... 25
The Inclusion of Consolidated Annual Accounts 26
Information concerning the Liabilities of the Issuer
of Bonds which are to be Admitted 27
Information about the Directors and Supervisory
Organs of the Issuer 28
Information about Current Performance
and Future Business Prospects of the Issuer........... 29
Information concerning the Auditing of the
Issuer's Annual Accounts and other Information
given in the Prospectus........................... 30
Information regarding Certificates
Representing Shares 31
Information concerning the Issuer of Certificates
which Represent Shares 32

Sub-Part Two
Contents of Prospectuses in Special Cases

Shares Based on Subscripton Rights 33
Securities of Issuers of Listed Securities 34
Securities with Conversion or Subscription Rights 35
Securities other than Shares by Reason of
Subscription Rights.............................. 36
Issuers Active in the Banking or Insurance Business 37
Bonds Continuously or Repeatedly Issued by Banks 38

221

Börsenzul. Verordnung

Gewährleistete Wertpapiere 39
Zertifikate, die Aktien vertreten 40
Verschmelzung, Spaltung, Übertragung, Umtausch,
Sacheinlagen 41
Schuldverschreibungen von Staaten,
Gebietskörperschaften,
zwischenstaatlichen Einrichtungen 42

Dritter Unterabschnitt
Veröffentlichung des Prospekts

Frist der Veröffentlichung 43
Veröffentlichung eines unvollständigen Prospekts ... 44

Vierter Unterabschnitt
Befreiung von der Pflicht,
einen Prospekt zu veröffentlichen

Befreiung im Hinblick auf bestimmte Wertpapiere ... 45
Befreiung im Hinblick auf bestimmte Anleger 46
Befreiung im Hinblick auf einzelne Angaben 47

Dritter Abschnitt
Zahlungsverfahren

Zulassungsantrag 48
Veröffentlichung des Zulassungsantrags 49
Zeitpunkt der Zulassung 50
Veröffentlichung der Zulassung 51
Einführung 52

Zweites Kapitel **Pflichten des Emittenten zugelassener Wertpapiere**

Erster Abschnitt
Zwischenbericht
Erster Unterabschnitt
Inhalt des Zwischenberichts

Allgemeine Grundsätze 53
Zahlenangaben 54

Admissions Regulation

Guaranteed Securities 39
Certificates Representing Shares 40
Merger, Split, Transfer, Exchange, Contributions
in Kind 41
Bonds Issued by Governments, Regional Authorities
and International Institutions 42

Sub-Part Three
Publication of the Prospectus

Time Limit for Publication 43
Publication of an Incomplete Prospectus 44

Sub-Part Four
Exemption from the Obligation
to Publish a Prospectus

Exemption relating to Specific Securities 45
Exemption relating to Specific Investors 46
Exemption relating to Specific Information 47

Part Three
Admisssions Procedure

Application for Admission 48
Publication of the Application for Admission 49
Date of Admission 50
Publication of Admission 51
Introduction 52

Chapter Two   **Obligations of an Issuer of Admitted Securities**

Part One
Interim Report
Sub-Part One
Contents of the Interim Report

General Principles 53
Figures Provided 54

223

Börsenzul. Verordnung

Erläuterungen 55
Konzernabschluß 56

Zweiter Unterabschnitt
Inhalt des Zwischenberichts in Sonderfällen

Anpassung der Zahlenangaben 57
Emittenten aus Drittstaaten 58
Zwischenberichte in mehreren Mitgliedstaaten
der Europäischen Wirtschaftsgemeinschaft 59
Befreiung im Hinblick auf einzelne Angaben 60

Dritter Unterabschnitt
Veröffentlichung des Zwischenberichts

Form und Frist der Veröffentlichung 61
Übermittlung an Zulassungsstelle 62

Zweiter Abschnitt
Sonstige Pflichten

Veröffentlichung von Mitteilungen 63
Änderungen der Rechtsgrundlage des Emittenten ... 64
Verfügbarkeit von Jahresabschluß und Lagebericht .. 65
Veröffentlichung zusätzlicher Angaben 66
Unterrichtung bei Zulassung an mehreren Börsen ... 67
Hinweis auf Prospekt 68
Zulassung später ausgegebener Aktien 69
Art und Form der Veröffentlichungen 70

Drittes Kapitel **Ordnungswidrigkeiten, Schlußvorschriften**
Ordnungswidrigkeiten 71

Admissions Regulation

Explanations 55
Consolidated Annual Accounts 56

Sub-Part Two
Contents of the Interim Report in Special Cases

Adjustment of Figures Provided 57
Issuers from Third Party States 58
Interim Reports Appearing in more than
One Member State of the European Economic
Community or another Contracting State of the
European Economic Area Treaty 59
Exemptions relating to Particular Items of Information . . 60

Sub-Part Three
Publication of the Interim Report

Time Limit and Form of Publication 61
Delivery of the Interim Report to the Listing Board 62

Part Two

Miscellaneous Obligations

Publication of Notifications 63
Changes of the Legal Basis of the Issuer 64
Availability of Annual Accounts and
Management Reports 65
Publication of Additional Information 66
Information in Cases of Admission to more than
one Stock Exchange 67
Reference to Prospectuses 68
The Admission of Shares Issued at a Later Date 69
Manner and Form of Publication 70

Chapter Three **Breach of Regulations and Final Provisions**
Breach of Regulations 71

Börsenzul. Verordnung

Erstes Kapitel
Zulassung von Wertpapieren zur amtlichen Notierung

Erster Abschnitt
Zulassungsvoraussetzungen

§ 1
Rechtsgrundlage des Emittenten

Die Gründung sowie die Satzung oder der Gesellschaftsvertrag des Emittenten müssen dem Recht des Staates entsprechen, in dem der Emittent seinen Sitz hat.

§ 2
Mindestbetrag der Wertpapiere

(1) Der voraussichtliche Kurswert der zuzulassenden Aktien oder, falls seine Schätzung nicht möglich ist, das Eigenkapital der Gesellschaft im Sinne des § 266 Abs. 3 Buchstabe A des Handelsgesetzbuchs, deren Aktien zugelassen werden sollen, muß mindestens zwei Millionen fünfhunderttausend Deutsche Mark betragen. Dies gilt nicht, wenn Aktien derselben Gattung an dieser Börse bereits amtlich notiert werden.

(2) Für die Zulassung von anderen Wertpapieren als Aktien muß der Gesamtnennbetrag mindestens fünfhunderttausend Deutsche Mark betragen.

(3) Für die Zulassung von Wertpapieren, die nicht auf einen Geldbetrag lauten, muß die Mindeststückzahl der Wertpapiere zehntausend betragen.

(4) Die Zulassungsstelle kann geringere Beträge als in den vorstehenden Absätzen vorgeschrieben zulassen, wenn sie überzeugt ist, daß sich für die zuzulassenden Wertpapiere ein ausreichender Markt bilden wird.

§ 3
Dauer des Bestehens des Emittenten

(1) Der Emittent zuzulassender Aktien muß mindestens drei Jahre als Unternehmen bestanden und seine Jahresabschlüsse für die drei dem Antrag

Admissions Regulation

Chapter One
Admission of Securities to Official Listing

Part One
Conditions for Admission

§ 1
The Legal Basis of the Issuer

The formation, memorandum and articles of association of an issuer must comply with the laws of the country in which the issuer has its principal place of business.

§ 2
Minimum Value of Securities

(1) The estimated market price of shares to be admitted or, if it is not possible to provide an estimate, the equity of the company according to § 266 sub-paragraph 3 letter A of the Commercial Code, shares in which are to be admitted, shall be at least two million five hundred thousand German Marks. This shall not apply where shares of the same class have already been officially listed on the same stock exchange.

(2) For the admission of securities other than in the form of shares, the total nominal value shall be at least five hundred thousand German Marks.

(3) For the admission of securities issued other than in an amount of money, the minimum number of securities shall be ten thousand.

(4) The Listing Board may allow securities to be issued for values or quantities lower than those referred to in the preceding sub-paragraphs, if it is satisfied that a sufficient market for the securities to be admitted will be formed.

§ 3
Duration of Existence of the Issuer

(1) An issuer of shares to be admitted must have existed as an enterprise for a minimum of three years and have published its annual accounts for the

Börsenzul. Verordnung

vorangegangenen Geschäftsjahre entsprechend den hierfür geltenden Vorschriften offengelegt haben.

(2) Die Zulassungsstelle kann abweichend von Absatz 1 Aktien zulassen, wenn dies im Interesse des Emittenten und des Publikums liegt.

§ 4
Rechtsgrundlage der Wertpapiere

Die Wertpapiere müssen in Übereinstimmung mit dem für den Emittenten geltenden Recht ausgegeben werden und den für das Wertpapier geltenden Vorschriften entsprechen.

§ 5
Handelbarkeit der Wertpapiere

(1) Die Wertpapiere müssen frei handelbar sein.

(2) Die Zulassungsstelle kann

1. nicht voll eingezahlte Wertpapiere zulassen, wenn sichergestellt ist, daß der Börsenhandel nicht beeinträchtigt wird und wenn in dem Prospekt (§ 13) auf die fehlende Volleinzahlung sowie auf die im Hinblick hierauf getroffenen Vorkehrungen hingewiesen wird oder, wenn ein Prospekt nicht zu veröffentlichen ist, das Publikum auf andere geeignete Weise unterrichtet wird;

2. Aktien, deren Erwerb einer Zustimmung bedarf, zulassen, wenn das Zustimmungserfordernis nicht zu einer Störung des Börsenhandels führt.

§ 6
Stückelung der Wertpapiere

Die Stückelung der Wertpapiere, insbesondere die kleinste Stückelung und die Anzahl der in dieser Stückelung ausgegebenen Wertpapiere, müssen den Bedürfnissen des Börsenhandels und des Publikums Rechnung tragen.

three financial years preceding application in accordance with appropriate regulations.

(2) The Listing Board may, notwithstanding the provisions of sub-paragraph 1, admit shares where doing so is in the interest of the issuer and the public.

§ 4

Legal Basis of Securities

Securities must be issued in accordance with the law applicable to the issuer and shall comply with the appropriate securities regulations.

§ 5

Negotiability of Securities

(1) Securities must be freely negotiable.

(2) The Listing Board may

1. admit securities which are not fully paid up provided that steps have been taken to ensure that stock exchange trading will not be adversely affected and provided that the prospectus (§ 13) states that payment has not been made in full and indicates the steps taken as a result or, if a prospectus is not to be published, the public is notified that payment in full has not been made by some other suitable means;

2. admit shares which need consent in order to be purchased, provided that the requirement of consent does not result in any disruption in stock exchange trading.

§ 6

Denomination of Securities

The denomination of securities, taking into particular consideration smaller denominations and the number thereof, must take into account the trading requirements of the stock exchange and the requirements of the public.

Börsenzul. Verordnung

§ 7
Zulassung von Wertpapieren einer Gattung oder einer Emission

(1) Der Antrag auf Zulassung von Aktien muß sich auf alle Aktien derselben Gattung beziehen. Er kann jedoch insoweit beschränkt werden, als die nicht zuzulassenden Aktien zu einer der Aufrechterhaltung eines beherrschenden Einflusses auf den Emittenten dienenden Beteiligung gehören oder für eine bestimmte Zeit nicht gehandelt werden dürfen und wenn aus der nur teilweisen Zulassung keine Nachteile für die Erwerber der zuzulassenden Aktien zu befürchten sind. In dem Prospekt (§ 13) ist darauf hinzuweisen, daß nur für einen Teil der Aktien die Zulassung beantragt wurde, und der Grund hierfür anzugeben; ist ein Prospekt nicht zu veröffentlichen, so ist das Publikum auf andere geeignete Weise zu unterrichten.

(2) Der Antrag auf Zulassung von anderen Wertpapieren als Aktien muß sich auf alle Wertpapiere derselben Emission beziehen.

§ 8
Druckausstattung der Wertpapiere

(1) Die Druckausstattung der Wertpapiere in ausgedruckten Einzelurkunden muß einen ausreichenden Schutz vor Fälschung bieten und eine sichere und leichte Abwicklung des Wertpapierverkehrs ermöglichen. Für Wertpapiere eines Emittenten mit Sitz in einem anderen Mitgliedstaat der Europäischen Wirtschaftsgemeinschaft oder in einem anderen Vertragsstaat des Abkommens über den Europäischen Wirtschaftsraum reicht die Beachtung der Vorschriften aus, die in diesem Staat für die Druckausstattung der Wertpapiere gelten.

(2) Bietet die Druckausstattung der Wertpapiere keinen ausreichenden Schutz vor Fälschung, so ist in dem Prospekt (§ 13) hierauf hinzuweisen; ist ein Prospekt nicht zu veröffentlichen, so ist das Publikum auf andere geeignete Weise zu unterrichten.

§ 9
Streuung der Aktien

(1) Die zuzulassenden Aktien müssen im Publikum eines Mitgliedstaats oder mehrerer Mitgliedstaaten der Europäischen Wirtschaftsgemeinschaft oder eines Vertragsstaates des Abkommens über den Europäischen Wirtschaftsraum ausreichend gestreut sein. Sie gelten als ausreichend gestreut,

Admissions Regulation

§ 7
Admission of Securities of one Class or one Issue

(1) An application for admission of shares must relate to all shares of the same class. It may, however, be limited where shares which are not to be admitted are part of a shareholding the purpose of which is to maintain a dominant influence over the issuer or which are not to be traded for a particular period provided that no prejudice is likely to be suffered as a result of partial admission by those acquiring such shares. The prospectus (§ 13) shall point out that admission has been applied for only for a part of the shares and shall state the reasons therefor; where a prospectus is not to be published, that information shall be provided to the public by some other suitable means.

(2) An application for the admission of securities which are not shares shall relate to all securities in the same issue.

§ 8
Printing of Securities

(1) Securities shall be printed in the form of individual certificates to provide adequate protection against forgery and to ensure that they can be safely and easily handled. In the case of securities of an issuer having its principal place of business in another state of the European Economic Community or in another contracting state of the European Economic Area Treaty, it shall be sufficient to comply with the regulations relating to the printing of securities in such state.

(2) If the method used in printing securities does not provide sufficient protection against forgery, that must be disclosed in the prospectus (§13); if the prospectus is not required to be published, the public shall be informed by some other suitable means.

§ 9
Distribution of Shares

(1) Shares to be admitted must be adequately distributed to be available to the public in one or more member states of the European Economic Community or in another contracting state of the European Economic Area Treaty. They shall be considered to be sufficiently available for distribution when at

Börsenzul. Verordnung

wenn mindestens fünfundzwanzig vom Hundert des Gesamtnennbetrages, bei nennwertlosen Aktien der Stückzahl, der zuzulassenden Aktien vom Publikum erworben worden sind oder wenn wegen der großen Zahl von Aktien derselben Gattung und ihrer breiten Streuung im Publikum ein ordnungsgemäßer Börsenhandel auch mit einem niedrigeren Vomhundertsatz gewährleistet ist.

(2) Abweichend von Absatz 1 können Aktien zugelassen werden, wenn

1. eine ausreichende Streuung über die Einführung an der Börse erreicht werden soll und die Zulassungsstelle davon überzeugt ist, daß diese Streuung innerhalb kurzer Frist nach der Einführung erreicht sein wird,

2. Aktien derselben Gattung innerhalb der Europäischen Wirtschaftsgemeinschaft oder innerhalb eines Vertragsstaates des Abkommens über den Europäischen Wirtschaftsraum amtlich notiert werden und eine ausreichende Streuung im Verhältnis zur Gesamtheit aller ausgegebenen Aktien erreicht wird oder

3. die Aktien außerhalb der Europäischen Wirtschaftsgemeinschaft oder außerhalb der anderen Vertragsstaaten des Abkommens über den Europäischen Wirtschaftsraum amtlich notiert werden und eine ausreichende Streuung im Publikum derjenigen Staaten erreicht ist, in denen diese Aktien amtlich notiert werden.

§ 10

Emittenten aus Drittstaaten

Aktien eines Emittenten mit Sitz in einem Staat außerhalb der Europäischen Wirtschaftsgemeinschaft oder außerhalb der anderen Vertragsstaaten des Abkommens über den Europäischen Wirtschaftsraum, die weder in diesem Staat noch in dem Staat ihrer hauptsächlichen Verbreitung an einer Börse amtlich notiert werden, dürfen nur zugelassen werden, wenn glaubhaft gemacht wird, daß die Notierung nicht aus Gründen des Schutzes des Publikums unterblieben ist.

§ 11

Zulassung von Wertpapieren mit Umtausch- oder Bezugsrecht

(1) Wertpapiere, die den Gläubigern ein Umtausch- oder Bezugsrecht auf andere Wertpapiere einräumen, können nur zugelassen werden, wenn die Wertpapiere, auf die sich das Umtausch- oder Bezugsrecht bezieht, an einer

Admissions Regulation

least twenty five percent of the total nominal value of shares to be admitted, or in the case of shares without any nominal value the actual number, have been acquired by the public or, where by reason of the large number of shares of the same class and their wide distribution to the public, orderly trading on the stock exchange can be safeguarded on the basis of a lower percentage.

(2) Notwithstanding the provisions of sub-paragraph 1, shares may be admitted where

1. sufficient distribution is likely to be achieved by the introduction of the shares to the stock exchange, and the Listing Board is satisfied that such distribution can be achieved within a short period of time after introduction,
2. shares of the same class are officially listed within the European Economic Community or another contracting state of the European Economic Area Treaty and sufficient distribution is likely to be achieved regarding the total number of shares to be issued or
3. the shares are to be officially listed outside the European Economic Community or another contracting state of the European Economic Area Treaty and sufficient distribution to the public has been achieved in those states where the shares have been officially listed.

§ 10

Issuers from Non-EEC States

Shares of an issuer having its principal place of business in a country outside the European Economic Community or another contracting state of the European Economic Area Treaty, which are not officially listed in such state or in the state where they are mainly distributed, may only be admitted if it can be demonstrated that listing has not been withheld in order to protect the public.

§ 11

Admission of Securities with Conversion or Subscription Rights

(1) Securities which grant their holders conversion or subscription rights in relation to other securities may only be admitted if the securities to which the conversion or subscription rights obtain have already been admitted

Börsenzul. Verordnung

inländischen Börse entweder zum Handel zugelassen oder in einen anderen organisierten Markt einbezogen sind oder gleichzeitig zugelassen oder einbezogen werden.

(2) Die Zulassungsstelle kann abweichend von Absatz 1 Wertpapiere zulassen, wenn die Wertpapiere, auf die sich das Umtausch- oder Bezugsrecht bezieht, zum Handel an einem Markt im Sinne des § 2 Abs. 1 des Wertpapierhandelsgesetzes zugelassen sind und wenn sich das Publikum im Inland regelmäßig über die Kurse unterrichten kann, die sich an dem Markt im Ausland im Handel in diesen Wertpapieren bilden. Der Prospekt für die Zulassung der Wertpapiere mit Umtausch- oder Bezugsrechten muß Angaben enthalten, wie sich das Publikum im Inland regelmäßig über die Kurse im Ausland unterrichten kann.

§ 12
Zulassung von Zertifikaten, die Aktien vertreten

(1) Zertifikate, die Aktien vertreten, können zugelassen werden, wenn

1. der Emittent der vertretenen Aktien den Zulassungsantrag mitunterzeichnet hat, die Voraussetzungen nach den §§ 1 bis 3 erfüllt und sich gegenüber der Zulassungsstelle schriftlich verpflichtet, die in den §§ 44 bis 44c des Börsengesetzes und §§ 62 bis 68 dieser Verordnung genannten Pflichten des Emittenten zugelassener Aktien zu erfüllen,

2. die Zertifikate die in den §§ 4 bis 10 genannten Voraussetzungen erfüllen und

3. der Emittent der Zertifikate die Gewähr für die Erfüllung seiner Verpflichtungen gegenüber den Zertifikatsinhabern bietet.

(2) Vertreten die Zertifikate Aktien eines Emittenten mit Sitz in einem Staat außerhalb der Europäischen Wirtschaftsgemeinschaft oder außerhalb eines anderen Vertragsstaates des Abkommens über den Europäischen Wirtschaftsraum und werden die Aktien weder in diesem Staat noch in dem Staat ihrer hauptsächlichen Verbreitung an einer Börse amtlich notiert, so ist glaubhaft zu machen, daß die Notierung nicht aus Gründen des Schutzes des Publikums unterblieben ist.

Admissions Regulation

to trading on a domestic stock exchange, are included on another organised market or are simultaneously admitted or included.

(2) Notwithstanding the provisions of sub-paragraph 1, the Listing Board may admit securities if the securities to which conversion or subscription rights obtain are admitted to trading on a market according to § 2 sub-paragraph 1 of the Securities Trading Act, and the public can obtain regular information domestically as to trading prices for the securities on the foreign markets. The prospectus for admission of securities with conversion or subscription rights must contain details as to how the public in Germany can obtain regular information on the price quotations abroad.

§ 12
Admission of Certificates Representing Shares

(1) Certificates representing shares may be admitted if

1. the issuer of the shares represented has joined in signing the application for admission, has complied with the requirements of §§ 1 to 3 and has given a written undertaking to the Listing Board to comply with the obligations of an issuer of admitted shares set out in §§ 44 to 44c of the Stock Exchange Act and §§ 62 to 68 of this Regulation,
2. the certificates comply with the requirements of §§ 4 to 10 and
3. the issuer of the certificates guarantees to comply with its obligations to holders of the certificates.

(2) If the certificates represent shares of an issuer having its principal place of business in a state outside the European Economic Community or another contracting state of the European Economic Area Treaty and if the shares are neither officially listed on a stock exchange in such a state or in a state where the shares are mainly distributed, steps must be taken to demonstrate that listing has not been withheld in order to protect the public.

Börsenzul. Verordnung

Zweiter Abschnitt
Prospekt (§ 36 Abs. 3 Nr. 2 des Börsengesetzes)

Erster Unterabschnitt
Prospektinhalt

§ 13
Allgemeine Grundsätze

(1) Der Prospekt muß über die tatsächlichen und rechtlichen Verhältnisse, die für die Beurteilung der zuzulassenden Wertpapiere wesentlich sind, Auskunft geben und richtig und vollständig sein. Er muß in deutscher Sprache und in einer Form abgefaßt sein, die sein Verständnis und seine Auswertung erleichtert. Der Prospekt ist von den Antragstellern (§ 36 Abs. 2 des Börsengesetzes) zu unterzeichnen.

(2) Der Prospekt muß vorbehaltlich der Vorschriften der §§ 33 bis 42 insbesondere Angaben enthalten über

1. die Personen oder Gesellschaften, die für den Inhalt des Prospekts die Verantwortung übernehmen (§ 14);

2. die zuzulassenden Wertpapiere (§§ 15 bis 17);

3. den Emittenten der zuzulassenden Wertpapiere (§§ 18 bis 29);

4. die Prüfung der Jahresabschlüsse des Emittenten der zuzulassenden Wertpapiere und anderer Angaben im Prospekt (§ 30).

Soweit vorgeschriebene Angaben nicht der Tätigkeit oder der Rechtsform des Emittenten entsprechen, sind sie durch angepaßte gleichwertige Angaben zu ersetzen.

(3) Ist der Emittent auf Grund gesetzlicher Vorschriften zur Aufstellung eines Konzernabschlusses verpflichtet, so sind die Angaben nach den §§ 20, 29 und 37 Abs. 1 und 2 sowohl für den Emittenten als auch für den Konzern zu machen. Die Zulassungsstelle kann gestatten, daß diese Angaben nur für den Emittenten oder nur für den Konzern in den Prospekt aufgenommen werden, wenn die nicht aufzunehmenden Angaben für die Beurteilung der Wertpapiere nicht von wesentlicher Bedeutung sind.

(4) Für die Zulassung von Zertifikaten, die Aktien vertreten, muß der Prospekt neben den Angaben, die für die Zulassung von Aktien vorgeschrieben

Admissions Regulation

Part Two

Prospectus (§ 36 Part 3 No. 2 of the Stock Exchange Act)

Sub-Part One

Contents of the Prospectus

§ 13

General Provisions

(1) The prospectus shall disclose all factual and legal matters essential for the purpose of assessing the securities to be admitted and such information as is provided shall be correct and complete. It shall be provided in the German language and in a form which facilitates understanding and evaluation. The prospectus shall be signed by the applicants (§ 36 sub-paragraph 2 of the Stock Exchange Act).

(2) Subject to the provisions of §§ 33 to 42, the prospectus shall contain information especially relating to:

1. the persons or companies responsible for the contents of the prospectus (§ 14);
2. the securities to be admitted (§§ 15 to 17);
3. the issuer of the securities to be admitted (§§ 18 to 29);
4. the auditing of the annual accounts of the issuer of the securities to be admitted and other information in the prospectus (§ 30).

If the information provided for above is not relevant to the business activity or legal form of the issuer, suitably adapted information of the same nature shall be provided in its place.

(3) If the issuer is required by law to provide consolidated annual accounts, the information required under §§ 20, 29 and 37, sub-paragraphs 1 and 2 shall be given for the issuer as well as for the concern on a consolidated basis. The Listing Board may allow this information to be given in the prospectus for only the issuer or the concern if the information which is not to be given is not of material significance for the purpose of assessing the securities.

(4) In the case of the admission of certificates representing shares, the prospectus shall contain information about the certificates (§ 31) and the

Börsenzul. Verordnung

sind, auch Angaben über die Zertifikate (§ 31) und deren Aussteller (§ 32) enthalten.

(5) Sind vorgeschriebene Angaben den nach § 21 Abs. 1 Nr. 1 und § 22 Abs. 1 in den Prospekt aufgenommenen Jahresabschlüssen unmittelbar zu entnehmen, so brauchen sie im Prospekt nicht wiederholt zu werden.

§ 14

Angaben über Personen oder Gesellschaften, die für den Inhalt des Prospekts die Verantwortung übernehmen

Der Prospekt muß Namen und Stellung, bei juristischen Personen oder Gesellschaften Firma und Sitz, der Personen oder Gesellschaften aufführen, die für den Inhalt des Prospekts die Verantwortung übernehmen; er muß eine Erklärung dieser Personen oder Gesellschaften enthalten, daß ihres Wissens die Angaben richtig und keine wesentlichen Umstände ausgelassen sind.

§ 15

Allgemeine Angaben über die Wertpapiere

(1) Der Prospekt muß über die Wertpapiere angeben

1. die Beschlüsse, Ermächtigungen, Genehmigungen und Eintragungen in das Handelsregister, welche die Grundlage für die Ausstellung und Ausgabe der Wertpapiere bilden;

2. die Art, Stückzahl und Nummern der Wertpapiere sowie den Gesamtnennbetrag der Emission oder einen Hinweis darauf, daß er nicht festgesetzt ist;

3. die Steuern, die in dem Staat, in dem der Emittent seinen Sitz hat oder in dem die Wertpapiere zur amtlichen Notierung zugelassen werden, auf die Einkünfte aus den Wertpapieren im Wege des Quellenabzugs erhoben werden; übernimmt der Emittent die Zahlung dieser Steuern, so ist dies anzugeben;

4. wie die Wertpapiere übertragen werden können und gegebenenfalls in welcher Weise ihre freie Handelbarkeit eingeschränkt ist;

5. die Börsen, bei denen ein Antrag auf Zulassung zur amtlichen Notierung gestellt worden ist oder noch gestellt werden wird sowie die Börsen, an denen Wertpapiere derselben Gattung bereits amtlich notiert werden;

issuer of the certificates (§ 32) in addition to providing the information required for the admission of shares.

(5) If the information prescribed under § 21 sub-paragraph 1 No.1 and § 22 sub-paragraph 1 is directly available from the annual accounts contained in the prospectus, it need not be repeated in the prospectus.

§ 14
Information on Persons or Companies Responsible for the Contents of the Prospectus

The prospectus shall state the names and positions or for legal entities or companies, the name and principal place of business of the persons or companies assuming responsibility for the contents of the prospectus; it shall contain a declaration by such persons or companies that to the best of their knowledge the information given is correct and no material information was omitted.

§ 15
General Information about the Securities

(1) The prospectus must contain the following information concerning the securities:

1. the resolutions, authorizations, approvals and entries in the commercial register on the basis of which the securities have come into existence and are issued;
2. the nature, number of units and numbers of the securities, and the total nominal value of the issue or a statement that this has not been determined;
3. the taxes to be withheld at source from the income derived from the securities in the country where the issuer has its principal place of business or where the securities are to be admitted for official listing; if the issuer undertakes to pay such taxes, a statement to that effect must be included;
4. the manner in which the securities are to be transferred and, if applicable, any restrictions on their free negotiability;
5. the stock exchanges where an application for admission to official listing has been or is to be made, and the stock exchanges where securities of the

Börsenzul. Verordnung

werden Wertpapiere derselben Gattung an anderen organisierten Märkten gehandelt, so sind diese Märkte anzugeben;

6. die Zahl- und Hinterlegungsstellen;
7. die einzelnen Teilbeträge, falls die Emission gleichzeitig in verschiedenen Staaten mit bestimmten Teilbeträgen ausgegeben oder untergebracht wird;
8. die Einzelheiten der Zahlung des Zeichnungs- oder Verkaufspreises, bei nicht voll eingezahlten Aktien auch der Leistung der Einlage;
9. das Verfahren für die Ausübung von Bezugsrechten, ihre Handelbarkeit und die Behandlung der nicht ausgeübten Bezugsrechte;
10. die Stellen, die Zeichnungen des Publikums entgegennehmen, sowie die für die Zeichnung oder den Verkauf der Wertpapiere vorgesehene Frist und die Möglichkeiten, die Zeichnung vorzeitig zu schließen oder Zeichnungen zu kürzen; dies gilt nicht für Schuldverschreibungen, die während einer längeren Dauer ausgegeben werden;
11. die Ausstattung ausgedruckter Stücke sowie die Einzelheiten und Fristen für deren Auslieferung, gegebenenfalls auch von Zwischenscheinen und anderen Urkunden einer vorübergehenden Verbriefung;
12. die Personen oder Gesellschaften, welche die gesamte Emission vom Emittenten übernehmen oder übernommen oder gegenüber dem Emittenten ihre Unterbringung garantiert haben; erstreckt sich die Übernahme oder die Garantie nicht auf die gesamte Emission, so ist der nicht erfaßte Teil der Emission anzugeben;
13. den Nettoerlös der Emission für den Emittenten, ausgenommen bei Schuldverschreibungen, die während einer längeren Dauer ausgegeben werden, sowie den vorgesehenen Verwendungszweck des Emissionserlöses;
14. die Wertpapier-Kenn-Nummer.

(2) Für die Zulassung von Aktien sind die Angaben nach Absatz 1 Nr. 7 bis 13 nur erforderlich, wenn die Ausgabe und Unterbringung der Aktien gleichzeitig mit der Zulassung stattfindet oder nicht länger als zwölf Monate vor der Zulassung stattgefunden hat.

(3) Für die Zulassung von anderen Wertpapieren als Aktien sind die Angaben nach Absatz 1 Nr. 8 bis 10 und 13 nur erforderlich, wenn die Ausgabe und Unterbringung der Wertpapiere gleichzeitig mit der Zulassung stattfindet oder nicht länger als drei Monate vor der Zulassung stattgefunden hat.

same class have already been officially listed; if securities of the same class being traded on other organised markets, such markets shall be identified;

6. the paying and depository agents;
7. the individual portions of the issue if the issue is taking place simultaneously in various states where individual portions are being issued or placed;
8. details of payment of the subscription or selling price, or for partially-paid shares, the amount of the capital contribution;
9. the procedure for exercising subscription rights, their negotiability and the way in which unexercised subscription rights are treated;
10. the offices where subscriptions from the public are accepted, the intended period of time for subscription or sale of the securities, and information about any rights to foreshorten the subscription period or to reduce subscriptions; this shall not apply to bonds issued over an extended period of time;
11. the getup of the printed certificates, details and time periods applicable to delivery of the same, and, if applicable, the same details for interim certificates and other documents temporarily representing the securities;
12. the persons or companies which are subscribing to the whole issue or have subscribed to the issue or have guaranteed placement of the issue; if the underwriting or guarantee does not extend to the whole of the issue, details of the portion not included shall be given;
13. the net proceeds of the issue for the issuer, except in the case of bonds issued over an extended period of time, as well as the intended purpose of the net proceeds;
14. the securities identification number.

(2) For the admission of shares, the information referred to in sub-paragraph 1 Nos. 7 to 13 is required only if the shares are issued and placed at the same time as they are admitted or no later than twelve months before they are admitted.

(3) For the admission of securities other than shares, the information referred to in sub-paragraph 1 Nos. 8 to 10 and No. 13 is required only if the securities are issued and placed at the same time as they are admitted or no later than three months before they are admitted.

Börsenzul. Verordnung

§ 16
Besondere Angaben über Aktien

(1) Für die Zulassung von Aktien muß der Prospekt zusätzlich folgendes angeben:

1. Angabe, ob die Aktien bereits untergebracht sind oder ob sie durch Einführung an der Börse im Publikum untergebracht werden sollen;

2. die Merkmale der Aktien, insbesondere den Nennbetrag je Aktie, bei nennwertlosen Aktien den rechnerischen Wert, die genaue Bezeichnung oder Gattung und die beigefügten Gewinnanteilscheine;

3. die mit den Aktien verbundenen Rechte, insbesondere das Stimmrecht, den Anspruch auf Beteiligung am Gewinn und am Erlös aus einer Liquidation sowie alle Vorrechte;

4. den Beginn der Dividendenberechtigung sowie die Verfallfrist für den Dividendenbezug unter Hinweis darauf, zu wessen Gunsten die Dividenden verfallen;

5. den Zeichnungs- oder Verkaufspreis, den Gesamtnennbetrag, bei nennwertlosen Aktien den rechnerischen Wert oder den dem gezeichneten Kapital gutgeschriebenen Betrag, sowie ein Emissionsagio und die offen auf Zeichner oder Käufer abgewälzten Kosten;

6. Auskunft über die Ausübung der Bezugsrechte der Aktionäre sowie über die Beschränkung oder den Ausschluß der Bezugsrechte unter Angabe der Gründe und der Personen, zugunsten deren die Bezugsrechte beschränkt oder ausgeschlossen wurden; bei Beschränkung oder Ausschluß der Bezugsrechte ist im Falle der Ausgabe von Aktien gegen Bareinlagen der Ausgabepreis zu begründen;

7. den Gesamtnennbetrag und die Zahl der untergebrachten Aktien, gegebenenfalls nach Gattungen getrennt;

8. den Betrag oder die Veranschlagung der Emissionskosten insgesamt oder pro Aktie, wobei die Gesamtvergütungen einschließlich der Provisionen der an der Durchführung der Emission beteiligten Personen und Gesellschaften gesondert auszuweisen sind;

9. die öffentlichen Kauf- oder Umtauschangebote für Aktien des Emittenten durch Dritte sowie die öffentlichen Umtauschangebote des Emittenten für Aktien anderer Gesellschaften im laufenden und im vorhergehenden Geschäftsjahr unter Angabe des Preises oder der Umtauschbedingungen und des Ergebnisses der Angebote;

Admissions Regulation

§ 16
Specific Information concerning Shares

(1) For the admission of shares, the prospectus must contain the following additional information:

1. a statement whether the shares have already been placed or whether it is intended that they be publicly placed by being introduced on the stock exchange;

2. the characteristics of the shares, in particular the nominal value per share or in the case of shares having no nominal value their calculated value, the exact designation or class of the shares and any profit participation certificates attaching to them;

3. any rights attaching to the shares, in particular voting rights, the right to a share of profit or any dividend arising out of liquidation, and any preferential rights;

4. the date when the entitlement to dividends begins, the statute of limitations when the payment of dividends are forfeited, and a note as to the persons to whom dividends so forfeited are to be paid;

5. the subscription or selling price, the total nominal value or in the case of shares with no nominal value their calculated value or amount credited to subscription capital, any issuing premium and any costs passed on to the subscriber or purchaser;

6. information as to the exercise of subscription rights of shareholders, any limitation or exclusion of subscription rights, information as to the reasons therefor and the identity of the persons for whose benefit such rights are limited or excluded; in the case of a limitation or exclusion of subscription rights, an explanation of the issue price must be given where shares are issued for cash;

7. the total nominal value and the number of shares placed, categorized by class, if appropriate;

8. the amount or an estimate of the issue costs expressed either in total or by share, such that all fees including commissions of any persons or companies involved in placing the issue are listed separately;

9. the public purchase or exchange offers for shares of the issuer by third parties, as well as the public exchange offers of the issuer for shares of other corporations in the current and preceding financial year, and infor-

Börsenzul. Verordnung

10. die Stellen, bei denen die Unterlagen für das Publikum einzusehen sind, aus denen die Einzelheiten der Verschmelzung, der Spaltung, der Einbringung der Gesamtheit oder eines Teils des Vermögens eines Unternehmens, des öffentlichen Umtauschangebots oder der Einbringung von Sacheinlagen ersichtlich sind, falls die Aktien aus einem dieser Anlässe ausgegeben worden sind;

11. den Zeitpunkt, von dem ab die Aktien amtlich notiert werden, soweit er bekannt ist;

12. die Zahl der dem Markt zur Verfügung gestellten Stücke und deren Nennbetrag, bei nennwertlosen Aktien ihr rechnerischer Wert, oder der Gesamtnennbetrag und gegebenenfalls der Ausgabepreis, wenn die Aktien durch Einführung an der Börse im Publikum untergebracht werden sollen;

13. die Zahl und Merkmale der Aktien derselben Gattung wie die zuzulassenden Aktien oder Aktien anderer Gattungen, die gleichzeitig mit der Ausgabe der zuzulassenden Aktien öffentlich oder nichtöffentlich gezeichnet oder untergebracht werden, unter Angabe des Vorgangs.

(2) Die Angaben nach Absatz 1 Nr. 6 bis 8 sind nur erforderlich, wenn die Ausgabe und Unterbringung der zuzulassenden Aktien gleichzeitig mit der Zulassung stattfindet oder nicht länger als zwölf Monate vor der Zulassung stattgefunden hat.

§ 17
Besondere Angaben über andere Wertpapiere als Aktien

Für die Zulassung von anderen Wertpapieren als Aktien muß der Prospekt zusätzlich angeben

1. die Stückelung der Wertpapiere;

2. den Ausgabepreis, ausgenommen bei Schuldverschreibungen, die während einer längeren Dauer ausgegeben werden, den Rückzahlungspreis und den Nominalzinssatz; sind mehrere Zinssätze vorgesehen, so sind die Bedingungen für den Wechsel des Zinssatzes anzugeben;

3. die Bedingungen für die Gewährung anderer Vorteile und deren Berechnung;

4. die Art der Tilgung der Wertpapiere einschließlich des Rückzahlungsverfahrens;

5. die Währung der Wertpapiere und sich hierauf beziehende Wahlmöglich-

Admissions Regulation

mation as to the price or conditions of exchange and the results of the offers;

10. the offices where the public can examine documents giving details of any merger, split, acquisition of all or part of the assets of a company, public exchange offer or contribution in kind for shares issued by reason of one of the foregoing;

11. the date when the shares are to be officially listed, if known;

12. the total number of shares available on the market, the nominal value, or for shares not having a nominal value their calculated value, or the total nominal value or issue price, if applicable, if the shares are to be publicly placed by being introduced on the stock exchange;

13. the number and characteristics of shares of the same class as the shares to be admitted or shares of other classes which are being subscribed or placed publicly or privately at the same time as the issue of the shares to be admitted, with details on the transaction.

(2) The information referred to in sub-paragraph 1 Nos. 6 to 8 is required only if the shares are issued and placed at the same time as they are admitted or no later than twelve months before the admission takes place.

§ 17

Specific Information concerning Securities Other than Shares

For the admission of securities other than shares the prospectus must contain, in addition, the following information:

1. the denomination of the securities;

2. the issue price, except in the case of bonds issued over an extended period of time, the redemption price and nominal interest rate; if more than one interest rate is anticipated, the criteria for a change in the applicable interest rate shall also be given;

3. any conditions applicable to the granting of any other benefits and the method of calculation thereof;

4. the method of redeeming the securities including the repayment procedures;

5. the currency of the securities and any applicable options; where secur-

Börsenzul. Verordnung

keiten; lauten die Wertpapiere auf Rechnungseinheiten, so ist deren vertragliche Regelung anzugeben;

6. die Laufzeit der Wertpapiere und alle zwischenzeitlichen Fälligkeitstermine;

7. den Beginn der Verzinsung und die Zinstermine;

8. die Fristen für die Vorlegung der Wertpapiere und Zinsscheine sowie für die Verjährung der Ansprüche auf Zinsen und Rückzahlung;

9. die Rendite und Methode ihrer Berechnung, sofern es sich nicht um Schuldverschreibungen handelt, die während einer längeren Dauer ausgegeben werden;

10. die Art und den Umfang der Gewährleistungsverträge zur Sicherung der Verzinsung und Rückzahlung der Wertpapiere und die Stellen, bei denen die Verträge hierüber vom Publikum einzusehen sind;

11. die Einsetzung eines Treuhänders oder eines Vertreters der Gesamtheit der Gläubiger, Name und Stellung oder Bezeichnung und Sitz des Treuhänders oder Vertreters, die wichtigsten Aufgaben und Befugnisse, die Regelungen für einen Wechsel in der Person des Treuhänders oder Vertreters und die Stellen, bei denen die Verträge über die Treuhand oder Vertretung vom Publikum einzusehen sind;

12. die Bestimmungen über eine Nachrangigkeit der Wertpapiere gegenüber anderen schon bestehenden oder künftigen Verbindlichkeiten des Emittenten;

13. die Rechtsordnung, nach der die Wertpapiere ausgegeben worden sind, das anwendbare Recht und den Gerichtsstand.

§ 18

Allgemeine Angaben über den Emittenten

Der Prospekt muß über den Emittenten angeben

1. die Firma, den Sitz und, wenn sich die Hauptverwaltung nicht am Sitz befindet, den Ort der Hauptverwaltung, die Zweigniederlassungen sowie das Geschäftsjahr;

2. das Datum der Gründung und, wenn er für eine bestimmte Zeit gegründet ist, die Dauer;

ities are issued in units of account, the contractual provisions in respect thereof shall be set out;
6. the maturity period of the securities, together with any intermediate maturity dates;
7. the date from which interest begins to accrue and the dates of payment of interest;
8. any time periods applicable to the presentation of the securities and interest certificates and the statute of limitations on claims for interest or repayment;
9. the yields and method of calculation, except in the case of bonds issued over an extended period of time;
10. the nature and extent of any guarantees securing the payment of interest and the repayment of the securities, together with details of the offices at which such guarantees may be examined by the public;
11. the appointment of a trustee or a representative of the whole body of creditors, the name and position or designation and principal place of business of such trustee or representative of such trustee, and information on the trustee's principal obligations and powers, the provisions for changing the trustee or representative and information on the offices where the trust deeds or representation deeds may be examined by the public;
12. any provisions relating to any subordination of the securities to any existing or future obligations of the issuer;
13. the legal provisions pursuant to which the securities are issued, the applicable law and the relevant venue governing any proceedings.

§ 18
General Information about the Issuer

The prospectus must give the following information in respect to the issuer:
1. the name of the company, principal place of business and, when its headquarters are not at the principal place of business, the location of its corporate headquarters, any branches, and its financial year;
2. date of incorporation and, where the issuer is incorporated for a fixed period, the duration;

Börsenzul. Verordnung

3. die Rechtsform und die für den Emittenten maßgebliche Rechtsordnung;
4. den in der Satzung oder im Gesellschaftsvertrag bestimmten Gegenstand des Unternehmens;
5. das Registergericht des Sitzes des Emittenten und die Nummer, unter der der Emittent in das Register eingetragen ist;
6. die Stelle, bei der die im Prospekt genannten Unterlagen, die den Emittenten betreffen, einzusehen sind;
7. eine kurze Beschreibung des Konzerns und der Stellung des Emittenten in ihm, falls der Emittent ein Konzernunternehmen ist.

§ 19
Angaben über das Kapital des Emittenten

(1) Der Prospekt muß über das Kapital des Emittenten angeben

1. die Höhe des gezeichneten Kapitals, die Zahl und Gattungen der Anteile, in die das Kapital zerlegt ist, unter Angabe ihrer Hauptmerkmale, die Höhe der ausstehenden Einlagen auf das gezeichnete Kapital unter Angabe der Zahl oder des Gesamtnennbetrages und der Art der Anteile, auf die noch Einlagen ausstehen, aufgeschlüsselt nach dem Grad ihrer Einzahlung;
2. den Nennbetrag der umlaufenden Wertpapiere, die den Gläubigern ein Umtausch- oder Bezugsrecht auf Aktien einräumen, unter Angabe der Bedingungen und des Verfahrens für den Umtausch oder Bezug;
3. die Zahl, den Buchwert und den Nennbetrag, bei nennwertlosen Aktien den rechnerischen Wert, der eigenen Aktien, die vom Emittenten oder einer Gesellschaft, an welcher der Emittent unmittelbar oder mittelbar mit einer Mehrheit der Anteile oder Stimmrechte beteiligt ist, erworben wurden und im Bestand gehalten werden, sofern die Bilanz sie nicht gesondert ausweist; für die Zulassung von Schuldverschreibungen sind diese Angaben nur erforderlich, wenn die eigenen Aktien mehr als fünf vom Hundert des gezeichneten Kapitals erreichen.

(2) Für die Zulassung von Aktien ist zusätzlich anzugeben

1. der Nennbetrag eines genehmigten oder bedingten Kapitals und die Dauer der Ermächtigung für die Kapitalerhöhung, der Kreis der Personen, die ein Umtausch- oder Bezugsrecht haben, sowie die Bedingungen und das Verfahren für die Ausgabe der neuen Aktien;

Admissions Regulation

3. the legal form of and law applicable to the issuer;
4. the objects of the company as they appear in its memorandum of association;
5. the court where the issuer is registered and the number under which the issuer is entered in the register;
6. the office where any documents relating to the issuer referred to in the prospectus may be examined;
7. if the issuer is part of a concern, a brief description and the status of the issuer within it.

§ 19
Information concerning the Capital of the Issuer

(1) The prospectus must contain the following information relating to the capital of the issuer:

1. the amount of the subscribed capital, the number and classes of shares into which the capital is divided, the principal characteristics thereof, the amount of unpaid capital in relation to subscribed capital, details of the total nominal capital and the nature of any shares not paid in full broken down by the proportion of paid to unpaid;
2. the nominal value of any securities in circulation which give their holders a right to conversion or subscription for shares, details concerning the conditions and procedure applicable to such conversion or subscription;
3. the number, book value and nominal value, or in the case of shares having no nominal value, the calculated value of any own shares purchased and held by the issuer or by any company, a majority of the shares or voting rights of which are held directly or indirectly by the issuer, except when such information is specifically available from the issuer's accounts; for the admission of bonds, this information is only required where any own-shares held represent more than five percent of the subscribed capital.

(2) In addition, for the admission of shares, the following information is to be provided:

1. the nominal value of any approved or conditional capital and the duration of the authorization applicable to any capital increase, information concerning any persons having conversion or subscription rights, and information concerning the conditions and procedures for application for the issue of new shares;

Börsenzul. Verordnung

2. die Zahl und Hauptmerkmale von Anteilen, die keinen Anteil am Kapital gewähren;

3. Bestimmungen der Satzung für eine Änderung des gezeichneten Kapitals und der mit den verschiedenen Aktiengattungen verbundenen Rechte, soweit die Bestimmungen von den gesetzlichen Vorschriften abweichen;

4. eine kurze Beschreibung der Vorgänge, welche die Höhe des gezeichneten Kapitals sowie die Zahl und die Gattungen der Aktien in den letzten drei Jahren verändert haben;

5. soweit sie dem Emittenten bekannt sind,

   a) die Personen oder Gesellschaften, deren unmittelbare oder mittelbare Beteiligung am gezeichneten Kapital des Emittenten mindestens fünf vom Hundert beträgt oder denen unmittelbar oder mittelbar mindestens fünf vom Hundert der Stimmrechte zustehen;

   b) die Personen oder Gesellschaften, die auf den Emittenten unmittelbar oder mittelbar einen beherrschenden Einfluß ausüben können, sowie die Anteile des gezeichneten Kapitals, die ihnen unmittelbar oder mittelbar Stimmrechte gewähren; dies gilt auch dann, wenn mehrere Personen oder Gesellschaften eine Vereinbarung getroffen haben, die es ihnen ermöglicht, gemeinsam einen beherrschenden Einfluß auf den Emittenten auszuüben.

§ 20

Angaben über die Geschäftstätigkeit des Emittenten

(1) Der Prospekt muß über die Geschäftstätigkeit des Emittenten folgende Angaben enthalten:

1. die wichtigsten Tätigkeitsbereiche unter Angabe der wichtigsten Arten der Erzeugnisse und Dienstleistungen; neue Erzeugnisse und Tätigkeiten sind auszuführen, wenn sie von Bedeutung sind;

2. die Umsatzerlöse im Sinne der für die Rechnungslegung geltenden handelsrechtlichen Vorschriften für die letzten drei, für die Zulassung von Schuldverschreibungen für die letzten zwei Geschäftsjahre;

3. den Standort und die Bedeutung solcher Betriebe des Emittenten, die jeweils mehr als zehn vom Hundert zum Umsatz oder zu den erzeugten Gütern oder erbrachten Dienstleistungen beitragen, sowie kurze Angaben über den bebauten und den unbebauten Grundbesitz;

Admissions Regulation

2. the number and principal characteristics of other issues which have no capital participation;

3. details of any provisions in the memorandum and articles of association relating to any variation in the authorized capital and the rights of the holders of shares of various classes in relation thereto as far as such provisions deviate from the legal norm;

4. a short description of any steps taken to vary the authorized capital or the number and classes of shares within the last three years;

5. as far as the issuer is aware, details of

   a) any person or company holding, directly or indirectly, at least five percent of the issuer's authorized capital or controlling, directly or indirectly, at least five percent of voting rights;

   b) any person or company able to exercise, whether directly or indirectly, a dominant influence over the issuer, the proportion of the authorized capital which gives such person or company voting rights, directly or indirectly, the same applies when a number of persons or companies have entered into an agreement making it possible for them to jointly exercise a dominant influence over the issuer.

§ 20

Information concerning the Business Activities of the Issuer

(1) The prospectus shall contain the following information concerning the business activities of the issuer:

1. the principal areas of business activities, information about the issuer's principal types of products and services; new products and types of business are also to be described if they are significant;

2. turnover applicable for accounting purposes for the last three financial years or for bond admissions, the last two financial years;

3. the locations and importance of any operations of the issuer which account for more than ten per cent of turnover, goods produced or services provided, brief details of any property, developed or undeveloped;

Börsenzul. Verordnung

4. bei Bergwerken, Öl- und Erdgasvorkommen, Steinbrüchen und ähnlichen Tätigkeitsbereichen, soweit sie von Bedeutung sind, eine Beschreibung der Lagerstätten, die Schätzung der wirtschaftlich nutzbaren Vorräte und die voraussichtliche Nutzungsdauer, die Dauer, die wesentlichen Bedingungen der Abbaurechte und die Bedingungen für deren wirtschaftliche Nutzung sowie den Stand der Erschließung;

5. Angaben über die Abhängigkeit des Emittenten von Patenten, Lizenzen, Verträgen oder neuen Herstellungsverfahren, wenn sie von wesentlicher Bedeutung für die Geschäftstätigkeit oder Rentabilität des Emittenten sind;

6. Gerichts- oder Schiedsverfahren, die einen erheblichen Einfluß auf die wirtschaftliche Lage des Emittenten haben können oder in den letzten zwei Geschäftsjahren gehabt haben,

7. Angaben über die Investitionen:

a) Zahlenangaben über die wichtigsten in den letzten drei Geschäftsjahren und im laufenden Geschäftsjahr vorgenommenen Investitionen einschließlich der Finanzanlagen;

b) Angaben über die wichtigsten laufenden Investitionen, mit Ausnahme der Finanzanlagen, mit Angaben über die geographische Verteilung dieser Investitionen (In- und Ausland) und über die Art ihrer Finanzierung (Eigen- oder Fremdfinanzierung);

c) Angaben über die wichtigsten vom Emittenten beschlossenen künftigen Investitionen mit Ausnahme der Finanzanlagen.

(2) Sind die Angaben nach Absatz 1 Nr. 1 bis 4 durch außergewöhnliche Ereignisse beeinflußt worden, so ist darauf hinzuweisen.

(3) Für die Zulassung von Aktien sind die Umsatzerlöse (Absatz 1 Nr. 2) nach Tätigkeitsbereichen sowie nach geographisch bestimmten Märkten aufzugliedern, soweit sich, unter Berücksichtigung der Organisation des Verkaufs von für die gewöhnliche Geschäftstätigkeit des Unternehmens typischen Erzeugnissen und der für die gewöhnliche Geschäftstätigkeit des Unternehmens typischen Dienstleistungen, die Tätigkeitsbereiche und geographisch bestimmten Märkte untereinander erheblich unterscheiden. Zusätzlich sind anzugeben

1. die durchschnittliche Zahl der Arbeitnehmer, möglichst nach Haupttätigkeitsbereichen aufgeschlüsselt, und ihre Entwicklung während der letzten drei Geschäftsjahre, wenn diese Entwicklung von Bedeutung ist;

Admissions Regulation

4. for mines, oil and gas resources, quarries and similar areas of operation where they are significant, details of deposits, an estimate of the economically available reserves, their prospective life span and any significant conditions attaching to any mineral rights or the extent to which they can be exploited, and information concerning the present state of development;

5. information concerning the extent to which the issuer is dependent on patents, licences, contracts or new manufacturing processes if these are of substantial significance to the business or profitability of the issuer;

6. details of any litigation or arbitration proceedings which could have a significant effect on the financial position of the issuer or may have done so in the last two financial years;

7. information concerning investments:

   a) figures relating to the most significant investments undertaken during the last three financial years and in the course of the current financial year, including details of financial assets;

   b) information concerning the most significant current investments with the exception of financial assets, information concerning the geographical spread of such investments (domestic and foreign) and the manner of their financing (equity or debt financing);

   c) information concerning the most significant future investments which the issuer has decided upon with the exception of financial asset investments.

(2) If any of the information referred to in sub-paragraph (1) Nos. 1 to 4 has been affected by any exceptional circumstances, explanatory information shall be provided.

(3) For the admission of shares, turnover (sub-paragraph 1 No.2) shall be broken down by individual areas of operation, as well as by geographically defined markets where, regarding the organisation of the sale of products which are typical for the ordinary conduct of business and the services provided which are typical for the ordinary conduct of business by the enterprise concerned, there are material differences between such areas of operation and such geographically defined markets. In addition, information shall be given concerning:

1. the average number of employees, broken down, if possible, by principal areas of operation and the developments thereof during the last three financial years if such developments are significant;

Börsenzul. Verordnung

2. Tätigkeiten auf dem Gebiet der Forschung und Entwicklung neuer Erzeugnisse und Verfahren während der letzten drei Geschäftsjahre, wenn diese Angaben von Bedeutung sind;

3. Unterbrechungen der Geschäftstätigkeit des Emittenten, die einen erheblichen Einfluß auf seine Finanzlage haben können oder in den letzten zwei Geschäftsjahren gehabt haben.

§ 21

Angaben über die Vermögens-, Finanz- und Ertragslage des Emittenten

(1) Der Prospekt muß über die Vermögens-, Finanz- und Ertragslage des Emittenten enthalten

1. die Bilanzen und Gewinn- und Verlustrechnungen des Emittenten einschließlich der Angaben, die statt in der Bilanz oder Gewinn- und Verlustrechnung im Anhang gemacht werden, für die letzten drei Geschäftsjahre in der Form einer vergleichenden Darstellung sowie den Anhang des letzten Geschäftsjahres (§ 22); für die Zulassung von Schuldverschreibungen muß sich die vergleichende Darstellung nur auf die letzten zwei Geschäftsjahre erstrecken;

2. eine Aufstellung über die Herkunft und Verwendung der Mittel für die letzten drei Geschäftsjahre (§ 23);

3. Einzelangaben über Unternehmen, an denen der Emittent Anteile besitzt (§ 24).

(2) Für die Zulassung von Aktien sind zusätzlich anzugeben:

1. das Ergebnis je Aktie für die letzten drei Geschäftsjahre (§ 25);

2. der Betrag der Dividende je Aktie für die letzten drei Geschäftsjahre (§ 25 Abs. 2).

(3) Für die Zulassung von Schuldverschreibungen sind zusätzlich der Gesamtbetrag der noch zurückzuzahlenden Anleihen, der Gesamtbetrag aller sonstigen Kreditaufnahmen und Verbindlichkeiten und der Gesamtbetrag der Eventualverbindlichkeiten zu einem möglichst zeitnahen und im Prospekt zu nennenden Stichtag anzugeben (§ 27); bestehen keine solchen Anleihen, Kreditaufnahmen oder Verbindlichkeiten, so ist im Prospekt hierauf hinzuweisen.

2. the research and development of new products and processes during the last three financial years, if such information is of significance;
3. any interruptions to the business operation of the issuer which could have a material effect on its financial position or have had such an effect in the last two financial years.

§ 21

Information about Net Worth, Financial Position and Results of the Issuer

(1) The prospectus shall contain the following information about the net worth, financial position and results of the issuer:

1. balance sheets and profit and loss accounts of the issuer including any information appearing in appendices instead of in the balance sheets and profit and loss accounts for the last three financial years, in the form of a comparative presentation, together with the appendices for the last financial year (§ 22); for the admission of bonds the comparative presentation need only deal with the last two financial years;
2. a statement about the source and application of funds for the last three financial years (§ 23);
3. detailed information about any enterprises in which the issuer holds shares (§ 24).

(2) For the admission of shares, additional information is to be given:

1. the net earnings per share for the last three financial years (§ 25);
2. the amount of dividends per share for the last three financial years (§ 25 sub-paragraph 2).

(3) In addition, for the admission of bonds, information shall be given on the total amount of bonds to be repaid, the total amount of all other borrowings and liabilities, and the total amount of contingent liabilities for the most recent possible date (§ 27); if there are no such bonds, borrowings or liabilities, a note to that effect shall appear in the prospectus.

Börsenzul. Verordnung

§ 22

Angaben aus der Rechnungslegung des Emittenten

(1) Ist der Emittent nur zur Aufstellung von Konzernabschlüssen verpflichtet, so sind sie gemäß § 21 Abs. 1 Nr. 1 in den Prospekt aufzunehmen; ist er auch zur Aufstellung von Einzelabschlüssen verpflichtet, so sind beide Arten von Jahresabschlüssen aufzunehmen. Die Zulassungsstelle kann dem Emittenten gestatten, nur Jahresabschlüsse der einen Art aufzunehmen, wenn die Jahresabschlüsse der anderen Art keine wesentlichen zusätzlichen Aussagen enthalten.

(2) Der Stichtag des letzten veröffentlichten Jahresabschlusses darf im Zeitpunkt des Antrags auf Zulassung zur amtlichen Notierung nicht länger als achtzehn Monate zurückliegen. In Ausnahmefällen kann die Zulassungsstelle diese Frist verlängern. Liegt der Stichtag des letzten in den Prospekt aufgenommenen Jahresabschlusses mehr als neun Monate zurück, so ist eine Zwischenübersicht für mindestens die ersten sechs Monate des laufenden Geschäftsjahres in den Prospekt aufzunehmen oder ihm beizufügen. Wurde diese Zwischenübersicht nicht geprüft, so ist dies anzugeben. Stellt der Emittent Konzernabschlüsse auf, so entscheidet die Zulassungsstelle, ob die Zwischenübersicht für den Konzern vorzulegen ist.

(3) Jede wesentliche Änderung nach Abschluß des letzten Geschäftsjahres oder nach dem Stichtag der Zwischenübersicht muß im Prospekt beschrieben werden.

(4) Entsprechen bei einem Emittenten mit Sitz außerhalb der Europäischen Wirtschaftsgemeinschaft oder außerhalb eines anderen Vertragsstaates des Abkommens über den Europäischen Wirtschaftsraum die Jahresabschlüsse nicht den Vorschriften im Geltungsbereich dieser Verordnung über den Jahresabschluß und den Lagebericht von Gesellschaften und geben sie kein den tatsächlichen Verhältnissen entsprechendes Bild von der Vermögens-, Finanz- und Ertragslage des Emittenten, so sind in den Prospekt ergänzende Angaben hierzu aufzunehmen.

§ 23

Aufstellung über die Herkunft und Verwendung der Mittel

Die Aufstellung gemäß § 21 Abs. 1 Nr. 2 hat als Bewegungsbilanz die Bilanzentwicklung im jeweiligen Berichtsjahr unter dem Gesichtspunkt der Mittelherkunft (Minderungen auf der Aktivseite und Mehrungen auf der Passivseite) und Mittelverwendung (Mehrungen auf der Aktivseite und Min-

Admissions Regulation

§ 22

Information about the Accounting Principles of the Issuer

(1) If the issuer is only obliged to prepare consolidated accounts, these shall be included in the prospectus in accordance with § 21 sub-paragraph 1 No.1; if the issuer is also obliged to prepare individual accounts, both types of accounts shall be included. The Listing Board may allow the issuer to include only one type of account if the other type does not provide material additional information.

(2) The closing date of the latest published annual accounts may not be longer than eighteen months before the time of application for admission to official listing. In exceptional cases, the Listing Board may extend this period. If the closing date for the last annual accounts included in the prospectus dates back more than nine months, then interim accounts for the period covering at least the first six months of the current financial year shall be included in the prospectus or shall be attached thereto. If such interim accounts are not audited, this shall be stated. If the issuer prepares consolidated accounts, the Listing Board shall decide whether consolidated interim accounts need to be presented.

(3) Any significant changes since the end of the last financial year or since the closing date of the interim accounts must be described in the prospectus.

(4) If the accounts of an issuer having its principal place of business outside the European Economic Community or another contracting state of the European Economic Area Treaty do not conform to the provisions applicable in the territory where this Regulation applies concerning accounts and management report of companies and if they do not give a true and fair view of the state of the net worth, financial position and results of the issuer, supplementary information shall be included in the prospectus.

§ 23

Information about the Source and Application of Funds

The information to be provided under § 21 sub-paragraph 1 No.2 shall indicate the manner in which funds have been applied, reflecting any changes in the balance sheet during the relevant financial year, having regard to the sources (decreases in assets and increases in liabilities) and applications (increases in assets and decreases in liabilities) of funds or in the form of

Börsenzul. Verordnung

derungen auf der Passivseite) oder in Form einer Finanzflußrechnung aufzuzeigen. Dabei sind die wesentlichen Positionen der Veränderungen einzeln und unsaldiert auszuweisen.

§ 24
Angaben über Beteiligungsunternehmen

(1) Über Unternehmen, an denen der Emittent unmittelbar oder mittelbar Anteile hält, deren Buchwert mindestens zehn vom Hundert seines Eigenkapitals beträgt oder die mit mindestens zehn vom Hundert zu seinem Jahresergebnis beitragen oder, falls der Emittent ein Konzernunternehmen ist, deren Buchwert mindestens zehn vom Hundert des konsolidierten Eigenkapitals darstellt oder die mit mindestens zehn vom Hundert zum konsolidierten Jahresergebnis des Konzerns beitragen, sind folgende Angaben in den Prospekt aufzunehmen:

1. Firma, Sitz und Tätigkeitsbereich;
2. Höhe des gezeichneten Kapitals und, sofern das Unternehmen seine Jahresabschlüsse veröffentlicht, Höhe der Rücklagen und den Jahresüberschuß oder Jahresfehlbetrag des Unternehmens;
3. Höhe der Anteile des Emittenten am gezeichneten Kapital des Unternehmens und hierauf noch einzuzahlender Betrag;
4. Höhe der Erträge des letzten Geschäftsjahres aus den Anteilen an dem Unternehmen.

(2) Für die Zulassung von Aktien sind zusätzlich der Buchwert der vom Emittenten gehaltenen Anteile und die Höhe der Forderungen und Verbindlichkeiten des Emittenten gegenüber dem Unternehmen anzugeben. Ferner sind über Unternehmen, die nicht unter Absatz 1 fallen, an denen der Emittent aber Anteile von mindestens zehn vom Hundert des gezeichneten Kapitals besitzt, die Firma und der Sitz sowie die Höhe des Kapitalanteils des Emittenten anzugeben; diese Angaben können unterbleiben, wenn sie für die Beurteilung der zuzulassenden Aktien von geringer Bedeutung sind.

(3) Die Angaben nach Absätzen 1 und 2 Satz 1 können unterbleiben, wenn der Emittent nachweist, daß die Anteile nur vorübergehend gehalten werden. Die Angaben nach Absatz 2 Satz 1 können ferner unterbleiben, wenn nach Ansicht der Zulassungsstelle dadurch das Publikum nicht irregeführt wird.

cash flow statements. Any significant positions of the variations are to be reported individually and unbalanced.

§ 24
Information about Subsidiaries or Affiliates

(1) The following information shall be given in the prospectus concerning any enterprises in which the issuer, whether directly or indirectly, owns shares if the book value thereof amounts to at least ten percent of the issuer's capital or contributes a minimum of ten percent towards the annual results of the issuer or, if the issuer is a member of a group of companies the book value of which represents at least ten percent of the consolidated capital or which contributes at least ten percent of the consolidated net results of the group:

1. company name, principal place of business, and business activities;
2. the amount of the subscribed capital and, if the enterprise publishes annual accounts, the amount of reserves and the annual profits or losses of the concern;
3. the extent of an issuer's share of the subscribed capital of the enterprise, with details of the amounts unpaid;
4. revenue derived during the last financial year from shareholdings in the enterprise.

(2) In addition, for the admission of shares, information shall be given on the book value of the shares in the enterprise held by the issuer and the amount of any receivables or liabilities of the issuer against the enterprise. The company name, principal place of business and proportion of shares held by the issuer shall be given for any enterprises which do not fall under sub-paragraph 1, but in which the issuer holds shares amounting to at least ten percent of the subscribed capital; such information may be omitted if it is of only minor importance for the purpose of assessing the shares to be admitted.

(3) The information referred to in sub-paragraphs 1 and 2 sentence 1 may be omitted if the issuer is able to demonstrate that the shares are being held only temporarily. The information required under sub-paragraph 2 sentence 1 may also be omitted if, in the opinion of the Listing Board, the public will not be thereby misled.

Börsenzul. Verordnung

§ 25
Angabe von Ergebnis und Dividende je Aktie

(1) Der Angabe nach § 21 Abs. 2 Nr. 1 ist der Jahresüberschuß oder Jahresfehlbetrag zugrunde zu legen, wenn der Emittent Einzelabschlüsse in den Prospekt aufnimmt. Nimmt der Emittent nur Konzernabschlüsse in den Prospekt auf, so hat er das auf jede Aktie entfallende konsolidierte Ergebnis des Geschäftsjahres für die letzten drei Geschäftsjahre anzugeben; diese Angabe ist zusätzlich zu der nach Satz 1 erforderlich, wenn der Emittent auch seine Einzelabschlüsse in den Prospekt aufnimmt.

(2) Hat sich in den letzten drei Geschäftsjahren die Zahl der Aktien des Emittenten insbesondere durch eine Erhöhung oder Herabsetzung des gezeichneten Kapitals oder durch Zusammenlegung der Aktien oder Teilung ihres Nennbetrags geändert, so sind die Ergebnisse je Aktie sowie die Beträge der Dividende je Aktie zu bereinigen, um sie vergleichbar zu machen. Die angewandten Berichtigungsformeln sind im Prospekt anzugeben.

§ 26
Aufnahme von Konzernabschlüssen

Werden in den Prospekt Konzernabschlüsse oder Angaben hieraus aufgenommen, so sind anzugeben

1. die angewandten Konsolidierungsmethoden; sie sind näher zu beschreiben, wenn sie nicht den Vorschriften oder einer allgemein anerkannten Methode im Geltungsbereich dieser Verordnung entsprechen;
2. die Firma und der Sitz der in den Konzernabschluß einbezogenen Unternehmen, wenn diese Angaben für die Beurteilung der Vermögens-, Finanz- und Ertragslage des Emittenten wichtig sind, wobei es genügt, diese Unternehmen bei den Angaben nach § 24 zu kennzeichnen;
3. für jedes der nach Nummer 2 anzugebenden Unternehmen der Betrag der insgesamt von Dritten gehaltenen Anteile an diesem Unternehmen, wenn die Jahresabschlüsse voll konsolidiert worden sind, und die für die Konsolidierung maßgebliche Quote, wenn quotenmäßig konsolidiert worden ist.

§ 25
Information Concerning Earnings and Dividends Per Share

(1) The information provided under § 21 sub-paragraph 2 No. 1 shall be based on annual profits or losses if the issuer includes individual annual accounts in the prospectus. If the issuer includes only consolidated annual accounts in the prospectus, the consolidated earnings per share in each financial year for the last three financial years shall be given; this information is required in addition to that required under sentence 1, if the issuer also includes individual accounts in the prospectus.

(2) If during the last three financial years the number of shares of the issuer has changed, in particular as a result of any increase or decrease in the subscribed capital, or as a result of any consolidation or splitting of stock, the earnings per share and the amounts of any dividends per share shall be adjusted to make them comparable. The adjustment formulae applied shall also be indicated.

§ 26
The Inclusion of Consolidated Annual Accounts

If consolidated annual accounts or information derived therefrom are included in the prospectus, the following information is to be given:

1. the principles applied to consolidation; such principles shall be described in detail if they do not comply with the provisions or principles generally accepted in the territory where this Regulation applies;

2. the name and principal place of business of any enterprises included in the consolidated accounts if that information is material for the purpose of assessing the net worth, financial position and results of the issuer; it shall suffice to provide information about these enterprises in the form referred to in § 24;

3. for each of the enterprises detailed pursuant to No.2 above, the total amount of shares held by any third parties in such enterprises for which annual accounts are fully consolidated, and in the case of quota consolidation, the quota applied.

Börsenzul. Verordnung

§ 27
Angabe der Verbindlichkeiten des Emittenten der zuzulassenden Schuldverschreibungen

Bei der Angabe der Gesamtbeträge der noch zu tilgenden Anleihen sowie der sonstigen Kreditaufnahmen und Verbindlichkeiten sind Teilbeträge, für die eine Gewährleistung besteht, jeweils gesondert auszuweisen. Stellt der Emittent konsolidierte Jahresabschlüsse auf, so sollen Verbindlichkeiten zwischen Konzernunternehmen grundsätzlich nicht berücksichtigt werden; erforderlichenfalls ist hierüber in den Prospekt eine Erklärung aufzunehmen.

§ 28
Angaben über Geschäftsführungs- und Aufsichtsorgane des Emittenten

(1) Der Prospekt muß über die Geschäftsführungs- und Aufsichtsorgane des Emittenten angeben

1. Name und Anschrift der Mitglieder der Geschäftsführungs- und Aufsichtsorgane und ihre Stellung beim Emittenten;
2. die wichtigsten Tätigkeiten dieser Personen, die sie außerhalb des Emittenten ausüben, soweit diese Tätigkeiten für die Beurteilung des Emittenten von Bedeutung sind.

(2) Für die Zulassung von Aktien sind zusätzlich anzugeben

1. die Angaben nach Absatz 1 für die Gründer des Emittenten, wenn die Gesellschaft vor weniger als fünf Jahren gegründet worden ist;
2. die den Mitgliedern der Geschäftsführungs- und Aufsichtsorgane für das letzte abgeschlossene Geschäftsjahr gewährten Gesamtbezüge (Gehälter, Gewinnbeteiligungen, Aufwandsentschädigungen, Versicherungsentgelte, Provisionen und Nebenleistungen jeder Art); diese Beträge sind für jedes Organ getrennt anzugeben;
3. die Gesamtbezüge im Sinne der Nummer 2, die den Mitgliedern der Geschäftsführungs- und Aufsichtsorgane des Emittenten von Unternehmen gewährt werden, die vom Emittenten abhängig sind und mit denen er einen Konzern bildet; diese Beträge sind für jedes Organ getrennt anzugeben;
4. die Gesamtzahl der Aktien des Emittenten, die von den Mitgliedern der Geschäftsführungs- und Aufsichtsorgane insgesamt gehalten werden, und die Rechte, die diesen Personen auf den Bezug solcher Aktien eingeräumt sind;

Admissions Regulation

§ 27

Information concerning the Liabilities of the Issuer of Bonds which are to be Admitted

In providing information as to the total amount outstanding in relation to bonds and other borrowings and liabilities, any partial amounts for which guarantees have been given are to be listed separately. If the issuer prepares consolidated accounts, inter-company liabilities should not generally be taken into account; if necessary, explanations are to be included in the prospectus.

§ 28

Information about the Directors and Supervisory Organs of the Issuer

(1) The prospectus shall provide the following information about the board of directors and the supervisory organs of the issuer:

1. the names and addresses of the members of the board of directors and of the supervisory organs and the positions they hold in the issuer;
2. the principal activities of these persons other than those for the issuer if such activities are of material significance in assessing the issuer;

(2) In addition, to admit shares, the following information is to be given:

1. the same information as in sub-paragraph 1 for the company founders, if the issuer was formed less than five years ago;
2. the total remuneration (including salaries, profit shares, allowances, insurance payments, commissions and benefits in kind of any description) paid to the members of the board of directors or supervisory organ in the last complete financial year; such amounts shall be indicated separately for each organ;
3. the total of all payments made, according to No. 2 above, to members of the board of directors and supervisory organs of the issuer by any enterprise controlled by the issuer in conjunction with which the issuer forms a concern; such amounts shall be stated separately for each organ;
4. the total number of shares of the issuer held by the members of the board of directors and supervisory organ in the aggregate, and details of any rights such persons have to subscribe for shares;

Börsenzul. Verordnung

5. die Art und der Umfang der Beteiligung von Mitgliedern der Geschäftsführungs- und Aufsichtsorgane an Geschäften außerhalb der Geschäftstätigkeit des Emittenten oder an anderen der Form oder der Sache nach ungewöhnlichen Geschäften des Emittenten während des laufenden und des vorhergehenden Geschäftsjahres; sind derartige ungewöhnliche Geschäfte in weiter zurückliegenden Geschäftsjahren getätigt und noch nicht endgültig abgeschlossen worden, so sind auch hierüber Angaben zu machen;

6. die Gesamthöhe der noch nicht zurückgezahlten Darlehen, die vom Emittenten den Mitgliedern der Geschäftsführungs- oder Aufsichtsorgane gewährt wurden, sowie der vom Emittenten für diese Personen übernommenen Bürgschaften und sonstigen Gewährleistungen;

7. die Möglichkeiten für die Beteiligung der Arbeitnehmer am Kapital des Emittenten.

§ 29

Angaben über den jüngsten Geschäftsgang und die Geschäftsaussichten des Emittenten

(1) Der Prospekt muß allgemeine Ausführungen über die Geschäftsentwicklung des Emittenten nach dem Schluß des Geschäftsjahres, auf das sich der letzte veröffentlichte Jahresabschluß bezieht, enthalten und dabei insbesondere die wichtigsten Tendenzen in der jüngsten Entwicklung der Erzeugung von Gütern und Erbringung von Dienstleistungen, des Absatzes, der Lagerhaltung und der Auftragsbestände sowie die jüngsten Tendenzen in der Entwicklung der Kosten und Erlöse angeben.

(2) Der Prospekt muß Angaben über die Geschäftsaussichten des Emittenten mindestens für das laufende Geschäftsjahr enthalten.

§ 30

Angaben über die Prüfung der Jahresabschlüsse des Emittenten und anderer Angaben im Prospekt

(1) Der Prospekt muß den Namen, die Anschrift und die Berufsbezeichnung der Abschlußprüfer, welche die Jahresabschlüsse der letzten drei Geschäftsjahre des Emittenten nach Maßgabe der gesetzlichen Vorschriften geprüft haben, angeben und eine Erklärung enthalten, daß die Jahresabschlüsse geprüft worden sind. Ferner sind die Bestätigungsvermerke einschließlich zusätzlicher Bemerkungen aufzunehmen; wurde die Bestätigung des Jahresabschlusses eingeschränkt oder versagt, so müssen der volle

Admissions Regulation

5. the nature and extent to which members of the board of directors or supervisory organ are concerned in transactions outside the scope of business conducted by the issuer or in any other business of the issuer if it is of an unusual nature whether as to form or subject matter during the current or preceding financial year; if any unusual transactions have been undertaken in the course of earlier financial years and are still not completed, information regarding the same shall also be supplied;
6. the total amount of any loans made by the issuer to members of the board of directors or supervisory organs which remain unpaid and any guarantees or other collateral given by the issuer for the benefit of such persons;
7. any employee options able to be exercised in respect to the issuer's share capital.

§ 29
Information about Current Performance and Future Business Prospects of the Issuer

(1) The prospectus shall contain general information about the development of the issuer's business since the end of the financial year to which the last published accounts relate, including in particular the most significant trends in the recent development regarding the production of goods and the performance of services, sales, stock levels and order books, in addition to the most recent trends in cost and revenue developments.

(2) The prospectus shall contain information about the issuer's business prospects for at least the current financial year.

§ 30
Information concerning the Auditing of the Issuer's Annual Accounts and other Information given in the Prospectus

(1) The prospectus shall state the names, addresses and professional designations of the auditors who have audited the issuer's annual accounts according to applicable law for the last three financial years and shall contain a declaration that the accounts have been audited. Furthermore, the auditors' opinion with any notes shall be included; if the auditors' opinion on the annual accounts contains any qualification or if no opinion has been given, the qualification or reasons for refusal to

Börsenzul. Verordnung

Wortlaut der Einschränkungen oder der Versagung und deren Begründung wiedergegeben werden.

(2) Sind sonstige Angaben des Prospekts von Abschlußprüfern geprüft, so ist darauf hinzuweisen. Absatz 1 Satz 2 gilt entsprechend.

§ 31
Angaben über Zertifikate, die Aktien vertreten

Der Prospekt muß über die zuzulassenden Zertifikate, die Aktien vertreten, angeben

1. die mit dem Zertifikat verbundenen Rechte unter Nennung der Ausgabebedingungen für die Zertifikate, des Zeitpunktes und des Ortes ihrer Veröffentlichung sowie der Rechtsvorschriften, nach denen die Zertifikate begeben worden sind, und des Gerichtsstands;

2. wie die mit den vertretenen Aktien verbundenen Rechte, insbesondere das Stimmrecht und das Recht auf Beteiligung an den Erträgen und am Liquidationserlös, durch den Zertifikatsinhaber ausgeübt werden; wird das Stimmrecht durch den Emittenten der Zertifikate ausgeübt, so ist anzugeben, ob und auf welche Weise er es ausübt und wie der Zertifikatsinhaber Weisungen für die Stimmrechtsausübung erteilen kann;

3. Gewährleistungen für die Ansprüche des Zertifikatsinhabers gegen den Emittenten der Zertifikate;

4. Möglichkeiten und Bedingungen für den Umtausch des Zertifikats in vertretene Aktien;

5. die Höhe der Provisionen und der Kosten, die vom Zertifikatsinhaber im Zusammenhang mit der Ausgabe der Zertifikate, der Einlösung der Gewinnanteilscheine, der Begebung zusätzlicher Zertifikate und dem Umtausch der Zertifikate gegen die vertretenen Aktien zu tragen sind;

6. die Rechtsvorschriften über die Steuern und Abgaben, die im Staat der Ausgabe der Zertifikate zu Lasten der Zertifikatsinhaber erhoben werden;

7. die nach § 15 Abs. 1 Nr. 4 und 5 erster Halbsatz und § 16 Abs. 1 Nr. 11 und 12 vorgeschriebenen Angaben mit der Maßgabe, daß an die Stelle der Aktien die Zertifikate treten.

Admissions Regulation

provide an opinion or reasons for qualification are to be included in full.

(2) If any other information in the prospectus is audited by auditors, a statement to that effect shall be included. Sub-paragraph 1 sentence 2 applies.

§ 31
Information regarding Certificates Representing Shares

The prospectus must contain the following information concerning any certificates which represent shares:

1. the rights attaching to the certificates including any conditions applicable to the issuing of the certificates, the date and place of publication and the legal provisions in accordance with which any certificates have been issued and the venue for any disputes;

2. how the rights attaching to any shares represented by the certificates, and in particular rights to vote and rights to share in profits and in any assets remaining after liquidation, may be exercised by the holder of the certificates; if a voting right is exercisable by the issuer of the certificates, a statement shall be included as to whether and how such voting rights may be exercised and how the holder of the certificates may give instructions how any voting rights may be exercised;

3. any guarantees relating to claims of the holder of any certificates against the issuer of the certificates;

4. the possibilities and conditions applicable to the exchange of the certificates for represented shares;

5. the amounts of any commissions and costs which are to be paid by the holder of the certificates in connection with the issue of the certificates, the payment of dividend coupons, the issue of additional certificates and the exchange of the certificates for shares;

6. the legal provisions relating to any taxes or duties levied by the state in which the certificates have been issued and which are to be paid by the holder of the certificates;

7. the information required under § 15 sub-paragraph 1 Nos. 4 and 5 first half sentence and § 16 sub-paragraph 1 Nos. 11 and 12, subject to the proviso that the certificates take the place of shares.

Börsenzul. Verordnung

§ 32
Angaben über den Emittenten der Zertifikate, die Aktien vertreten

Der Prospekt muß über den Emittenten der zuzulassenden Zertifikate, die Aktien vertreten, enthalten

1. die Angaben nach § 18 Nr. 1 bis 3, § 19 Abs. 1 Nr. 1 und § 28 Abs. 1;
2. die Anteilseigner, denen mehr als fünfundzwanzig vom Hundert des gezeichneten Kapitals des Emittenten oder der hieraus auszuübenden Stimmrechte gehören;
3. den Gegenstand des Unternehmens; werden neben der Ausgabe der Zertifikate weitere Tätigkeiten ausgeübt, so sind deren Merkmale anzugeben und die treuhänderischen Tätigkeiten gesondert aufzuführen;
4. eine Zusammenfassung des Jahresabschlusses des letzten abgeschlossenen Geschäftsjahres; § 22 Abs. 2 Satz 3 bis 5 und Abs. 3 ist anzuwenden.

Zweiter Unterabschnitt

Prospektinhalt in Sonderfällen

§ 33
Aktien auf Grund von Bezugsrechten

(1) Für die Zulassung von Aktien, die den Aktionären des Emittenten auf Grund ihres Bezugsrechts zugeteilt werden, kann die Zulassungsstelle einen Prospekt billigen, der nur die Angaben gemäß den §§ 14 und 15 Abs. 1 und 2, den §§ 16 und 18 Nr. 1, 6 und 7, § 19 Abs. 1 Nr. 1 und 3 und Abs. 2 Nr. 1 und 5, § 20 Abs. 1 Nr. 5, 6 und 7 Buchstabe b und c und Abs. 3 Satz 2 Nr. 3, § 22 Abs. 2 Satz 3 bis 5 und Abs. 3 und 4, § 28 Abs. 1 und 2 Nr. 1 bis 6 sowie den §§ 29 und 30 enthält, wenn Aktien des Emittenten an dieser Börse bereits amtlich notiert werden.

(2) Werden die zugeteilten Aktien durch Zertifikate vertreten, so hat der Prospekt vorbehaltlich der Regelung des § 40 neben den Angaben nach Absatz 1 die Angaben gemäß § 18 Nr. 3 sowie den §§ 31 und 32 Nr. 4 zu enthalten.

§ 32

Information concerning the Issuer of Certificates which Represent Shares

The prospectus shall contain the following information concerning any issuer of certificates representing shares which are to be admitted:

1. the information required under § 18 Nos. 1 to 3, § 19 sub-paragraph 1 No.1 and § 28 sub-paragraph 1;
2. details of any shareholders who hold more than twenty-five percent of the subscribed capital in the issuer or the voting rights exercisable as a result;
3. the objects of the company; if, besides the issuing of certificates, other types of business are undertaken, details thereof shall be given and any trust activities undertaken shall be separately described;
4. a summary of the accounts for the last financial year; § 22 sub-paragraph 2 sentences 3 to 5 and sub-paragraph 3 apply.

Sub-Part Two

Contents of Prospectuses in Special Cases

§ 33

Shares Based on Subscription Rights

(1) For the admission of shares which are issued to shareholders of the issuer on the basis of subscription rights, the Listing Board may approve a prospectus containing only the information provided for under §§ 14 and 15 sub-paragraphs 1 and 2, §§ 16 and 18 Nos. 1, 6 and 7, § 19 sub-paragraph 1 Nos. 1 and 3 and sub-paragraph 2 Nos. 1 and 5, § 20 sub-paragraph 1 Nos. 5, 6 and 7 letters b and c and sub-paragraph 3 sentence 2 No. 3, § 22 sub-paragraph 2 sentences 3 to 5 and sub-paragraphs 3 and 4, § 28 sub-paragraphs 1 and 2 No. 1 to 6, and §§ 29 and 30 if the issuer has shares which are already officially listed on the stock exchange.

(2) If any shares allotted are represented by certificates, the prospectus shall, subject to the provisions of § 40, contain the information required under § 18 No. 3 and §§ 31 and 32 No. 4, in addition to the information described in sub-paragraph 1 above.

Börsenzul. Verordnung

§ 34
Wertpapiere von Emittenten börsennotierter Wertpapiere

(1) Für die Zulassung von anderen Wertpapieren als Aktien kann die Zulassungsstelle einen Prospekt billigen, der nur Angaben gemäß den §§ 14 und 15 Abs. 1 und 3, den §§ 17 und 18 Nr. 1, 6 und 7, § 19 Abs. 1 Nr. 1, § 20 Abs. 1 Nr. 6, § 21 Abs. 3, § 22 Abs. 2 Satz 3 bis 5 und Abs. 3 und 4, den §§ 27 und 28 Abs. 1 sowie den §§ 29 und 30 enthält, wenn Wertpapiere des Emittenten an dieser Börse bereits amtlich notiert werden.

(2) Der Prospekt muß den letzten festgestellten Jahresabschluß des Emittenten enthalten. Stellt der Emittent sowohl einen Einzelabschluß als auch einen Konzernabschluß auf, so sind beide Arten von Jahresabschlüssen aufzunehmen. Die Zulassungsstelle kann dem Emittenten gestatten, nur den Jahresabschluß der einen Art aufzunehmen, wenn der Jahresabschluß der anderen Art keine wesentlichen zusätzlichen Aussagen enthält.

(3) Die Absätze 1 und 2 gelten für die in § 35 Abs. 1 genannten Wertpapiere.

§ 35
Wertpapiere mit Umtausch- oder Bezugsrecht auf Aktien

(1) Für die Zulassung von anderen Wertpapieren als Aktien, die den Gläubigern ein Umtausch- oder Bezugsrecht auf Aktien einräumen, hat der Prospekt folgende Angaben zu enthalten:

1. die Art der zum Umtausch oder Bezug angebotenen Aktien und der mit ihnen verbundenen Rechte;
2. die Bedingungen und das Verfahren für den Umtausch und den Bezug sowie die Fälle, in denen die Bedingungen oder das Verfahren geändert werden können;
3. die Angaben gemäß § 14;
4. die Angaben gemäß den §§ 18 bis 30 mit Ausnahme des § 21 Abs. 3 und des § 27;
5. die Angaben gemäß § 15 Abs. 1 und 3 sowie § 17.

(2) Ist der Emittent der zuzulassenden Wertpapiere nicht zugleich der Emittent der zum Umtausch oder Bezug angebotenen Aktien, so sind die Angaben nach Absatz 1 Nr. 1 bis 3 sowie über den Emittenten der Aktien die Angaben nach Absatz 1 Nr. 4 und über den Emittenten der zuzulassenden

Admissions Regulation

§ 34

Securities of Issuers of Listed Securities

(1) For the admission of securities other than shares, the Listing Board may approve a prospectus containing only the information required under §§ 14 and 15, sub-paragraphs 1 and 3, §§ 17 and 18, Nos. 1, 6 and 7, § 19 sub-paragraph 1 No. 1, § 20 sub-paragraph 1 No. 6, § 21 sub-paragraph 3, § 22 sub-paragraph 2 sentences 3 to 5 and sub-paragraphs 3 and 4, §§ 27 and 28 sub-paragraph 1 and §§ 29 and 30, if the issuer has shares which are already officially listed on the stock exchange.

(2) The prospectus shall contain the issuer's last audited annual accounts. If the issuer prepares individual accounts as well as consolidated accounts, both types of accounts shall be included. The Listing Board may allow the issuer to include only one type of annual accounts if the other accounts do not contain additional material information.

(3) Sub-paragraphs 1 and 2 shall not apply to securities of the kind referred to in § 35 sub-paragraph 1.

§ 35

Securities with Conversion or Subscription Rights

(1) For the admission of securities other than shares giving creditors a right to conversion or subscription for shares, the prospectus shall contain the following information:

1. details of the kinds of shares offered in exchange or for subscription and the rights connected thereto;
2. the conditions and procedures applicable to conversion and subscription and information on cases where such conditions and procedures may be amended;
3. the information required under § 14;
4. the information required under §§ 18 to 30, but excluding § 21 sub-paragraph 3 and § 27;
5. the information required under § 15 sub-paragraphs 1 and 3 as well as § 17.

(2) If the issuer of the securities to be admitted is not also the issuer of the shares offered for conversion or for subscription, the information required under sub-paragraph 1 Nos. 1 to 3 and the information concerning the issuer of the shares under sub-paragraph 1 No. 4, and for

271

Börsenzul. Verordnung

Wertpapiere neben den Angaben nach Absatz 1 Nr. 5 die Angaben gemäß den §§ 18 und 19 Abs. 1, § 20 Abs. 1 und 2, § 21 Abs. 1 und 3, den §§ 22, 23 und 24 Abs. 1 und 3, den §§ 26, 27 und 28 Abs. 1 sowie den §§ 29 und 30 aufzunehmen.

(3) Ist der Emittent der zuzulassenden Wertpapiere eine Gesellschaft im Sinne des § 37 Abs. 3 Nr. 1, so brauchen neben den Angaben nach Absatz 1 Nr. 1 bis 3 über diesen Emittenten nur die Angaben gemäß § 15 Abs. 1 und 3, den §§ 17, 18 und 19 Abs. 1, § 21 Abs. 1 Nr. 1 und 2 und Abs. 3, den §§ 22, 23, 27 und 28 Abs. 1 sowie den §§ 29 und 30 aufgenommen zu werden.

§ 36
Wertpapiere außer Aktien auf Grund von Bezugsrechten

Für die Zulassung von in § 35 Abs. 1 genannten Wertpapieren, die den Aktionären des Emittenten auf Grund eines Bezugsrechts zugeteilt werden, kann die Zulassungsstelle, sofern Aktien des Emittenten an dieser Börse bereits amtlich notiert werden, einen Prospekt billigen, der nur die Angaben gemäß den §§ 14 und 15 Abs. 1 und 3, den §§ 17 und 18 Nr. 1, 6 und 7, § 19 Abs. 1 Nr. 1 und 3 und Abs. 2 Nr. 1 und 5, § 20 Abs. 1 Nr. 5, 6 und 7 Buchstabe b und c und Abs. 3 Satz 2 Nr. 3, § 22 Abs. 2 Satz 3 bis 5 und Abs. 3 und 4, § 28 Abs. 1 und 2 Nr. 1 bis 6 sowie den §§ 29, 30 und 35 Abs. 1 Nr. 1 und 2 enthält; § 34 Abs. 2 ist anzuwenden.

§ 37
Bank- oder Versicherungsgeschäfte betreibende Emittenten

(1) Für die Zulassung von Wertpapieren eines Emittenten, der überwiegend den Betrieb von Bankgeschäften im Sinne des § 1 Abs. 1 Satz 2 des Gesetzes über das Kreditwesen zum Gegenstand des Unternehmens hat, sind an Stelle der Angaben nach den §§ 20 und 29 anzugeben

1. die hauptsächlichen Geschäftsbereiche des Emittenten, seine wichtigsten Zweigniederlassungen im In- und Ausland sowie die Gerichts- oder Schiedsverfahren, die einen erheblichen Einfluß auf die wirtschaftliche Lage des Emittenten haben können oder in den letzten zwei Geschäftsjahren gehabt haben;

Admissions Regulation

the issuer of the securities to be admitted, in addition to the information required under sub-paragraph 1 No. 5 and the information required under §§ 18 and 19 sub-paragraph 1, § 20 sub-paragraphs 1 and 2, § 21 sub-paragraphs 1 and 3, §§ 22, 23 and 24 sub-paragraphs 1 and 3, §§ 26, 27 and 28 sub-paragraph 1, and §§ 29 and 30 shall be included.

(3) If the issuer of the securities to be admitted is a company according to § 37 sub-paragraph 3 No. 1, in addition to the information concerning the issuer according to sub-paragraph 1 Nos. 1 to 3, the only other information required to be included is that under § 15 sub-paragraphs 1 and 3, §§ 17, 18 and 19 sub-paragraph 1, § 21 sub-paragraph 1 Nos. 1 and 2 and sub-paragraph 3, §§ 22, 23, 27 and 28 sub-paragraph 1, and §§ 29 and 30.

§ 36
Securities other than Shares by Reason of Subscription Rights

For the admission of shares of the kind referred to in § 35 sub-paragraph 1, which are issued to shareholders of the issuer on the basis of subscription rights, the Listing Board may, if the issuer already has shares officially listed on the stock exchange, approve a prospectus containing only the information required under §§ 14 and 15 sub-paragraphs 1 and 3, §§ 17 and 18 Nos. 1, 6 and 7, § 19 sub-paragraph 1 Nos. 1 and 3, and sub-paragraph 2 Nos. 1 and 5, § 20 sub-paragraph 1 Nos. 5, 6 and 7 letters b and c and sub-paragraph 3 sentence 2 No. 3, § 22 sub-paragraph 2 sentences 3 to 5 and sub-paragraphs 3 and 4, § 28 sub-paragraphs 1 and 2 Nos. 1 to 6, and § 29, 30 and 35 sub-paragraph 1 Nos. 1 and 2; § 34 sub-paragraph 2 shall apply.

§ 37
Issuers Active in the Banking or Insurance Business

(1) For the admission of securities of an issuer carrying on business predominantly in banking within the meaning of § 1 sub-paragraph 1 sentence 2 of the Banking Act, the information set out below shall be provided in place of that referred to in §§ 20 and 29:
1. the issuer's principal areas of business, principal domestic and foreign branches, and details of any litigation or arbitration which could have, or

Börsenzul. Verordnung

2. die Geschäftsentwicklung des Emittenten nach dem Schluß des Geschäftsjahres, auf das sich der letzte veröffentlichte Jahresabschluß bezieht; dabei sind insbesondere die wichtigsten Tendenzen in der jüngsten Entwicklung der hauptsächlichen Geschäftsbereiche sowie die jüngsten Tendenzen in der Entwicklung der Aufwendungen und Erträge anzugeben.

(2) Für die Zulassung von Wertpapieren eines Emittenten, der überwiegend den Betrieb von Versicherungsgeschäften zum Gegenstand des Unternehmens hat, sind an Stelle der Angaben nach den §§ 20 und 29 anzugeben

1. die hauptsächlichen Geschäftsbereiche des Emittenten sowie die Gerichts- und Schiedsverfahren, die einen erheblichen Einfluß auf die wirtschaftliche Lage des Emittenten haben können oder in den letzten zwei Geschäftsjahren gehabt haben;
2. die Geschäftsentwicklung des Emittenten nach dem Schluß des Geschäftsjahres, auf das sich der letzte veröffentlichte Jahresabschluß bezieht; dabei sind insbesondere die wichtigsten Tendenzen in der jüngsten Entwicklung der Beitragseinnahmen, der Schäden, der Kosten und der Erträge aus Kapitalanlagen sowie der Bestände in der Lebensversicherung anzugeben.

(3) Absatz 1 gilt entsprechend für die Zulassung von Wertpapieren, deren Emittent eine Gesellschaft ist, die

1. ein verbundenes Unternehmen ist und ausschließlich die Beschaffung von Finanzierungsmitteln für andere mit ihm verbundene Unternehmen zum Gegenstand des Unternehmens hat oder
2. einen Bestand an Wertpapieren, Lizenzen oder Patenten besitzt und ausschließlich die Verwaltung dieses Bestandes zum Gegenstand des Unternehmens hat.

§ 38

Von Kreditinstituten dauernd oder wiederholt ausgegebene Schuldverschreibungen

(1) Für die Zulassung von Schuldverschreibungen, deren Emittent

1. Schuldverschreibungen während einer längeren Dauer oder wiederholt ausgibt,
2. befugt Einlagen oder andere rückzahlbare Gelder des Publikums entgegennimmt und Kredite für eigene Rechnung gewährt,
3. regelmäßig seine Jahresabschlüsse veröffentlicht und

Admissions Regulation

have had any material effect on the financial position of the issuer within the last two financial years;

2. the development of the issuer's business since the close of the financial year to which the issuer's last published annual accounts relate; information shall be given in particular on the most important trends in the recent development of the issuer's principal areas of business, and information about recent trends in expenditure and income.

(2) For the admission of securities of an issuer carrying on business predominantly in insurance, the information set out below shall be provided in place of that referred to in §§ 20 and 29:

1. the issuer's principal areas of business, and details of any litigation or arbitration which could have, or have had within the last two financial years any material effect on the financial position of the issuer;

2. the developments in the issuer's business since the close of the financial year to which the issuer's last published annual accounts relate; information shall be given in particular on the most important trends in the recent development of premium income, claims, investment costs and returns and the inventory of life policies.

(3) Sub-paragraph 1 shall apply in the case of the admission of securities issued by a company which

1. is an associated company and whose business consists exclusively in raising funds for other associated companies, or

2. owns securities, licences or patents and whose sole object is the administration thereof.

§ 38

Bonds Continuously or Repeatedly Issued by Banks

(1) For the admission of bonds the issuer of which

1. issues bonds over an extended period or on a repeated basis,

2. is authorised to accept deposits or other repayable monies from the public grant loans on its own account,

3. regularly publishes annual accounts and

Börsenzul. Verordnung

4. innerhalb der Europäischen Wirtschaftsgemeinschaft oder innerhalb eines anderen Vertragsstaates des Abkommens über den Europäischen Wirtschaftsraum durch ein besonderes Gesetz oder auf Grund eines besonderen Gesetzes geschaffen worden ist oder geregelt wird oder einer öffentlichen Aufsicht zum Schutz der Anleger untersteht,

muß der Prospekt mindestens die Angaben nach § 14 erster Halbsatz, § 15 Abs. 1 und 3 und § 17 sowie Angaben über Ereignisse enthalten, die nach dem Abschlußstichtag des letzten veröffentlichten Jahresabschlusses des Emittenten eingetreten und für die Beurteilung der Schuldverschreibungen wichtig sind. Dieser Jahresabschluß muß dem Publikum am Sitz des Emittenten oder bei seinen Zahlstellen zur Verfügung gestellt werden.

(2) Ein Emittent gibt im Sinne des Absatzes 1 wiederholt Schuldverschreibungen aus, wenn in den zwölf Kalendermonaten, die dem Zulassungsantrag vorausgegangen sind, mindestens drei Emissionen von Schuldverschreibungen des Emittenten an einer Börse innerhalb der Europäischen Wirtschaftsgemeinschaft oder innerhalb eines anderen Vertragsstaates des Abkommens über den Europäischen Wirtschaftsraum eingeführt worden sind.

(3) Sind seit der letzten Veröffentlichung eines gemäß den §§ 13 bis 37 und 39 bis 41 erstellten Prospekts für die Zulassung von Wertpapieren dieses Emittenten mehr als drei Jahre vergangen, kann die Zulassungsstelle einen solchen Prospekt fordern, wenn dies zum Schutze des Publikums und für einen ordnungsgemäßen Börsenhandel notwendig ist.

§ 39

Gewährleistete Wertpapiere

(1) Für die Zulassung von anderen Wertpapieren als Aktien, für deren Verzinsung oder Rückzahlung eine juristische Person oder Gesellschaft die Gewährleistung übernommen hat, muß der Prospekt enthalten

1. über den Emittenten die Angaben gemäß den §§ 14 und 15 Abs. 1 und 3, den §§ 17, 18 und 19 Abs. 1, § 20 Abs. 1 und 2, § 21 Abs. 1 und 3, den §§ 22, 23 und 24 Abs. 1 und 3, den §§ 26, 27 und 28 Abs. 1 sowie den §§ 29 und 30;

2. über die Person oder Gesellschaft, welche die Gewährleistung übernommen hat, die Angaben gemäß den §§ 18 und 19 Abs. 1, § 20 Abs. 1 und 2, § 21 Abs. 1 und 3, den §§ 22, 23 und 24 Abs. 1 und 3, den §§ 26, 27 und 28 Abs. 1 sowie den §§ 29 und 30.

Admissions Regulation

4. has been established or is subject to regulation within the European Community or another contracting state of the European Economic Area Treaty or has been created or is regulated by a special Act or by virtue of a special Act or is subject to public supervision for the protection of investors,

the prospectus shall contain as a minimum requirement the information provided for in § 14 first half sentence, § 15 sub-paragraphs 1 and 3 and § 17, and information concerning any events which have occurred after the closing date of the last published accounts of the issuer and which are material for assessment of the bonds. Such annual accounts shall be made available to the public at the principal place of business of the issuer or at the offices of its paying agents.

(2) An issuer issues bonds on a repeated basis according to sub-paragraph 1 if in the course of the twelve calendar months preceding the application for admission at least three issues of bonds have been introduced by the issuer on a stock exchange within the European Economic Community or another contracting state of the European Economic Area Treaty.

(3) If more than three years have passed since the last publication of a prospectus prepared in accordance with §§ 13 to 37 and 39 to 41 for the admission of securities by the issuer, the Listing Board may require such a prospectus should it be necessary for the protection of the public and for orderly trading on the stock exchange.

§ 39
Guaranteed Securities

(1) For the admission of securities other than shares for which the payment of principal and interest has been guaranteed by a legal entity or company, the prospectus shall contain

1. for the issuer, the information required under §§ 14 and 15 sub-paragraph 1 and 3, §§ 17, 18 and 19 sub-paragraph 1, § 20 sub-paragraphs 1 and 2, § 21 sub-paragraphs 1 and 3, §§ 22, 23 and 24 sub-paragraphs 1 and 3, §§ 26, 27 and 28 sub-paragraph 1, and §§ 29 and 30;

2. about the person or company giving the guarantee, the information required under §§ 18 and 19 sub-paragraph 1, § 20 sub-paragraphs 1 and 2, § 21 sub-paragraphs 1 and 3, §§ 22, 23 and 24 sub-paragraphs 1 and 3, §§ 26, 27 and 28 sub-paragraph 1, and §§ 29 and 30.

Börsenzul. Verordnung

(2) Ist der Emittent oder die Person oder Gesellschaft, welche die Gewährleistung übernommen hat, ein Unternehmen, das überwiegend den Betrieb von Bankgeschäften im Sinne des § 1 Abs. 1 Satz 2 des Gesetzes über das Kreditwesen oder von Versicherungsgeschäften zum Gegenstand des Unternehmens hat, oder eine im § 37 Abs. 3 genannte Gesellschaft, so ist insoweit § 37 Abs. 1 und 2 anzuwenden. Ist der Emittent eine Gesellschaft im Sinne des § 37 Abs. 3 Nr. 1, ist § 35 Abs. 3 anzuwenden.

(3) Haben mehrere Personen oder Gesellschaften die Gewährleistung übernommen, muß der Prospekt über jede von ihnen die vorgeschriebenen Angaben enthalten. Die Zulassungsstelle kann eine Kürzung dieser Angaben zulassen, wenn sie die Aussagekraft des Prospekts nicht wesentlich beeinträchtigt.

(4) Die Verträge, mit denen die Gewährleistung übernommen worden ist, müssen vom Publikum am Sitz des Emittenten oder bei seinen Zahlstellen eingesehen werden können. Auf Verlangen sind Vervielfältigungen der Verträge an Personen auszuhändigen, die sich über die Wertpapiere unterrichten wollen.

§ 40
Zertifikate, die Aktien vertreten

(1) Für die Zulassung von Zertifikaten, die Aktien vertreten, kann die Zulassungsstelle von der Verpflichtung befreien, in den Prospekt die Angaben nach § 32 Nr. 4 über den Emittenten der Zertifikate aufzunehmen, wenn er ein Unternehmen mit Sitz in einem Mitgliedstaat der Europäischen Wirtschaftsgemeinschaft oder in einem anderen Vertragsstaat des Abkommens über den Europäischen Wirtschaftsraum ist, das befugt Einlagen oder andere rückzahlbare Gelder des Publikums entgegennimmt und Kredite für eigene Rechnung gewährt sowie durch ein besonderes Gesetz oder auf Grund eines besonderen Gesetzes geschaffen worden ist oder geregelt wird oder einer öffentlichen Aufsicht zum Schutz der Anleger untersteht.

(2) Absatz 1 gilt auch, wenn der Emittent der Zertifikate

1. eine Gesellschaft ist, deren Anteile in Höhe von mindestens fünfundneunzig vom Hundert einem Unternehmen nach Absatz 1 gehören, das gegenüber den Inhabern der Zertifikate eine unbedingte und unwiderrufliche Gewährleistung übernommen hat, und wenn die Gesellschaft und das Unternehmen rechtlich oder tatsächlich derselben Aufsicht unterliegen oder

Admissions Regulation

(2) If the issuer or person or company giving the guarantee is an enterprise which carries on predominantly banking business within the meaning of § 1 sub-paragraph 1 sentence 2 of the Banking Act or insurance business or is a company of the kind referred to in § 37 sub-paragraph 3, then § 37 sub-paragraphs 1 and 2 shall apply. If the issuer is a company within the meaning of § 37 sub-paragraph 3 No. 1, then § 35 sub-paragraph 3 shall apply.

(3) If more than one person or company has guaranteed the securities, the prospectus shall contain such information about each of them. The Listing Board may allow abridged information to be given, provided that doing so does not materially detract from the value of the information in the prospectus.

(4) The contracts pursuant to which the guarantee is given shall be available for inspection by the public at the principal place of business of the issuer or at the offices of its paying agents. Copies of the contracts shall be provided on demand to any person seeking information regarding the securities concerned.

§ 40
Certificates Representing Shares

(1) For the admission of certificates representing shares, the Listing Board may dispense with the requirements to include in the prospectus the information referred to in § 32 No. 4 regarding the issuer of the certificates if the issuer is an enterprise having its principal place of business in a member state of the European Economic Community or another contracting state of the European Economic Area Treaty and is authorised to accept deposits or other repayable monies from the public and to extend credits for its own account and has been created or is regulated by a special Act or by virtue of a special Act or is subject to public supervision for the protection of depositors.

(2) Sub-paragraph 1 shall also apply if the issuer of the certificates

1. is a company at least ninety five per cent of the shares of which are owned by an enterprise of the kind referred to in sub-paragraph 1 and which has given an unconditional and irrevocable guarantee for the benefit of the holders of the certificates, and if the company or enterprise is legally or actually subject to the same supervision or

Börsenzul. Verordnung

2. ein administratiekantor in den Niederlanden ist, das besonderen Vorschriften für die Verwahrung und die Verwaltung der von den Zertifikaten vertretenen Aktien unterliegt.

(3) Ist der Emittent der Zertifikate eine Wertpapiersammelbank (§ 1 Abs. 3 des Depotgesetzes) oder eine von Wertpapiersammelbanken getragene Einrichtung, so kann die Zulassungsstelle von der Verpflichtung befreien, die Angaben nach § 32 in den Prospekt aufzunehmen.

§ 41
Verschmelzung, Spaltung, Übertragung, Umtausch, Sacheinlagen

Für die Zulassung von Wertpapieren, die bei einer Verschmelzung, Spaltung, Übertragung des gesamten oder eines Teils des Vermögens eines Unternehmens, einem öffentlichen Umtauschangebot oder als Gegenleistung für Sacheinlagen ausgegeben worden sind, müssen zusätzlich zur Veröffentlichung des Prospekts die Unterlagen, aus denen sich die Einzelheiten dieses Vorgangs ergeben, sowie, wenn der Emittent im Falle des § 3 Abs. 2 noch keinen Jahresabschluß veröffentlicht hat, die Eröffnungsbilanz, die auch nur vorläufig aufgestellt sein kann, vom Publikum am Sitz des Emittenten oder bei seinen Zahlstellen eingesehen werden können. Die Zulassungsstelle kann von der Verpflichtung nach Satz 1 befreien, wenn der Vorgang, in dessen Zusammenhang die Wertpapiere ausgegeben worden sind, mehr als zwei Jahre zurückliegt.

§ 42
Schuldverschreibungen von Staaten, Gebietskörperschaften, zwischenstaatlichen Einrichtungen

(1) Für die Zulassung von Schuldverschreibungen, die von Staaten emittiert werden, muß der Prospekt insbesondere Angaben enthalten über

1. die geographischen und staatsrechtlichen Verhältnisse;
2. die Zugehörigkeit zu zwischenstaatlichen Einrichtungen;
3. die Wirtschaft, insbesondere ihre Struktur, Produktionszahlen der wesentlichen Wirtschaftszweige, Entstehung und Verwendung des Bruttosozialprodukts und des Volkseinkommens, die Beschäftigung, Preise und Löhne;
4. den Außenhandel, die Zahlungsbilanz und die Währungsreserven;

Admissions Regulation

2. is an *administratiekantor* in the Netherlands, subject to specific provisions relating to the safekeeping and administration of shares represented by certificates.

(3) If the issuer of the certificates is a securities clearing and depositing bank (§ 3 sub-paragraph 3 of the Securities Deposit Act) or an institution established by a securities clearing and depositing bank, the Listing Board may dispense with the requirement to include in the prospectus the information provided for in § 32.

§ 41
Merger, Split, Transfer, Exchange, Contributions in Kind

For the admission of securities issued in connection with a merger, split, transfer of the whole or part of the undertaking of an enterprise, a public exchange offer or in consideration for contributions in kind, in addition to publication of the prospectus, the documents containing details of such transactions and the opening balance, which may be a provisional opening balance if under § 3 sub-paragraph 2 the issuer has not yet published annual accounts, must be available for inspection by the public at the issuer's principal place of business or at the offices of its paying agents. The Listing Board may dispense with the requirements of sentence 1 if the transaction, in the context of which the securities were issued, is more than two years old.

§ 42
Bonds Issued by Governments, Regional Authorities and International Institutions

(1) For the admission of bonds issued by governments, the prospectus must contain information about

1. relevant geographical and constitutional matters;
2. membership of international institutions;
3. the economy, in particular its structure, production figures for significant branches of the economy, how the gross national product and the gross national income are generated and applied, the level of employment, price levels and salaries and wages;
4. foreign trade, balance of payments and currency reserves;

Börsenzul. Verordnung

5. den Staatshaushalt und die Staatsverschuldung;
6. die jährlichen Fälligkeiten der bestehenden Verschuldung;
7. die Erfüllung der Verbindlichkeiten aus bisher ausgegebenen Schuldverschreibungen.

Die Angaben gemäß den Nummern 3 bis 5 sind jeweils für die letzten drei Jahre aufzunehmen.

(2) Für die Zulassung von Schuldverschreibungen, die von Gebietskörperschaften oder von zwischenstaatlichen Einrichtungen emittiert werden, ist Absatz 1 sinngemäß anzuwenden.

Dritter Unterabschnitt
Veröffentlichung des Prospekts

§ 43

Frist der Veröffentlichung

(1) Der Prospekt muß mindestens drei Werktage vor der Einführung der Wertpapiere veröffentlicht werden. Findet vor der Einführung der Wertpapiere ein Handel mit amtlicher Notierung der Bezugsrechte statt, muß der Prospekt mindestens drei Werktage vor dem Beginn dieses Handels veröffentlicht werden. Die Zulassungsstelle kann diese Fristen verkürzen, wenn der Emittent darlegt, daß ihm sonst ein für ihn unvorhersehbarer und auch unter Berücksichtigung der Interessen des Publikums nicht zu rechtfertigender Nachteil drohe; in besonderen Ausnahmefällen kann die Zulassungsstelle gestatten, daß der Prospekt nach der Eröffnung, aber vor Beendigung des Handels der Bezugsrechte veröffentlicht wird.

(2) Der Prospekt darf erst veröffentlicht werden, wenn er von der Zulassungsstelle gebilligt worden ist.

§ 44

Veröffentlichung eines unvollständigen Prospekts

Werden bei Schuldverschreibungen, die gleichzeitig mit ihrer öffentlichen ersten Ausgabe zugelassen werden, einzelne Ausgabebedingungen erst kurz vor der Ausgabe festgesetzt, so kann die Zulassungsstelle gestatten, daß ein

5. the national budget and national debt;
6. the annual maturities of any existing indebtedness;
7. the performance of obligations arising from bonds previously issued.

Information provided pursuant to Nos. 3 to 5 shall be given for the last three years.

(2) For the admission of bonds issued by regional authorities or international institutions, sub-paragraph 1 shall apply mutatis mutandis.

Sub-Part Three
Publication of the Prospectus

§ 43
Time Limit for Publication

(1) The prospectus shall be published at least three working days prior to the introduction of the securities. If trading with official quotation of subscription rights takes place prior to the introduction of the securities, the prospectus shall be published at least three working days prior to the commencement of such trading. The Listing Board may reduce this period if the issuer demonstrates that there is a likelihood that it may suffer some unforeseen and unfair disadvantage, even taking the interests of the public into consideration; in exceptional circumstances, the Listing Board may permit publication of the prospectus after the commencement, but prior to the termination of trading in the subscription rights.

(2) The prospectus may be published only after it has been approved by the Listing Board.

§ 44
Publication of an Incomplete Prospectus

If individual conditions applying to an issue of bonds which are admitted at the same time as their initial public issue are stipulated only shortly before issue, the Listing Board may permit publication of a prospectus which does not contain these conditions, but which contains information as to how

Börsenzul. Verordnung

Prospekt veröffentlicht wird, der dies Bedingungen nicht enthält und insoweit Auskunft darüber gibt, wie diese Angaben nachgetragen werden. Diese Angaben müssen vor der Einführung der Wertpapiere gemäß § 36 Abs. 4 des Börsengesetzes veröffentlicht werden; die Veröffentlichung kann nachträglich vorgenommen werden, wenn die Schuldverschreibungen während einer längeren Dauer und zu veränderlichen Preisen ausgegeben werden.

Vierter Unterabschnitt

Befreiung von der Pflicht, einen Prospekt zu veröffentlichen

§ 45

Befreiung im Hinblick auf bestimmte Wertpapiere

Die Zulassungsstelle kann von der Pflicht, einen Prospekt zu veröffentlichen, ganz oder teilweise befreien

1. wenn die zuzulassenden Wertpapiere

    a) Gegenstand einer öffentlichen ersten Ausgabe waren oder

    b) bei einem öffentlichen Umtauschangebot, einer Verschmelzung, Spaltung, Übertragung des gesamten oder eines Teils des Vermögens eines Unternehmens oder als Gegenleistung für Sacheinlagen ausgegeben worden sind

    und wenn innerhalb von zwölf Monaten vor ihrer Zulassung im Geltungsbereich dieser Verordnung eine schriftliche Darstellung veröffentlicht worden ist, die am Sitz des Emittenten und bei seinen Zahlstellen dem Publikum zur Verfügung steht und den für den Prospekt vorgeschriebenen Angaben entspricht, und alle seit der Erstellung dieser schriftlichen Darstellung eingetretenen wesentlichen Änderungen gemäß § 36 Abs. 4 des Börsengesetzes und § 43 Abs. 1 dieser Verordnung veröffentlicht werden;

2. wenn die zuzulassenden Wertpapiere Aktien sind, die

    a) nach einer Kapitalerhöhung aus Gesellschaftsmitteln den Inhabern an derselben Börse amtlich notierter Aktien zugeteilt werden,

    b) nach der Ausübung von Umtausch- oder Bezugsrechten aus anderen Wertpapieren als Aktien ausgegeben worden sind und Aktien der Gesellschaft, deren Aktien zum Umtausch oder Bezug angeboten worden sind, an derselben Börse amtlich notiert werden oder

Admissions Regulation

the details will later be provided. Such information shall be published prior to the introduction of the securities pursuant to § 36 sub-paragraph 4 of the Stock Exchange Act; publication may be made subsequently when the bonds are issued over an extended period and at variable prices.

Sub-Part Four

Exemption from the Obligation to Publish a Prospectus

§ 45

Exemption relating to Specific Securities

The Listing Board may grant an exemption from the obligation to publish a prospectus in whole or part

1. if the securities to be admitted

    a) have been the subject of an initial public issue or

    b) have been issued in connection with a public tender offer, a merger, split, transfer of the whole or part of the undertaking of an enterprise or as consideration for contributions in kind

    and provided that a written description has been published within three months prior to their admission in the territory where this Regulation applies, and that this description is available to the public at the principal place of business of the issuer and at the offices of its paying agents and provides the information required of a prospectus, and provided that all material changes which have occurred since the preparation of such description are published pursuant to § 36 sub-paragraph 4 of the Stock Exchange Act and § 43 sub-paragraph 1 of this Regulation;

2. if the securities to be admitted are shares which

    a) are allotted to holders of shares officially listed on the same stock exchange in connection with a capital increase out of retained earnings, or

    b) have been issued as shares in connection with the exercise of conversion or subscription rights attached to other securities and if the shares of the company whose shares are offered for conversion or subscription are officially listed on the same stock exchange or

Börsenzul. Verordnung

    c) an Stelle von an derselben Börse amtlich notierten Aktien ausgegeben worden sind, ohne daß mit der Ausgabe dieser neuen Aktien eine Änderung des gezeichneten Kapitals verbunden war

und wenn die in den §§ 15 und 16 vorgeschriebenen Angaben gemäß § 36 Abs. 4 des Börsengesetzes und § 43 Abs. 1 dieser Verordnung veröffentlicht werden oder

3. wenn die zuzulassenden Wertpapiere

    a) Wertpapiere sind, die an einer anderen inländischen Börse zur amtlichen Notierung zugelassen sind und wenn für diese Wertpapiere ein Prospekt veröffentlicht worden ist;

    b) Aktien sind, deren Zahl, geschätzter Kurswert oder Nennbetrag, bei nennwertlosen Aktien deren rechnerischer Wert, niedriger ist als zehn vom Hundert des entsprechenden Werts der Aktien derselben Gattung, die an derselben Börse amtlich notiert werden, und der Emittent die mit der Zulassung verbundenen Veröffentlichungspflichten erfüllt; Aktien, die sich nur in bezug auf den Beginn der Dividendenberechtigung unterscheiden, gelten als Aktien derselben Gattung;

    c) an Arbeitnehmer überlassene Aktien sind und Aktien derselben Gattung an derselben Börse amtlich notiert werden; Aktien, die sich nur in bezug auf den Beginn der Dividendenberechtigung unterscheiden, gelten als Aktien derselben Gattung;

    d) Aktien sind, die als Vergütung für den teilweisen oder gänzlichen Verzicht der persönlich haftenden Gesellschafter einer Kommanditgesellschaft auf Aktien auf ihre satzungsgemäßen Rechte bezüglich der Gewinne ausgegeben werden und wenn Aktien derselben Gattung an derselben Börse bereits amtlich notiert werden; Aktien, die sich nur in bezug auf den Beginn der Dividendenberechtigung unterscheiden, gelten als Aktien derselben Gattung;

    e) Schuldverschreibungen sind, die von Gesellschaften oder juristischen Personen mit Sitz in einem Mitgliedstaat der Europäischen Wirtschaftsgemeinschaft oder in einem anderen Vertragsstaat des Abkommens über den Europäischen Wirtschaftsraum ausgegeben werden, die ihre Tätigkeit unter einem Staatsmonopol ausüben und die durch ein besonderes Gesetz oder auf Grund eines besonderen Gesetzes geschaffen worden sind oder geregelt werden oder für deren Schuldverschreibungen ein Mitgliedstaat der Europäischen Wirtschaftsgemeinschaft oder eines seiner Bundesländer oder ein anderer Vertragsstaat des

Admissions Regulation

c) have been issued instead of shares officially listed on the same stock exchange, without any modification to the subscribed capital in connection with the issue of such new shares

and if the information required pursuant to §§ 15 and 16 is published pursuant to § 36 sub-paragraph 4 of the Stock Exchange Act and § 43 sub-paragraph 1 of this Regulation or

3. if the securities to be admitted are

   a) securities which have been admitted to official listing on another domestic stock exchange and a prospectus has been published for such securities;

   b) shares the number of which, estimated market value or nominal value or for shares not having a nominal value their calculated value, is less than ten per cent of the corresponding value of shares of the same class which are officially listed on the same stock exchange, and the issuer has complied with the publication obligations for the admission the publication of which is not to be older than three years; any shares which differ only on the commencement of entitlement to dividends shall be treated as of the same class;

   c) shares given to employees and of the same class officially listed on the same stock exchange; any shares which differ only on the commencement of entitlement to dividends shall be treated as the same class;

   d) shares issued in consideration of the waiver, in part or in full, by the personally liable members of a commercial partnership limited by shares of their rights to profits under the memorandum and articles, and if shares of the same class are already officially listed on the same stock exchange; any shares which differ only on the commencement of entitlement to dividends shall be treated as the same class;

   e) bonds issued by companies or legal entities which have their principal place of business in a member state of the European Economic Community or another contracting state of the European Economic Area Treaty which carry out its activities as a state monopoly and which have been established by a specific Act or on the basis of a specific Act or are regulated by such an Act or for whose bonds a member state of the European Economic Community or another contracting state of

Börsenzul. Verordnung

Abkommens über den Europäischen Wirtschaftsraum oder eines seiner Bundesländer die unbedingte und unwiderrufliche Gewährleistung für ihre Verzinsung und Rückzahlung übernommen hat;

f) Schuldverschreibungen sind, die von juristischen Personen mit Sitz in einem Mitgliedstaat der Europäischen Wirtschaftsgemeinschaft oder in einem anderen Vertragsstaat des Abkommens über den Europäischen Wirtschaftsraum ausgegeben werden, die keine Gesellschaften sind, durch ein besonderes Gesetz geschaffen worden sind und deren Tätigkeit nach diesem Gesetz ausschließlich darin besteht, unter behördlicher Aufsicht durch die Ausgabe von Schuldverschreibungen Kapital aufzunehmen und mit diesen aufgenommenen sowie mit von einem Mitgliedstaat der Europäischen Wirtschaftsgemeinschaft oder von einem anderen Vertragsstaat des Abkommens über den Europäischen Wirtschaftsraum bereitgestellten Mitteln die Erzeugung von Gütern und Erbringung von Dienstleistungen zu finanzieren, und deren Schuldverschreibungen für die Zulassung zur amtlichen Notierung durch innerstaatliches Recht den Schuldverschreibungen rechtlich gleichgestellt sind, die vom Staat ausgegeben werden oder für deren Verzinsung und Rückzahlung der Staat die Gewährleistung übernommen hat;

g) Zertifikate sind, die Aktien vertreten und im Austausch gegen die vertretenen Aktien ausgegeben worden sind, ohne daß mit der Ausgabe dieser neuen Zertifikate eine Änderung des gezeichneten Kapitals verbunden war, und Zertifikate, die diese Aktien vertreten, an derselben Börse amtlich notiert werden,

und wenn Angaben über die Zahl und Art der zuzulassenden Wertpapiere und die Bedingungen ihrer Ausgabe gemäß § 36 Abs. 4 des Börsengesetzes und § 43 Abs. 1 dieser Verordnung veröffentlicht werden.

§ 46
Befreiung im Hinblick auf bestimmte Anleger

Die Zulassungsstelle kann für die Zulassung von anderen Wertpapieren als Aktien gestatten, daß Angaben, die nach dieser Verordnung vorgeschrieben sind, nicht oder nur in zusammengefaßter Form in den Prospekt aufgenommen werden, wenn die zuzulassenden Wertpapiere nach ihren Merkmalen in der Regel nur von Anlegern erworben werden, die mit der Anlage in solchen Wertpapieren besonders vertraut sind und diese Wertpapiere in der Regel nur untereinander handeln. Dies gilt nicht für Angaben, die für diese Anleger von wesentlicher Bedeutung sind.

Admissions Regulation

the European Economic Area Treaty or one of its federal states has given an unconditional and irrevocable guarantee for the payment of interest and principal;

f) bonds issued by legal entities having their principal place of business in a member state of the European Economic Community or another contracting state of the European Economic Area Treaty, which are not companies and are established by a specific Act and which carry out business pursuant to this Act solely for the purpose of raising capital under governmental supervision by issuing bonds and by financing with such funds and with funds provided by a member state of the European Economic Community or another contracting state of the European Economic Area Treaty, for the production of goods and the rendering of services, and whose bonds are, for the purposes of admission to official listing, treated under domestic law as legally equivalent to bonds issued by the government or to bonds for the payment of interest and principal for which the government has given its guarantee;

g) certificates representing shares issued in exchange for the represented shares, without a change in subscribed capital having occurred in the context of the issuance of such securities, and, if certificates representing such shares are listed on the same stock exchange,

and if information about the number and type of securities to be admitted and the terms of issue are published according to § 36 sub-paragraph 4 of the Stock Exchange Act and § 43 sub-paragraph 1 of this Regulation.

§ 46
Exemption relating to Specific Investors

For the admission of securities other than shares, the Listing Board may allow the information prescribed by this Regulation to be omitted from the prospectus or included in summary form if the securities to be admitted are, by reason of their characteristics, normally purchased only by investors who have particular experience in investing in such securities and who normally trade such securities only among themselves. This shall not apply to information which is of material significance for such investors.

Börsenzul. Verordnung

§ 47

Befreiung im Hinblick auf einzelne Angaben

Die Zulassungsstelle kann gestatten, daß einzelne Angaben, die nach dieser Verordnung vorgeschrieben sind, nicht in den Prospekt aufgenommen werden, wenn sie der Auffassung ist, daß

1. diese Angaben nur von geringer Bedeutung und nicht geeignet sind, die Beurteilung der Vermögens-, Finanz- und Ertragslage und der Entwicklungsaussichten des Emittenten zu beeinflussen,
2. die Verbreitung dieser Angaben dem öffentlichen Interesse zuwiderläuft oder
3. die Verbreitung dieser Angaben dem Emittenten erheblichen Schaden zufügt, sofern die Nichtveröffentlichung das Publikum nicht über die für die Beurteilung der zuzulassenden Wertpapiere wesentlichen Tatsachen und Umstände täuscht.

Dritter Abschnitt

Zulassungsverfahren

§ 48

Zulassungsantrag

(1) Der Zulassungsantrag ist schriftlich zu stellen. Er muß Firma und Sitz der Antragsteller, Art und Betrag der zuzulassenden Wertpapiere sowie ein überregionales Börsenpflichtblatt, in dem der Antrag veröffentlicht werden soll, angeben; weitere Börsenpflichtblätter können angegeben werden. Ferner ist anzugeben, ob ein gleichartiger Antrag zuvor oder gleichzeitig an einer anderen inländischen Börse oder in einem anderen Mitgliedstaat der Europäischen Wirtschaftsgemeinschaft oder in einem anderen Vertragsstaat des Abkommens über den Europäischen Wirtschaftsraum gestellt worden ist oder alsbald gestellt werden wird.

(2) Dem Antrag sind ein Entwurf des Prospekts und die zur Prüfung der Zulassungsvoraussetzungen erforderlichen Nachweise beizufügen. Der Zulassungsstelle sind auf Verlangen insbesondere vorzulegen

Admissions Regulation

§ 47

Exemption relating to Specific Information

The Listing Board may allow information to be omitted from a prospectus which is otherwise prescribed by this Regulation, if it is of the view that

1. such information is of only minor significance and not likely to influence the net worth, financial position, results and prospective business development of the issuer,
2. the dissemination of such information would be contrary to the public interest or
3. the dissemination of such information would cause substantial prejudice to the issuer, provided that its non-publication would not mislead the public about any facts or matters which are of material significance in assessing the securities to be admitted.

Part Three

Admissions Procedure

§ 48

Application for Admission

(1) Application for admission shall be made in writing. It shall state the firm name and principal place of business of the applicant, the nature and quantity of the securities to be admitted, and the identity of a national authorized journal for mandatory stock exchange publication in which the application is to be published; further authorized journals may be stated. In addition, it shall contain a statement as to whether a similar application has been or is to be made in the near future to any other domestic stock exchange or any stock exchanges in any other member state of the European Economic Community or another contracting state of the European Economic Area Treaty.

(2) A draft of the prospectus and all documentation necessary for the purpose of checking the admission requirements shall be annexed to the application. The Listing Board may in particular require the following to be submitted:

Börsenzul. Verordnung

1. ein beglaubigter Auszug aus dem Handelsregister nach neuestem Stand;
2. die Satzung oder der Gesellschaftsvertrag in der neuesten Fassung;
3. die Genehmigungsurkunden, wenn die Gründung des Emittenten, die Ausübung seiner Geschäftstätigkeit oder die Ausgabe der Wertpapiere einer staatlichen Genehmigung bedarf;
4. die Jahresabschlüsse und die Lageberichte für die drei Geschäftsjahre, die dem Antrag vorausgegangen sind, einschließlich der Bestätigungsvermerke der Abschlußprüfer;
5. ein Nachweis über die Rechtsgrundlage der Wertpapierausgabe;
6. im Falle ausgedruckter Einzelurkunden ein Musterstück jeden Nennwertes der zuzulassenden Wertpapiere (Mantel und Bogen);
7. im Falle einer Sammelverbriefung der zuzulassenden Wertpapiere die Erklärung des Emittenten, daß

a) die Sammelurkunde bei einer Wertpapiersammelbank (§ 1 Abs. 3 des Depotgesetzes) hinterlegt ist und bei einer Auflösung der Sammelurkunde die Einzelurkunden gemäß Nummer 6 vorgelegt werden und

b) er auf Anforderung der Zulassungsstelle die Sammelurkunde auflösen wird, wenn er gegenüber den Inhabern der in der Sammelurkunde verbrieften Rechte verpflichtet ist, auf Verlangen einzelne Wertpapiere auszugeben;

8. im Falle des § 3 Abs. 2 die Berichte über die Gründung und deren Prüfung (§ 32 Abs. 1, § 34 Abs. 2 des Aktiengesetzes).

§ 49
Veröffentlichung des Zulassungsantrags

Der Zulassungsantrag ist von der Zulassungsstelle auf Kosten der Antragsteller im Bundesanzeiger und in dem im Antrag angegebenen Börsenpflichtblatt sowie durch Börsenbekanntmachung zu veröffentlichen.

§ 50
Zeitpunkt der Zulassung

Die Zulassung darf nicht vor Ablauf von drei Werktagen seit der ersten Veröffentlichung des Zulassungsantrags erfolgen.

Admissions Regulation

1. current certified extracts from the Commercial Register;
2. a current version of the memorandum and articles of association;
3. any documents of authorization if the formation of the issuer, the carrying out of its business or the issue of securities requires government authorization;
4. the annual accounts and management reports for the three financial years preceding the application, including the auditors' opinion;
5. evidence of the legal basis on which the securities are to be issued;
6. in the case of individually printed certificates, a sample certificate for each nominal value of the securities to be admitted (certificate and coupon sheet);
7. in the case of a collective certificate for the securities to be admitted, a declaration by the issuer that
   a) the collective certificate has been deposited with a securities clearing and depositing bank (§ 1 sub-paragraph 3 of the Securities Deposit Act) and that in case of any exchange of the collective certificate, individual certificates in accordance with No. 6 will be provided, and
   b) the issuer will exchange the collective certificate at the request of the Listing Board if the issuer is required by the holders of the rights represented by the collective certificate to issue individual securities if requested to do so;
8. for cases falling under § 3 sub-paragraph 2, the reports on formation and an audit report in respect thereof (§ 32 sub-paragraph 1, § 34 sub-paragraph 2 of the Stock Corporation Act).

§ 49
Publication of the Application for Admission

The application for admission shall be published by the Listing Board at the expense of the applicant in the Federal Gazette and in the authorized journal referred to in the application and by announcement on the stock exchange.

§ 50
Date of Admission

Admission shall not be granted before the expiry of three working days after initial publication of the application for admission.

Börsenzul. Verordnung

§ 51
Veröffentlichung der Zulassung

Die Zulassung ist in die Veröffentlichung des Prospekts aufzunehmen. Ist ein Prospekt nicht zu veröffentlichen, so wird die Zulassung von der Zulassungsstelle auf Kosten der Antragsteller im Bundesanzeiger und in dem Börsenpflichtblatt, in dem der Antrag veröffentlicht worden ist, sowie durch Börsenbekanntmachung veröffentlicht.

§ 52
Einführung

(1) Vorbehaltlich des § 43 Abs. 1 Satz 3 dürfen die zugelassenen Wertpapiere frühestens am dritten Werktag nach der ersten Veröffentlichung des Prospekts oder, wenn kein Prospekt zu veröffentlichen ist, nach der Veröffentlichung der Zulassung eingeführt werden.

(2) Sind seit der Veröffentlichung des Prospekts Veränderungen bei Umständen eingetreten, die für die Beurteilung des Emittenten oder der einzuführenden Wertpapiere von wesentlicher Bedeutung sind, so sind die Veränderungen in einem Nachtrag zum Prospekt zu veröffentlichen. Auf diesen Nachtrag sind die Vorschriften über den Prospekt und dessen Veröffentlichungen entsprechend anzuwenden.

Admissions Regulation

§ 51
Publication of Admission

The admission shall be included when the prospectus is published. If no prospectus is to be published, the admission shall be published by the Listing Board at the applicant's expense in the Federal Gazette and in the authorized journal where the application has been published and by announcement on the stock exchange.

§ 52
Introduction

(1) Subject to § 43 sub-paragraph 1 sentence 3, the securities to be admitted may be introduced no sooner than the third working day after first publication of the prospectus or, if no prospectus is to be published, after publication of the admission.

(2) If, following publication of the prospectus, any changes of circumstances occur which are of material significance for the assessment of the issuer or the securities to be admitted, such changes shall be published in a supplement to the prospectus. The provisions relating to the prospectus and the manner of its publication shall also apply to the supplement.

Börsenzul. Verordnung

Zweites Kapitel
Pflichten des Emittenten zugelassener Wertpapiere

Erster Abschnitt
Zwischenbericht

Erster Unterabschnitt
Inhalt des Zwischenberichts

§ 53
Allgemeine Grundsätze

Der Zwischenbericht muß eine Beurteilung ermöglichen, wie sich die Geschäftstätigkeit des Emittenten in den ersten sechs Monaten des Geschäftsjahres entwickelt hat. Er muß Zahlenangaben über die Tätigkeit und die Ergebnisse des Emittenten im Berichtszeitraum sowie Erläuterungen hierzu enthalten und vorbehaltlich der Vorschrift des § 58 Satz 2 in deutscher Sprache abgefaßt sein.

§ 54
Zahlenangaben

(1) Die Zahlenangaben müssen mindestens den Betrag der Umsatzerlöse und das Ergebnis vor oder nach Steuern im Sinne der für die Rechnungslegung geltenden handelsrechtlichen Vorschriften ausweisen. Zu jeder Zahlenangabe ist die Vergleichszahl für den entsprechenden Zeitraum des Vorjahres anzugeben.

(2) Hat der Emittent für den Berichtszeitraum Zwischendividenden ausgeschüttet oder schlägt er dies vor, so sind bei den Zahlenangaben das Ergebnis nach Steuern für den betreffenden Zeitraum und der ausgeschüttete oder zur Ausschüttung vorgeschlagene Betrag auszuweisen.

(3) Sind die Zahlenangaben durch einen Abschlußprüfer geprüft worden, so sind der Bestätigungsvermerk einschließlich zusätzlicher Bemerkungen sowie Einschränkungen oder seine Versagung vollständig wiederzugeben.

Chapter Two
Obligations of an Issuer of Admitted Securities

Part One

Interim Report

Sub-Part One

Contents of the Interim Report

§ 53

General Principles

The interim report shall make it possible to assess the development of the issuer's business during the first six months of the financial year. It shall contain figures relating to business operations and the results of the issuer for the reporting period and explanations and shall, subject to the provisions of § 58 sentence 2, be in the German language.

§ 54

Figures Provided

(1) The figures provided shall at a minimum indicate the amount of turnover and results before or after tax in accordance with current accounting and commercial law provisions. For each set of figures, comparative figures for the corresponding period of the previous year shall also be provided.

(2) If the issuer has paid interim dividends during the reporting period or proposes to do so, the results after tax for the relevant period and details of any distribution or proposed distribution shall be given in the figures.

(3) If the figures provided have been audited, the auditors' opinion, including any notes and qualifications or confirmation of their refusal to issue an opinion, shall be set out in full.

Börsenzul. Verordnung

(4) Einem Emittenten, dessen Aktien nur an inländischen Börsen zur amtlichen Notierung zugelassen sind, kann die Zulassungsstelle gestatten, das Ergebnis in Form einer geschätzten Zahlenangabe auszuweisen, wenn der Emittent darlegt, daß sich nur dadurch für ihn im Hinblick auf den zusätzlichen Aussagewert unverhältnismäßig hohe Kosten vermeiden lassen oder andere Gründe diese Ausnahme rechtfertigen. Aus dem Zwischenbericht muß für das Publikum deutlich erkennbar sein, daß es sich um geschätzte Zahlen handelt.

§ 55

Erläuterungen

In den Erläuterungen sind in dem Umfang, der für die Beurteilung der Entwicklung der Geschäftstätigkeit und der Ergebnisse des Emittenten erforderlich ist, die Umsatzerlöse aufzugliedern und Ausführungen zu machen über Auftragslage, Entwicklung der Kosten und Preise, Zahl der Arbeitnehmer, Investitionen sowie über Vorgänge von besonderer Bedeutung, die sich auf das Ergebnis der Geschäftstätigkeit auswirken können. Soweit besondere Umstände die Entwicklung der Geschäftstätigkeit beeinflußt haben, ist hierauf hinzuweisen. Die Erläuterungen müssen einen Vergleich mit den Vorjahresangaben ermöglichen. Soweit möglich, haben sich die Erläuterungen auch auf die Aussichten des Emittenten für das laufende Geschäftsjahr zu erstrecken.

§ 56

Konzernabschluß

Veröffentlicht der Emittent einen Konzernabschluß, so kann er den Zwischenbericht entweder für die Einzelgesellschaft oder für den Konzern aufstellen. Enthält die nicht gewählte Form nach Auffassung der Zulassungsstelle wichtige zusätzliche Angaben, so kann die Zulassungsstelle von dem Emittenten die Veröffentlichung dieser Angaben verlangen.

Admissions Regulation

(4) The Listing Board may permit an issuer whose shares are only admitted to official listing on a domestic stock exchange to state its results in the form of an estimate if the issuer demonstrates that the costs of providing full figures are disproportionately high and that it is justifiable regarding the value of those figures or for other reasons. If estimated figures are used, it shall be made clear to the public that the figures are estimates.

§ 55

Explanations

The explanations shall be sufficient to enable an assessment to be made of the development of operations and results of the issuer and shall break down the turnover and statements relating to the order books, development of costs and prices, the number of employees, investments and events of particular significance which could have an adverse effect on the results of the business. If unusual circumstances have influenced the development of business operations, this is to be stated. The explanations must make it possible to compare the given information with that for the previous year. As far as possible, the explanations shall also deal with the issuer's business prospects for the current financial year.

§ 56

Consolidated Annual Accounts

If the issuer publishes consolidated accounts, it may prepare its interim report either for the individual company concerned or on a consolidated basis. If, in the opinion of the Listing Board, the form not adopted contains material information, the Listing Board may require the issuer to publish such information.

Börsenzul. Verordnung

Zweiter Unterabschnitt

Inhalt des Zwischenberichts in Sonderfällen

§ 57

Anpassung der Zahlenangaben

(1) Ist die Angabe von Umsatzerlösen im Hinblick auf die Tätigkeit des Emittenten nicht geeignet, eine den tatsächlichen Verhältnissen entsprechende Beurteilung der Geschäftstätigkeit des Emittenten zu ermöglichen, so ist die Angabe um eine der Tätigkeit des Emittenten entsprechend angepaßte Zahlenangabe zu ergänzen.

(2) Emittenten, die überwiegend den Betrieb von Bankgeschäften im Sinne des § 1 Abs. 1 Satz 2 des Gesetzes über das Kreditwesen zum Gegenstand des Unternehmens haben, müssen an Stelle der Umsatzerlöse und des Ergebnisses die Bilanzsumme und die in der Anlage dieser Verordnung aufgeführten Posten aus der Bilanz und der Gewinn- und Verlustrechnung angeben sowie über die Entwicklung der Eigenhandelsgeschäfte in Wertpapieren, Devisen und Edelmetallen berichten. § 55 ist im übrigen sinngemäß anzuwenden.

(3) Emittenten, die überwiegend den Betrieb von Versicherungsgeschäften zum Gegenstand des Unternehmens haben, müssen an Stelle der Umsatzerlöse und des Ergebnisses die Beitragseinnahmen in den wichtigsten Versicherungszweigen sowie die Bestände in der Lebensversicherung angeben und in den Erläuterungen auch über die Ergebniskomponenten für Schäden, Kosten und Erträge aus Kapitalanlagen berichten. § 55 ist im übrigen sinngemäß anzuwenden.

§ 58

Emittenten aus Drittstaaten

Veröffentlicht ein Emittent, der nicht dem Recht eines Mitgliedstaates der Europäischen Wirtschaftsgemeinschaft oder eines anderen Vertragsstaates des Abkommens über den Europäischen Wirtschaftsraum unterliegt, außerhalb der Europäischen Wirtschaftsgemeinschaft oder außerhalb eines anderen Vertragsstaates des Abkommens über den Europäischen Wirtschaftsraum einen Zwischenbericht, so kann ihm die Zulassungsstelle gestatten, diesen Bericht an Stelle des nach § 44b des Börsengesetzes vorgeschriebenen Zwischenberichts in deutscher Sprache zu veröffentlichen, wenn er Auskünfte gibt, die den Aus-

Sub-Part Two

Contents of the Interim Report in Special Cases

§ 57

Adjustment of Figures Provided

(1) If as a result of the issuer's type of business the statements of turnover provided do not allow an assessment to be made of the true circumstances of the issuer's business, then the statement of turnover shall be supplemented by information in the form of figures to provide a true picture of the issuer's business activity.

(2) Issuers, whose principal objects of business are the conduct of banking business according to § 1 sub-paragraph 1 sentence 2 of the Banking Act shall, instead of information on turnover and results, state the amount of its balance sheet total and the information listed in the appendix of this Regulation derived from the balance sheet and profit and loss accounts, and shall report on the development of own-account trading in securities, foreign exchange and precious metals. In all other respects, § 55 shall apply.

(3) Issuers, whose principal objects of business are the conduct of insurance business shall, in place of information about turnover and results, state their premium revenue broken down by reference to principal areas of insurance business and the inventory of life insurance policies, and shall by way of explanations also report revenue results regarding damages claims and costs and income from capital investments. In all other respects, § 55 shall apply.

§ 58

Issuers from Third Party States

If an issuer, not subject to the laws of a member state of the European Economic Community or another contracting state of the European Economic Area Treaty, publishes an interim report outside the European Economic Community or another contracting state of the European Economic Area Treaty, the Listing Board may allow the issuer to publish the report in the German language in place of the interim report provided for under § 44 b of the Stock Exchange Act, if that report contains information equivalent to the information required under §§ 53 to 57. The Listing Board may also allow the report to be prepared in another language if it is not unusual for that

Börsenzul. Verordnung

künften nach den Vorschriften der §§ 53 bis 57 gleichwertig sind. Die Zulassungsstelle kann auch gestatten, daß dieser Bericht in einer anderen Sprache abgefaßt ist, wenn diese Sprache auf dem Gebiet der Wertpapieranlage in ausländischen Werten innerhalb des Geltungsbereichs dieser Verordnung nicht unüblich ist und eine ausreichende Unterrichtung des Publikums im Hinblick auf die angesprochenen Anlegerkreise dadurch nicht gefährdet erscheint.

§ 59
Zwischenberichte in mehreren Mitgliedstaaten der Europäischen Wirtschaftsgemeinschaft

Ist ein Zwischenbericht auch in einem anderen Mitgliedstaat der Europäischen Wirtschaftsgemeinschaft oder in einem anderen Vertragsstaat des Abkommens über den Europäischen Wirtschaftsraum zu veröffentlichen, so stimmt die Zulassungsstelle mit der entsprechenden Stelle des anderen Staates die Anforderungen an den Zwischenbericht ab, um nach Möglichkeit zu erreichen, daß eine einheitliche Fassung veröffentlicht werden kann.

§ 60
Befreiung im Hinblick auf einzelne Angaben

Die Zulassungsstelle kann gestatten, daß einzelne Angaben nicht in den Zwischenbericht aufgenommen werden, wenn sie der Auffassung ist, daß

1. die Verbreitung dieser Angaben dem öffentlichen Interesse zuwiderläuft oder

2. die Verbreitung dieser Angaben dem Emittenten erheblichen Schaden zufügt, sofern die Nichtveröffentlichung das Publikum nicht über die für die Beurteilung der Aktien des Emittenten wesentlichen Tatsachen und Umstände täuscht.

Dritter Unterabschnitt

Veröffentlichung des Zwischenberichts

§ 61
Form und Frist der Veröffentlichung

(1) Der Zwischenbericht ist innerhalb von zwei Monaten nach dem Ende des Berichtszeitraums entweder durch Abdruck in mindestens einem überre-

language to be used in relation to investments in foreign securities within the territory where this Regulation applies and if there does not appear to be a danger of the public not being sufficiently informed in respect to the targeted group of investors.

§ 59
Interim Reports Appearing in more than One Member State of the European Economic Community or another Contracting State of the European Economic Area Treaty

If an interim report must also be published in another member state of the European Economic Community or another contracting state of the European Economic Area Treaty, the Listing Board shall agree with the relevant authority of the other state on the requirements of the interim report to ensure, if possible, that the report is published in a uniform version.

§ 60
Exemptions relating to Particular Items of Information

The Listing Board may allow particular items of information to be omitted from an interim report if it is of the opinion that

1. the dissemination of such information would be contrary to the public interest or
2. the dissemination of such information would cause substantial damage to the issuer so long as its non-publication would not mislead the public about facts and circumstances which are material in assessing the issuer's shares.

Sub-Part Three

Publication of the Interim Report

§ 61
Time Limit and Form of Publication

(1) The interim report is to be published within two months of the end of the reporting period either by publication in at least one national authorized

Börsenzul. Verordnung

gionalen Börsenpflichtblatt oder im Bundesanzeiger oder als Druckschrift zu veröffentlichen, die dem Publikum bei den Zahlstellen auf Verlangen kostenlos zur Verfügung gestellt wird. Wird der Zwischenbericht nicht im Bundesanzeiger veröffentlicht, so ist im Bundesanzeiger ein Hinweis darauf bekanntzumachen, wo der Zwischenbericht veröffentlicht und für das Publikum zu erhalten ist.

(2) Bei Emittenten, die überwiegend den Betrieb von Rückversicherungsgeschäften zum Gegenstand des Unternehmens haben, ist der Zwischenbericht innerhalb von sechs Monaten gemäß Absatz 1 Satz 1 zu veröffentlichen.

(3) Die Zulassungsstelle kann die Fristen für die Veröffentlichung verlängern, wenn der Emittent darlegt, daß ihm die Einhaltung dieser Frist aus für ihn nicht vorhersehbaren Gründen nicht möglich ist oder daß andere Gründe vorliegen, die auch nach Würdigung der Interessen des Publikums eine Verlängerung der Fristen rechtfertigen.

§ 62

Übermittlung an Zulassungsstelle

Der Emittent ist verpflichtet, den Zwischenbericht spätestens mit seiner ersten Veröffentlichung in einem Mitgliedstaat der Europäischen Wirtschaftsgemeinschaft oder in einem anderen Vertragsstaat des Abkommens über den Europäischen Wirtschaftsraum den Zulassungsstellen der Börsen, an denen die Aktien zur amtlichen Notierung zugelassen sind, und gleichzeitig den entsprechenden Stellen der anderen Mitgliedstaaten der Europäischen Wirtschaftsgemeinschaft oder der anderen Vertragsstaaten des Abkommens über den Europäischen Wirtschaftsraum, in denen die Aktien zur amtlichen Notierung zugelassen sind, zu übermitteln.

Zweiter Abschnitt

Sonstige Pflichten

§ 63

Veröffentlichung von Mitteilungen

(1) Der Emittent zugelassener Aktien muß die Einberufung der Hauptversammlung und Mitteilungen über die Ausschüttung und Auszahlung von Dividenden, die Ausgabe neuer Aktien und die Ausübung von Umtausch-, Bezugs- und Zeichnungsrechten veröffentlichen.

journal, in the Federal Gazette, or in printed form available to the public upon demand and free of charge at the offices of the paying agents. If an interim report is not published in the Federal Gazette, notice shall be published in the Federal Gazette indicating where the interim report is published and available to the public.

(2) In the case of issuers whose principal business is reinsurance, the interim report shall be published within seven months according to the provisions of sub-paragraph 1, sentence 1 above.

(3) The Listing Board may extend the time for publication if the issuer demonstrates that it cannot comply with these time limits for unforeseen reasons, or if there are other reasons justifying a time extension, also considering the interests of the public.

§ 62

Delivery of the Interim Report to the Listing Board

The issuer is obliged to deliver the interim report to the Listing Board of the stock exchange where the shares are admitted to official quotation and at the same time to the relevant offices of any other member states of the European Economic Community or another contracting state of the European Economic Area Treaty where the shares are admitted to official listing by no later than the date of first publication of the interim report in a member state of the European Economic Community or another contracting state of the European Economic Area Treaty.

Part Two

Miscellaneous Obligations

§ 63

Publication of Notifications

(1) An issuer of admitted shares shall publish details of the holding of any general shareholders' meetings and any notices of declaration and payments of dividends, the issue of any new shares and the exercise of any conversion or subscription rights.

Börsenzul. Verordnung

(2) Der Emittent zugelassener anderer Wertpapiere als Aktien muß Mitteilungen über die Ausübung von Umtausch-, Zeichnungs- und Kündigungsrechten sowie über die Zinszahlung, die Rückzahlungen, die Auslosungen und die früher gekündigten oder ausgelosten, noch nicht eingelösten Stücke veröffentlichen. Der Emittent zugelassener Schuldverschreibungen muß ferner die Einberufung der Versammlung der Schuldverschreibungsinhaber veröffentlichen.

§ 64
Änderungen der Rechtsgrundlage des Emittenten

(1) Der Emittent zugelassener Aktien muß beabsichtigte Änderungen seiner Satzung spätestens zum Zeitpunkt der Einberufung der Hauptversammlung, die über die Änderung beschließen soll, der Zulassungsstelle mitteilen.

(2) Der Emittent zugelassener anderer Wertpapiere als Aktien muß beabsichtigte Änderungen seiner Rechtsgrundlage, welche die Rechte der Wertpapierinhaber berühren, spätestens zum Zeitpunkt der Einberufung des Beschlußorgans, das über die Änderung beschließen soll, der Zulassungsstelle mitteilen.

§ 65
Verfügbarkeit von Jahresabschluß und Lagebericht

(1) Der Emittent der zugelassenen Wertpapiere hat den Jahresabschluß und den Lagebericht unverzüglich nach der Feststellung dem Publikum bei den Zahlstellen zur Verfügung zu stellen, sofern nicht der Jahresabschluß und Lagebericht im Geltungsbereich dieser Verordnung veröffentlicht worden ist.

(2) Stellt der Emittent sowohl einen Einzelabschluß als auch einen Konzernabschluß auf, so sind beide Arten von Jahresabschlüssen nach Maßgabe des Absatzes 1 dem Publikum zur Verfügung zu stellen. Die Zulassungsstelle kann dem Emittenten gestatten, nur den Jahresabschluß der einen Art zur Verfügung zu stellen, wenn der Jahresabschluß der anderen Art keine wesentlichen zusätzlichen Aussagen enthält.

(3) Die Zulassungsstelle kann Zusammenfassungen oder Kürzungen des Jahresabschlusses zulassen, soweit eine ausreichende Unterrichtung des Publikums gewährleistet bleibt und auf die Stelle hingewiesen wird, bei der die vollständige Fassung verfügbar oder veröffentlicht ist.

Admissions Regulation

(2) An issuer of admitted securities other than shares shall publish details about the exercise of any conversion, subscription or redemption rights, the payment of interest, the repayment of any principal sums, advance redemption and any bonds previously redeemed or drawn, but not yet presented for payment. The issuer of admitted bonds shall also publish details on the convening of any meeting of bondholders.

§ 64
Changes of the Legal Basis of the Issuer

(1) An issuer of admitted shares shall notify the Listing Board of any proposed changes to its memorandum or articles of association no later than the date of the calling of the shareholders' meeting at which such changes are to be put to a vote.

(2) An issuer of admitted securities other than shares shall notify the Listing Board of any proposed changes of its legal basis which might affect the rights of the holders of any securities no later than the date of the calling of a meeting of the body entitled to vote on such changes.

§ 65
Availability of Annual Accounts and Management Reports

(1) An issuer of admitted securities shall make available at the offices of its paying agent its annual accounts and management reports as soon as they have been approved unless the accounts and reports have been published within the territory where this Regulation applies.

(2) If an issuer prepares both individual and consolidated accounts, then both shall be made available to the public in accordance with sub-paragraph 1. The Listing Board may allow an issuer to provide its annual accounts in one form only if the accounts of the type not to be provided do not contain essential additional information.

(3) The Listing Board may allow annual accounts to be provided in summary or abbreviated form if sufficient information is available to the public and if information is given as to where complete documentation is available or published.

Börsenzul. Verordnung

(4) Entsprechen bei Emittenten mit Sitz außerhalb der Europäischen Wirtschaftsgemeinschaft oder außerhalb eines anderen Vertragsstaates des Abkommens über den Europäischen Wirtschaftsraum der Jahresabschluß oder der Lagebericht nicht den Vorschriften im Geltungsbereich dieser Verordnung über den Jahresabschluß und den Lagebericht von Gesellschaften und geben sie kein den tatsächlichen Verhältnissen entsprechendes Bild von der Vermögens-, Finanz- und Ertragslage des Emittenten, so hat der Emittent ergänzende Angaben hierzu dem Publikum bei den Zahlstellen zur Verfügung zu stellen.

§ 66
Veröffentlichung zusätzlicher Angaben

(1) Der Emittent der zugelassenen Wertpapiere muß jede Änderung der mit den Wertpapieren verbundenen Rechte unverzüglich veröffentlichen.

(2) Der Emittent zugelassener anderer Wertpapiere als Aktien muß ferner unverzüglich veröffentlichen

1. die Aufnahme von Anleihen, insbesondere die für sie übernommenen Gewährleistungen;

2. bei Wertpapieren, die den Gläubigern ein Umtausch- oder Bezugsrecht auf Aktien einräumen, alle Änderungen der Rechte, die mit den Aktien verbunden sind, auf die sich das Umtausch- oder Bezugsrecht bezieht.

(3) Absatz 2 Nr. 1 gilt nicht

1. für Emittenten, die ihren Sitz im Geltungsbereich dieser Verordnung oder in einem anderen Mitgliedstaat der Europäischen Wirtschaftsgemeinschaft oder in einem anderen Vertragsstaat des Abkommens über den Europäischen Wirtschaftsraum haben und durch ein besonderes Gesetz oder auf Grund eines besonderen Gesetzes geschaffen worden sind oder geregelt werden, wenn für die Verzinsung und Rückzahlung der zugelassenen Wertpapiere ein Mitgliedstaat der Europäischen Wirtschaftsgemeinschaft oder eines seiner Bundesländer oder ein anderer Vertragsstaat des Abkommens über den Europäischen Wirtschaftsraum oder eines seiner Bundesländer die Gewährleistung übernommen hat;

2. für die in § 41 des Börsengesetzes und in § 38 dieser Verordnung bezeichneten Schuldverschreibungen.

Admissions Regulation

(4) If an issuer has its principal place of business outside the European Economic Community or another contracting state of the European Economic Area Treaty and its annual accounts or management reports do not comply with the provisions valid in the territory of this regulation regarding annual accounts and management reports, and they fail to give a true and fair view of the issuer regarding its net worth, financial position and results, the issuer must make available to the public the appropriate additional information at the offices of its paying agents.

§ 66
Publication of Additional Information

(1) An issuer of admitted securities shall be obliged to publish forthwith details of any changes in the rights attaching to its securities.

(2) An issuer of admitted securities other than shares shall in addition publish forthwith

1. details of the taking up of any debentures and in particular any warranties given in connection therewith;
2. in the case of securities granting creditors conversion or subscription rights in shares, any variations of the rights arising out of those shares to which such rights of conversion or subscription relate.

(3) Sub-paragraph 2 No.1 shall not apply to

1. issuers having their principal place of business in the territory where this Regulation applies or in another member state of the European Economic Community or another contracting state of the European Economic Area Treaty which have been created or are regulated by a special Act, provided that the member state of the European Economic Community or another contracting state of the European Economic Area Treaty or a federal state thereof has guaranteed the payment of principal and interest of the admitted securities;
2. bonds of the type referred to in § 41 of the Stock Exchange Act and § 38 of this regulation.

Börsenzul. Verordnung

§ 67
Unterrichtung bei Zulassung an mehreren Börsen

(1) Sind Wertpapiere eines Emittenten an mehreren inländischen Börsen zur amtlichen Notierung zugelassen, so muß der Emittent an diesen Börsenplätzen dieselben Angaben veröffentlichen.

(2) Sind zugelassene Wertpapiere auch außerhalb des Geltungsbereichs dieser Verordnung an einer Börse zur amtlichen Notierung zugelassen und hat der Emittent dort Angaben veröffentlicht, die für die Bewertung der Wertpapiere Bedeutung haben können, so muß er im Geltungsbereich dieser Verordnung zumindest gleichwertige Angaben veröffentlichen.

§ 68
Hinweis auf Prospekt

Veröffentlichungen, in denen die Zulassung von Wertpapieren eines Emittenten zur amtlichen Notierung angekündigt und auf die wesentlichen Merkmale der Wertpapiere hingewiesen wird, müssen einen Hinweis auf den Prospekt und dessen Veröffentlichung enthalten. Die Veröffentlichungen sind unverzüglich der Zulassungsstelle zu übermitteln.

§ 69
Zulassung später ausgegebener Aktien

(1) Der Emittent zugelassener Aktien ist verpflichtet, für später öffentlich ausgegebene Aktien derselben Gattung wie der bereits zugelassenen die Zulassung zur amtlichen Notierung zu beantragen, wenn ihre Zulassung einen Antrag voraussetzt. § 7 Abs. 1 Satz 2 und 3 bleibt unberührt.

(2) Der Antrag nach Absatz 1 ist spätestens ein Jahr nach der Ausgabe der zuzulassenden Aktien oder, falls sie zu diesem Zeitpunkt nicht frei handelbar sind, zum Zeitpunkt ihrer freien Handelbarkeit zu stellen. Findet vor der Einführung der Aktien ein Handel mit amtlicher Notierung der Bezugsrechte statt und muß ein Prospekt veröffentlicht werden, so ist der Antrag unter Beachtung der in § 43 Abs. 1 Satz 2 und 3 für die Prospektveröffentlichung bestimmten Fristen zu stellen.

Admissions Regulation

§ 67
Information in Cases of Admission to more than one Stock Exchange

(1) If an issuer has securities which are admitted to official listing on more than one domestic stock exchange, the issuer shall publish the same information at those stock exchanges.

(2) If admitted securities are also admitted to official listing on a stock exchange outside the territory where this Regulation applies and if an issuer publishes in such other territory information which could be relevant to the evaluation of the securities concerned, then the issuer shall publish equivalent information within the territory where this Regulation applies.

§ 68
Reference to Prospectuses

Any publication announcing the admission of securities of an issuer to official listing which contains information regarding the essential characteristics of those securities, shall make reference to the prospectus and the publication thereof. Any publication shall be submitted forthwith to the Listing Board.

§ 69
The Admission of Shares Issued at a Later Date

(1) An issuer of admitted shares is obliged to apply for the admission to official listing of shares publicly issued at a later date if such shares are of the same class as shares already admitted and where the admission thereof requires an application to be made. § 7 sub-paragraph 1 sentences 2 and 3 shall not be affected thereby.

(2) An application under sub-paragraph 1 shall be made no later than one year after the issue of the shares to be admitted or where such shares cannot be freely traded, at the time when such shares can be freely traded. If, prior to the introduction of the shares, subscription rights are traded with official quotation, and if a prospectus has to be published, application must be made in accordance with the time limits applicable to publication of the prospectus as set out in § 43 sub-paragraph 1 sentences 2 and 3.

Börsenzul. Verordnung

§ 70
Art und Form der Veröffentlichungen

(1) Veröffentlichungen auf Grund der §§ 63, 66 und 67 sind in deutscher Sprache in einem oder mehreren Börsenpflichtblättern vorzunehmen; in jedem Fall muß die Veröffentlichung in einem überregionalen Börsenpflichtblatt erfolgen.

(2) Die Zulassungsstelle kann gestatten, daß bei umfangreichen Mitteilungen oder Angaben eine Zusammenfassung gemäß Absatz 1 veröffentlicht wird, wenn die vollständigen Angaben bei den Zahlstellen kostenfrei erhältlich sind und in der Veröffentlichung hierauf hingewiesen wird.

(3) Die Veröffentlichungen nach den Absätzen 1 und 2 sind unverzüglich der Zulassungsstelle zu übermitteln.

Drittes Kapitel
Ordnungswidrigkeiten, Schlußvorschriften

§ 71
Ordnungswidrigkeiten

(1) Ordnungswidrig im Sinne des § 90 Abs. 2 Nr. 1 des Börsengesetzes handelt, wer vorsätzlich oder leichtfertig entgegen

1. § 43 Abs. 1 einen Prospekt nicht rechtzeitig veröffentlicht oder

2. § 43 Abs. 2 einen Prospekt veröffentlicht, ehe er von der Zulassungsstelle gebilligt worden ist.

(2) Ordnungswidrig im Sinne des § 90 Abs. 2 Nr. 2 des Börsengesetzes handelt, wer vorsätzlich oder leichtfertig entgegen

1. §§ 63, 70 Abs. 1 die Veröffentlichungen nicht, nicht richtig, nicht vollständig oder nicht in der vorgeschriebenen Art oder Form vornimmt oder

2. § 66 Abs. 1, § 70 Abs. 1 Änderungen der Rechte, die mit den Wertpapieren verbunden sind, nicht, nicht richtig, nicht vollständig, nicht in der vorgeschriebenen Art oder Form oder nicht rechtzeitig veröffentlicht.

§ 70
Manner and Form of Publication

(1) Notices given under §§ 63, 66 and 67 of this Regulation shall be in the German language and shall be published in one or more authorized journals; in each case, publication of the notice shall follow in a national authorized journal.

(2) The Listing Board may allow, for extensive information or data, a summary to be published, provided that complete information is available free of charge at the offices of the paying agents and a notice to that effect is contained in the publication.

(3) Publication in accordance with sub-paragraphs 1 and 2 shall be sent forthwith to the Listing Board.

Chapter Three
Breach of Regulations and Final Provisions

§ 71
Breach of Regulations

(1) Any person who intentionally or recklessly

1. fails to publish a prospectus in accordance with § 43 sub-paragraph 1 on time
2. publishes a prospectus in accordance with § 43 sub-paragraph 2 before approval by the Listing Board

shall be guilty of a breach of regulation under § 90 sub-paragraph 2 No.1 of the Stock Exchange Act.

(2) Any person who intentionally or recklessly

1. fails to publish or publishes incorrect or incomplete information or in a form other than that prescribed under §§63 to 70 sub-paragraph 1 or
2. fails to publish information on changes in rights connected with securities or publishes incorrect or incomplete information or in a form other than that prescribed or fails to publish such information on time under § 66 sub-paragraph 1 or § 70 sub-paragraph 1

is guilty of a breach of regulation under § 90 sub-paragraph 2 No. 2 of the Stock Exchange Act.

Wertpapier-Verkaufsprospektgesetz (VerkaufsprospektG)

vom 13. Dezember 1990 (BGBl. I, S. 2749), zuletzt geändert durch Artikel 8 des Zweiten Finanzmarktförderungsgesetzes vom 26. Juli 1994 (BGBl. I, S. 1779)

Inhaltsübersicht

		§
Erster Abschnitt	**Anwendungsbereich**	
	Grundregel	1
	Ausnahmen im Hinblick auf die Art des Angebots	2
	Ausnahmen im Hinblick auf bestimmte Emittenten	3
	Ausnahmen im Hinblick auf bestimmte Wertpapiere	4
Zweiter Abschnitt	**Angebot von Wertpapieren, für die eine amtliche Notierung beantragt ist**	
	Prospektinhalt	5
	Zulassungsstelle	6
Dritter Abschnitt	**Angebot von Wertpapieren, für die eine amtliche Notierung nicht beantragt ist**	
	Prospektinhalt	7
	Hinterlegungsstelle	8
Vierter Abschnitt	**Veröffentlichung des Verkaufsprospekts**	
	Frist und Form der Veröffentlichung	9
	Veröffentlichung eines unvollständigen Verkaufsprospekts	10
	Veröffentlichung ergänzender Angaben	11
	Hinweis auf Verkaufsprospekt	12
Fünfter Abschnitt	**Verletzung des Prospektpflicht**	
	Unrichtiger Verkaufsprospekt	13

Act Governing Sales Prospectuses for Securities
(Securities Sales Prospectus Act)
of December 13, 1990 (Federal Gazette I 2749), last amended by Article 8 of the Second Financial Market Advancement Law of July 26, 1994 (Federal Gazette I 1779),

Table of Contents

§

Chapter One	**Area of Application**	
	Ground Rule	1
	Exceptions with Regard to the Type of Offer for Sale	2
	Exceptions with Regard to Specific Issuing Bodies	3
	Exceptions with Regard to Specific Securities	4
Chapter Two	**Offer for Sale of Securities for which Application is made for an Official Listing**	
	Contents of Prospectus	5
	Listing Board	6
Chapter Three	**Offer for Sale of Securities for which no Application is made for an Official Listing**	
	Contents of Prospectus	7
	Depositing Agent	8
Chapter Four	**Publication of the Sales Prospectus**	
	Notice Requirement and Form of Publication	9
	Publication of an Incomplete Sales Prospectus	10
	Publication of Supplementary Details	11
	Reference to the Sales Prospectus	12
Chapter Five	**Infringement of the Obligation concerning Prospectuses**	
	Incorrect Sales Prospectus	13

315

VerkaufsprospektGesetz

§

Sechster Abschnitt **Verfahren in der Europäischen Wirtschaftsgemeinschaft; Gebühren; Bußgeldvorschriften**

Zusammenarbeit in der Europäischen
Wirtschaftsgemeinschaft 14
Angebot in mehreren Mitgliedsstaaten der
Europäischen Wirtschaftsgemeinschaft oder in
anderen Vertragsstaaten des Abkommens über den
Europäischen Wirtschaftsraum 15
Gebühren 16
Bußgeldvorschriften 17

Sales Prospectus Act

§

Chapter Six	**Procedures in the European Economic Community; Charges; Fining Provisions**

Cooperation in the European Economic
Community 14
Offer for Sales in Several Member States of
the European Economic Community or in other
Contracting States of the European
Economic Area Treaty 15
Fees 16
Fining Provisions 17

VerkaufsprospektGesetz

Erster Abschnitt

Anwendungsbereich

§ 1
Grundregel

Für Wertpapiere, die erstmals im Inland öffentlich angeboten werden und nicht zum Handel an einer inländischen Börse zugelassen sind, muß der Anbieter einen Prospekt (Verkaufsprospekt) veröffentlichen, sofern sich aus den §§ 2 bis 4 nichts anderes ergibt.

§ 2
Ausnahmen im Hinblick auf die Art des Angebots

Ein Verkaufsprospekt muß nicht veröffentlicht werden, wenn die Wertpapiere

1. nur Personen angeboten werden, die beruflich oder gewerblich für eigene oder fremde Rechnung Wertpapiere erwerben oder veräußern;

2. einem begrenzten Personenkreis angeboten werden;

3. nur den Arbeitnehmern von ihrem Arbeitgeber oder von einem mit seinem Unternehmen verbundenen Unternehmen angeboten werden;

4. nur in Stückelungen von mindestens achtzigtausend Deutsche Mark oder nur zu einem Kaufpreis von mindestens achtzigtausend Deutsche Mark je Anleger erworben werden können oder wenn der Verkaufspreis für alle angebotenen Wertpapiere achtzigtausend Deutsche Mark nicht übersteigt;

5. Teil einer Emission sind, für die bereits im Inland ein Verkaufsprospekt veröffentlicht worden ist.

§ 3
Ausnahmen im Hinblick auf bestimmte Emittenten

Ein Verkaufsprospekt muß nicht veröffentlicht werden, wenn die Wertpapiere

1. von einem Staat oder einer seiner Gebietskörperschaften oder einer internationalen Organisation des öffentlichen Rechts, der mindestens ein Mit-

Sales Prospectus Act

Chapter One
Area of Application

§ 1
Ground Rule

In the case of securities publicly offered for sale for the first time on the domestic market and not admitted to trading on a domestic stock exchange, the person making the offer must publish a prospectus (sales prospectus), if no other factors emerge from §§ 2 to 4.

§ 2
Exceptions with Regard to the Type of Offer for Sale

A sales prospectus does not have to be published if the securities

1. are solely offered for sale to persons who, for professional or commercial reasons, are acquiring or disposing of securities on their own or someone else's account;
2. are offered for sale to a restricted group of people;
3. are solely offered for sale to employees by their employer or by a company associated with the company;
4. can only be acquired in denominations of at least eighty thousand German Marks or at a purchase price of at least eighty thousand German Marks per investor or if the selling price for all securities offered for sale does not exceed eighty thousand German Marks;
5. are part of an issue for which a sales prospectus has already been published on the domestic market.

§ 3
Exceptions with Regard to Specific Issuing Bodies

A sales prospectus does not have to be published, if the securities

1. are issued by a state or one of its regional administrative authorities or an international public institution to which at least one member state of the European Economic Community or another contracting state of the European Economic Area Treaty belongs;

VerkaufsprospektGesetz

gliedstaat der Europäischen Wirtschaftsgemeinschaft oder ein anderer Vertragsstaat des Abkommens über den Europäischen Wirtschaftsraum angehört, ausgegeben werden;

2. Schuldverschreibungen sind, die von

   a) einem inländischen Kreditinstitut oder der Kreditanstalt für Wiederaufbau oder

   b) einem Unternehmen mit Sitz in einem anderen Staat, das ein § 1 des Gesetzes über das Kreditwesen entsprechendes Bankgeschäft betreibt, regelmäßig seine Jahresabschlüsse veröffentlicht und innerhalb der Europäischen Wirtschaftsgemeinschaft oder innerhalb eines anderen Vertragsstaates des Abkommens über den Europäischen Wirtschaftsraum durch ein besonderes Gesetz oder aufgrund eines besonderen Gesetzes geschaffen worden ist oder geregelt wird oder einer öffentlichen Aufsicht zum Schutz der Anleger untersteht,

   ausgegeben werden, das in den zwölf Kalendermonaten vor dem Angebot während einer längeren Dauer oder wiederholt Schuldverschreibungen öffentlich angeboten hat; ein wiederholtes Angebot ist gegeben, wenn in dem angegebenen Zeitraum mindestens drei Emissionen von Schuldverschreibungen innerhalb der Europäischen Wirtschaftsgemeinschaft oder innerhalb eines anderen Vertragsstaates des Abkommens über den Europäischen Wirtschaftsraum öffentlich angeboten worden sind;

3. Anteilscheine sind, die von einer Kapitalanlagegesellschaft oder ausländischen Investmentgesellschaft ausgegeben werden und bei denen die Anteilinhaber ein Recht auf Rückgabe der Anteilscheine haben;

4. Schuldverschreibungen sind, die von einer Gesellschaft oder juristischen Person mit Sitz in einem Mitgliedstaat der Europäischen Wirtschaftsgemeinschaft oder in einem anderen Vertragsstaat des Abkommens über den Europäischen Wirtschaftsraum ausgegeben werden, die ihre Tätigkeit unter einem Staatsmonopol ausübt und die durch ein besonderes Gesetz oder auf Grund eines besonderen Gesetzes geschaffen worden ist oder geregelt wird oder für deren Schuldverschreibungen ein Mitgliedstaat der Europäischen Wirtschaftsgemeinschaft oder eines seiner Bundesländer oder ein anderer Vertragsstaat des Abkommens über den Europäischen Wirtschaftsraum oder eines seiner Bundesländer die unbedingte und unwiderrufliche Gewährleistung für ihre Verzinsung und Rückzahlung übernommen hat.

Sales Prospectus Act

2. are bonds, issued by
   a) a domestic credit institution or the 'Kreditanstalt für Wiederaufbau' or
   b) a company with its principal place of business in another state, which conducts banking operations in accordance with § 1 of the Banking Act, publishes its annual accounts regularly and has been created or is regulated by a special Act or by virtue of a special Act or is subject to public supervision for the protection of investors within the European Economic Community or within another contracting state of the European Economic Area Treaty,

   which has publicly offered bonds for sale in the twelve calendar months before the offer over a longer period or on repeated occasions; a repeated offer for sale has occurred if, during the above-mentioned period, at least three bond issues have been publicly offered for sale within the European Economic Community or within another contracting state of the European Economic Area Treaty;

3. are certificates issued by an investment company or foreign investment company and for which the owners of the shares have a right to return the certificates;

4. are bonds issued by a company or legal entity with its principal place of business in a member state of the European Economic Community or in another contracting state of the European Economic Area Treaty which conducts its business under a state monopoly and which has been created or is regulated by a special Act or by virtue of a special Act or for whose bonds a member state of the European Economic Community or one of its Federal States or another contracting state of the European Economic Area Treaty or one of its Federal States has taken on an unconditional and irrevocable guarantee with respect to interest payments and redemption.

VerkaufsprospektGesetz

§ 4

Ausnahmen im Hinblick auf bestimmte Wertpapiere

(1) Ein Verkaufsprospekt muß nicht veröffentlicht werden, wenn die Wertpapiere

1. Euro-Wertpapiere sind, für die nicht öffentlich geworben wird und die nicht im Wege von Geschäften im Sinne des Gesetzes über den Widerruf von Haustürgeschäften und ähnlichen Geschäften angeboten werden;

2. Aktien sind, für die ein Antrag auf Zulassung zur amtlichen Notierung an einer inländischen Börse gestellt ist, deren Zahl, geschätzter Kurswert oder Nennwert, bei nennwertlosen Aktien deren rechnerischer Wert, niedriger ist als 10 vom Hundert des entsprechenden Wertes der Aktien derselben Gattung, die an derselben Börse amtlich notiert sind, und wenn der Emittent die mit der Zulassung verbundenen Veröffentlichungspflichten erfüllt; Aktien, die sich nur in bezug auf den Beginn der Dividendenberechtigung unterscheiden, gelten als Aktien derselben Gattung;

3. Aktien sind, für die kein Antrag auf Zulassung zur amtlichen Notierung an einer inländischen Börse gestellt ist und deren Zahl, geschätzter Kurswert oder Nennwert, bei nennwertlosen Aktien deren rechnerischer Wert, niedriger ist als 10 vom Hundert des entsprechenden Wertes der Aktien derselben Gattung, die an einer inländischen Börse zum Handel zugelassen sind, sofern den Anlegern Informationen über den Emittenten zur Verfügung stehen, die den im Dritten Abschnitt vorgeschriebenen Angaben gleichwertig und auf dem neuesten Stand sind; Aktien, die sich nur in bezug auf den Beginn der Dividendenberechtigung unterscheiden, gelten als Aktien derselben Gattung;

4. Aktien sind, die den Aktionären nach einer Kapitalerhöhung aus Gesellschaftsmitteln zugeteilt werden;

5. Zertifikate sind, die anstelle von Aktien derselben Gesellschaft ausgegeben werden und mit deren Ausgabe keine Änderung des gezeichneten Kapitals verbunden ist;

6. nach der Ausübung von Umtausch- oder Bezugsrechten aus anderen Wertpapieren als Aktien ausgegeben werden, sofern im Inland bei der Ausgabe dieser Wertpapiere ein Zulassungs- oder Verkaufsprospekt veröffentlicht worden ist;

7. bei einem öffentlichen Umtauschangebot oder einer Verschmelzung von Unternehmen angeboten werden;

§ 4

Exceptions with Regard to Specific Securities

(1) A sales prospectus need not be published if the securities

1. are Eurosecurities which are not publicly advertised and are not offered for sale in the course of transactions as defined by the Act covering the cancellation of door-to-door sales and similar transactions;

2. are shares for which an application has been made for admission to official quotation on a domestic stock exchange, if the number, estimated market value or par value of such shares, and for shares with no par value their calculated value, is less than 10 per cent of the corresponding value of the shares of the same class which are officially quoted on the same stock exchange, and if the issuer meets the publication requirements associated with the admission; shares which differ solely with respect to the beginning of the dividend entitlement are counted as shares of the same class;

3. are shares for which no application has been made for admission to official quotation on a domestic stock exchange, and whose number, estimated market value or par value, and in the case of shares with no par value their calculated value, is less than 10 per cent of the corresponding value of the shares of the same class which are admitted to trading on a domestic stock exchange, provided investors have access to the most recent information on the issuer which equates to the particulars laid down in Chapter III; shares which differ merely in respect to the beginning of the dividend entitlement are counted as shares of the same class;

4. are shares alloted to shareholders following an increase in share capital from corporate funds;

5. are certificates issued in place of the same company's shares and the issue of which involves no change in the subscribed capital;

6. are issued as shares following the exercise of conversion or subscription rights from other securities if a sales prospectus was published domestically when these securities were issued;

7. are offered for sale in the context of a public tender offer or a company merger;

VerkaufsprospektGesetz

8. Schuldverschreibungen mit einer vereinbarten Laufzeit von weniger als einem Jahr sind.

(2) Euro-Wertpapiere im Sinne von Absatz 1 Nr. 1 sind Wertpapiere, die

1. ein Konsortium übernimmt oder zu übernehmen verspricht und vertreibt, dessen Mitglieder ihren Sitz nicht alle in demselben Staat haben,
2. zu einem wesentlichen Teil nicht in dem Staat angeboten werden, in dem der Emittent seinen Sitz hat, und
3. nur über ein Kreditinstitut oder ein anderes Finanzinstitut gezeichnet oder erstmals erworben werden dürfen.

Zweiter Abschnitt
Angebot von Wertpapieren, für die eine amtliche Notierung beantragt ist

§ 5
Prospektinhalt

Ist für die öffentlich angebotenen Wertpapiere ein Antrag auf Zulassung zur amtlichen Notierung an einer inländischen Börse gestellt, so sind auf den Inhalt des Verkaufsprospekts die Vorschriften des § 38 Abs. 1 Nr. 2, Abs. 2 des Börsengesetzes in Verbindung mit den §§ 13 bis 40 und 47 der Börsenzulassungs-Verordnung entsprechend anzuwenden.

§ 6
Zulassungsstelle

(1) Der Verkaufsprospekt muß vor der Veröffentlichung von der Zulassungsstelle der Börse, bei welcher der Zulassungsantrag gestellt ist, gebilligt werden. Wird der Zulassungsantrag gleichzeitig bei mehreren inländischen Börsen gestellt, so hat der Emittent die für die Billigung des Verkaufsprospekts zuständige Zulassungsstelle zu bestimmen. Die Zulassungsstelle hat innerhalb von 15 Börsentagen nach Eingang des Verkaufsprospekts über den Antrag auf Billigung zu entscheiden.

Sales Prospectus Act

8. are bonds with an agreed maturity period of less than one year;

(2) Eurosecurities within the meaning of sub-paragraph 1 No. 1 are securities

1. which a consortium, the members of which do not all have their principal place of business in the same state, buys or promises to buy and sells,
2. a significant proportion of which are not offered for sale in the state where the issuer has its principal place of business, and
3. which may only be subscribed for or first acquired via a credit institution or other financial institution.

Chapter Two

Offer for Sale of Securities for which Application is made for an Official Listing

§ 5

Contents of Prospectus

If in the case of securities publicly offered for sale an application is made for admission to official listing on a domestic stock exchange, the provisions of § 38 sub-paragraph 1 No. 2 and sub-paragraph 2 of the Stock Exchange Act in conjunction with §§ 13 to 40 and § 47 of the Stock Exchange Admissions Regulation must be applied as appropriate to the contents of the sales prospectus.

§ 6

Listing Board

(1) Before publication, the sales prospectus must be approved by the Listing Board of the stock exchange where the application for admission is made. If the application for admission is made simultaneously to several domestic stock exchanges, the issuer must specify the Listing Board competent to approve the sales prospectus. The Listing Board must reach a decision on the application for approval within 15 exchange trading days of the receipt of the sales prospectus.

VerkaufsprospektGesetz

(2) Die Zulassungsstelle überwacht die Einhaltung der Pflichten, die sich aus dem öffentlichen Angebot für den Anbieter ergeben.

(3) Die Zulassungsstelle hat dem Anbieter auf Verlangen eine Bescheinigung über die Billigung des Verkaufsprospekts auszustellen.

Dritter Abschnitt
Angebot von Wertpapieren, für die eine amtliche Notierung nicht beantragt ist

§ 7
Prospektinhalt

(1) Ist für die öffentlich angebotenen Wertpapiere ein Antrag auf Zulassung zur amtlichen Notierung an einer inländischen Börse nicht gestellt, so muß der Verkaufsprospekt die Angaben enthalten, die notwendig sind, um dem Publikum ein zutreffendes Urteil über den Emittenten und die Wertpapiere zu ermöglichen.

(2) Die Bundesregierung wird ermächtigt, durch Rechtsverordnung mit Zustimmung des Bundesrates die zum Schutz des Publikums erforderlichen Vorschriften über den Inhalt des Verkaufsprospekts zu erlassen, insbesondere über

1. die Personen oder Gesellschaften, die für den Inhalt des Verkaufsprospekts die Verantwortung übernehmen,

2. die angebotenen Wertpapiere und

3. den Emittenten der Wertpapiere sowie sein Kapital und seine Geschäftstätigkeit, seine Vermögens-, Finanz- und Ertragslage, seine Geschäftsführungs- und Aufsichtsorgane und seine Geschäftsaussichten.

(3) In die Rechtsverordnung nach Absatz 2 können auch Vorschriften aufgenommen werden über Ausnahmen, in denen von der Aufnahme einzelner Angaben in den Verkaufsprospekt abgesehen werden kann,

1. wenn beim Emittenten, bei den angebotenen Wertpapieren, bei ihrer Ausgabe oder beim Kreis der mit der Wertpapierausgabe angesprochenen Anleger besondere Umstände vorliegen und den Interessen des Publi-

Sales Prospectus Act

(2) The Listing Board supervises adherence to the obligations arising from the public offer for sale in respect to the offerer.

(3) The Listing Board must issue the person making the offer, upon demand, a certificate of approval of the sales prospectus.

Chapter Three

Offer for Sale of Securities for which no Application is made for an Official Listing

§ 7

Contents of Prospectus

(1) If, in the case of securities which are publicly offered for sale, an application is not made for admission to official listing on a domestic stock exchange, the sales prospectus must contain such necessary particulars to enable the public to make an accurate judgment concerning the issuer and the securities.

(2) The Federal Government is authorised, by Regulation with the approval of the Bundesrat, to pass any provisions required for the protection of the public with regard to the contents of the sales prospectus, particularly in respect to

1. the persons or companies assuming responsibility for the contents of the sales prospectus,
2. the securities offered for sale and
3. the issuer of the securities along with its capital and business activity, net worth, finance and earnings position, management and supervisory bodies and business prospects.

(3) Provisions can also be incorporated into the Regulation according to sub-paragraph 2 concerning exceptions, whereby the inclusion of certain details in the sales prospectus can be disregarded,

1. if special circumstances exist in respect to the issuer, the securities offered for sale, their issue or the group of investors approached in

VerkaufsprospektGesetz

kums durch eine anderweitige Unterrichtung ausreichend Rechnung getragen ist oder

2. mit Rücksicht auf die geringe Bedeutung einzelner Angaben oder einen beim Emittenten zu befürchtenden erheblichen Schaden.

§ 8
Hinterlegungsstelle

Der Anbieter muß den Verkaufsprospekt vor seiner Veröffentlichung dem Bundesaufsichtsamt für den Wertpapierhandel (Bundesaufsichtsamt) übermitteln.

Vierter Abschnitt
Veröffentlichung des Verkaufsprospekts

§ 9
Frist und Form der Veröffentlichung

(1) Der Verkaufsprospekt muß mindestens drei Werktage vor dem öffentlichen Angebot veröffentlicht werden.

(2) Ist die Zulassung zur amtlichen Notierung beantragt, so ist der Verkaufsprospekt zu veröffentlichen

1. durch Abdruck in den Börsenpflichtblättern, in denen der Zulassungsantrag veröffentlicht wurde oder veröffentlicht wird, oder

2. durch Bereithalten zur kostenlosen Ausgabe bei den im Verkaufsprospekt genannten Zahlstellen und bei den Zulassungsstellen der Börsen, bei denen die Zulassung beantragt ist; in den Börsenpflichtblättern, in denen der Zulassungsantrag veröffentlicht wurde oder veröffentlicht wird, ist bekanntzumachen, bei welchen Stellen der Verkaufsprospekt bereitgehalten wird.

(3) Ist die Zulassung zur amtlichen Notierung nicht beantragt, so ist der Verkaufsprospekt in der Form zu veröffentlichen, daß er entweder in einem überregionalen Börsenpflichtblatt bekanntgemacht oder bei den im Ver-

connection with the securities issue, and the interests of the public are sufficiently taken into consideration through the medium of other information or

2. because of the minor importance of certain details or a major loss to be feared on the part of the issuer.

§ 8

Depositing Agent

Before publication, the person making the offer must forward the sales prospectus to the Federal Supervisory Authority for Securities Trading (Federal Supervisory Authority).

Chapter Four

Publication of the Sales Prospectus

§ 9

Notice Requirement and Form of Publication

(1) The sales prospectus must be published at least three working days before the public offer for sale.

(2) If an application is made for admission to official quotation, the sales prospectus must be published

1. by printing in the authorised journals for the publication of mandatory stock exchange announcements (authorised journals), in which the application for admission was or is being published, or

2. by being held for free issue in the paying offices named in the sales prospectus and at the Listing Board of the stock exchanges at which application was made for admission; a notice must be placed in the authorised journals in which the application for admission was published or is being published, stating at which offices the sales prospectus is held.

(3) If an application is not made for admission to official quotation, the sales prospectus must be published in the form of publication in a national authorised journal or held for free issue at the paying offices named in the

VerkaufsprospektGesetz

kaufsprospekt benannten Zahlstellen zur kostenlosen Ausgabe bereitgehalten wird; im letzteren Fall ist in einem überregionalen Börsenpflichtblatt bekanntzumachen, daß der Verkaufsprospekt bei den Zahlstellen bereitgehalten wird. Außerdem ist im Bundesanzeiger der Verkaufsprospekt oder ein Hinweis darauf bekanntzumachen, wo der Verkaufsprospekt veröffentlicht und für das Publikum zu erhalten ist.

§ 10
Veröffentlichung eines unvollständigen Verkaufsprospekts

Werden einzelne Angebotsbedingungen erst kurz vor dem öffentlichen Angebot festgesetzt, so darf der Verkaufsprospekt ohne diese Angaben veröffentlicht werden, sofern er Auskunft darüber gibt, wie diese Angaben nachgetragen werden, und sofern sie vor dem Angebot gemäß § 9 Abs. 2 und 3 veröffentlicht werden.

§ 11
Veröffentlichung ergänzender Angaben

Sind seit der Veröffentlichung des Verkaufsprospekts Veränderungen eingetreten, die für die Beurteilung des Emittenten oder der Wertpapiere von wesentlicher Bedeutung sind, so sind die Veränderungen während der Dauer des öffentlichen Angebots in einem Nachtrag zum Verkaufsprospekt zu veröffentlichen. Auf diesen Nachtrag sind die Vorschriften über den Verkaufsprospekt und dessen Veröffentlichung entsprechend anzuwenden.

§ 12
Hinweis auf Verkaufsprospekt

Veröffentlichungen, in denen das öffentliche Angebot von Wertpapieren angekündigt und auf die wesentlichen Merkmale der Wertpapiere hingewiesen wird, müssen einen Hinweis auf den Verkaufsprospekt und dessen Veröffentlichung enthalten. In Fällen, in denen ein Antrag auf Zulassung zur amtlichen Notierung an einer inländischen Börse gestellt ist, sind die Veröffentlichungen unverzüglich der Zulassungsstelle zu übermitteln.

Sales Prospectus Act

sales prospectus; in the latter case a notice must be placed in one of the national authorised journals that the sales prospectus is held at the paying offices. In addition, a notice on the sales prospectus or a reference to it must be placed in the Federal Gazette and details given as to where the sales prospectus is published and obtainable by the public.

§ 10
Publication of an Incomplete Sales Prospectus

If certain offer conditions are finalised only shortly before the public offer for sale, the sales prospectus may be published without these particulars, provided that it gives information on how these details will be subsequently added and provided that they are published in advance of the offer for sale under the terms of § 9, sub-paragraphs 2 and 3.

§ 11
Publication of Supplementary Details

If changes have occurred since the publication of the sales prospectus which are of great importance in assessing the issuer or the securities, the changes must be published during the period of the public offer for sale in a supplement to the sales prospectus. The legal provisions for the sales prospectus and its publication must be applied to this supplement as appropriate.

§ 12
Reference to the Sales Prospectus

Publications in which the public offer for sale of securities is announced and where reference is made to the distinctive features of the securities, must contain a reference to the sales prospectus and its publication. In cases where an application is made for admission to official quotation on a domestic stock exchange, the publications must be forwarded without delay to the Listing Board.

VerkaufsprospektGesetz

Fünfter Abschnitt
Verletzung der Prospektpflicht

§ 13
Unrichtiger Verkaufsprospekt

Sind Angaben in einem Verkaufsprospekt unrichtig oder unvollständig, so sind die Vorschriften der §§ 45 bis 48 des Börsengesetzes mit der Maßgabe entsprechend anzuwenden, daß der Ersatzanspruch in fünf Jahren seit der Veröffentlichung des Verkaufsprospekts verjährt.

Sechster Abschnitt
Verfahren in der Europäischen Wirtschaftsgemeinschaft; Gebühren; Bußgeldvorschriften

§ 14
Zusammenarbeit in der Europäischen Wirtschaftsgemeinschaft

(1) Sollen die Wertpapiere auch in anderen Mitgliedstaaten der Europäischen Wirtschaftsgemeinschaft oder in anderen Vertragsstaaten des Abkommens über den Europäischen Wirtschaftsraum öffentlich angeboten werden, so hat derjenige, der zur Veröffentlichung des Verkaufsprospekts verpflichtet ist, den zuständigen Stellen dieser Staaten den Entwurf des Verkaufsprospektes, den er in diesen Staaten verwenden will, zu übermitteln.

(2) Die Zulassungsstellen und das Bundesaufsichtsamt arbeiten untereinander und mit den zuständigen Stellen in den anderen Mitgliedstaaten der Europäischen Wirtschaftsgemeinschaft oder in den anderen Vertragsstaaten des Abkommens über den Europäischen Wirtschaftsraum im Rahmen ihrer Aufgaben und Befugnisse zusammen und übermitteln sich gegenseitig die hierfür erforderlichen Angaben, soweit die Amtsverschwiegenheit gewährleistet ist; insoweit unterliegen die Mitglieder der Zulassungsstellen und des Bundesaufsichtsamtes sowie die für diese Stellen tätigen Personen nicht der Pflicht zur Geheimhaltung.

(3) Sollen Wertpapiere eines Emittenten mit Sitz in einem anderen Mitgliedstaat der Europäischen Wirtschaftsgemeinschaft oder in einem anderen Vertragsstaat des Abkommens über den Europäischen Wirtschaftsraum, mit

Sales Prospectus Act

Chapter Five

Infringement of the Obligation concerning Prospectuses

§ 13

Incorrect Sales Prospectus

If particulars contained in a sales prospectus are incorrect or incomplete, the provisions of §§ 45 to 48 of the Stock Exchange Act must be applied as appropriate, with the proviso that the entitlement to compensation lapses five years after the publication of the sales prospectus.

Chapter Six

Procedures in the European Economic Community; Charges; Fining Provisions

§ 14

Cooperation in the European Economic Community

(1) Should the securities also be offered for sale publicly in other member states of the European Economic Community or in other contracting states of the European Economic Area Treaty, the person who is responsible for publishing the sales prospectus must forward the draft of the sales prospectus he wishes to use in these states to the competent administrative authorities of these states.

(2) The Listing Board and the Federal Supervisory Authority work with each other and together with the competent administrative authorities in the other member states of the European Economic Community or in the other contracting states of the European Economic Area Treaty within the framework of their responsibilities and powers and forward to each other the requisite details, as long as official secrecy is guaranteed; in this connection the members of the Listing Board and the Federal Supervisory Authority as well as persons working for these administrative authorities are not subject to the obligation to maintain secrecy.

(3) Should securities linked to share subscription rights issued by a body with its principal place of business in another member state of the European Economic Community or in another contracting state of the European Eco-

VerkaufsprospektGesetz

denen Bezugsrechte für Aktien verbunden sind, im Inland öffentlich angeboten werden und ist die Zulassung zur amtlichen Notierung an einer inländischen Börse beantragt, so hat die Zulassungsstelle vor ihrer Entscheidung über den Antrag auf Billigung des Verkaufsprospektes eine Stellungnahme der zuständigen Stelle des anderen Staates einzuholen, sofern die Aktien des Emittenten in diesem Staat zur amtlichen Notierung zugelassen sind.

§ 15
Angebot in mehreren Mitgliedstaaten der Europäischen Wirtschaftsgemeinschaft oder in anderen Vertragsstaaten des Abkommens über den Europäischen Wirtschaftsraum

(1) Sollen Wertpapiere eines Emittenten mit Sitz in einem anderen Mitgliedstaat der Europäischen Wirtschaftsgemeinschaft oder in einem anderen Vertragsstaat des Abkommens über den Europäischen Wirtschaftsraum gleichzeitig oder annähernd gleichzeitig in diesem Staat und im Inland öffentlich angeboten werden und ist die Zulassung zur amtlichen Notierung bei einer inländischen Börse beantragt, so hat die Zulassungsstelle vorbehaltlich des Absatzes 2 den von der zuständigen Stelle des anderen Staates gebilligten Verkaufsprospekt ohne weitere Prüfung zu billigen, sofern ihr eine Übersetzung des Verkaufsprospekts in die deutsche Sprache sowie eine Bescheinigung der zuständigen Stelle des anderen Staates über die Billigung des Verkaufsprospekts vorliegt.

(2) Hat die zuständige Stelle des anderen Mitgliedstaates oder des anderen Vertragsstaates des Abkommens über den Europäischen Wirtschaftsraum für einzelne Angaben im Verkaufsprospekt eine Befreiung erteilt oder Abweichungen von den im Regelfall vorgeschriebenen Angaben zugelassen, so billigt die Zulassungsstelle den Verkaufsprospekt nach Absatz 1 nur, wenn

1. die Befreiung oder Abweichung nach diesem Gesetz oder auf Grund dieses Gesetzes zulässig ist,

2. im Inland dieselben Bedingungen bestehen, welche die Befreiungen rechtfertigen, und

3. die Befreiung oder Abweichung an keine weitere Bedingung gebunden ist, welche die Zulassungsstelle veranlassen würde, die Befreiung oder Abweichung abzulehnen.

(3) Sollen Wertpapiere eines Emittenten mit Sitz in einem anderen Mitgliedstaat oder in einem anderen Vertragsstaat des Abkommens über den

nomic Area Treaty be offered for sale publicly on the domestic market and if application has been made for admission to official quotation on a domestic stock exchange, before making its decision on the application for approval of the sales prospectus, the Listing Board must obtain a statement from the competent authority of the other state, insofar as the shares of the issuer in this state are admitted to official quotation.

§ 15
Offer for Sale in Several Member States of the European Economic Community or in other Contracting States of the European Economic Area Treaty

(1) Should securities from an issuer with its principal place of business in another member state of the European Economic Community or in another contracting state of the European Economic Area Treaty be publicly offered for sale simultaneously or almost simultaneously both in this state and domestically and if an application has been made for admission to official quotation on a domestic stock exchange, the Listing Board, except as provided in sub-paragraph 2, must approve without further review the sales prospectus approved by the competent authority of the other state, provided that it has access to a translation of the sales prospectus in the German language and written confirmation from the competent authority of the other state of approval of the sales prospectus.

(2) If the competent authority of the other member state of the European Economic Community or the other contracting state of the European Economic Area Treaty has granted an exemption with respect to certain particulars in the sales prospectus or has authorised variations to normally stipulated particulars, the Listing Board will only approve the sales prospectus in accordance with sub-paragraph 1 if

1. the exemption or variation is permissible under the terms of this Act or by virtue of this Act,
2. the same conditions exist domestically to justify the exemptions, and
3. the exemption or variation is not linked to any further condition which would cause the Listing Board to refuse the exemption or variation.

(3) Should securities from an issuer with its principal place of business in another member state or in another contracting state of the European Economic Area Treaty be publicly offered for sale simultaneously or almost

VerkaufsprospektGesetz

Europäischen Wirtschaftsraum gleichzeitig oder annähernd gleichzeitig in diesem Staat und im Inland öffentlich angeboten werden und ist die Zulassung zur amtlichen Notierung bei einer inländischen Börse nicht beantragt, so kann als Verkaufsprospekt eine Übersetzung des von der zuständigen Stelle des anderen Staates gebilligten Verkaufsprospekts in die deutsche Sprache veröffentlicht werden, sofern dem Bundesaufsichtsamt die Übersetzung des Verkaufsprospekts in die deutsche Sprache sowie eine Bescheinigung der zuständigen Stelle des anderen Staates über die Billigung des Verkaufsprospekts vorliegt.

(4) Sollen Wertpapiere eines Emittenten mit Sitz außerhalb des Geltungsbereichs dieses Gesetzes sowohl in einem anderen Mitgliedstaat oder in einem anderen Vertragsstaat des Abkommens über den Europäischen Wirtschaftsraum, der nicht der Sitzstaat ist, als auch im Inland öffentlich angeboten werden, so sind die Vorschriften der Absätze 1 bis 3 entsprechend anzuwenden, wenn der Emittent bestimmt, daß der Verkaufsprospekt von der zuständigen Stelle des anderen Staates gebilligt werden soll.

§ 16
Gebühren

(1) In der Gebührenordnung nach § 5 des Börsengesetzes sind die Gebühren zu regeln, die von der Zulassungsstelle für die Billigung des Verkaufsprospekts zu erheben sind.

(2) Das Bundesaufsichtsamt erhebt für die Hinterlegung von Verkaufsprospekten eine Gebühr. Diese beträgt bei einem Gesamtausgabepreis der Wertpapiere von

- bis zu 5 Millionen Deutsche Mark: 750 Deutsche Mark
- bis zu 50 Millionen Deutsche Mark: 1000 Deutsche Mark
- über 50 Millionen Deutsche Mark: 1500 Deutsche Mark

Die Gebühren werden nach den Vorschriften des Verwaltungs-Vollstreckungsgesetzes beigetrieben.

§ 17
Bußgeldvorschriften

(1) Ordnungswidrig handelt, wer vorsätzlich oder leichtfertig einen Verkaufprospekt

Sales Prospectus Act

simultaneously both in that state and domestically and if an application is not made for admission to official quotation on a domestic stock exchange, a translation of the sales prospectus approved by the competent authority of the other state can be published in the German language as the sales prospectus, provided that the Federal Supervisory Authority has access to the translation of the sales prospectus in the German language and written confirmation from the competent board of the other state regarding approval of the sales prospectus.

(4) Should securities from an issuer with its principal place of business outside the jurisdiction of this Act be publicly offered for sale both in another member state or in another contracting state of the European Economic Area Treaty which is not the state where the principal place of business is located, as well as domestically, the provisions of sub-paragraphs 1 to 3 must be applied as appropriate, if the issuer specifies that the sales prospectus should be approved by the competent board of the other state.

§ 16

Fees

(1) Fees levied by the Listing Board for the approval of the sales prospectus must lie within the fee scale in § 5 of the Stock Exchange Act.

(2) The Federal Supervisory Authority levies a charge for the deposition of sales prospectuses. This varies according to the total issue price of the securities as follows

- up to 5 million German Marks: 750 German Marks
- up to 50 million German Marks: 1,000 German Marks
- over 50 million German Marks: 1,500 German Marks.

The charges are collected in accordance with the provisions of the Administrative Enforcement Act.

§ 17

Fining Provisions

(1) A person is deemed to be in infringement of these regulations if he intentionally or recklessly

VerkaufsprospektGesetz

1. entgegen § 1 oder § 9 Abs. 1 nicht oder nicht rechtzeitig veröffentlicht,
2. veröffentlicht, bevor dieser nach § 6 Abs. 1 Satz 1 gebilligt worden ist,
3. entgegen § 8 nicht oder nicht rechtzeitig übermittelt oder
4. entgegen § 9 Abs. 2 oder 3 eine Veröffentlichung oder eine Bekanntmachung nicht oder nicht in der vorgeschriebenen Form vornimmt.

(2) Die Ordnungswidrigkeit kann in den Fällen des Absatzes 1 Nr. 1, 2 und 4 mit einer Geldbuße bis zu einhunderttausend Deutsche Mark, in den Fällen des Absatzes 1 Nr. 3 mit einer Geldbuße bis zu fünfzigtausend Deutsche Mark geahndet werden.

(3) Verwaltungsbehörde im Sinne des § 36 Abs. 1 Nr. 1 des Gesetzes über Ordnungswidrigkeiten ist in den Fällen

1. des Absatzes 1 Nr. 1 und 4, wenn für die öffentlich angebotenen Wertpapiere kein Antrag auf Zulassung zur amtlichen Notierung an einer inländischen Börse gestellt wurde, und
2. des Absatzes 1 Nr. 3

das Bundesaufsichtsamt für den Wertpapierhandel.

1. does not publish or does not publish at the appropriate time a sales prospectus contrary to §§ 1 or 9 sub-paragraph 1,
2. publishes a sales prospectus before it has been approved in accordance with § 6 sub-paragraph 1 sentence 1,
3. does not forward or does not forward at the appropriate time a sales prospectus contrary to § 8 or
4. does not produce or does not produce in the prescribed form a publication or a notice contrary to § 9, sub-paragraph 2 or 3.

(2) In the case of sub-paragraph 1 No. 1, 2 and 4, infringement of the regulations can be punished with a fine of up to one hundred thousand German Marks; in the case of sub-paragraph 1 No. 3, with a fine of up to fifty thousand German Marks.

(3) The relevant administrative authority under the terms of § 36, sub-paragraph 1 No. 1 of the Breaches of Regulation Act is the Federal Supervisory Authority, in the case of

1. sub-paragraph 1 No. 1 and 4, if for securities which have been publicly offered for sale no application has been made for admission to official quotation on a domestic stock exchange, and
2. sub-paragraph 1 No. 3.